on screen ...
James Bond

every movie, every star

Andrew Wild

sonicbondpublishing.com

Sonicbond Publishing Limited
www.sonicbondpublishing.co.uk
Email: info@sonicbondpublishing.co.uk

First Published in the United Kingdom 2021
First Published in the United States 2021

British Library Cataloguing in Publication Data:
A Catalogue record for this book is available from the British Library

ISBN 978-1-78952-010-1

Typeset in ITC Garamond & ITC Avant Garde
Printed and bound in England

Graphic design and typesetting: Full Moon Media

on screen ...
James Bond

every movie, every star

Andrew Wild

sonicbondpublishing.com

Also by Andrew Wild

Local history

108 Steps Around Macclesfield (Sigma Press, 1994 / 2nd edition, Rumble Strips, 2018)
Exploring Chester (Sigma Press, 1996 / re-publication, Rumble Strips, 2018)
Ever Forward (MADS, 1997)

Biographies

Play On (Twelfth Night, 2009)
One for the Record (Avalon, 2013 / 2nd edition, 2018)

Music

Pink Floyd Song by Song (Fonthill, 2017)
Queen On Track (Sonicbond, 2018)
The Beatles: An A-Z Guide to Every Song: On Track (Sonicbond, 2019)
Solo Beatles 1969-1980 On Track (Sonicbond, 2020)
Crosby, Stills & Nash On Track (Sonicbond, 2020)
Dire Straits On Track (Sonicbond, 2021)
Fleetwood Mac in the 1970s (Sonicbond, 2021)
Eric Clapton: Solo On Track (Sonicbond, 2021)

Plays

The Difficult Crossing (Stagescripts, 2016)
A Difficult Man (Rumble Strips, 2021)

The 'Thank You' List

To Robin 'Trolly' Smith, Tom Barrow and Ian Taylor
for correspondence.

To Stephen Lambe, for sending the contract.

To Nick Jackson, with whom I've seen the last
however many Bond films, and who selflessly carried
out proofreading for this book.

To Chris, Maddie, Mimi and Jules, who each watched
a handful of these films with us.

To Rosie and Amy, for endless patience.

And to Amanda, always.

To the memories of Sir Roger Moore
(14 October 1927–23 May 2017)
and
Sir Sean Connery
(25 August 1930–31 October 2020)

Tho' much is taken, much abides; and though
We are not now that strength which in old days
Moved earth and heaven; that which we are, we are;
One equal temper of heroic hearts,
Made weak by time and fate, but strong in will
To strive, to seek, to find, and not to yield.
Tennyson, *Ulysses*

on screen ...
James Bond

Contents

Introduction

> The screen goes dark ... a pulsating, staccato beat fills the theatre. A series of white dots march across the screen in rhythm to the music ... one grows in size and we find ourselves suddenly looking down a telescopic sight. A man walks into range and the sight moves to follow him ... he spins around ... drops to one knee and fires directly at us. A red veil slowly descends over the screen and the telescope sight begins to waver ... then sags downward, shrinks ... and is once again a white dot.
>
> *James Bond in the Cinema*, John Brosnan, 1972.

For me, it's Roger Moore, trotting between absurd scenarios with a ready quip. For my kids, Daniel Craig, aloof, dangerous and brooding. For my mother and father, Sean Connery, effortlessly charismatic with a hint of danger. Every generation remembers going to the cinema to see their first James Bond film, their first James Bond actor, and the first time they saw the iconic opening gun barrel sequence.

In 1962, the first James Bond film, *Dr. No*, was a gamble. The 'Swinging Sixties' were about to begin–the James Bond films were a major part of them – and the aspirational lifestyle they depict were very much part of the art, music and fashion revolution that defined the decade. But no one could have predicted that the first Bond film would spawn twenty-four sequels (so far).

'The Bond films ... occupy a significant place in cinema history,' writes James Chapman. 'They mark the transition of the spy thriller from the netherland of the B-movie to the glossy, big-budget world of the A-feature.' [1]

The films' success are a wry combination of change and consistency. In the official series, we've had six different lead actors, four Moneypennys, three Qs, four Ms. There have been twelve directors and twenty credited screenwriters. But crucially, there has always been someone called Broccoli sitting in the producer's chair: Albert R 'Cubby' Broccoli from 1962 to 1995, his daughter Barbara Broccoli from 1995 to date. Likewise, the influence of co-producers Harry Salzman (1962-1974) and Cubby's stepson Michael G. Wilson (1985-date) must not be underestimated.

Success begets success, yes. But there's much more than producers' self-interest and desire for a fast buck to the James Bond films. The *Twilight* saga and the *Pirates of the Caribbean* series took millions at the box office but can hardly be considered part of the bedrock culture of a generation.

This book revisits and analyses all twenty-five official James Bond films – as well as the two attempts to steal some of that lucrative Bond audience. It's been fun re-watching these films. They have been part of my life since 1976, when *From Russia With Love* and *Goldfinger* were shown on TV. The following year I went to see *The Spy Who Loved Me* at my local cinema, The Forum in Romiley, Stockport.

> James Bond: In my country, Major, the condemned man is usually allowed a final request.

Major Anya Amasova: Granted.
James Bond: Let's get out of these wet things.

Andrew Wild
Rainow, Cheshire, 2018-2020

[1]*Licence to Thrill: A Cultural History of the Bond Films* (2000).

1953–1966: The Literary Canon

The scent and smoke and sweat of a casino are nauseating at three in the morning. Then the soul-erosion produced by high gambling – a compost of greed and fear and nervous tension – becomes unbearable and the senses awake and revolt from it. James Bond suddenly knew that he was tired. He always knew when his body or his mind had had enough and he always acted on the knowledge. This helped him to avoid staleness and the sensual bluntness that breeds mistakes.

Opening lines from Ian Fleming's first James Bond novel, *Casino Royale*.[1]

Before the films, there were the books: eleven novels and a collection of short stories published during author Ian Fleming's lifetime – one each year from 1953 to 1964 – then posthumous publication of a final novel in 1965 and a mop-up of three short stories collected in paperback in 1966. [2]

Ian Fleming was 'a curious and complex person … both clever and conceited'. [3] 'Beneath the sybaritic exterior', Ben McIntyre notes, 'Fleming was a driven man, intensely observant, with an internal sense of romance and drama that belied his public languor and occasional cynicism'. [4]

Born in 1908, Fleming came from a privileged background – he was the grandson of the founder of the merchant bank Robert Fleming & Co. His father, Valentine, was an MP from 1910 until 1917, and was killed on the Western Front. Valentine's obituary was written by Winston Churchill. [5]

Ian Fleming, the second of four sons, was educated at Eton, Sandhurst, and the universities of Munich and Geneva. His father's will was restrictive, so unlike many of his peers, he needed to earn a living, although he was never short of money. After failing the entrance exam for the Foreign Office, he had spells at Reuters and two City banking firms. Fleming twice visited Moscow in the 1930s. While working for Britain's Naval Intelligence Division during the Second World War, he was involved in planning Operation *GoldenEye*, and in the planning and oversight of two intelligence units, 30 Assault Unit and T-Force. Fleming's wartime service and his subsequent career as a journalist provided much of the background, detail and depth of the James Bond novels.

Upon demobilisation in 1945, Fleming became the Foreign Manager for *The Sunday Times*. He was a bridge-playing friend with the paper owner Lord Kemsley and his generous contract allowed him to take three months holiday every winter in Jamaica. It was here, in his house *GoldenEye*, that Fleming wrote *Casino Royale* in January and February 1952. [6]

Published in April 1953, this first novel is hard-hitting, inventive and, at times, shocking. *Casino Royale* contains many of the ingredients which coloured the later Bond novels and, in time, the films – a glamorous setting, a beautiful but flawed woman, a hideous villain, and much luxury, violence and sex. That famous opening scene is set in a casino: the introduction to the lead character in the first James Bond film *Dr. No*. is almost identical. Gambling in casinos was illegal in the UK until 1960, so from the opening moments of both the first Bond book and film we are in territory that was utterly unfamiliar to the majority of British readers and viewers. To war-ravaged Great Britain in 1953, with rationing still in place, the Bond stories were pure escapism and, to a large degree, fantastic and aspirational. Fleming himself understood this. 'James Bond is the author's pillow fantasy,' he told a reporter in 1963. 'It's very much like the Walter Mitty syndrome – the feverish dream of the author of what he might have been: bang, bang, bang, kiss, kiss, kiss, that sort of stuff. It's what you'd expect of an adolescent mind, which I happen to possess.'

Fleming's routine would be to plot and research his stories during the summer and autumn, write them in Jamaica in the winter, then polish and correct the proofs during the spring and summer. The hardback first edition would follow the next spring, by which time the next book would have been written. The second Bond novel, *Live and Let Die*, written in 1953 and published in April 1954, established both Fleming's annual routine and his racy writing style –fast-moving, taut, sexy, diligently researched, and underpinned by vivid powers of descriptive writing. Whereas some of Fleming's plots would verge on fantasy, and many character traits would reappear from book to book (talkative villains and nebulous evil organisations; cartoon henchmen; food snobbery; athletic, slightly-tanned women with 'fine' breasts and short fingernails; Bond's self-reliance, cruel mouth and comma of hair), readers of the Bond novels would grow to expect a hard, humourless lead character compared to the one later portrayed on film. Indeed, it's the complete lack of humour in Fleming's Bond novels that make them funny. There are also the outdated attitudes to women, sexuality and race, with heavy overtones of sadism and snobbery that can jar the modern reader.

Writer and historian Simon Winder suggests that Fleming was 'a handsome but banal philandering toff; self-confident but only through staying within the vast ramparts of class distain; intelligent but only because the usual arbitrary scraps of elite education had stuck to him. In fact, he is very much like Bond, but minus the action and adventure and plus the golfing chums'. [7] Fleming himself was asked on the radio programme *Desert Island Discs* 'Is there much of you in it?' The author replied: 'I hope not … I certainly haven't got his guts nor his very lively appetites.' [8]

A further ten books followed annually. *From Russia With Love* (1957) became Fleming's first overwhelming success, boosted by a visit from the British Prime Minister Anthony Eden to the *GoldenEye* estate and the publication of Fleming's previous books in paperback in 1956, and by a serialisation in *The Daily Express* newspaper, first in an abridged, multi-part form (April 1957) and then as a comic strip (February to May 1960). An article in *Life* (March 1961) listed *From Russia With Love* as one of President John F. Kennedy's ten favourite books. [9]

Ian Fleming soon became the best-selling thriller writer in both the US and the UK. Of the first eighteen books to sell a million copies in the UK, no fewer than ten were Bond thrillers. *For Your Eyes Only*, published in 1960, collected five short stories. Some of these were Fleming's adaptations of treatments for a television series that was never made. [10]

This proposed TV series was just one of several attempts to film James Bond.

[1] Copyright the Ian Fleming Estate.

[2] Since Fleming's death, a number of other authors have written continuation works: Kingsley Amis (1968, *Colonel Sun*, a direct sequel to the Fleming books), John Gardener (sixteen books, 1981-1996: Bond is the same character in the same extended timeline of the Fleming books, but by now getting a little long in the tooth), Raymond Benson (six books, 1997-2002, applies a floating timeline to ensure Bond is of appropriate contemporary age), Sebastian Faulks (one book, *Devil May Care*, 2008, set in the 1960s), Jeffery Deaver (one book, *Carte Blanche*, 2011, Bond's birthdate is reset to 1980), William Boyd (one book, *Solo*, 2013, set after the events of *Colonel Sun* in 1969), Anthony Horowitz (since 2014, two books set within or before the Fleming time line: 1957 [*Trigger Mortis*] and 1950 [*Forever and a Day*].)

[3] *Grace and Favour, the memoirs of Loelia, Duchess of Westminster* (1961). She was one of Fleming's many close woman friends (and possibly lover), and provided the name of James Bond's secretary in the early novels.

[4] *For Your Eyes Only: James Bond and Ian Fleming* (2009).

[5] Churchill ended his obituary for Fleming's father with these poetic words: 'As the war lengthens and intensifies and the extending lists appear, it seems as if one watched at night a well-loved city whose lights, which burn so bright, which burn so true, are extinguished in the darkness one by one.' A framed copy was treasured by Ian Fleming throughout his life.

[6] Fleming always pronounced 'Royale' as in 'Royal family'.

[7] *The Man Who Saved Britain: A Personal Journey into the Disturbing World of James Bond* (2006).

[8] First broadcast on 8 August 1963.

[9] Following Kennedy's endorsement, Fleming saw the sales of his books skyrocket. The other books listed in *Life* were *Montrose and Leadership* by John Buchan (1930), *Melbourne* by Lord David Cecil (1954), *Marlborough: His Life and Times* (book one) by Winston Churchill (1933),*John Quincy Adams and the Foundations of American Foreign Policy* by Samuel Flagg Bemis (1949), *Ordeal of the Union vol 2: The Emergence of Lincoln* by Allan Nevins (1950), *The Price of Union* by Herbert Agar (1942),*John C Calhoun American Portrait* by Margaret L Coit (1950), *Byron in Italy* by Peter Quennell (1941) and *The Red and the Black* by Stendhal (1830). As Sandipan Deb writes 'No one has read any of the other nine, including, one suspects, JFK.' Interestingly, Kennedy and Fleming had in fact met, in Washington DC on 13 March 1960. Urban myths persist that both Kennedy and Lee Harvey Oswald were reading Bond books on the night before Kennedy's assassination: it is true that Kennedy watched *From Russia With Love* the night he left before Dallas – as related in the obituary of Arthur M Schlesinger Jr., author of *One Thousand Days: John F Kennedy in the White House* (1965). As for Oswald, there's bound to be a conspiracy theory somewhere online.

[10] Another two were incorporated into Anthony Horowitz's Bond novels *Trigger Mortis* (2015) and *Forever and a Day* (2018).

1954-1962: Getting Bond on Screen

United Artists' decision to back three films – *Dr. No, Tom Jones* and *A Hard Day's Night*–was to have a revolutionary effect on the film industry.
Robert Murphy, *Sixties British Cinema* (1992)

The road to the release of *Dr. No* in 1962 was long and winding. The first stirrings of a film version of Fleming's hero were felt in January 1954. British film producer, director and screenwriter Alexander Korda had read a proof copy of *Live and Let Die* and wrote to Ian Fleming saying how much he'd enjoyed it. [1] Korda asked Fleming if he'd be interested in writing for films and Fleming responded a few days later: 'I think my next book ... is an expansion of a film story I've had in my mind since the war – a straight thriller with particularly English but also general appeal, set in London and on the White Cliffs of Dover, and involving the destruction of London by a V2. I have never written a film synopsis ... but if your office would care to send me along a specimen, I will dash it off and send it on to you from Jamaica.' [2]

Although Korda was initially interested, he later withdrew and Fleming completed his third Bond novel, *Moonraker*, that spring. [3]

Fleming sold the US TV rights for *Casino Royale* to Columbia Broadcasting in 1954. A fifty-minute version – retitled *Too Hot to Handle* – was broadcast live on 21 October 1954 as part of the weekly TV drama series *Climax!* Forty-four-year-old Barry Nelson plays 'Jimmy Bond' and Peter Lorre, some years down the line from *The Maltese Falcon*, is suitably unsettling as Le Chiffre. Fading Hollywood starlet Linda Christian plays Vesper, but otherwise, this version is no more than a curio. [4]

The film rights for Fleming's debut novel were duly sold in March 1955 and those for *Moonraker* that October. The rights for *Casino Royale* went to producer Gregory Bathoff but, for now, nothing came of the deal. The buyer for *Moonraker* was the actor John Payne, who was known equally for drama (*To the Shores of Tripoli*, 1942) and comedy (*Miracle on 34th Street*, 1947). Payne – aged 43 in 1955 – saw himself taking the lead role in a film version of *Moonraker* with Maureen O'Hara as Gala Brand. But the option was not taken up and duly expired in 1956. At around the same time, British character actor Ian Hunter and the Rank Organisation bought an advance option for *Moonraker*. [5] Rank did not develop the material further and sold them back to Fleming in 1959. [6]

Meanwhile, in the summer of 1956, Fleming began working with television producer Henry Morgenthau III on a film for American TV which would have followed the adventures of secret agent James Gunn in the Caribbean. A 28-page pilot script was written, but Morgenthau failed to raise the finance and the idea was abandoned. Fleming reshaped some of the ideas into his next novel, *Dr. No*, published in 1958. It is this book that so irritated reviewer Paul Johnson that he would write: 'There are three basic ingredients ...

all unhealthy, all thoroughly English: the sadism of a schoolboy bully, the mechanical, two-dimensional sex-longings of a frustrated adolescent, and the crude, snob-cravings of a suburban adult.' Sex, snobbery and sadism. Johnson, of course, missed the point. Fleming's books are not works of art and were never intended to be. But as fast-paced, fantastic thrillers, Fleming's Bond novels were, and remain, popular with readers who want to escape the drudgery of their daily grind.

Around this time, Fleming met shipping millionaire Aristotle Onassis in Monte Carlo to discuss scripting a film about the casino. They reached a verbal agreement which was seemingly never followed up. A short time later, in June 1958, Fleming discussed a Bond TV series with American producer Maurice Winnick who wanted to adapt OO7 for CBS television. Fleming wrote a number of plot ideas, but again the project fell away. Some of the ideas would be worked into short stories in the 1960 book *For Your Eyes Only*, mostly written in January and February 1959.

In May 1959, Fleming met Irish film producer Kevin McClory at Claridges in London. The link was Fleming's close friend Ivar Bryce. [7] Bryce had co-produced McClory's pet project *The Boy and the Bridge*, filmed at the end of 1958 and released soon after this first meeting. Fleming and McClory were both mercurial talents and worked well together. With screenwriter Jack Wittingham, they developed the idea for a film to be called *Longitude 78 West*, later renamed *Thunderball*. [8] Thus begins the complicated gestation of the fourth James Bond film.

An article in *The Daily Express* claimed that McClory wanted Trevor Howard for the role as the English actor, then aged 46, looked as if he had 'lived it up enough' to be OO7. Fleming noted that 'Howard is not my idea of Bond, not by a long way,' Fleming told *The Daily Express* in April 1959. 'It is nothing personal against him. I think he's a very fine actor. But don't you think he's a bit old to be Bond?' Fleming favoured Peter Finch, who would later win an Oscar for his role as the crazed news presenter in *Network* (1977). In a series of letters between Fleming and McClory, sold at auction in 2018, the names of Richard Todd (*The Dam Busters*), Stanley Baker (*The Cruel Sea*) and Richard Burton (*Look Back in Anger*) were also mooted. By the end of the year, Bryce's interest had waned. McClory was still keen, but without a financial backer. With the project seemingly stalled, Fleming novelised the work into his ninth book, *Thunderball*, completed in Jamaica in January and February 1960 and published in March 1961. Aggrieved that Fleming had infringed his copyright, McClory sued Fleming. The case came to court in 1963 – stress that no doubt hastened Fleming's early death. [9]

Elsewhere, in 1959, Albert R. 'Cubby' Broccoli at Warwick Films expressed an interest in adapting the Bond novels. His partner at Warwick, Irving Allen, was unenthusiastic. Broccoli was a larger-than-life character who had started in the post-room at 20th Century Fox in the 1930s and would befriend Howard Hughes, the American business magnate, investor, pilot, engineer, film director and philanthropist. Broccoli founded Warwick with Allen in 1953 and moved to Britain to fulfil his ambition to be an independent film producer. Bankrolled by Hughes, he produced *The Red Beret*, directed by future Bond director Terence Young, and another eighteen films over the next seven years. Broccoli's 1959 attempt to gain the rights to the Bond films ended in failure. But here was an itch that he was determined to scratch. 'My father believed you could achieve whatever you wanted to, whatever you desired,' said his daughter Barbara Broccoli in 2012. 'If you worked hard, any dream was possible.' [10]

Meanwhile, Ian Fleming's next move was rather remarkable. Having assigned theatrical rights to his American agent MCA in 1959, a year later his head was turned by Ann Marlow, a glamorous actor-turned-producer. He assigned TV rights to her, 'in a fit of romantic largesse'. [11] They had met over smoked salmon, scrambled eggs and champagne in New York and Fleming assigned the rights by scribbling on a Sardi's menu and signing his name below. [12] In June 1961, Fleming was ready to sell a six-month option on the film rights to his published and future James Bond novels and short stories to Harry Saltzman, a Canadian film producer based in the UK. [13] Saltzman co-produced such ground-breaking films as *Look Back in Anger* (1959) and *Saturday Night and Sunday Morning* (1960) – films with a very British social realism that would transfer to the James Bond series, and ground, at least for the first few films, the more extreme flights of fantasy. Harry Saltzman's offer interested Fleming. But with TV rights assigned to Ann Marlow, and with no self-respecting film producer wanting to be undercut by the potential sale of TV rights to a property they had optioned, Fleming found himself having to obsequiously extract himself from his short-sighted deal. He wrote to Marlow on 3 July 1961. 'You really are an angel, and I am not in the least bit surprised that you should feel rather 'miffed'. All I can do at the moment is to order you a small memento from Cartier in token of my esteem and affection.' [14]

Towards the end of Saltzman's option period, screenwriter Wolf Mankowitz introduced him to Albert Broccoli. Saltzman and Broccoli formed Eon Productions for the express purpose of producing Bond films. The buzz surrounding James Bond started to get louder. Even *Pravda* would take note: 'It is no accident that sham agents of the Soviet counter-intelligence, represented in caricature form, invariably figure in the role of Bond's opponents, because Bond kills right and left the men Fleming wanted to kill – Russians, Reds and Yellows. Bond is portrayed as a sort of white archangel, destroying the impure races.' [15]

Eon's biggest challenges were to find a studio to fund the project and an actor who at least *looked* like the literary Bond. It is in *From Russia With Love* – the fifth Bond novel, and one of the best – that we get the most detailed description of Bond's physical features.

> It was a dark, clean-cut face, with a three-inch scar showing whitely down the sunburned skin of the right cheek. The eyes were wide and level under

straight, rather long black brows. The hair was black, parted on the left, and carelessly brushed so that a thick black comma fell down over the right eyebrow. The longish straight nose ran down to a short upper lip below which was a wide and finely drawn but cruel mouth. The line of jaw was straight and firm.
from Ian Fleming's *From Russia With Love.* [16]

As is often the way, many separate strands came together at once, leading Eon to both United Artists and Sean Connery. In 1961, David Picker, Vice President of United Artists, received a tip-off from his cousin's husband, suggesting that the Bond books would make good films. He called Doris Vidor, daughter of Warner Bros. studio co-founder and long-time president Harry Warner, and wife of director Charles Vidor, who also worked for United Artists. '[I] asked her to check on the rights to the James Bond books, whose author, Ian Fleming, was represented by MCA,' Picker wrote in his autobiography. 'Her response was quick. He was represented by Bob Fenn at MCA London and they were not for sale.' [17] Still hoping to secure the right, Picker persisted. He wanted Alfred Hitchcock to direct the first Bond film for United Artists. That idea fell through, but some months later, Picker was visited by Harry Salzman and Albert Broccoli. 'We own the rights to James Bond,' Salzman simply said. He had bought an option from Ian Fleming earlier in 1961. Finally, everything aligned.

Eon signed a deal with United Artists for financial backing and distribution of seven films. Eon also agreed to pay Ian Fleming $100,000 for each title used, plus a percentage of the net profits from each film. Astutely, Saltzman and Broccoli bought the rights to the character James Bond, ensuring that they could continue to make James Bond films once the source novels had all been mined. They created a separate company, Danjaq, specifically to administer copyright and trademarks for James Bond on screen. A press announcement was made that same month. As for the actor who would play Bond, with a series of films planned from the beginning, clearly no established star would commit themselves to more than one film. 'Our theory was that if we cast a virtually unknown actor', Cubby Broccoli wrote in his memoirs, 'the public would be more likely to accept him as a character. We wanted to build the actor into the role, so that he would grow with it.' [18]

Patrick McGoohan, from TV's *Danger Man*, was a credible early candidate, but was uneasy about the sex and violence. Broccoli noted that James Fox, a year ahead of his breakthrough in *The Servant,* was considered, as was Roger Moore, soon to be cast as *The Saint* (1962-1969). Moore had met Broccoli and Saltzman over 'the tables of the gaming tables in London's Curzon Street'. [19] According to Broccoli, Moore was 'slightly too young, perhaps a shade too pretty'. [20] Moore confirms in his memoirs that he was never approached for *Dr. No*.

Patricia Lewis, the show-business editor of *The Daily Express* fuelled the speculation. In June 1961, Lewis reported that Harry Saltzman was planning to screen-test Patrick Allen – a character actor from many British films of the

1950s and was 'also thinking about Michael Craig [best known as a stage actor at that time] and Patrick McGoohan'. Presumably, with the approval of Eon, Patricia Lewis launched a competition in *The Daily Express* to find the perfect Bond. In her article 'In Search of a He-Man', she invited 'every tough-talking type' to have 'a crack at landing this plum role'. Applicants were invited to submit their acting résumés and vital statistics to Lowndes Film Productions [one of Salzman's companies] in Soho Square, London. The winner would be announced as James Bond and be rewarded with a three-year contract to star in two Bond films a year. Patricia Lewis announced in *The Daily Express* on 21 September 1961 that Peter Anthony had won the competition. She quoted Broccoli as saying that Anthony had 'a Greg Peck quality that's instantly arresting'. Certainly, contemporary pictures show Anthony as sophisticated and handsome with a hint of menace. Peter Anthony had potential, clearly, but was too risky to cast. [21]

The search continued.

'An unprecedented number of talented young actors emerged in the early 60s,' notes Robert Murphy in *Sixties British Cinema*. 'Albert Finney, Tom Courtney, Alan Bates and Terence Stamp had established themselves ... by 1962.' Stamp, Bates or Finney could have taken on James Bond at a pinch. Indeed, Stamp was one of over 400 actors who were considered as a replacement for Sean Connery in 1967-1968. They would all have been more suitable than David Niven, Richard Burton, James Stewart (Ian Fleming's suggestions), Richard Johnson (later the cinematic Bulldog Drummond, 1967-1971; the preference of *Dr. No* director Terence Young), Peter Lawford (United Artists' recommendation), Cary Grant or James Mason (both Cubby Broccoli's, both in their fifties). Robert Shaw, later to play Red Grant in the second Bond film, was also mentioned. Other names suggested included Michael Redgrave and Trevor Howard, both by then probably too old, and certainly too famous. [22]

'While all the discussions about the casting of Bond were going on', wrote producer Cubby Broccoli, 'one face kept coming back to my mind. It belonged to an actor I had met the year before in London. He was Sean Connery.'

Thomas Sean Connery was born on 25 August 1930, in Fountainbridge, Edinburgh. The son of a lorry driver and laundress, he had a modest upbringing. Known during his youth as 'Tommy', Connery enjoyed comic books and visits to the cinema, and quit school aged 13 to work as a milkman for the St. Cuthbert's Co-operative Society. He joined the Royal Navy in 1946 but was released from service after three years on medical grounds. Back in Edinburgh, Connery took various jobs, including shovelling coal, bricklaying, lifeguarding, labouring, polishing coffins and posing as a model at the Edinburgh Art School. A member of the Dunedin Weightlifting Club, he travelled to London in 1953 to take part in Mr Universe. Here, Connery received his first break: while in London, he auditioned for a local casting director, who asked him to join the chorus of the musical *South Pacific*, playing at the Theatre Royal, Drury Lane since 1951. He started his film career in 1954, as an extra in *Lilacs in the Spring* alongside Anna Neagle. Over the next few years, Connery was cast in many films and TV programmes, including his first lead role as a down-on-his-luck boxer in an acclaimed BBC production of *Requiem for a Heavyweight* in 1957. Twentieth-Century Fox studios gave him a seven-year contract worth around £6,000 a year, but was unable to find suitable parts for him. Instead, they loaned him out to other studios, and he was cast in *Action of the Tiger* (MGM, 1957), *Another Time, Another Place* (Paramount, 1958) and *Darby O'Gill and the Little People* (Walt Disney, 1959). *Action of the Tiger* was crucial in the James Bond story, as it was directed by Terence Young, who would later take charge of three of the first four Bond films. Connery was most often seen on TV in this period. He portrayed Hotspur in a BBC adaptation of *An Age of Kings* (1960), appeared in the TV movie *Without the Grail* (1960), ITV's *The Pets* (1960), the title role of *Macbeth* (1961) for the Canadian Broadcast Corporation, Alexander the Great in Terence Rattigan's *Adventure Story* (1961), and Vronsky in *Anna Karenina* (1961) for BBC Television. Connery was eventually given second billing in two feature films: *The Frightened City* (1961), a crime drama with Herbert Lom in which Connery's character is killed off in the first twenty minutes, and *On the Fiddle* (1961, retitled *Operation Snafu* in the US when first released in 1965). He was one of many familiar names to have small parts in the large ensemble cast of *The Longest Day* (1962). [23]

'Connery … had a strength and energy about him which I found riveting,' wrote Cubby Broccoli. 'Everything about Connery … was convincingly James Bond.' 'Connery's James Bond', writes Andrew Spicer, '… that extraordinary synthesis of the tough guy and the debonair'. [24] 'We all knew this guy had something,' Harry Saltzman would recall. 'We signed him without a screen test. We all agreed, he was 007.' United Artists weren't so sure. 'No. Keep trying,' they telegrammed. 'Harry called me from London,' writes David Picker of UA. 'He was coming to New York with some films and stills [of] Sean Connery. I saw the clips. He was attractive. I was neither over- nor under-whelmed. I asked Harry if he was the best he could find, and his answer was 'He's the richest man in the poor house'.'

Awarding the role to Sean Connery was a risk – but Broccoli and Saltzman were seasoned gamblers, and their wager paid off. Spectacularly. 'In retrospect', notes Roy Armes in *A Critical History of British Cinema*, 'it is clear that Saltzman and Broccoli were right in all the crucial decisions, most important the casting of Sean Connery as Bond. Connery … was able to bring to the role a combination of toughness and nonchalance which made Fleming's rather preposterous comic strip hero an authentic vehicle for the audience's dreams of action and affluence.' Connery's Bond was suave, charming, deadly, nonchalant, cocky and masculine but with questionable scruples. Initially unconvinced, author Ian Fleming famously called Connery an 'overgrown stuntman'. He only relented after the pair had lunch at The Savoy, where another guest, the Marchioness of Milford Haven (or perhaps Ivar Bryce's teenage niece, sources cannot agree), assured Fleming that Connery had 'it'. 'I never got introduced to Fleming until I was well into the movie,' Sean Connery told Melvyn Bragg in 2008. 'But I know he was not [initially] happy with me as the choice. What was it he called me, or told somebody? That I was an over-developed stunt man. He never said it to me. When I did eventually meet him, he was very interesting, erudite and a snob – a real snob. But his company was very good for a limited time for me.'

Fleming later noted, 'the man they have chosen for Bond, Sean Connery, is a real charmer – fairly unknown, but a good actor with the right looks and physique. One thing I put my foot down about when they planned the first film was to choose an unknown actor who wasn't yet typed. Yes, Sean is a good choice.' [25]

To many, Sean Connery is James Bond. [26]

Screenwriter Richard Maibaum agrees: 'Sean Connery was absolutely perfect. Apart from physically being a great specimen and good-looking, he had a basic irony about him. Also, he was a much better actor than most people thought. You believed all of the physical stuff that Sean did.' [27]

The Bond films in the sixties, seventies, eighties and nineties were about escapism – glamorous, colourful and tongue-in-cheek, with luxurious locations, big stunts, larger-than-life villains and an indestructible hero. Occasionally, they tripped over into pure fantasy – *You Only Live Twice*, *Moonraker* – and just sometimes, we saw elements of honest realism – *The Living Daylights*, *For Your Eyes Only*, *On Her Majesty's Secret Service*. At all times, as with Fleming's novels, they were fantastic and aspirational. 'Bond is, quite simply, a stylish, fast-shooting, high-living, sexually liberated advertisement for all the things the ordinary Britons had never had, yet dreamed of,' suggests Ben McIntyre. 'The finest food and drink, smart clothes, fast cars, leisure time, casinos, exotic foreign travel, swimming in warm waters.'

Roger Moore:

> In an era when travel was the reserve of the rich, post-war rationing and rebuilding was still a vivid memory, and fine living consisted of a night out at the pictures followed by a fish-and-chip supper, James Bond offered something exciting – something previously unimaginable. [28]

'[The Bond films] display the attractions of a material life richer and more adventurous than Joe Lampton could ever have dreamed of,' writes Robert Murphy in *Sixties British Cinema*. [29] 'Cars that fly and swim and have customised flame-throwers, endless supplies of cool drinks, sleek women, strange and exciting locations. The energy and panache of … the Bond films, the success of British pop music and the development of the myth of Swinging London made British society suddenly exciting, charismatic and fashionable.'

That energy lasted right through sixteen films and four Bond actors to the end of the 1980s. [30] In Bond's modern update of 1995, Pierce Brosnan combined the charisma, urbanity and sex appeal of Connery with the wit and polish of Moore and extended the series' appeal, without too much change, through to the early 2000s. But the Austin Powers films of 1997-2002 poked fun at Bond as the super-suave not-so-secret agent. The first two Jason Bourne films (2002-2004) rewrote the rules of the blockbuster thriller. Major change became inevitable. With Daniel Craig's five films from 2006 to 2021, Bond has become more emotionally complex, more human, more vulnerable. He makes mistakes, he falls in love, he gets hurt, he bleeds. By far, the best actor to have played James Bond, Craig himself, has said 'The question I keep asking myself while playing the role is, 'Am I the good guy or just a bad guy who works for the good side?'' [31] This echoes James Bond's own words in an Ian Fleming novel: 'History is moving pretty quickly these days, and the heroes and villains keep on changing parts.' [32]

The basic formula of the Bond film remains essentially the same. But, crucially, the main character – whilst still the ultimate male fantasy – has evolved, adapted and been re-invented by the actor of the moment. Connery: lithe, virile, charismatic, cocksure. Lazenby: physical, charming, handsome. Moore: wry, smart, self-mocking. Dalton: saturnine, professional, dangerous. Brosnan: smooth, shrewd, efficient. Craig: taciturn, tough, driven, dark.

The remarkable success of the twenty-five James Bond films can be attributed to many factors – the strength and imagination of Ian Fleming's original novels, the consistency of the creative and production teams, the skill and wit of the screenplays.

> Natalya Simonova (in *GoldenEye*): How can you act like this? How can you be so cold?
> Bond: It's what keeps me alive.
> Natalya: No, it what keeps you alone.

'The appeal of Bond is global,' suggests Ben MacIntyre. 'But … it helps to be British, male and slightly naff: interested in gizmos, sex without commitment, saving the world, clunking *double entendres*, ironic self-mockery and, above all, embracing a particular sort of loneliness.' [33]

In the final analysis, every James Bond film comes down to one key point: Bond lives a glamorous, exciting life and we live vicariously through him.

[1] 1893-1956. Hungarian born and a pioneer film-maker in Hungary, Vienna and Berlin, he moved to Hollywood in 1926, then relocated to London in 1932 to make such well-regarded films as *Elephant Boy* (1937), *The Third Man* (1949), *Cry, The Beloved Country* (1951) and *Richard III* (1956), amongst many others. It's intriguing to speculate how Korda might have produced Bond.

[2] Reproduced in *The Man with the Golden Typewriter* edited by Fergus Fleming, 2015. Copyright the Ian Fleming Estate.

[3] Ironically, the resultant book, *Moonraker*, would be the very last Fleming novel to be

used as the basis for a film. Even then only the characters of Bond, M and Drax – and practically none of Fleming's story – would carry through from the book to the film.

[4] Performed live, the episode was lost for decades until a black and white kinescope was located by film historian Jim Schoenberger in 1981. The story that Peter Lorre as Le Chiffre gets up and leaves the set after being killed appears to be apocryphal. It's available on the 2011 BluRay release of the 1967 film version.

[5] *The Life of Ian Fleming* (1966)

[6] A hoax article, published on 1 April 2004, claimed that a shooting script and forty minutes of footage from a 'forgotten' 1956 film version of *Moonraker* had been discovered in the estate of the (fictional) producer Dayton Mace. The film was said to have been directed by Orson Welles with Dirk Bogarde as 007, Peter Lorre as Willy Krebs and Welles himself as Sir Hugo Drax.

[7] Bryce and Fleming had first met as children in 1917, and again as schoolboys at Eton. They both worked for William Stephenson, the head of British Security Coordination, during the Second World War. Fleming visited Bryce in Jamaica in 1941 and resolved to buy a house there after the war. Fleming bought land in Jamaica in 1945 and built his house *GoldenEye*, where he would spend each winter until his death in 1964. All of the James Bond books were written at *GoldenEye*. Fleming would name Bond's CIA agent friend after Ivar Bryce's middle name, Felix.

[8] 78 degrees west is the longitude of the island of Grand Bahama.

[9] Future versions of the novel were credited as 'based on a screen treatment by Kevin McClory, Jack Whittingham, and Ian Fleming', in that order. The whole sorry tale is told in Robert Sellers' absorbing book *The Battle for Bond* (2007).

[10] Quoted in *Everything or Nothing*, Stevan Riley's terrific 50th-anniversary documentary film.

[11] Andrew Lycett in *Ian Fleming* (1996).

[12] Sardi's was then, and still is, located at 234 West 44th Street, New York, just off Broadway.

[13] With the exception of *Casino Royale*, which he had previously sold. By this time, the rights had passed from Gregory Ratoff to his widow, and then, in December 1960, to producer Charles K Feldman.

[14] Reproduced in *The Man With the Golden Typewriter* edited by Fergus Fleming, 2015. Copyright the Ian Fleming Estate.

[15] 30 September 1965, reproduced in *James Bond: A Celebration* (1987).

[16] Copyright the Ian Fleming Estate.

[17] *Musts, Maybes, and Nevers: A Book About the Movies* (2013).

[18] *When the Snow Melts–The Autobiography of Cubby Broccoli* (1999).

[19] Roger Moore in *Bond on Bond* (2012).

[20] *When the Snow Melts–The Autobiography of Cubby Broccoli* (1999).

[21] For the record, the other finalists were Gordon Cooper, a sales rep from Warrington; Anthony Clements, a salesman from Bolton; Frank Ellement, a teacher turned actor from London; Michael Ricketts, an engineer from Hadleigh, and Bob Simmons, a former Army Physical Training Instructor. Simmons would work as a stuntman/stunt coordinator on ten of the Bond films from 1962 to 1985.

[22] Cary Grant and Cubby Broccoli were friends – Grant was best man at the producer's wedding in 1959. James Mason, Grant's co-star in *North by Northwest*, was offered the part but he refused to commit to more than two films. He turned down the role of Hugo Drax in 1979's *Moonraker*. Terence Stamp would have made a great Bond villain. He might yet.

[23] Three actors later cast as Bond villains also appeared in *The Longest Day*: Gert Fröbe (Auric Goldfinger, *Goldfinger*, 1964), Curd Jürgens (Karl Stromberg, *The Spy Who Loved Me*, 1977), and Walter Gotell (Morzeny in *From Russia With Love* and six appearances as General Gogol, 1977-1987).
[24] *Typical Men–The Representation of Masculinity in Popular British Cinema* (2003).
[25] First sentence from a letter to Blanche Blackwell, 25 October 1961. Reproduced in *The Man with the Golden Typewriter* edited by Fergus Fleming, 2015. Copyright the Ian Fleming Estate. Connery and Fleming would not meet until 1962, during location filming for *Dr. No*. Second sentence from a December 1963 interview with Peter Haining, reproduced in *James Bond: A Celebration* (1987).
[26] Possibly co-incidentally, possibly not, Connery in 1962 bears an uncanny resemblance to the comic strip James Bond, running each day in *The Daily Express* from July 1958. Eleven Bond stories had been serialised by the time *Dr. No* was released. Connery was never able to shake off the Bond image. Even after quitting in 1967, he would return to the role twice, and give broad winks to his past role in both *Indiana Jones and the Last Crusade* (1989) and *The Rock* (1996).
[27] *James Bond: A Celebration* (1987).
[28] *Bond on Bond* (2012).
[29] Joe Lampton is the ambitious hero of *Room at the Top*, the first of the new wave of British kitchen sink realism film dramas, released in 1959.
[30] Notwithstanding the considerable acting chops of Timothy Dalton, his two films used the same creative teams – notably the director and writers – as the later Moore films.
[31] *Parade* (2012).
[32] *Casino Royale* by Ian Fleming, copyright the Ian Fleming Estate.
[33] *For Your Eyes Only: Ian Fleming and James Bond* (2009).

1962–1971: No, Mr. Bond. I expect you to die!

Dr. No

Harry Saltzman & Albert R Broccoli Present Ian Fleming's *Dr. No* starring Sean Connery
'The First James Bond Film!'
Release Date: 5 October 1962. Running time: 109 minutes. Distributed by United Artists. Producers: Harry Salzman (1 of 9), Albert R Broccoli (1 of 17).
James Bond: Sean Connery (1 of 7), M: Bernard Lee (1 of 11), Boothroyd (proto-Q): Peter Burton, Moneypenny: Lois Maxwell (1 of 14), Leiter: Jack Lord And Joseph Wiseman (Dr. No) with Ursula Andress (Honey Ryder), Anthony Dawson (Dent), John Kitzmiller (Quarrel), Zena Marshall (Miss Taro), Eunice Grayson (Sylvia Trench) (1 of 2).
Director: Terence Young (1 of 3). Screenplay: Richard Maibaum (1 of 13), Johanna Harwood and Berkely Mather (1 of 2). Production Design: Ken Adam (1 of 7). Main titles by Maurice Binder (1 of 14). Music: Monty Norman. Theme performed by John Barry Orchestra. Cinematography: Ted Moore (1 of 7). Edited by Peter Hunt (1 of 5).

Plot

James Bond is sent to Jamaica to investigate the disappearance of the head of station and his secretary. With the assistance of Felix Leiter of the CIA and Quarrel, a resourceful fisherman, Bond starts to unravel a wider plot. After two attempts on his life, Bond follows the trail of clues to the island of Crab Key. Here, Bond and Quarrel meet Honey Ryder, a native shell-diver. Quarrel is killed and Bond and Honey are captured by Dr. No, a reclusive scientist and member of SPECTRE, who is sabotaging the US missile programme. Bond escapes, rescues Honey and kills Dr. No.

Cast

With Sean Connery in place, another crucial casting decision was Bernard Lee as the irascible M, head of M16.

> M looked like any member of any of the clubs in St James's Street. Dark grey suit, stiff white collar, the favourite dark blue bowtie with spots, rather loosely tied, the thin black cord of the rimless eyeglass…the keen sailor's face, with the clear, sharp sailor's eyes.
> From Ian Fleming's, *Moonraker.* [1]

M is introduced early in the film to kick off the plot – a trope that would last right through until the series' reboot with *Casino Royale*. Lee would portray M in eleven Bond films, rarely getting more than five minutes of screen time. A busy actor, he would exercise his formidable skills in over one hundred films across more than forty years, perhaps most noticeably as the spy Harry

Houghton in *Ring of Spies* (1964). M's secretary, Moneypenny is played by Canadian-born Lois Maxwell. She had attended the Royal Academy of Dramatic Arts with Roger Moore and was a jobbing actor when she was offered either Moneypenny or Bond's girlfriend Sylvia Trench in *Dr. No*. She chose wisely and appeared in each of the first fourteen Bond films through to *A View to a Kill* in 1985. She also appeared with Roger Moore in episodes of *The Saint* and *The Persuaders!* Bond's scenes with M and Moneypenny 'create a sense of stability in contrast to the exotic, dangerous and usually foreign settings in which Bond carries out his missions'. [2]

Joseph Wiseman had a long career in live theatre, especially on Broadway. He was cast as the half-Chinese *Dr. No* by Harry Salzman, who remembered him from *The Detective Story* (1951). 'I had no idea what I was letting myself in for,' he said later. 'I had no idea it would achieve the success it did. As far as I was concerned, I thought it might be just another Grade B Charlie Chan mystery.'

Ian Fleming had another actor in mind for the film's protagonist: his step-cousin and golf buddy, Christopher Lee. 'Before any of his stories had been screened', Lee wrote in his autobiography, 'he said to me, 'I want you to play Dr. No, if you will. You'd suit the part.' I said 'wonderful!' I really did look forward to playing this power-crazed character who 'looked like a giant venomous worm wrapped in a grey tin-foil'. But I was to be disappointed. No call came as … they had found Joseph Wiseman.' [3] This is the first of many 'what ifs' in Bond casting lore.

And, of course, there's twenty-six-year-old Swiss-born Ursula Andress. Andress made a few films in Italy in 1954-1955 and tried her luck in Hollywood from early 1955. Despite being signed to Paramount and later Columbia, she made no films there. She did, however, marry actor and director John Derek. [4] *Dr. No* was her first major film role.

'Kirk Douglas and everybody came over for my birthday,' she remembers. 'We were all laughing while we were reading the script, because we thought nothing could be worse. I figured no one would ever see it, so I might as well try it.' [5]

Andress' birthday is 19 March, so if her story is true then she had the script as early as March 1961, three months before Eon signed with UA, and was cast sometime before Sean Connery. This seems unlikely. Fans of her later films might be surprised by her voice in *Dr. No*. Her speaking scenes were dubbed by German actress Monica 'Nikki' van der Zyl. Van der Zyl dubbed actors' voices in ten Bond films, including Sylvia Trench (*Dr. No*, *From Russia With Love*), Kerim's girl (*From Russia With Love*), Jill Masterson (*Goldfinger*), Domino (*Thunderball*), Kissy Suzuki (*You Only Live Twice*), Olympe (*On Her Majesty's Secret Service*), Marie (*Diamonds Are Forever*), Solitaire (*Live and Let Die*), Chew Mee (*The Man With the Golden Gun*), Corinne Dufour (*Moonraker*) and unnamed private jet attendant (*Moonraker*). [6] Andress' singing voice was provided by Betty Diana Coupland, the wife of composer Monty Norman.

Theme Song

The familiar 'James Bond Theme', with the motif written by Monty Norman and arranged and orchestrated by John Barry, kicks off over fifty years of the most successful film series of all.

Production

Dr. No was filmed between January and March 1962 at Pinewood Studios, Buckinghamshire and on location in the UK and Jamaica.

Observations

Dr. No is a glamorous, classy film, cleverly written, tightly directed, beautifully designed and gorgeously shot. We need to pay tribute here to Richard Maibaum, Terence Young, Peter Hunt, Ken Adam and Ted Moore – four perfect, inspired choices to work on *Dr. No*.

Richard Maibaum, a writer who had some success in the theatre before being lured to Hollywood, was deft at creating basic ideas for others or providing necessary nip and tuck to other writers' material. He was credited as co-writer of twelve Bond films from 1962 to 1989: his only sole writing credit for a Bond film was *On Her Majesty's Secret Service*, which followed Fleming's original novel closely. Maibaum came to Cubby Broccoli's attention through an association with Alan Ladd – he co-wrote and produced the 1949 remake of *The Great Gatsby*. Maibaum adapted *Hell Below Zero* for Broccoli's Warwick Films in 1953, also starring Ladd. So, when Ladd was signed for *The Red Beret*, Cubby's first film for Warwick Pictures, released later that year, Maibaum was signed too. This led to *The Cockleshell Heroes* for Warwick and, eventually, to *Dr. No*. Maibaum's key contribution was the addition of a touch of comedy to Fleming's resolutely humourless books. 'What we have to do', he said in 1987, 'is to spoof ourselves and quite rightly the audience has the last laugh'.[7] For *Dr. No*, Maibaum retooled an earlier script by English screenwriter Wolf Mankowitz. According to Martin Sterling and Gary Morecombe in their admirable book *Martinis, Guns and Girls*, Mankowitz feared that *Dr. No* would be a disaster, and insisted on having his name removed from the film's credits.

Terence Young directed three of the first four Bond films and also worked on *The Red Beret*. Born in Shanghai, Young had begun his film career as a screenwriter in 1939. After his national service, he turned to directing: his first credit was for *Corridor of Mirrors*, a Gothic romance released in 1948 which featured 26-year-old Christopher Lee in his first film role. By the time of *The Red Beret*, Young had directed several well-received films.

'We were lucky in one sense,' writes Cubby Broccoli. 'I believe that Terence Young, like Ian Fleming, subconsciously saw himself as James Bond. He had a fair claim to the fantasy. He certainly had the background. He'd read the books, too, was a *bon viveur* and knew the odd countess here and there.'

'It was a question of timing,' Young said. 'I think we arrived not only in the right year, but the right week of the right month. We hit the audiences at *precisely* the right moment. I think the first [Bond] picture was the most perfectly timed film ever made. I don't think when I took on *Dr. No* I had a very clear conception of what I was going to do. The original Ian Fleming story was diabolically childish – like something straight out of a Grade B thriller. All Fleming stories are like that. The only way I thought we could do a Bond film was to heat it up a bit, to give it a sense of humour, to make it as cynical as possible.' [8]

And as Lois Maxwell said: 'Terence took Sean under his wing. He took him to dinner, to his tailor, showed him how to walk, how to talk, even how to eat.' [9]

Editor Peter Hunt keeps *Dr. No* moving at a cracking pace. 'I was a top English film editor in those days,' he said in 1997. 'Harry Saltzman ... came across to England and the first film he made was *Look Back in Anger*, which starred Richard Burton. The war was over, and I was editing, and Harry had always wanted to use me. When he made a film he'd call me and say, 'Come on, let's make a film together', and each time I was either in the middle of a film, or about to do another film, so I had never been able to do it. But we kept on good terms, and it was Harry who got a hold of me when he was doing *Dr. No*. It happened that I wasn't do anything else at that time. I've known Terence since I was a boy; I'd been assistant on several films with him, and I'd always liked him. So all of that sort of slotted into place, and I found myself editing *Dr. No*.' [10]

Hunt subsequently edited *From Russia With Love*, *Goldfinger*, *Thunderball* and *You Only Live Twice*, and directed *On Her Majesty's Secret Service*.

The *look* of the early Bond films can be attributed to Ken Adam and Ted Moore. Designer Ken Adam, veteran of seven Bond films from 1962 to 1979 was as important to *Dr. No* as Sean Connery. The visual identity of these early Bond films – Adam designed *Goldfinger*, *Thunderball* and *You Only Live Twice* in the 1960s – was very much a part of the films' aspirational storytelling. Adam, a German-born Jew, fled the Nazis and came to the UK in 1934 and was an RAF fighter pilot in the Second World War. He started his career in films as a draughtsman in 1947, progressed through the ranks of the design teams and had worked with Albert Broccoli on *In the Nick* (1959) and *The Trials of Oscar Wilde* (1960). '*Dr. No* was a very small budget film,' Adam told Sascha Braun in 2004. 'Terence Young was a friend of mine; I had also worked for the two producers Cubby Broccoli and Harry Saltzman. I was no stranger to them. I had a meeting with Terence which took exactly five minutes. He said: 'Ken, I leave the concepts of the settings to you to provide it. But how you design them is your Business.' So I went back to England and to Pinewood. The ideas came then really. The first thing that happened, I called in all the Heads of Construction at Pinewood and said, please let me have any new material that is on the market. They came up with stainless steel and copper finishes and so on which then inspired me to go way out in my design. Because at that time I hadn't seen any contemporary film which reflected the electronic age, the age of computers we were living in. So that gave me an opportunity to do that and at the same time keep the whole thing not completely realistic – tongue-in-cheek. Bigger than life, you know?' [11]

Adam's work on *Dr. No* attracted the attention of Stanley Kubrick and led to his spectacular work on *Dr. Strangelove* (1963). Adam was knighted in 2003 and died in 2016, aged 95, after a quite remarkable life.

Ted Moore, *Dr. No*'s cinematographer, had filmed the much-admired *The Trials of Oscar Wilde*. Moore gives *Dr. No* crisp framing, vibrant colours and a lush, grand cinematography which helped create a feeling of luxury in the Bond films. Moore would go on be involved in another six of the Bond series: *From Russia With Love* (for which he won a BAFTA), *Goldfinger*, *Thunderball*, *Diamonds Are Forever*, *Live and Let Die* and *The Man With the Golden Gun*.

Dr. No establishes a number of series tropes, most of which were present in Fleming's books. Umberto Eco, later a best-selling author of fiction, edited one of the first Bond studies in 1966 and identified the following scheme, with elements present in almost every novel, if not always in the same sequence: [12]

M moves and gives a task to Bond.
The villain moves and appears to Bond (perhaps in alternating forms) [i.e., more than one villainous character].
Bond moves and gives a first check to the villain, or the villain gives a first check to Bond.
Woman moves and shows herself to Bond.
Bond consumes woman, possesses her or begins consumption.
The villain captures Bond, with or without the woman, or at different moments.
The villain tortures Bond, with or without the woman.
Bond conquers the villain (kills him, or kills his representative or helps at their killing).
Bond convalescing enjoys woman, whom he then loses.

The original novel of *Dr. No* follows this exact narrative. The majority of the Bond films that followed also use this basic structure, with variations, starting with the first.

Dr. No opens with Maurice Binder's now-classic gun barrel/silhouette motif, accompanied by the refrain from the 'James Bond Theme'. It's not Sean Connery we see in the gun barrel, but stunt man and stand-in Bob Simmons – it's him in the next two films as well.

'The opening twenty seconds or so [of *Dr. No*]', claims Simon Winder, 'are the most important in British cinema'. [13]

The mission here is mere police work. In the original book, Bond is recovering from his near-death encounter with Rosa Klebb at the end of *From Russia With Love*. The opening scene of the film portrays a handsome, hard, well-dressed man who wins at cards, is called away on a secret assignment, meets and flirts with a beautiful woman and vanishes into the night. That the words 'Bond. James Bond' are almost the first ever spoken by this cinematic icon of the 20th century says much about how important the character has become, and how entrenched in popular culture, over the last sixty-five years. He is sent to Jamaica to investigate the disappearance of Commander Strangways, the head of station. In the early Jamaican scenes, Connery looks uncomfortable. As Sinclair McKay has pointed out: 'Sean Connery's Bond, a deliberately classless, modern figure, never looks at ease in this place. This is a world of black servants and white men calling impatiently for drinks.' [14] 'Although Connery's Bond retained the easy, confident élan of the clubland hero', writes Andrew Spicer, 'he is clearly not from that world'. [15]

But when asked to fight, walk, gamble, kill a spider or simply flair his nostrils, Connery is magnetic: physically lithe, devastatingly handsome and sexually intimidating without being out of reach. In many ways, it was Connery's everyman appeal that helped the public accept him as James Bond – especially in the US. Connery's Scottish burr travelled well, was a novelty to many American viewers and kept him out of the often-clichéd portrayals of the English class system. [1]

Roy Armes confirms. 'The James Bond series totally recast[s] the source material,' he writes, 'so that the upper-class Englishness of Ian Fleming's original gives way to the more classless virility of the Hollywood action from hero'. [17]

At the beginning of his first scene with Moneypenny, Bond tosses his hat onto the hat stand. He does this again in *From Russia With Love* ('For my next miracle'). And then we see subtle variants through the rest of the films of the 1960s: Moneypenny tosses his hat onto the rack in *Goldfinger*; Bond readies himself to toss his hat in *Thunderball* but is disappointed to find the rack right next to the door, and in *You Only Live Twice*, Bond tosses his Naval Commander's cap instead of his usual trilby. Lazenby's hat toss in *On Her Majesty's Secret Service* is easily the coolest and most effortless – he opens the office door, tosses the hat across the room and turns to Moneypenny before he even sees it land on the hook. The hat toss would be absent in the 1970s, but re-appeared in *For Your Eyes Only*, with comic variations in the final two Moore films. There's also a smart toss of Bond's top hat in the middle of the Day of the Dead scene which opens *Spectre*.

Bond travels to Jamaica – scenes were filmed in and around Kingston, Falmouth, Port Royal, Mammee Bay, Dunn's River Falls and Ocho Rios. Here he meets Felix Leiter, his recurring CIA contact. Leiter is played by Jack Lord, later to become world-famous as Steve McGarrett in *Hawaii Five-O*, which ran from 1968 to 1980. We also have Bond's first kill. Professor Dent, working for Dr. No, attempts to kill Bond by placing a tarantula in his bed. Bond later encounters Dent in a tense scene. Dent's assassination is brutal and controversial, Bond shooting Dent even though the villain's gun is empty: 'That's a Smith and Wesson. And you've had your six.'

Bond is assisted by the black Cayman Islander, Quarrel. Bond's relationship with Quarrel, is that of respect, friendship and equality. For 1962, this is most unusual and very refreshing. We'll ignore the barked command to 'fetch my shoes!' This marks the first of a series of usually older, roguish father-figure male characters with whom Bond forms an immediate tie: Kerim Bay (*From Russia With Love*), Tiger Tanaka (*You Only Live Twice*) Marc-Ange Draco (*On Her Majesty's Secret Service*), Milos Columbo (*For Your Eyes Only*), Valentin Zukovsky (*GoldenEye* and *The World Is Not Enough*) and René Mathis (*Casino Royale* and *Quantum of Solace*). And, of course, Bernard Lee's and Ralph Fiennes' versions of M. This is a trope carried over from the Fleming books.

Bond's investigations lead to the island of Crab Key. When he meets bikini-clad Honey Ryder – Ursula Andress at her most appealing. 'Fleming saw her [Ryder] as 'Botticelli's Venus seen from behind', writes Cubby Broccoli. 'We visualised her as a very sexy broad who looked pretty good from the front as well.'

The first sight of Andress emerging, glistening and gorgeous, from the sea, not only gave us one of the most resonant images in the film series, but also the first of the great Bond one-liners, delivered with a wry confidence.

> Honey: And what are you doing here? Are you looking for shells?
> Bond: No. I'm just looking.

The literary Bond would never have uttered this line. We see here the films diverging from their source material; some might say dumbing down, others making them more appealing to a wide audience. Andress, for better or worse, set the template for the female lead in the Bond series: '… beautiful for sure, and sassy and sporty; she is also sexually available, and unlikely to make a fuss when killed off, either literally or metaphorically, at the end of the last instalment to make way for a new love interest'. [18]

In the original novels, all of the female leads bore an imperfection: Honeychile has a broken nose, Tiffany Case was gang-raped as a teenager; Vesper Lynd is being blackmailed; Tracy di Vicenzo suffers from depression; Domino Petacchi has one leg shorter than the other. In the films, as Anthony Burgess observed in *The Listener* (1966): '[they] tend … to be nothing more animated centrefolds. In the books they are credible and lovable because of some humanising flaw.' [19]

Joseph Wiseman's performance as Dr. No, when we finally meet him, is taut and menacing. In a subtle plot change, No is not an independent agent, as depicted in the novel, but part of SPECTRE, a criminal organisation that had first formally appeared in the book *Thunderball* (1960). SPECTRE, or its leader Ernst Stavro Blofeld, would comprise Bond's chief antagonist in five of the next six Bond films (1963-1971), and would be revealed, in an unlikely retcon, as being directly or indirectly responsible for the events of the five Craig-era films (2006-2021).

The scene where the villain serves Bond dinner in a grand room, explains his nefarious plan and allows Bond to escape is necessary exposition but hardly likely. This would occur more than once in the Bond films and has been widely parodied. Bond escapes by crawling through an air shaft: an assault course of deadly intent. This is taken directly from the book. The film ramps the tension by excluding the musical score for the whole of this scene. Bond tracks down his enemy, too easily overloads the nuclear reactor and knocks No into the reactor pool. He escapes the island with Honey in the first of the romantic Bond-gets-the-girl final scenes.

It's clear that the film is feeling its way. The spirit of Fleming's Bond is there, and much of Fleming's original plot remains intact. But there are important changes: it's less violent, jokey, often tongue-in-cheek. In particular, the assault course of pain which pushed the reader to the finale in the novel is toned down and the battle with the giant squid has, quite rightly, been excised. But there is violence – Bond still bleeds, and Quarrel is still burned to death. Dr. No is killed by falling into a nuclear reactor and Felix Leiter is added – otherwise, the film follows the book almost scene for scene. [20]

It is notable that *Dr. No* went on general release in the UK *on the same day* that The Beatles' debut single came out. Within six weeks, the ground-breaking TV series *That Was the Week That Was* would lampoon establishment figures. Bond, The Beatles and the satire boom: the sixties had finally begun. More seriously, the first Russian missiles were installed in Cuba that same month, giving *Dr. No* a chilling prescience that no one involved could have predicted.

Dr. No was a huge success, grossing $6m around the world. It was the first Bond film to be shown on UK television: 28 October 1975. The simple formula is established here: 'star, action, storyline, gadgetry, exotic locations, Ken Adam's modernist designs, music, logo, and a parade of athletic 'Bond girls', changed for each film.' [21] A second Bond film, quickly greenlighted following the success of *Dr. No*, would swerve the direct involvement of the KGB as portrayed in Fleming's 1957 novel by using the more generic SPECTRE as the protagonist. Audiences would soon be queuing around the block to see it.

> Pleasant is the last word I expected to choose for the first film of one of Ian Fleming's James Bond novels. But *Dr. No* has managed to cut out the nastiness, the sadism which in this novel at any rate so unbalances plot and human interest. Here the story's the thing: a ridiculous thing of Secret Agent versus Master Mind, but the rewriting and direction ensure that you don't take anything very seriously – not even the nuclear reactor to-do which has taken the place of those very specific tortures. Sean Connery is a delightful Bond, stunningly handsome and nicely light-hearted as he pursues the forces of evil from his glossy London world to an even glossier Jamaica. But his metamorphosis produces one jarring note and an important one; the callous killings now seem the more callous. That problem will have to be worked out before the Bond image is set for a series.
> *Punch*, 17 October 1962

IF you haven't yet made the acquaintance of Ian Fleming's suave detective, James Bond, in the author's fertile series of mystery thrillers akin to the yarns of Mickey Spillane, here's your chance to correct that misfortune in one quick and painless stroke. This lively, amusing picture is not to be taken seriously as realistic fiction or even art, any more than the works of Mr. Fleming are to be taken as long-hair literature. It is strictly a tinselled action-thriller, spiked with a mystery of a sort. And, if you are clever, you will see it as a spoof of science-fiction and sex. It's not the mystery that entertains you, it's the things that happen along the way – the attempted kidnapping at the Jamaica airport, the tarantula dropped onto Bond's bed, the seduction of the Oriental beauty, the encounter with the beautiful blond bikini-clad Ursula Andress on the beach of Crab Key. And it's all of these things happening so smoothly in the lovely Jamaica locale, looking real and tempting in colour, that recommend this playful British film.
New York Times, 30 May 1963

From Russia With Love

Albert R Broccoli & Harry Saltzman Present Ian Fleming's *From Russia With Love* starring Sean Connery
'James Bond is Back!'
Release Date: 10 October 1963. Running time 115 minutes. Distributed by United Artists. Producers: Harry Salzman (2 of 9), Albert R Broccoli (2 of 17).
James Bond: Sean Connery (2 of 7), M: Bernard Lee (2 of 11), Q: Desmond Llewelyn (1 of 17), Moneypenny: Lois Maxwell (2 of 14).
And Lotte Lenya (Rosa Klebb) with Daniela Bianchi (Tatiana Romanova), Robert Shaw (Donald 'Red' Grant), Pedro Armendáriz (Ali Kerim Bey), Eunice Gayson (Sylvia Trench) (2 of 2), Walter Gotell (Morzeny), Vladek Sheybal (Kronsteen).
Director: Terence Young (2 of 3). Screenplay: Richard Maibaum (2 of 13), Berkely Mather (2 of 2). Production design: Syd Cain (1 of 3). Main titles by Robert Brownjohn (1 of 2). Music: John Barry (1 of 11). Theme song performed by Matt Munro. Cinematography: Ted Moore (2 of 7). Edited by Peter Hunt (2 of 5).

Plot

A chess grandmaster devices a SPECTRE plot to avenge the death of *Dr. No*. Rosa Klebb, formerly of SMERSH, recruits a clerk at the Soviet consulate in Istanbul as a double agent. She offers to defect and will bring a Russian encryption device, the Lektor, but only if James Bond accompanies her. They leave Turkey on the Orient Express but are tracked and intercepted by Donald 'Red' Grant, SPECTRE's chief assassin.

Cast

Along with the crucial return of Connery, Lee and Maxwell, and a second appearance by Eunice Grayson as Sylvia Trench – picnicking with Bond in a punt, with a bottle of Taittinger Blanc de Blanc chilling in the river – the producers made two important casting decisions. Calculating, cold-blooded Rosa Klebb was played by Lotte Lenya – an audacious but inspired choice. [22] Lenya was a singer, stage performer and monologist, and the widow of composer Kurt Weill. Coming late to film acting, she would be nominated for an Oscar in 1961 and would later appear in the original Broadway cast of the musical *Cabaret*. Her cold portrayal of Rosa Klebb is one of the most unforgettable in the entire film series: her look of disgust when Morzeny touches her elbow is priceless. The casting of Robert Shaw as the psychopathic Grant was fortuitous. *From Russia With Love* was his first major film role after years of fleeting appearances and much theatre work: his whispered line 'don't make it tougher on yourself' is obsequious, smooth and startlingly threatening. With his profile raised, Shaw would be nominated for an Oscar for playing Henry VIII in *A Man for All Seasons* (1966) and later take memorable roles in *The Sting* (1973) and *Jaws* (1975). A talented writer as well as actor, Shaw died in 1978, aged 51. Shaw's magnetic portrayal as the blond homicidal paranoid would be revisited many times in the series: Hans in *You Only Live Twice*; Peter Franks in *Diamonds Are Forever*; Erich Kriegler in *For Your Eyes Only*; Venz in *A View to a Kill*; Necros in *The Living Daylights*; Richard Stamper in *Tomorrow Never Dies*.

Twenty-one-year-old Dianella Bianchi, who plays the very sexy Tatiana Romanova, is an Italian actor previously runner-up in the 1960 Miss Universe contest. Bianchi had a heavy Roman accent, so her voice was dubbed by the British Shakespearean actor Barbara Jefford. Jefford would later do the same for dubbing Molly Peters as Patricia Fearing, Bond's physiotherapist in *Thunderball* and for Caroline Munro as Naomi, Stromberg's pilot in *The Spy Who Loved Me*. The reading of the line 'I suppose that would depend on the man' is perfect. German actor Elga Andersen was the first choice to play Tatiana but director Terence Young was unable to get her casting approved by the producers.

Mexican actor Pedro Armendáriz plays Kerim Bey, head of station in Istanbul. Armendáriz steals scene after scene ('He is my son … He is also my son. All of my key employees are my sons.', 'back to the salt mines'). Armendáriz was diagnosed with inoperable cancer during filming and the production moved to Britain to allow his scenes to be completed without delay: he shot himself in Los Angeles in June 1963 after assuring financial security for his family. Tov Kronsteen, the chess master and SPECTRE'S Chief of Planning, was portrayed by the highly regarded Polish-born Vladek Sheybal.

We also have our first sight of Bond's long-term nemesis Ernst Stavro Blofeld, although he is called 'Number 1' by Klebb and Kronsteen and is given a simple question mark in the end credits. The role, complete with white cat and the SPECTRE ring, was played by Anthony Dawson – Professor Dent in *Dr. No* – with the voice dubbed by Viennese actor Eric Pohlmann. Both would jointly reprise the role in *Thunderball*. The character of Morzeny was played by busy German actor Walter Gotell, who had appeared in a previous Young/Broccoli/Maibaum collaboration, *The Red Beret* (1953), and would later return to the series six times as KGB head General Gogol between 1977 and 1987. Perhaps most importantly, *From Russia With Love* marks the debut of Desmond Llewelyn as Q, although he is not named as such in this film: the credits read 'Boothroyd', as per the Fleming book, but he is only addressed as 'the equipment officer'. Q is first seen in the background as Bond enters M's office. This low-key scene introduced the most enduring character in the film series. Llewelyn, who had worked with director Terence Young in *They Were Not Divided* in 1950 appeared as the permanently exasperated Q in all but one of the series' films until his death in 1999. Zora, one of the fiery gypsy women was played by Martine Beswick, later to be cast as the ill-fated Paula Caplan, Bond's CIA ally in *Thunderball*.

Theme Song

The concept of a song that played over the titles of a Bond film was a year away. *From Russia With Love* uses an instrumental theme by John Barry. The vocal version, by Matt Munro, 'the singing bus conductor', plays over the end titles but has been the inclusion of choice on every Bond theme compilation album since.

Production

From Russia With Love was filmed between April and August 1963 at Pinewood Studios, Buckinghamshire and on location in the UK, Turkey, and Italy.

Observations

Ian Fleming's original novel, his fifth, published in April 1957, is a taut thriller. The opening page has some of Fleming's best descriptive writing:

> A blue and green dragon-fly flashed out from among the rose bushes at the end of the garden and hovered in mid-air a few inches above the base of the man's spine. It had been attracted by the golden shimmer of the June sunshine on the ridge of fine blond hairs above the coccyx. A puff of breeze came off the sea. The tiny field of hairs bent gently. The dragon-fly darted nervously sideways and hung above the man's left shoulder, looking down. The young grass below the man's open mouth stirred. A large drop of sweat rolled down the side of the fleshy nose and dropped glittering into the grass. That was enough. The dragon-fly flashed away through the roses and over the jagged glass on top of the high garden wall. [23]

So, the source material was strong, and Richard Maibaum and Berkely Mather's screenplay retained the best elements from the book, especially the cold, ruthless KGB assassin 'Red' Grant, played with an underlying menace by a blond-rinsed, buffed Robert Shaw.

From Russia With Love is an atmospheric film, with many twists, memorable performances and some truly unforgettable scenes, including a notorious gypsy dance sequence that ends with a gun battle, a quietly menacing back-street assassination where the victim appears through the lips of a poster of Anita Ekberg (sly product placement ahoy!) and a tense showdown with arch-villain Rosa Klebb. Sean Connery, Robert Shaw as Red Grant ('homicidal maniac – superb material') and Lotte Lenya are simply perfect. This is where the Bond series finds its feet. 'If *Dr. No* is Fleming's beaches, calypso bars and Jamaican seascapes, *From Russia With Love* is Fleming's Europe, shadowy basilicas, private bureaus and crosswire politics... double agent betrayals and duplicity. And sexuality drives the plot.' [24]

The film opens with the series' first pre-credits sequence. A huge room, a chess game. Deception. Darkness. James Bond is stalked and, seemingly, killed. Floodlights. Russians.

A very English country house – Heatherden Hall, near Pinewood – was used for Spectre Island. This is the same location where Oddjob knocks the head off the statue in *Goldfinger* and where OO9 expires with the Fabergé egg in *Octopussy*.

The projected lap-dancing main titles are now a trademark of graphic designer Robert Brownjohn. Brownjohn, an American domiciled in London, created the title for only the second and third Bond films. But Maurice Binder, who would provide the next twelve sets of main titles, would follow his lead with writhing bodies, silhouettes and phallic symbolism. Brownjohn died aged just 44 in 1970.

The first 65 pages of Fleming's book springs the trap. In the film, these are condensed into a tight, taut ten minutes. Initially, very little is revealed about the enigmatic Ernst Stavro Blofeld, Bond's nemesis in three of the books and seven of the films. Referred to as 'Number 1', Blofeld is first seen in his luxury yacht. He strokes a white cat and discusses a plan to avenge the death of Dr No – in the original novel, the plot was hatched by the SMERSH, the Soviet counterintelligence agency who were Bond's main adversaries in four of Fleming's first seven books. Number 1 puts Rosa Klebb, an ex-SMERSH operative and the organisation's Number 3, in charge of a plan to manipulate Bond into stealing a Lektor cryptographic device from the Soviets and for him 'to be killed with ignominy'.

We are seventeen minutes into the film before we meet Bond, who is relaxing with Sylvia Trench (or, 'reviewing an old case', as Bond puts it) in a scene filmed at Hurley Lock on the River Thames. We also see the first of several gadgets – a pager – and Bond's green Bentley, looking very old-fashioned for 1963. Bond meets M ('But I've never even heard of a Tatiana Romanova') and Q, at this stage, simply 'the equipment officer from Q branch'. This, of course, is the first of seventeen appearances by the much-loved Desmond Llewelyn. Soon, Bond flies to Turkey. The stock footage of a jet plane was very aspirational for 1963. 'Bond was the ideal role model for the Swinging Sixties', writes Dominic Sandbrook, 'a classless hero moving through a world of foreign travel, consumer luxuries and disposable pleasures'. [25]

Istanbul, an exotic location, features in many scenes in the central part of the film. The mosque section was filmed at the Blue Mosque, Firuz Ağa Mosque, Hagia Sophia Cathedral and Nuruosmaniye Mosque. The underground boat ride takes place in the Basilica Cistern, and a building on the Halaskargazi Avenue doubles for the Russian embassy. Pedro Armendáriz steals every scene he's in. Bond sees Tania for the first time through the periscope that sees into the Russian embassy. 'Things are shaping up nicely from this angle', he quips.

The gunfight at the gypsy camp uses an upbeat, syncopated, percussion-heavy march called 'OO7'. This is heard in many of the Bond films of the 60s and 70s, almost as a second Bond theme, notably during the climactic underwater fight in *Thunderball*, the flight of Little Nellie in *You Only Live Twice*, the destruction of Blofeld's Headquarters in *Diamonds Are Forever* and the Amazon river chase in *Moonraker*. This is the first truly effective use of the talents of John Barry, composer for twelve of the Bond films. Barry established extensive orchestral scoring with, from *Goldfinger* onwards, a popular music theme song that keeps pace with changing tastes. For the Bond films from 1963 to 1985, his music 'combine[s] jazz-inflected big band brass and sweeping, romantic string lines with classic songwriting skills that continue to provide a template for contemporary musicians working on the series'. [26]

Bond's reward for helping during the gunfight seems to have been to have sex with both women. 'This might take some time', Connery says with a smirk. The assassination scene follows immediately, and then Bond returns to the hotel to find Tania in his bed: all told, a tiring evening. As Ben McIntyre wryly observes, 'Bond's sex life attained levels of priapism that would merit serious medical attention or industrial supplies of Viagra in a real human being'.

The long section on the train builds the tension. The scenes purporting to be at representing Istanbul, Belgrade and Zagreb stations were all filmed at different places at the main Sirkeci Terminal in Istanbul.

An online conspiracy theory suggests that the man in the white shirt seen herding cows as the train passes is Ian Fleming himself. The jury's out on that one.

When Grant has been rumbled, the tension is ramped as he waits for his moment to kill Bond.

> Bond: 'Old man?' Is that what you chaps in SMERSH call each other?
> Grant: SMERSH? I'm not with them.
> Bond: Of course... SPECTRE. And it wasn't a Russian show at all. You've been playing us off against each other, haven't you? And it was SPECTRE who killed the Russian agent in the mosque. You?
> Grant: Oh, I don't mind talking. I get a kick out of watching the great James Bond find out what a bloody fool he's been making of himself. We're pros, Mr. Bond. We sweated your recognition code out of one of your men in Tokyo...

before he died. I've been keeping tabs on you. I've been your guardian angel. Saved your life at the Gypsy camp.
Bond: Oh, yes. I'm much obliged.

The savage, violent fight between Bond and Grant took three weeks to film. The catalyst is Bond's booby-trapped attaché case, a device taken from the novel where it appears as a 'smart little bag' with hidden ammunition, gold sovereigns and crucially, a flat throwing knife. From this inauspicious start, we can draw a straight line to the invisible car of *Die Another Day* via cigarette rocket darts (*You Only Live Twice*), prosthetic third nipple (*The Man With the Golden Gun*), ski pole gun (*The Spy Who Loved Me*), fake horse mini-jet trailer (*Octopussy*), ice-berg boat (*A View to A Kill*), and man-eating sofa (*The Living Daylights*). Did we mention the flame-throwing bagpipes?

Back to 1963. The helicopter and boat chase scenes were not in the original novel but were added to create an extended action climax. The former was inspired by the crop-dusting scene in Alfred Hitchcock's *North by Northwest* (1959). These scenes were filmed in Scotland, at Crinan, Lochgilphead and Loch Craignish, in Argyll and Bute. They feel tacked on. The final scene, Bond and Titania in Venice, is very obviously studio-bound with back projection. Bond returns to Venice in *Moonraker* (1979) and *Casino Royale* (2006).

With twice the budget of *Dr. No* – Syd Cain's sumptuous designs spend every penny – *From Russia With Love* is luscious to watch. Despite the troubled production, including a helicopter crash that nearly did for director Terence Young and a shooting delay after Dianella Bianchi was injured in a car crash, the final result is magnificent. In many ways, the film version of *From Russia With Love* is the closest to Ian Fleming's source material: the film plays it straight. There are no characters with silly names, no scenes in space, no gadgets that are introduced solely to allow Bond to triumph. SPECTRE's plan involves a cryptographic device and a minor sex scandal, not world domination.

'I think [*From Russia With Love*] shows Bond to the best advantage,' said Terence Young. 'The tone was set in *Dr. No*, but completed in *From Russia With Love*. I have heard that during the filming of the other pictures my successors have watched my films to see what they could find in them to cannibalise. Mind you, it was easier for those of us who started the whole thing!' [27]

Alexander Walker in *Hollywood, England*, his seminal study of the British film industry in the 1960s, notes:

> By the time *From Russia With Love* was screened in the autumn of 1963, the Bond formula had been well and truly processed: the outsize action, the superman panache, the self-parody, the eroticism that carried just a hint of what the then-fashionable term dubbed 'kinky', and the brutality which was so nonchalantly dealt out that the moral shock was absorbed almost before

the blows landed or the bullets struck home. From mid-1963, when audiences everywhere had discovered their novelty-dimension, the Bond films became established as a world cult.

And that cult was about to deliver the best Bond film of all.

Goldfinger

Albert R Broccoli & Harry Saltzman Present Sean Connery as Agent OO7 in Ian Fleming's *Goldfinger*
'James Bond is Back in Action! Everything he Touches Turns to Excitement!'
Release date: 9 September 1964. Running time: 110 minutes. Distributed by United Artists. Producers: Harry Salzman (3 of 9), Albert R Broccoli (3 of 17)
James Bond: Sean Connery (3 of 7), M: Bernard Lee (3 of 11), Q: Desmond Llewelyn (2 of 17), Moneypenny: Lois Maxwell (3 of 14), Leiter: Cec Linder.
And Gert Fröbe (Auric Goldfinger) with Honor Blackman (Pussy Galore), Oddjob (Harold Sakata), Shirley Eaton (Jill Masterson), Tania Mallet (Tilly Masterson), Martin Benson (Mr. Solo), Austin Willis (Simmons), Margaret Nolan (Dink).
Director: Guy Hamilton (1 of 4). Screenplay by Richard Maibaum (3 of 13), Paul Dehn. Production design: Ken Adam (2 of 7). Main titles: Robert Brownjohn (2 of 2). Music: John Barry (2 of 11). Theme song performed by Shirley Bassey. Cinematography: Ted Moore (3 of 7). Edited by Peter Hunt (3 of 5).

Plot

Bond is returning via Miami Beach from a job in Latin America when he is instructed by his CIA contact to observe powerful bullion dealer Auric Goldfinger who the Bank of England suspects is stockpiling huge amounts of gold. Bond plays Goldfinger at golf, then tracks him to Switzerland where he uncovers a bigger plot – to raid Fort Knox and irradiate the world's gold supply. Along the way, Bond avoids Goldfinger's hat-toting bodyguard and charms his personal pilot, the sexy Pussy Galore.

Cast

Goldfinger himself is played by the German actor Gert Fröbe who embodies the role splendidly: short-tempered, menacing, narcissistic, cruel and insane – he's the perfect Bond villain, henchman in tow and world domination plans intact. As Adrian Turner writes: 'Goldfinger is Hitler, Mabuse, Dr Strangelove and Robert Maxwell all rolled into one.' [28] Fröbe spoke little English and despite being dubbed by stage actor Michael Collins, his performance dominates the film.

Appearing in many German films from 1948, Fröbe is also familiar to English-speaking audiences from roles in *The Longest Day* (1962, also featuring a pre-Bond Sean Connery), *Those Magnificent Men in Their Flying Machines* (1965) and the Broccoli-produced *Chitty Chitty Bang Bang* (1968). He had been cast as Goldfinger after impressing the producers and director as a child killer in the Spanish/Swiss/German film *Es Geschah am Hellichten Tag [It Happened in Broad Daylight]* (1958).

He also has the greatest single line in any Bond film:

> Bond: Do you expect me to talk?
> Goldfinger: No Mr Bond. I expect you to die!

Intriguingly, another actor considered for the chief antagonist in the third Bond film was Theodore Bikel, Oscar-nominated for *The Defiant Ones* in 1958 and as Captain von Trapp in the original Broadway production of *The Sound of Music* (1959). He is perhaps best known as the Hungarian phonetics expert in *My Fair Lady* (1964). This is just one of the many 'what-ifs' in Bond casting lore that culminate as the delicious if unfulfilled thought of Sean Connery as Kincade in *Skyfall*.

Pussy Galore was memorably portrayed by Honor Blackman and is a much bigger character in the film. Her relationship with Bond is expanded and it is her ultimate switching of sides that provides Bond with the leverage to defeat Goldfinger. In the book, Bond leaves a message under the rim of the aeroplane loo in the vain (but correct) hope that it would be found by a cleaner. Shirley Eaton plays Jill Masterson and became an icon: the gold-painted corpse. Eaton had appeared in three of the early Carry On films: *Carry on Sergeant* (1958), *Carry on Nurse* (1959: including the brilliant daffodil scene) and *Carry on Constable* (1960).

Theme Song

For the first time, we have a title song: both *Dr. No* and *From Russia With Love* used instrumental themes under the titles, but 'Goldfinger' – horns blasting, Shirley Bassey wailing, everything turned to twelve – is three minutes of sheer bombast. The song gave Bassey her only top 40 hit in the US. Co-composer Anthony Newley's sparse, jazzy demo – no big brassy horns or full-on vocal, just a louche lounge jazz arrangement which is very unsettling – was released in 1992 on the first version of the compilation album *The Best of Bond...James Bond*.

Production

Goldfinger was filmed between January and August 1964 at Pinewood Studios, Buckinghamshire and on location in the UK, Switzerland and the US.

Observations

'It's near impossible to watch *Goldfinger* and see through the golden haze that 60s pop culture has bestowed on it,' writes Mark O'Connell. Nevertheless, *Goldfinger* is the best James Bond film: every sequel that followed merely tries to copy its style, panache and sheer *joie de vivre*. From the exciting opening sequence, through the gold-painted corpse, assured performances from the lead actors, especially Sean Connery, the unexpected tension of the golf scenes, the gadget-heavy car and the remarkable design of Ken Adam's Fort Knox set – the 'cathedral of gold' – everything about this film is, quite simply, magnificent.

The pre-credit sequence is one of the series' best. Starting with a very tongue-in-cheek sight gag of a decoy duck on Bond's submerged head, our hero destroys a Latin American drugs laboratory, hooks up with an exotic dancer and avoids being killed after seeing an assassin reflected in his lover's eye. He despatches his would-be killer by throwing an electric heater into a bathtub. There are two great lines in this opening section. When asked why he carries a gun, Bond replies: 'I have a slight inferiority complex.' And, of course, after electrocuting his aggressor, he quips 'Shocking. Simply shocking.' [29]

'It seems to me', said Guy Hamilton, 'that if I could do the pre-credits sequence … and make you laugh … I could take [you] for a great big ride … we're going to take you to wonderful places, we're going to show you beautiful girls, we're going to have some suspense, and we're going to have some laughs. So let's enjoy it!' [30]

After the title sequence, we switch to a glorious aerial shot of the Fontainebleau Hotel in Miami Beach. Simon Winder writes:

> The camera lovingly dwells on ... swimming pools, the sunshine, the bathing suits, the vast hotel rooms', 'All topped off with a blaring big-band jazz soundtrack. We are now terribly used to America – and Britain has taken on so many of its features – but in these moments of *Goldfinger* we still get a glimpse into the America that made the books and early films so vivid, that must have made its original British viewers smart. [31]

A perfect edit cuts from the diver at the outdoor pool to the shot of the same diver seen underwater. Bond's recurring CIA contact Felix Leiter sees Cec Linder taking over the role from Jack Lord, who wanted co-star billing and more money. Amazingly, only Linder travelled to Florida during production (for the scene where he turns away from the underwater swimming pool porthole). Sean Connery, Gert Fröbe, Shirley Eaton, Margaret Nolan, who plays Dink, and Austin Willis as Junius Du Pont, Goldfinger's card victim, all filmed their parts on a soundstage at Pinewood. Apparently, Sean Connery didn't travel to the US *at all* for *Goldfinger*.

The scene between Bond and Dink here is blatantly sexist: 'Run along dear, man talk,' mutters Bond as he pats his buxom masseur on the behind. [32] Simon Winder says of this scene, 'Bond is ... slapping the bottom and saying goodbye to any tenuous hope that a female audience might be watching. He is also slapping the bottom and saying goodbye to a whole framework of ideas and assumptions that had once seemed so cosily in place and which have rotted away around a once harmlessly stupid little line of script.' [33]

Leiter tells Bond that M has a new mission for him: the observation of Auric Goldfinger, an international jeweller who is suspected of smuggling. In the book, Bond is employed by Junius Du Pont, a rich American businessman whom he had met in the first Bond book, *Casino Royale*, to find out how Goldfinger is cheating at cards. Bond agrees and within minutes, he has discovered not only Goldfinger's methods but his semi-clad subordinate Jill Masterson. Bond drawls: 'My dear girl, there are some things that just aren't done, such as drinking Dom Perignon '53 above the temperature of 38 degrees Fahrenheit. That's just as bad as listening to the Beatles without earmuffs.' I guess Paul McCartney had forgotten or forgiven this when he agreed to write the theme song for *Live and Let Die*.

Goldfinger's comeuppance, as Bond discovers Jill Masterson whispering instructions into his ear, is delicious. After fifteen minutes, as Bond inspects the contents of a fridge, a shadow on the wall shows a bulky figure wearing a brimmed hat. This is our first glimpse of Oddjob. Here is a new type of screen villain, visually striking, dependably foreign – a top-notch physical foil for Bond. Oddjob was the first of many memorably grotesque silly henchmen in the Bond films, some based on Fleming creations, others the work of the screenwriters: Wint and Kidd, Tee Hee, Nick Nack, Jaws, May Day, Stamper, Zao, Mr Hinx ...

Harold Sakata, who unforgettably portrayed the mute Oddjob, was a Hawaiian wrestler discovered by Guy Hamilton. Bond is knocked out with a single blow to the neck. [34] When he awakes, we are presented with the image of the murdered Jill, her entire body covered in gold paint.

'Iconic' is an overused word, but this single image is a defining moment in the Bond series.

Jill's death is implausible, but her legacy – and that of actor Shirley Eaton – is significant. Here we have a screen death that provides lots of spectacle but no logic. Until the Craig-era reboot, most Bond films would find irrational, sometimes silly, deaths: Baron Samedi being thrown into a coffin of venomous snakes (*Live and Let Die*); Kanaga swallowing a compressed air pellet (*Live and Let Die*); Hugo Drax ejected into space (*Moonraker*); Whitaker crushed by a bust of the Duke of Wellington (*The Living Daylights*); Milton Krest's encounter with a decompression chamber (*Licence To Kill*); Boris Grishenko frozen by liquid nitrogen (*GoldenEye*); Elliot Carver and the sea drill (*Tomorrow Never Dies*).

We then have two stock scenes which were included in nearly every Bond film over the next 25 years: Bond's briefing with M, although Connery's Bond isn't quite such a smug know-all as Moore's, and the much-played 'now pay attention, 007' scene where Bond is given a gadget or two by Q. In this case, it's the now-legendary Aston Martin DB5. In the novel, the Aston Martin (a DB Mark III) was given reinforced bumpers, a compartment for a Colt 45 and headlights that can change colour. But the modifications went to incredible lengths on-screen: bug tracker, machine guns, oil slick, smokescreen, passenger ejector seat, tyre slashers, bullet-proof glass and revolving license plates. It's the first of nine screen appearances for the DB5. The others were in *Thunderball*, *GoldenEye*, *Tomorrow Never Dies*, *The World Is Not Enough*, *Casino Royale*, *Skyfall*, *Spectre* and *No Time To Die*. [35]

And, in the middle of a spy thriller, we have a game of golf, with Stoke Park Country Club sitting in for the fictional Royal St Marks. It's a tribute to the writers, director and actors that what could be six minutes of tedium is spellbinding, tense and beautifully filmed. The denouement, when Bond out-cheats Goldfinger and is warned to stay away, is most satisfying.

The plot moves to Geneva. Bond has placed a tracker on Goldfinger's Rolls Royce. The car tracking scenes were filmed on roads near Realp. The exterior of the Pilatus Aircraft factory in Stans, just south of Lucerne, served as the exterior of Goldfinger's factory.

Tilly Masterson is introduced, looking to avenge her sister and put a spanner in Bond's plans. Her attempt to snipe Goldfinger was shot in the Furka Pass, 12km west of Realp. Bond and Goldfinger's men take part in a car chase, filmed at Pinewood and the adjacent Black Park.

Bond is captured and Tilly is killed, but an overhead reference to 'Operation Grand Slam' prevents his castration by laser. The music in this still-wonderful scene is very effective, building in pitch and intensity. The moment when the laser is switched off comes as a great relief to the audience. And also to Sean Connery, no doubt, as the smouldering table was created for real by a technician, Bert Luxford, with a blowtorch hiding underneath.

Bond also meets 'Pooshy' Galore. The name Pussy Galore is taken directly from the novel and this was the only time that Fleming gave a double entendre name to one of his characters. [36] The films' scriptwriters would, regrettably, follow suit, with Plenty O'Toole (*Diamonds Are Forever*), Chew Mee (*The Man With the Golden Gun*), Holly Goodhead (*Moonraker*), Bibi Dahl (*For Your Eyes Only*), Penelope Smallbone (*Octopussy*), Jenny Flex (*A View to A Kill*), Xenia Onatopp (*GoldenEye*), Molly Warmflash (*The World Is Not Enough*) and Strawberry Fields (*Quantum of Solace*).

Bond: Who are you?
Galore: Pussy Galore.
Bond: I must be dreaming.

Bond's original scripted response was 'I know, but what's your name'. This was judged to be too strong by the production team. Pussy is, of course, lesbian and 'immune' to his charms. This is explicit in the book, but 'tiptoed around in the film ... and effectively available for viewers who are happy with a very stifled set of code words'. [37]

The plot of the Fleming novel has two fatal flaws. Firstly, Goldfinger decides not to kill Bond when Bond suggests that he should work for him. Bond is allowed to stay alive in *Goldfinger* (the film) to allow him to mislead MI6 into believing he has things in hand. Thin, but workable. Bond is flown from Geneva to Goldfinger's stud farm near Fort Knox, Kentucky. The airport scene was filmed at RAF Northolt in west London, about 8 miles from Pinewood Studios. This same location was used as a Cuban airbase in *Octopussy* and an Azerbaijani airbase in *The World Is Not Enough*.

In a scene that is visually wonderful but entirely pointless within the plot, other than to demonstrate his megalomania, Goldfinger meets with several organized crime bosses telling them of his plan and them immediately killing them all. Except, that is, for Mr Solo, who has 'a pressing engagement'. [38]

Roger Ebert writes:

> This stretch of the film is founded on a fundamental absurdity. Goldfinger has assembled the heads of all the Mafia families of America at his Kentucky farm. He pushes buttons, and the most elaborate presentation in movie history unfolds. Screens descend from the ceiling. Film of Fort Knox is shown. The floor itself rolls back, and a vast scale model of the fort rises on hydraulic lifters (with Bond hidden inside). Goldfinger tells the mobsters what he plans to do, Bond listens in, and then shutters fall to lock the Mafioso in the room, and they are immediately killed with poison gas. My question: Why bother to show them that expensive presentation if you're only going to kill them afterward? My best guess: Goldfinger had workmen crawling all over the place for weeks, constructing that presentation, and he wanted to show it to somebody. [39]

We then move towards the film's climax: the raid on Fort Knox. Astonishingly, the external scenes were filmed on the Army post close to Fort Knox, and on the approach to the real Bullion Depository.

Goldfinger's motives are improved within the film. Rather than simply wanting the gold for himself, he wants to irradiate the US gold supply and therefore makes his own stash more valuable: Operation Grand Slam. Goldfinger puts this plan into effect by neutralizing the military force of soldiers stationed at Fort Knox with nerve gas, sprayed from the air. In his second plot hole, Fleming has Goldfinger poisoning the Fort Knox water supply. In the film the Fort Knox residents and military personnel play dead when the airborne nerve gas is replaced by a harmless substance. This is simply nonsense.

Before this, Bond and Galore match judo moves. They fight until Bond is able to gain the upper hand and seduce Pussy. And here we have one of the most uncomfortable scenes in the film series. Nothing about this seems remotely consensual – Connery leers as he forces himself on her. As Ben MacIntyre suggests, with regard to the books on which the first films were based: Bond's approach to sex grew directly out of Fleming's own distinctive attitudes to women, which in turn were shaped by the times he lived in, the class he occupied, and his own psychological and sexual preoccupations.' [40]

Different times, yes, but still inexcusable.

Look closely during the raid and you'll see Cubby's stepson and future screenwriter and producer Michael G. Wilson appearing as one of Goldfinger's soldiers at Fort Knox. This was the first of many cameos for Wilson. [41]

The interior scenes of Fort Knox were filmed at Pinewood on one of Ken Adam's spectacular sets. The US Treasury would not give the producers permission to film within the genuine location, so the Fort Knox we see in *Goldfinger* is the product of Adam's brilliant imagination. Adam later told UK daily newspaper *The Guardian*:

> No one was allowed in Fort Knox [the bullion depository], but because Cubby Broccoli had some good connections and the Kennedys loved Ian Fleming's books, I was allowed to fly over it once. It was quite frightening – they had machine guns on the roof. I was also allowed to drive around the perimeter, but if you got out of the car, there was a loudspeaker warning you to keep away. There was not a chance of going in it, and I was delighted because I knew from going to the Bank of England vaults that gold isn't stacked very high and it's all underwhelming. It gave me the chance to show the biggest gold repository in the world as I imagined it, with gold going up to heaven. I came up with this cathedral-type design.

The exterior sets were constructed on the Fort Knox campus – 'within shouting distance of the real thing', according to Cubby Broccoli, 'under the alert security of the US military'. The aerial shots, amazingly, show the genuine Fort Knox depository.

The final battle is furious. Bond is trapped in the vault with Oddjob – footsteps echoing ominously. Bond despatches Oddjob but is unable to defuse the bomb: Connery's panicked expression is priceless. The timer ends at OO7 seconds – but Bond's line, 'What kept you? Three more ticks and Goldfinger would've hit the jackpot', shows that this was a post-production edit.

In an unlikely conclusion, Bond is flying to the White House for a meeting with the President when Goldfinger emerges, pointing a pistol at Bond. They struggle, the gun goes off, Goldfinger is sucked outside, Bond and Pussy escape by parachute, and once again, we have the requisite romantic closing scene.

Goldfinger was directed by Guy Hamilton. Terence Young, the director of *Dr. No* and *From Russia With Love*, declined in favour of *The Amorous Adventures of Moll Flanders*. Hamilton had turned Bond down in 1962, but his work on *Goldfinger*, and three other Bond films in the 1970s, has pace and a glossy, sophisticated style. Add a pre-credits sequence that stands alone from the main storyline, tongue-in-cheek humour, the Q briefing, some unlikely deaths and hole-ridden plotting and we have, three films in, the classic Bond formula – iconic, yes, but also easily-parodied.

The film grossed $50m around the world. Ian Fleming would not reap his reward. He died of a heart attack on 12 August 1964, less than a month before the film's premiere in London's Leicester Square. He had seen some of the early rushes of *Goldfinger*. 'He was pleased with what he saw,' wrote Cubby Broccoli. [42]

Rene MacColl wrote in *The Daily Express*, 13 August 1964:

> James Bond, his inspired secret agent, was an amalgam of all the daydreams of not only Fleming himself, but of several million men all over the world. He hit it just right. Bond became absolutely compulsive reading. And as Britain jumped into prosperity, into an understanding of winemanship, motorcarmanship, hotelmanship, travelmanship and, above all, expertise about women, Fleming became a sort of high priest of the secret life of all the Walter Mittys all over the world.

'They're reading too much into the man,' Fleming once said. 'He's not that important.'

Goldfinger, meanwhile, was the first Bond blockbuster. In fact, the first blockbuster *per se*. *The Daily Telegraph* declared:

> The film, which arrived in London this week comes about as near a comprehensive definition as any filmgoer could wish to see. To begin with, it holds the attention of the audience from brazen start to fantastic finish – well, not quite to the silly end, perhaps, but then we can't have everything. Every foot of it is made with the shrewdest sense of how to work on the spectator's responses: the result is an extraordinarily lively relationship between the audience and the screen; and above all the film leaves us as it finds us; unmoved but not unamused, and feeling that the time has been agreeably spent in a satisfactorily light-hearted way. Seldom in the history of the modern cinema can so many clichés have been pressed into such active service with so few yawns; and the reason is clear enough. Every now and again, the narrative insists on gently sending itself up, as if assuring us that the film is perfectly aware of its fundamental absurdity but anxious that we should share the joke on terms of mutual one-upmanship. It's a sort of Brecht's alienation effect.

Roger Ebert:

> Of all the Bonds, *Goldfinger* is the best, and can stand as a surrogate for the others. If it is not a great film, it is a great entertainment, and contains all the elements of the Bond formula that would work again and again. The Broccoli-Saltzman formula found its lasting form in the making of *Goldfinger*. It probably contains more durable images than any other title in the series. The outline was emerging in the first two films, and here it is complete. [43]

Eric Shorter in *The Daily Telegraph*, 1964:

> One again wishes that Sean Connery could be made to seem a shade more human as Bond; and Gert Fröbe's Goldfinger, though nicely in character, also acts like an automaton. Or is one merely being nostalgic about the

> performances of a vanished generation? Humphrey Bogart, say, as Bond, and Sidney Greenstreet as Goldfinger: wouldn't that have been richer casting? Still, if the players do not possess or are not allowed very much depth of personality, the cult itself, the ingredients of sex and violence, brilliantly fills the former gap. And unlike the old Chicago melodramas, no one dares to moralise in the world of OO7. Their standard of living is too high for that.

Goldfinger **is the film against which all past and future Bonds will be measured. At the premiere, a stampede of five thousand female fans smashed through the plate-glass entrance of the Odeon cinema in London's Leicester Square. The object of their affection, Sean Connery, had not even bothered to turn up.**

Thunderball

Albert R Broccoli and Harry Saltzman Present Sean Connery in Ian Fleming's *Thunderball*.
'Look Out! Remember… there is only one James Bond and *Thunderball*'s the Biggest of them All!'
Release date: 9 December 1965. Running time: 130 minutes. Distributed by United Artists. Producers: Harry Salzman (4 of 9), Albert R Broccoli (4 of 17), Kevin McClory James Bond: Sean Connery (4 of 7), M: Bernard Lee (4 of 11), Q: Desmond Llewelyn (3 of 17), Moneypenny: Lois Maxwell (4 of 14), Leiter: Rik van Nutter. And Adolfo Celi (Emilio Largo) with Claudine Auger (Domino), Luciana Paluzzi (Fiona Volpe), Martine Beswick (Paula Caplan), Guy Doleman (Count Lippe), Molly Peters (Patricia Fearing).
Director: Terence Young (3 of 3). Screenplay by Richard Maibaum (4 of 13), John Hopkins. Based on a story by Kevin McClory, Jack Whittingham and Ian Fleming. Production design: Ken Adam (3 of 7). Main Titles by Maurice Binder (2 of 14). Music by John Barry (3 of 11). Theme song performed by Tom Jones. Cinematography: Ted Moore (4 of 7). Edited by Peter Hunt (4 of 5).

Plot

SPECTRE steals two nuclear warheads, intending to hold the world to ransom. James Bond tracks them to the Bahamas. Here, he meets the beautiful Domino. Bond leads a daring underwater battle to retrieve the nuclear weapons and is forced into a thrilling confrontation with SPECTRE agent Emilio Largo on board his boat, the Disco Volante.

Cast

SPECTRE's Number Two and the primary antagonist, Emilio Largo, is played by the experienced Italian actor Adolfo Celi. His lines were dubbed by Robert Rietty, to hide Celi's thick and distinctive Sicilian accent. Active in films since 1933, Rietty had dubbed the voice of John Strangways in *Dr. No*, and would go

on to provide the on-screen voices of Tiger Tanaka in *You Only Live Twice* and the not-at-all-Blofeld-honestly character in *For Your Eyes Only*. Rietty would be cast as an Italian Minster of State in *Never Say Never Again*.

Broccoli and Saltzman's first choice for the fascinating, enigmatic, world-weary Domino was Raquel Welsh. At that time, Welsh was signed to Twentieth Century Fox and had been cast in small roles in *A House Is Not a Home* (1964) and *Roustabout* (1964) with Elvis Presley, and a featured role in *A Swingin' Summer* (1965). Welsh was signed for the role of Domino but was recalled by Fox to play a major role in her breakthrough film *Fantastic Voyage*. Julie Christie met Cubby Broccoli and Terence Young but wasn't selected, going on to make *Darling* and *Dr. Zhivago* that same year. French actor Claudine Auger had been runner-up in the 1958 Miss World competition and was on holiday in Nassau when she was spotted by Kevin McClory, who suggested that she audition for Domino in *Thunderball*. Originally planned as an Italian character – Dominetta Vitali in the original novel – the part was rewritten to suit a French woman, renamed Dominique Derval. Claudine Auger's heavily accented English was deemed too thick by the filmmakers. Nikki Van der Zyl, who dubbed Ursula Andress' voice in *Dr. No* was brought back to dub Auger's lines. *Thunderball* launched Auger into a successful European movie career, including *Anyone Can Play* (1968, with Ursula Andress) and *Black Belly of the Tarantula* (1971, with Barbara Bach and Barbara Bouchet: Moneypenny in the 1967 *Casino Royale*).

Leather-clad Luciana Paluzzi as Fiona Volpe, a character invented for the film, remains not only one of the best Bond villains but one of the sexiest women to ever appear in a Bond film. Paluzzi had auditioned for the part of Domino, and when that role went to Claudine Auger, Paluzzi was cast as Volpe. She is the first female character to use her sexuality as a weapon – a concept taken to absurd lengths in *GoldenEye*. Volpe is Italian for 'fox'. As Robert Caplan writes:

> Bond seeks to reposition Fiona, whom he knows is a SPECTRE associate, by sleeping with her, as he does with Pussy Galore. But unlike Pussy Galore, Fiona is inherently evil and not merely an accessory to the villain's scheme. Rather, Fiona is an integral part of SPECTRE's mission and, as such, cannot be persuaded to join Bond's cause.

Martine Beswick, who had played one of the gypsy women in *From Russia With Love*, gets a bigger part here as the unfortunate Paula Caplan. Rik van Nutter as a forgettable Leiter was married to Anita Ekberg (qv: *From Russia With Love*). We should also mention the scientist Ladislav Kutze, played by UK-based Czech actor George Pravda. He is taken aback by the sounds of Largo torturing Domino, and, during the climactic fight scene, turns against Largo and throws the nuclear detonator (and himself) overboard. And there is a tiny uncredited cameo by André Maranne as SPECTRE No. 10. He is more familiar as Sergeant François Chevalier in six of the *Pink Panther* films, 1964 to 1983.

Producer Kevin McClory appears as a man sitting and smoking a cigar as Bond enters the Nassau Casino.

Theme Song

Belted out by Tom Jones, the nearest that we can get to a male Shirley Bassey, the original plan was to use a song called 'Mr Kiss Kiss Bang Bang' by Dionne Warwick, later re-recorded by Bassey herself. Johnny Cash's submission was rejected, therefore a quick replacement was needed when United Artists requested that the film's name was included in the lyrics. It's a Bond theme, it's Tom Jones, what more do you need to know?

Production

Thunderball was filmed between February and May 1965 at Pinewood Studios, Buckinghamshire and on location in France, the UK, the Bahamas and the US (Coral Gables, Florida – frogmen parachuting into the sea).

Observations

The fourth James Bond film in just four years, the story of *Thunderball* begins in May 1959, when Ian Fleming met Irish film producer Kevin McClory, with a view to creating the first James Bond film together.

McClory's career in films began as a boom operator at Shepperton Studios in the mid-1950s, including some jobs for Cubby Broccoli's Warwick Films. He wrote and directed the 1957 film *The Boy and the Bridge*, which was part-funded by Ian Fleming's close friend Ivor Bryce. Thus these two main protagonists, the languid Englishman and the magnanimous Irishmen, met and wrote the outline for what was originally planned as the first James Bond film. This was developed into a full shooting script by British screenwriter Jack Whittingham. When the film idea fell through, Fleming novelised the work into his ninth Bond book. The novel, however, only credited Ian Fleming. McClory and Whittingham sued Fleming, which led to a settlement in 1963. McClory was granted the film rights to the novel and successfully negotiated with Eon to use the book as the basis of the fourth Bond film. Broccoli and Saltzman employed two further screenwriters to develop a new script for *Thunderball*. All of this means that the film credit should read 'Written by Richard Maibaum and John Hopkins, based on the book by Ian Fleming, based on an original screenplay by Jack Whittingham, based on the original story by Kevin McClory, Jack Whittingham, and Ian Fleming'.

Set mostly in Nassau, Terence Young returned to direct his third and final Bond film with his usual élan and style. The film opens in as low key a manner as you can imagine: at a funeral, filmed at Château d'Anet near Dreux, 8km west of Paris. Bond, of course, realises that Colonel Jacques Bouvar, a SPECTRE operative played by stuntman Bob Simmons, is disguised as his own widow. Bond fights him, throttles him and escapes. With a jetpack. So, five minutes into the fourth Bond film, we have a gadget that exists for its own sake. This raises many questions. Did he use the jetpack to get into the chateau? If so, why wasn't he seen? If not, how does it get there? Does he carry on in the boot of his car, on the off chance? In any event, this was a case of spectacle ahead of credibility. Here's an early glimpse of the debacles of *Diamonds Are Forever*, *Moonraker* and *A View to a Kill*.

Bond's classic Aston Martin DB5 makes a second appearance, now fitted with water jets. A neat faded cut leads to Maurice Binder's sub-ocean opening titles. The SPECTRE board meeting has been heavily parodied over the years: once again, Number 1 (the still unnamed Blofeld) is portrayed by Anthony Dawson and dubbed by Eric Pohlmann. Number 2, Emilio Largo, introduces their latest audacious scheme – to hijack two nuclear bombs. The exteriors were filmed on the Avenue d'Eylau in Paris. The scene shifts to Shrublands, a health clinic where Bond has been sent to improve his health. The exterior is Chalfont Park House in Gerrards Cross, close to Pinewood studios. By a credibility-stretching coincidence, Bond disrupts SPECTRE's plans. He also seduces (or sexually assaults) his physiotherapist Patricia Fearing, memorably played by Molly Peters, whose screen career was unfortunately short-lived. Bond's technique here is troubling – coercion though blackmail – with echoes of the creepy barn scene with Pussy Galore in *Goldfinger*. Connery's wry 'see you later, irrigator', however, is one of the best puns of the series.

We are also introduced to Fiona Volpe, played by Luciana Paluzzi. The film comes to life when she is on screen. Her very sexy exchange with the luckless pilot Derval sets her character immediately:

Derval: You'll be here when I come back?
Fiona: Mm hmm.
Derval: But I may not be in the mood then.
Fiona: Do you wanna bet?
Derval: You know your François, huh?
Fiona: I know me.

Following an unusual MI6 briefing scene, with all of the Double-O agents in attendance, the action moves to Nassau. [44] Some of the sequences as the hijacked plane is hidden underwater are spectacular and technically brilliant. Kudos here to second-unit director Ricou Browning.

Bond arrived to investigate. We get some charged dialogue when Bond and Domino first meet.

Domino: How do you know my friends call me Domino?
Bond: It's on the bracelet on your ankle.
Domino: So ... what sharp little eyes you've got.
Bond: Wait 'til you get to my teeth.

Bond joins Domino for some amorous activity underwater. 'I hope we didn't frighten the fish,' he quips afterwards.

Bond meets Largo at the casino. Largo wears a SPECTRE ring. They play blackjack.

Largo: Someone has to lose.
Bond: Yes, I thought I saw a spectre at your shoulder.
Largo: What do you mean?
Bond: The spectre of defeat. That your luck was due to change.
Largo: We'll soon find out.

Q makes a typically bad-tempered appearance in a startling pineapple-print shirt and with some fairly mundane gadgets. And, at Largo's villa, director Terence Young places his camera into a swimming pool full of sharks for the film's best single shot: a fisheye view from below, filtered through a victim's blood.

Back to Fiona Volpe. Volpe and Bond's exchanges crackle with sexual energy. We see Bond standing in the doorway between their hotel rooms as Fiona takes a bath.

Volpe: Aren't you in the wrong room, Mr. Bond?
Bond: Not from where I'm standing.
Volpe: Since you're here, would you mind giving me something to put on?

Bond casually hands Fiona her slippers and casually sinks into a chair with a look of extreme self-satisfaction, almost entitlement. Then, later:

Bond: Vanity has its dangers.
Volpe: Vanity, Mister Bond, is something you know so much about.
Bond: My dear girl, don't flatter yourself. What I did this evening was for king and country. You don't think it gave me any pleasure, do you?
Volpe: But of course. I forgot your ego, Mr Bond. James Bond, who only has to make love to a woman and she starts to hear heavenly choirs singing. She repents and immediately turns to the side of right and virtue. What a blow it must have been, you having a failure.
Bond: Oh well you can't win them all.

Volpe is killed off too soon, shot in the back with a bullet meant for Bond.

An article from *Time*, December 1965, reads:

If *Thunderball's* gimmickry seems to overreach at times, actor Connery gains assurance from film to film, by now delivering all his soppiest Jimcracks martini-dry. He is hilariously astringent when he drops a limp dancing partner at a nightclubber's ringside table, saying: 'D'you mind if my friend sits this one out? She's just dead.' And indeed she is.

This scene, with pummelling drums and fast cuts to quickly build tension, was reworked in *The Spy Who Loved Me* when Max Kalba is killed by Jaws.

The final underwater battle is a slow ballet of grace and brutality. This is in complete contrast to the fistfight on Largo's ship, which is vicious, despite some unconvincing rear projection and judicious speeding up of the frame rate. Domino's final decision gives the character some closure.

Thunderball is utterly outlandish and retreads some of the Bond tropes: a scene in a casino, the appearance of the DB5, Blofeld's hidden face. But it has the dream Bond team at the peak of their powers: Sean Connery (by now inseparable from the Bond persona), Terence Young (director), Ken Adam (designer), John Barry (composer), Maurice Binder (titles) and Peter Hunt (editor). It might have been formulaic, but it was very classy with effortless style and swagger nevertheless.

Its leading man, however, was starting to tire:

> I find that fame tends to turn one from an actor and a human being into a piece of merchandise, a public institution. Well, I don't intend to undergo that metamorphosis. It's got so one needs the constitution of a rugby player. [45]

> THE popular image of James Bond as the man who has everything, already magnificently developed in three progressively more compelling films, is now being cheerfully expanded beyond any possible chance of doubt in this latest and most handsome screen rendering of an Ian Fleming novel, *Thunderball*.
>
> Richard Maibaum and John Hopkins sprinkle their gaudy fabrication with the very best sight and verbal gags. *Thunderball* is pretty, too, and it is filled with such underwater action as would delight Capt. Jacques-Yves Cousteau. Diving saucers, aqualungs, frogman outfits and a fantastic hydrofoil yacht that belongs to the head man of SPECTRE are devices of daring and fun. So it is in this liveliest extension of the cultural scope of the comic strip. Machinery of the most way-out nature become the instruments and the master, too, of man. Connery is at his peak of coolness and nonchalance with the girls. Adolfo Celi is piratical as the villain with a black patch over his eye. Claudine Auger, a French beauty winner, is a tasty skin-diving dish and Luciana Paluzzi is streamlined as the inevitable and almost insuperable villainous girl. The colour is handsome. The scenery in the Bahamas is an irresistible lure. Even the violence is funny.
>
> *New York Times*, 22 December 1965

Casino Royale

Casino Royale is Too Much... for One James Bond!
Release date: 13 April 1967. Running time: 131 minutes. Distributed by Columbia.
Produced by Charles K. Feldman, Jerry Bresler.
Starring Peter Sellers, Ursula Andress, David Niven, Woody Allen, Joanna Pettet,

Orson Welles, Daliah Lavi, Deborah Kerr.
Directors: Ken Hughes, John Huston, Joseph McGrath, Robert Parrish, Val Guest, Richard Talmadge. Screenplay by Wolf Mankowitz, John Law, Michael Sayers. Music: Burt Bacharach. Cinematography: Jack Hildyard, Nicolas Roeg, John Wilcox. Edited by Bill Lenny.

Background

The film industry was slow, at first, in responding to the success of the Bond films. But, perhaps unusually, it was the British Carry On team that were first off the blocks, with *Carry On Spying* filmed in February and March 1964 and released that June. [46]

Other copycats and parodies followed the huge success of *Goldfinger*: stand up *The Spy with My Face* (1965, the first of nine film spin offs from *The Man from UNCLE*); *The Ipcress File* and its sequels (Len Deighton, 1965-1967); Morecombe and Wise's catastrophic *The Intelligence Men* (1965); *The Spy Who Came in From the Cold* and *The Deadly Affair* (John Le Carre, 1965-1966); *The Quiller Memorandum* (1965); *Operations Crossbow* (1965); two Charles Vine films with Tom Adams (1965-1966); four Matt Helm films starring Dean Martin (1966-1968); the Dr. Goldfoot films with Vincent Price (1965-1966); *Our Man Flint* and its sequel (1966-1967); *Arabesque* (1966); the Bulldog Drummond adaptation *Deadlier Than the Male* (1967), and the notorious *Operation Kid Brother* featuring Sean Connery's non-acting sibling (1967). It seemed that anyone could find a virile actor, surround him with sexy women, cobble together a spy story and release a film.

The most infamous of these was based on a book by Ian Fleming: Charles Feldman's 1967 version of *Casino Royale*. Ian Fleming sold the film rights for his first novel to producer Gregory Ratoff in 1955. Ratoff died in 1960. 'At one time, I had tried to buy the film rights of [Fleming's book *Casino Royale*] from Gregory Ratoff's widow,' writes Cubby Broccoli. 'She sold her interest to Gregory's agent, Charlie Feldman.' Feldman held onto them until the huge success of the Eon Bond films. He decided to produce his own Bond film, and even asked Cubby Broccoli to loan Sean Connery and to co-produce *Casino Royale*. Broccoli understandably refused. Instead, Feldman contracted Peter Sellers to play Bond paying him a million dollar salary to do so.

Observations

This version of *Casino Royale* is a spoof. The trailer says that it is 'indescribably funny'. It's certainly indescribable. Cubby Broccoli later recalled that 'It was a mess of a picture'. '[Feldman] made a terrible mistake in trying to make it into a farce,' says David Picker. [47]

Bond, Vesper and Le Chiffre are in place, but the plot bears only a passing resemblance to Fleming's novel. Remarkably, the cast includes David Niven, Peter Sellers, Ursula Andress, Orson Welles, John Huston, Woody Allen, Deborah Kerr, Jacqueline Bisset, Deborah Kerr, George Raft, Jean-Paul

Belmondo, Peter O'Toole, William Holden, Bernard Cribbins, Ronnie Corbett, Charles Boyer, John Wells, Derek Nimmo, Graham Stark, Alexandra Bastedo, Chic Murray and Vladek Sheybal (Kronsteen, the chess master in *From Russia With Love*).

It was directed by six people. Any film directed by committee is bound to be bewildering. But it all could have been so different. Feldman, possibly in 1963, perhaps earlier, had commissioned Ben Hecht to write a screenplay for *Casino Royale*. Hecht was a prodigious screenwriter, and the recipient of the first-ever Oscar for best screenplay for *Underworld* in 1929, an award he would win again for *The Scoundrel* in 1936. Perhaps his best-known work was *Notorious* for Alfred Hitchcock (1946), for which he was nominated once again for best screenplay, his sixth Oscar nod. Author Jeremy Duns discovered his early *Casino Royale* screenplays in the Newberry Library in Chicago, where they had been stored since 1979. 'These drafts are a master-class in thriller writing, he said, 'from the man who arguably perfected the form with *Notorious*. All the pages in Hecht's papers are gripping, but the material from April 1964 is phenomenal, and it's easy to imagine it as the basis for a classic Bond adventure. It has all the excitement and glamour you would expect from a Bond film.' [48] Duns concludes that Hecht's April 1964 screenplay 'could have made for an extraordinary Bond film'. [49]

Initially, Scottish director Joe McGrath was signed up. McGrath had filmed some of the Beatles' promo clips and several episodes of *Not Only but Also*, so had credentials within the Swinging London milieu. Production commenced at Shepperton in January 1966, with Peter Sellers as the main character, but with an incomplete script, ultimately credited to Wolf Mankowitz, John Law and Michael Sayers. Writer Terry Southern, who had worked on *Dr. Strangelove*, was hired by Sellers to script his lines. There was on-set tension between McGrath and Sellers, however, which culminated in a fist fight between star and director: never a good omen for harmonious film-making. Sellers quit but then returned once McGrath himself was sacked. Experienced directors Val Guest, John Houston and Robert Parrish all directed new scenes, until Sellers quit for good. Sellers appears in around thirty-five minutes of the final film.

After Sellers' departure, the script was re-vamped further. Woody Allen was brought in as Dr. Noah, and a character called Mata Bond was added. Finally, David Niven was hired as Sir James Bond in an attempt to link the story together. These scenes were directed by Ken Hughes, who had worked for Broccoli's Warwick Films, including *The Trials of Oscar Wilde* (1960). Hughes would go on to direct another Fleming story: *Chitty Chitty Bang Bang* (1968). The final brawl sequence was principally directed by Richard Talmage and filmed by Nicolas Roeg.

So, in place of Sean Connery, six characters were deputized under the name James Bond, including Sellers, Joanna Pettit as Mata Bond – the love child of Mata Hari and the real James Bond – Niven, Allen, Daliah Lavi as 'The Detainer', and an actor kept on contract by Feldman for two years to play Bond, Terence 'Coop' Cooper. Ursula Andress is Vesper Lynd: her sex appeal doesn't quite atone for her lack of acting talent and heavy Swiss accent. William Holden, Bert Kwouk, George Raft, John Le Mesurier, Sterling Moss, Peter O'Toole and Andress' then husband Jean Paul Belmondo were pulled in for blink-and-you'll-miss them cameos. Lord only knows how six-time Oscar nominee Deborah Kerr agreed to take part. Q is Catweazle. There is a chimpanzee in a ginger wig. And the Keystone Cops. Future Darth Vader David Prowse appears as Frankenstein's monster. One character is abducted by aliens. I'm not making any of this up.

The film opens with Evelyn Tremble's version of James Bond (Sellers) meeting Mathis of the Deuxième Bureau in a pissoir in Paris. Tremble checks Mathis' 'credentials'. That's about the level we're operating at here. The first thirty minutes are almost unwatchable as we meet the retired Sir James Bond (Niven), who is visited by M (John Huston in a ginger wig) and representatives of the CIA (William Holden), the KGB and the French Special Police.

> M: He plays Debussy every afternoon from sunset until it's too dark to read the music. Stands on his head a lot, eats royal jelly. Lets his intestines down and washes them by hand. Something he learned during his sojourn in Tibet.

Bond declines to return to service. His mansion is destroyed by a mortar attack at the orders of M, who is killed in the explosion. Bond travels to Scotland to return M's wig ('it's an hairloom') to his widow Fiona. We then have an excruciating section as a stuttering Sir James fends off SMERSH agents pretending to be Fiona and her eleven daughters. Awful 'we're all doomed' Scottish accents abound. The otherwise admirable Deborah Kerr – Anna in *The King and I*, let's not forget – is simply bad. There is a grouse shoot. The birds are remote-control bombs. Sir James is promoted to head of MI5 (yes, MI5) after a chase involving a remote-control milk float.

> Sir James: Bring me up to date. Who's on what assignment?
> Hadley (Derek Nimmo): It's not a happy picture.
> Sir James: Why the black flags?
> Hadley: They've been liquidated, I'm afraid. Finland – stabbed to death in a ladies' sauna bath, Sir. Madrid – burnt in a blazing bordello, sir. And Tokyo, sir – garrotted in a geisha house.
> Sir James: It's depressing that 'secret agent' has become synonymous with 'sex maniac'. Incidentally, where is my namesake? [a reference to Bond of the Eon film series]
> Hadley: He's now doing television.

We have a fleeting scene with Woody Allen in front of a firing squad, then Connery-alike Terence Cooper in training, and the introduction of Ursula Andress as Vesper Lynd. Finally, we have elements of the original Fleming novel. Lynd is a retired agent who recruits baccarat expert Evelyn Tremble (Sellers) to play cards against SMERSH agent Le Chiffre. We are forty-six minutes into the film before we see Peter Sellers, who acquits himself well. If the entire film had been able to focus on Sellers then, who knows, it might not have been a disaster. After fifteen minutes of focussed film-making, we suddenly switch to another story entirely. The next twenty minutes follow the adventures of the delightful Mata Bond, who takes a taxi from London to Berlin to infiltrate 'International Mothers' Help', an au pair service that is a cover for a SMERSH training centre. This section of the film is gently bonkers.

Tremble/Bond is seduced by Miss Goodthighs, an early role for Jacqueline Bisset, who would have been a good choice for a female lead in the official series.

> Miss Goodthighs: Very sexy pants you're wearing, James.
> Bond: Yes, they're the new double-O-fronts.

We also have, I think, a smart sight gag – there is a copy of the book *How To Speak Japanese* next to Bond's bed. Is this a neat reference to his next assignment, then being filmed by Eon?

And then, a song. Sample lyrics:

> James Bond playing at Casino Royale
> He won a lot of money and a gal at Casino Royale
> Oh, he's not really such a wonderful spy
> But winning lots of money and a gal, he's a fabulous guy

Meanwhile, the next twenty minutes follows the original story quite closely – the card game, Vesper's abduction and Bond's torture. A glimpse of what might have been.

The film now falls apart before our eyes. Vesper kills Tremble/Bond with a gun hidden in bagpipes. Mata Bond is kidnapped by a UFO which lands in Trafalgar Square. Sir James and Moneypenny go to the Casino Royale to rescue her and here they discover the underground headquarters of Dr. Noah, Sir James' nephew Jimmy Bond in a Nehru jacket. Noah reveals that he plans to use biological warfare to make all women beautiful and kill all men over 4 feet 6 inches tall. Sir James, Moneypenny, Mata and Cooper (remember him?) battle SMERSH with American and French support arriving to add to the chaos. Eventually, an atomic pill that Noah has swallowed explodes, destroying the casino with everyone inside, putting us out of our misery.

Astonishingly, such was the drawing power of James Bond in 1967, *Casino Royale* had its premiere at the Odeon, Leicester Square, in the presence of Her Majesty the Queen. It was a box office success and is now very much in the 'cult film' category. 'If I'd have known that I was making a cult film', quipped Val Guest forty years later, 'I would have asked for more money'. [50]

If we're very generous, then *Casino Royale* has its moments: the music, the titles, one or two good set pieces, Joanna Pettit, Jacqueline Bisset. Its most positive legacy is the wonderful Dusty Springfield song 'The Look of Love'. But don't waste your weekend watching it: stick on *Austin Powers: International Man of Mystery* instead. Or *The Bourne Supremacy*. Or *Johnny English*. Or even *Die Another Day*. Anything.

At one time or another, *Casino Royale* undoubtedly had a shooting schedule, a script and a plot. If any one of the three ever turns up, it might be the making of a good movie.

In the meantime, the present version is a definitive example of what can happen when everybody working on a film goes simultaneously berserk.

Lines and scenes are improvised before our very eyes. Skilful cutting builds up the suspense between two parallel plots – but, alas, the parallel plots never converge. No matter; they are forgotten. Visitors from Peter O'Toole to Jean-Paul Belmondo are pressed into service. Peter Sellers, free at last from every vestige of discipline, goes absolutely gaga.

This is possibly the most indulgent film ever made. Anything goes. Consistency and planning must have seemed the merest whimsy. One imagines the directors (there were five, all working independently) waking in the morning and wondering what they'd shoot today. How could they lose? They had bundles of money, because this film was blessed with the magic name of James Bond.

Perhaps that was the problem. When Charles Feldman bought the screen rights for *Casino Royale* from Ian Fleming back in 1953, nobody had heard of James Bond, or Sean Connery for that matter. But by the time Feldman got around to making the movie, Connery was firmly fixed in the public imagination as the redoubtable OO7. What to do?

Feldman apparently decided to throw all sanity overboard. Instead of one Bond, he determined to have five or six. The senior Bond is Sir James Bond (David Niven). He is called out of retirement to meet a terrible threat by SMERSH.

Unfortunately, the threat is never explained. Other Bonds are created on the spot. Peter Sellers is the baccarat-playing Bond. He meets Le Chiffre (Orson Welles) in a baccarat game. Why? The movie doesn't say.

The five directors were given instructions only for their own segments, according to the publicity, and none knew what the other four were doing. This is painfully apparent.

There are some nice touches, of course. Woody Allen rarely fails to be funny, and the massive presence of Welles makes one wish Le Chiffre had been handled seriously.

But the good things are lost, too often, in the frantic scurrying back and forth before the cameras. The steady hand of Terence Young, who made the original Bond films credible despite their gimmicks, is notably lacking here.

I suppose a film this chaotic was inevitable. There has been a blight of these unorganized comedies, usually featuring Sellers, Allen, and-or Jonathan Winters, in which the idea is to prove how zany and clever everyone is when he throws away the script and goes nuts in front of the camera.

In comedy, however, understatement is almost always better than excess.

Sellers was the funniest comedian in the movies when he was making those lightly directed low-budget pictures like *I'm All Right, Jack*. Now he is simply self-infatuated and wearisome. And so are the movies he graces.

One wishes Charlie Feldman had sat down one bright morning, early in the history of this film, and announced that everyone simply had to get organized.

Roger Ebert, *Chicago Sun-Times*, 1 May 1967

You Only Live Twice

Harry Saltzman and Albert R Broccoli Present Sean Connery in Ian Fleming's *You Only Live Twice*

'…and TWICE is the only way to live!'

Release Date: 12 June 1967. Running time: 117 minutes. Distributed by United Artists. Producers: Harry Salzman (5 of 9), Albert R Broccoli (5 of 17).

James Bond: Sean Connery (5 of 7), M: Bernard Lee (5 of 11), Q: Desmond Llewelyn (4 of 17), Moneypenny: Lois Maxwell (5 of 14).

And Donald Pleasance (Blofeld) with Akiko Wakabayashi (Aki), Tetsuro Tamba (Tiger Tanaka), Mie Hama (Kissy Suzuki), Teru Shimada (Osato), Karin Dor (Helga Brandt), Charles Gray (Dikko Henderson).

Director: Lewis Gilbert (1 of 3). Screenplay: Roald Dahl. Production design: Ken Adam (4 of 7). Main titles: Maurice Binder (3 of 14). Music: John Barry (4 of 11). Theme song performed by Nancy Sinatra. Cinematography: Freddie Young. Edited by Peter Hunt (5 of 5).

Plot

James Bond travels to Japan to investigate the disappearance of US and Soviet space vehicles. He finds SPECTRE's secret volcano hideout and comes face to face with his nemesis, Ernst Stavro Blofeld.

Cast

Finally, we get to see Blofeld's face, after teases as SPECTRE Number One in *From Russia With Love* and *Thunderball*. We are not disappointed: the cat, the scar, the bald head, the penetrating stare. Blofeld is played here by British actor Donald Pleasance. Active since discharge from the RAF in 1946, Pleasance often played evil or fanatical characters. He was familiar to British TV viewers from his roles in *The Adventures of Robin Hood* (1956-1958), and in films such as *Look Back in Anger* (1959), *Dr. Crippen* (1962), *Fantastic Voyage* (1966), and many others. In the US he was nominated for Tony Awards for *The Caretaker* (1962)

and *Poor Bitos* (1965). Globally he had perhaps made his biggest impact as Colin Blythe, the good-natured forger in *The Great Escape* (1963). After *You Only Live Twice*, Pleasance would achieve two more Tony nominations and play the psychiatrist, Dr. Samuel Loomis, in five of the *Halloween* films (1978-1995). But it is as Blofeld that Pleasance is best remembered; his interpretation has become very familiar in popular culture, for better or worse.

Producer Harry Saltzman had originally hired Czech actor and playwright Jan Werich to play Blofeld. Werich's benevolent appearance didn't work for the part and he was released after a week of shooting. Experienced character actor Charles Gray plays Dikko Henderson, Bond's contact in Japan. Active on stage and TV in the 1960s, Grey's film breakthrough was opposite Peter O'Toole, Omar Sharif and Donald Pleasance in *The Night of the Generals* (1967). Japanese actor Tetsurõ Tamba is perfectly cast as the head of the Japanese secret service, Tiger Tanaka. Tamba appeared in many Japanese films in the 1950s and 1960s and would play the lead in two very popular police series on Japanese TV between 1968 and 1982. He also appeared in *The 7th Dawn* (1964) directed by Lewis Gilbert. In *You Only Live Twice*, Tamba was dubbed by Robert Rietti, who had also voiced Strangways in *Dr. No* and Largo in *Thunderball*. Tanaka was initially offered to Toshirô Mifune, who turned the part down to appear in *Grand Prix* (1966).

Akiko Wakabayashi and Mie Hama were both very popular actors in Japan. Akiko Wakabayashi had 25 Japanese films to her credit since 1961, and Mie Hama had made more than sixty films before she was cast as Kissy. They appeared together in the *Key of Keys* (1965), a James Bond parody (English version: *What's Up, Tiger Lily?*), and this attracted them to the producers of the James Bond series. Neither could speak English when cast – they also swapped roles before filming commenced. As with Sylvia Trench, Jill Masterson and Domino, Hama's voice was re-dubbed by Nikki van der Zyl. Helga Brandt – another no-nonsense sexy redhead who could be Fiona Volpe's sister – was played by German actor Karin Dor, selected from over fifty potentials. English-Chinese actor Bert Kwouk, who appeared in dozens of films and TV series over forty years, appears as SPECTRE Number Three. He had previously taken a small role in *Goldfinger* and played Cato Fong in seven of the *Pink Panther* films (1964-1993).

Theme Song

Sung by Nancy Sinatra. Her hit version is a contemporary re-recording and quite different to the dramatic theme used in the film. Alternative versions performed by Julie Rogers and Lorraine Chandler are also available.

Production

You Only Live Twice was filmed between July 1966 and March 1967 at Pinewood Studios, Buckinghamshire, and on location in Norway, Gibraltar, Japan, the US and Spain.

Observations

After four simply fabulous films, Bond parodies itself, as a Scotsman pretending to be English dresses up as a Japanese fisherman to rescue the Russian and American space programmes from a megalomaniac who has a hide-out in a hollowed volcano.

Sample lines of dialogue (casual racism warning):

Bond: Why do Chinese girls taste different from all other girls?
Ling: You think we better, huh?
Bond: No, just different. Like Peking Duck is different from Russian Caviar. But I love them both.
Ling: Darling, I give you very best duck.

Although *You Only Live Twice* is not the series' first wholly original James Bond film – Bond's infiltration of the Japanese fishing village, and the characters of Blofeld, Tanaka and Kissy are from the novel – it does differ significantly from Ian Fleming's book, the last to be published during his lifetime. The screenplay is credited to Road Dahl, best known at that time for the books *James and the Giant Peach* (1961) and *Charlie and the Chocolate Factory* (1964) and recommended to the producers by David Picker at United Artists. Dahl had written a film for Picker with the working title *The Bells of Hell Go Ding-a-Ling-a-Ling*. The film was never made. 'The important thing about that little story,' Dahl told Tom Soter in 1980, 'is that Picker saw this screenplay, which had been made up from nothing. At the time, he was talking to Broccoli and Saltzman about how to do *You Only Live Twice*. They thought of me and I got a call from Broccoli: 'Would you do a Bond script?' I said yes and went up to see them. There were Broccoli and Saltzman, and they said, 'You know, it will have to be completely invented. You can use the Japanese scenes and the names of the characters, but we need an entirely new plot.' So, I said, 'Well, all right.' 'It was Ian Fleming's worst book, with no plot in it which would ever make a movie. I didn't know what the hell Bond was going to do.' [51]

A nine-page treatment had previously been written by Sidney Boehm in November 1965. Boehm was an American screenwriter and former crime reporter. His treatment, which sticks close to Fleming's novel, was expanded to a full screenplay in early 1965, but seemingly none of his ideas were used. TV writer Harold Jack Bloom accompanied the producers to Japan and completed a second screenplay. Several of Bloom's ideas were used in the final script, including Bond's fake death and burial at sea, the ninja attack and the attacks on the Russian and American space programmes. Bloom is credited with 'additional story material' for the film.

You Only Live Twice is the first 'epic' Bond film: suspending disbelief is a prerequisite. Filming commenced only two years after the publication of the last fully realised Ian Fleming novel. [52] The first forty-five minutes are terrific: a tense thriller, tightly edited, set in unfamiliar territory. The director, Lewis

Gilbert, had made his mark with *Alfie* (1966) after twenty years of success making documentaries and very British low budget feature films such as *The Good Die Young* (1954), *Reach for the Sky* (1956) and *The Admirable Crichton* (1957).

> I had just made *Alfie* when Cubby and Harry came to me and asked me to do Bond number five. At first, I turned them down because I did not know what I could possibly offer them. Cubby called and said, 'You're turning down the biggest audience in the world.' And I thought, that's absolutely true. [53]

Gilbert returned to direct two other films in the Bond series, and died in 2018, aged 97.

The pre-credits scene is, in turns nonsense, and very satisfying. The film opens with an American spacecraft being hijacked – the score here is terrific. The establishing shot of the UK/US/Russia crisis meeting is radar domes on a military base in Mågerø, Norway. And then James Bond fakes his own death in Hong Kong ('At least he died on the job. He would have wanted it that way') and is buried at sea, with Gibraltar standing in for Hong Kong in a fun and witty scene that culminates in Bond being rescued by divers – the underwater scenes were filmed in the Bahamas – and taken aboard a British Navy submarine. 'Request permission to come aboard, sir!'

Bond meets M and Moneypenny. This is the first Bond film when 007 does not visit MI6 headquarters for his briefing, a trick re-used in *The Man With the Golden Gun* (covert offices in the wreck of the RMS Queen Elizabeth in Hong Kong harbour) and *The Spy Who Loved Me* (Scottish naval base and inside an Egyptian pyramid). Bond travels to Japan – beautifully photographed – and meets Dikko Henderson, played by sinister and underused Charles Grey. Bond breaks into the offices of a chemical company (exteriors were filmed at Hotel New Otani, Tokyo) and is rescued by a mysterious woman. So far, so good. But his introduction to Tiger Tanaka is ridiculous – a chase from the Kuramae Kokugikan sumo hall leads to a hidden trap door and lengths of aluminium piping, very freely adapted from a scene in Fleming's novel. [54]

> Tiger Tanaka: I must say I am disappointed with the ease with which I could pull you in. The one thing my honourable mother taught me long ago was never to get into a car with a strange girl. But you, I'm afraid, will get into anything. With any girl.

Clues take Bond to a ship called the Ning-Po at Kobe docks. Director Lewis Gilbert provides a stunningly filmed fight across the roofs of the dock warehouses, which culminates in a very neat stuntman-for-Connery switcheroo. Bond is captured and we meet again, the Volpe-alike Helga Brandt. She chooses an over-ambitious, illogical and doomed-to-failure scheme to kill Bond by threatening him, releasing him, bedding him, betraying him, then jumping out of a plane leaving him behind. Brandt – a redhead, like Fiona Volpe – gets to swim with the piranhas, a very Dahlesque idea.

The scenes with Little Nellie, the DIY autogyro are classic Bond. Both 'OO7' and 'The James Bond Theme' are used to great effect as Bond uses his gadgets to dispatch four model helicopters. These aerial scenes were filmed over Torremolinos in Spain, an inspired last-minute replacement for another car chase.

A plan takes shape and the film falls over. We'll skip over the risible scenes when Bond is 'disguised' as a Japanese fisherman, principally by the addition of eyelids and wig to replace the one Connery was already wearing. The film drags for twenty minutes while OO7 trains to be a ninja in what seems like a single afternoon – filmed at Himeji castle not far from Kobe and in the gardens of the Hotel New Otani in Tokyo. Bond then participates in an elaborate Japanese marriage ceremony which took place at the ancient and very beautiful Kumanonachi Taisha shrine, nestled in the Kii Mountains, near Kii Katsuura, 250km south of Osaka.

There is cheeky line when Kissy Suzuki turns down Bond's advances.

> Bond: Is this the only room there is?
> Kissy: Yes. That is your bed. I shall sleep over there.
> Bond: But we're supposed to be married. We must keep up appearances. We're on our honeymoon.
> Kissy: No honeymoon. This is business.

Bond pushes aside his oysters and utters, with evident disappointment, 'I won't need these then.'

Bond and Kissy disguise themselves as a fisherman and diver and investigate a local cave. These scenes were filmed in the region of Bonotsucho Akime, on the southernmost top of the Japanese peninsula, around 1,500km west of Tokyo. Pursuing the lead further, they climb a volcano and discover, yes!, that Blofeld's base is inside. Bond and Kissy climb up to the summit from the coast. In reality, Mount Shinmoedake is a couple of hours' drive inland.

Luckily – massive plot hole warning – Bond has handily packed his rubber suckers and exploding cigarettes. Making it up as he goes along, Bond ultimately tries to replace one of the astronauts. There is a neat bit of direction after Bond is exposed for carrying his air conditioner into the space capsule. He is brought to Blofeld who orders his helmet to be removed. Instead of looking at Blofeld – the first time they have been face-to-face, let's not forget – Bond looks at Osato. Connery stares him down and Osato looks away. In the next shot, Bond gets a first look at Blofeld. He is intrigued and doesn't know what to make of him.

> Blofeld: James Bond. Allow me to introduce myself. I am Ernst Stavro Blofeld. They told me you were assassinated in Hong Kong.

Bond: Yes, this is my second life.
Blofeld: You only live twice, Mr. Bond.

Screenwriter Roald Dahl attended the location shoot in Japan. 'Nobody ever got close to Sean, you know,' he said later. 'He's Scottish and they have a peculiar kind of reticence. The crew and Freddie Young – the chief cameraman and a lovely fellow – and everyone else all stood a round at the end of a hot day and had drinks and beer, and Sean accepted all these. He was the only man making a million in the film and he never stood anyone a round. This was known. They all talked about it. He is not an attractive personality. Sean happened to fit exactly into the Bond image. Somehow, Bond didn't need personality; he was just a tough guy. The quips were all given to him by us, you see. All of them. There was damn little acting for him to do. He walked through it, you know. Literally.' [55]

The real highlight is Ken Adam's production design. Every interior is magnificent, culminating in that famous volcano lair: the finale with Tanaka's ninjas dropping in from the ceiling is still outrageous and electrifying in equal measures. The 'blow-up-the-set' finale is undeniably spectacular, even if the back-projection and flowing lava visual effects are pants.

You Only Live Twice is not the best Bond film of the 60s, but cinematically, it might be the best made. It certainly turned a corner in the Bond series. After the out-of-character diversion of *On Her Majesty's Secret Service*, the Bond films would become increasingly fantastic and sometimes downright silly in the Roger Moore era. Despite not looking 100% engaged, Connery's charisma enables him to easily out-Bond Roger Moore or George Lazenby.

In July 1966, mid-way through the football World Cup finals, the set had some important visitors: members of Alf Ramsey's England team who visited Pinewood as a distraction from their forthcoming game against Mexico. 'Photographers are allowed in to record the moment when Ramsey's players meet a succession of movie stars,' writes Henry Winter. 'One picture captures Sean Connery, who is filming the latest Bond film *You Only Live Twice*, looking respectfully at Bobby Moore – OO7 and No. 6 in the same frame.'

Although there's a lot more science-fiction than there is first-vintage James Bond in *You Only Live Twice*, the fifth in a series of veritable Bond films with Sean Connery, there's enough of the bright and bland bravado of the popular British super-sleuth mixed into this melee of rocket-launching to make it a bag of good Bond fun. This noisy and wildly violent picture is evidently pegged to the notion that nothing succeeds like excess. Through it all, Connery paces with his elegant nonchalance a little more non than usual (he is evidently getting slightly bored) but altogether able in the clinches and in tossing off the gags of Roald Dahl. The sex is minimal. But then, Bond is getting old. And so, I would guess, is anybody who can't get a few giggles from this film.
New York Times, 14 June 1967

On Her Majesty's Secret Service

'Far Up! Far Out! Far More!'
Release date: 18 December 1969. Running time 140 minutes. Distributed by United Artists. Producers: Harry Salzman (6 of 9), Albert R Broccoli (6 of 17)
James Bond: George Lazenby, M: Bernard Lee (6 of 11), Q: Desmond Llewelyn (5 of 17), Moneypenny: Lois Maxwell (6 of 14).
And Telly Savalas (Blofeld) with Diana Rigg (Tracy), Gabriele Ferzetti (Marc-Ange Draco), Ilse Steppat (Irma Bunt), Angela Scoular (Ruby Bartlett), George Baker (Sir Hilary Bray).
Director: Peter Hunt. Screenplay by Richard Maibaum (5 of 13). Additional dialogue by Simon Raven. Production design: Syd Cain (3 of 3). Main titles: Maurice Binder (4 of 14). Music by John Barry (5 of 11). Theme song performed by the John Barry Orchestra. Cinematography: Michael Reed. Edited by John Glen (1 of 3).

Plot

Still on Blofeld's trail, James Bond meets criminal overlord Marc-Ange Draco after saving his wayward daughter from suicide. Draco helps trace Blofeld to the Swiss Alps, where Bond disrupts Blofeld's plans for destroying the UK agriculture industry with germ warfare. Bond and Tracy marry, but Blofeld delivers tragic revenge.

Cast

Sean Connery publicly stated 'never again' after *You Only Live Twice*. That film offered 'the usual array of incredible gadgetry, but the formula was already signs showing of becoming purely mechanical.' [56] As Alexander Walker writes, '[Connery] was tired of being increasingly subordinated to production hyperbole, proxy stunt-men and scene-stealing gimmickry.' [57]

It's ironic, then, that the sixth Bond film would deliberately play down the overstatement, outrageous plotting plot and silly tricks of *You Only Live Twice* in favour of an almost straight film version of Ian Fleming's best novel.

'Sean was a good Bond,' writes Cubby Broccoli. 'But he was never going to be the only one.'

'I would have loved to have Connery,' says director Peter Hunt, 'Because if we had had him, it would have been the best of the lot. But at that time, we couldn't, so there was really no point in wishing that we could. I think we were like two weeks off of shooting, when one had to say, 'Who are we going with? We're supposed to be starting, but we haven't got a Bond yet'.' [58]

Eon and UA began the thankless task of recruiting a new Bond. They would, of course, repeat this process in 1970 and 1972. They considered Roger Moore once again. Moore was friendly with the producers and had attended the first screening of *Dr. No*, and the other films in the series, at Eon's London offices.

Roger Moore: 'Around the time of *You Only Live Twice* in 1967, Harry and Cubby spoke to me about the possibility of taking over the role. The Bond adventure they discussed was planned for filming in Cambodia. When all hell broke loose in that country [when the Government was overthrown between 1968 and 1970] ... the plans were scrapped. I continued making *The Saint* and was unavailable when they re-grouped [for] *On Her Majesty's Secret Service*.'

UA's David Picker wanted Australian tennis player John Newcombe. Broccoli and Saltzman again turned to Richard Burton but could not match the fee he was asking for. Oliver Reed was briefly considered. 'Oliver Reed was very near the top of [our] list,' Cubby Broccoli said in a later interview. 'Oliver already had a public image; he was well known and working hard at making himself even better known. We would have had to destroy that image and rebuild Oliver Reed as James Bond – and we just didn't have the time or the money.'

A young British actor called Timothy Dalton, twenty-two at the time, had made a big impression as Philip II in *The Lion in Winter*. But Dalton felt the task of replacing Connery was too great. Peter Hunt favoured Michael Billington, a young actor who would test for Bond many times between 1972 and 1983. But Broccoli and Saltzman saw a TV advert for Fry's chocolate. The story of how Australian model and used-car salesman George Lazenby (born 5 September 1939) won the role of James Bond based on a 'chance' encounter with Cubby Broccoli and a screen-test fight scene when he bloodied the nose of stuntman Yuri Borionko has been well-documented. [59] By October 1968, Lazenby was reported as being one of five serious contenders. The others were British actor John Richardson who had played opposite Ursula Andress in *She* (1965) and Raquel Welch in *One Million Years BC* (1966); Anthony Rogers, a British actor from the films *El Dorado* (1966), with John Wayne, and *Camelot* (1967), with Richard Harris; Robert Campbell, a handsome American actor with very little experience; and Hans de Vries who had taken a small role in *You Only Live Twice*. [60]

Broccoli and Saltzman had gambled on Sean Connery and had hit the jackpot. They would gamble again with the appointment of George Lazenby. Over the years, Lazenby's portrayal of Bond has, unfairly, been reduced to an answer in a trivia quiz. Stories of his clashes with co-star Diana Rigg and ego-driven belief that a single Bond film would make a lasting international superstar are rife. But the question remains – not was Lazenby the right choice compared to Sean Connery, but was he a good Bond in his own right? The answer must be 'yes'. In fact, despite Lazenby's lack of acting chops, his single Bond film must rank as one of the best in the series – thanks to a top-notch source novel (the last to be filmed more or less intact), a sparkling script, sure and firm direction from Peter Hunt – who had been involved in the series from the start – and tight editing from John Glen.

Glen is a major contributor to the James Bond series. In addition to editing and directing the second unit on *On Her Majesty's Secret Service*, *The Spy Who Loved Me* and *Moonraker*, he would also direct the final three Moore films and both Dalton entries. Glen started his working life as a messenger boy in 1945, aged 13. He was later employed in the visual and sound editorial departments of Shepperton Studios on films such as *The Third Man* (1949) and *The Wooden Horse* (1950). He also worked on *The Italian Job* (1969), *Superman* (1978) and *The Wild Geese* (1978, with Roger Moore). Glen was promoted to the rank of director for all five of Bond films of the 1980s and all of his films are strong on action. His 2001 memoirs *For My Eyes Only* is a must-read for any Bond fan.

George Lazenby benefited from the experienced acting of Diana Rigg as Tracy and Telly Savalas as Blofeld. Like Honor Blackman, Diana Rigg was familiar from TV's *The Avengers*. Her character had a Flemingesque name: Emma Peel – M[ale] Appeal. Rigg had considerable acting chops, having been active with the Royal Shakespeare Company between 1959 and 1964.

Rigg explained that she took the part to sex up her image. 'At the end of all that pulchritude, there's me,' she said. 'And, let's face it, I'm not exactly all teeth and tits, am I?' She also hoped the role would 'make me better known in America'. It didn't quite do the job. [61] Director Peter Hunt wanted Brigitte Bardot to play Tracy and travelled to France to meet her, but she was committed to *Shalako* with Sean Connery. Catherine Deneuve said 'non'. Of all the Bond series' female leads, only Rigg has been able to continue with a critically acclaimed film, theatre and TV career. She was made a Dame in 1994 for services to drama and died in 2020.

American-born to Greek parents, Telly Savalas, charismatic and unfashionably bald, had made his mark in *Birdman of Alcatraz* (1962), *Battle of the Bulge* (1965) and *The Dirty Dozen* (1967). He is most familiar as the eponymous Kojak in the acclaimed, ground-breaking TV series between 1973-1978 and 1985-1990. Savalas died in 1994. German actor Ilse Steppat was perfectly cast as Irma Bunt in her only English-speaking role. Unfortunately, she died the week of the film's release.

We should also mention Gabriele Ferzetti as Marc-Ange Draco, Tracy's father and head of the Union Corse, the Corsican mafia. Ferzetti was an experienced actor with dozens of Italian films to his credit from 1942 onwards. In *On Her Majesty's Secret Service*, Ferzetti's voice was dubbed by British actor David de Keyser who performed much-uncredited voice work in the 1960s, 1970s and 1980s and has a small role in *Diamonds Are Forever*.

Many of Blofeld's 'Angels of Death' would have successful careers in films and TV: Catharina von Schell (*Space 1999* and several more), Joanna Lumley (*The New Avengers*, *Sapphire and Steel*, *Absolutely Fabulous* and many others), Julie Ege (*Up Pompeii*), Jenny Hanley (*Magpie*) and Zaheera (many Bollywood films in the 1970s and 1980s). Angela Scoular, as Lancastrian chicken-lover Ruby Bartlett, had appeared in the 1967 version of *Casino Royale*, would marry actor Leslie Phillips and have a chequered and ultimately tragic life. Anouska Hempel is now best known as an interior designer to the rich and famous.

Theme Song

A pounding John Barry instrumental, with a powerful synthesised bass, plays over the main titles. Barry also wrote the love song 'We Have All the Time in the World', which accompanies the Bond/Tracy love montage.

Production

On Her Majesty's Secret Service was filmed between October 1968 and May 1969 at Pinewood Studios, Buckinghamshire and on location in Portugal, Switzerland and the United Kingdom.

Observations

Fleming's best book, *On Her Majesty's Secret Service*, was published in 1963. It was the first he would write after the surprise success of the film version of *Dr. No*, and is in turns wistful, melancholic and downright exciting. In the original book, the casino scene is set in the Casino Royale in Royale-les-Eaux in northern France: it is revealed that Bond goes there each year, visiting Vesper Lynd's grave nearby. This gives a real depth to the plot, much of which transferred to the film version. Two years before, Bond had been battling a megalomaniac with a white Persian cat who stole spaceships from a base within a hollowed-out Japanese volcano. In *On Her Majesty's Secret Service*, we have a Bond film of a very different stripe. The story is driven not by a megalomaniac gold fetishist, a stolen nuclear warhead or a Russian decoding machine. It starts (and ends) with a woman, and because of this Bond, and the film as a whole, is more human and less of a caricature.

'Fleming had created the character of Tracy with much care,' writes Sandipan Deb. 'She possessed indomitable *joie de vivre* and was also a manic depressive. She loved life and wanted to commit suicide. She was enormously confident and deeply vulnerable. She was a wealthy high-living slut looking for a man who would be the love of her life, to whom she would surrender totally and stand by him, forever.'

Many of these character traits find their way into the film. It is Diana Rigg's performance throughout, as well as Lazenby's better moments and less arrogant characterisation acting against her, that drive an emotional resonance that was unusual in a Bond film. In many ways, Tracy transfers her recklessness and vulnerability to Bond, a character trait not seen again until *Casino Royale* (2006).

The plot follows the book closely: from the introductory car chase and beach, the scenes with Draco, the cover story of the College of Arms, Bond's visit to Piz Gloria, the ski chase, the escape by car, M's house, the assault on Piz Gloria, the bob-sleigh chase and the heart-breaking final scene. It's also a very dialogue-heavy film, from Tracy distracting egotistic Blofeld by discussing poetry, to the long scene between Draco and Bond. Credit here should go to industrious British writer Simon Raven, his only contribution to the series.

Following a new gun barrel scene – Lazenby drops to one knee – the lengthy pre-titles scene opens with M and Q at MI6 headquarters. We then switch to

Bond driving his Aston Martin DV5, face half-hidden. He is burned off by an attractive woman in a scene straight from the book:

> If there was one thing that set James Bond really moving in life, with the exception of gun-play, it was being passed at speed by a pretty girl; and it was his experience that girls who drove competitively like that were always pretty – and exciting. [62]

The chase leads to the beach and we finally see Bond's face as he introduces himself with, what else, 'my name is Bond, James Bond'. Bond despatches two goons, and Lazenby's physicality here is terrific. These scenes were filmed at Praia do Guincho on the Atlantic coast, west of Lisbon. There is a sly acknowledgement to Sean Connery in 'this never happened to the other fella', and we are into the titles sequence: the mandatory naked silhouettes. The sequence, with its instrumental theme music, reprises the villains and female leads of the first five Bond films. This was surely designed to reassure the audience that this was simply the next chapter in an ongoing series.

The opening scene in the casino, filmed at Palácio Estoril Hotel in Estoril and again taken directly from the book, once again places Bond and the audience into familiar territory. The seeds of Bond's relationship with Tracy are sown ('Please stay alive. At least for tonight.') before Bond is pulled up by Draco's men. The next several minutes are very satisfactory, as Lazenby trades lines with Gabriele Ferzetti in a well-written and carefully directed scene. Note also the whistling midget caretaker played by Norman McGlen, one of the Oompa Loompas from *Willy Wonka and the Chocolate Factory*.

Back in London, the obligatory scene with Moneypenny is one of the best. In fact, this may be Lois Maxwell's finest outing as M's ever-hopeful secretary. In a sparkling scene, Bond pinches Moneypenny's bum and describes her as 'Britain's last line of defence'. The requisite double entendres are subtle and witty.

> Bond: Moneypenny, what would I do without you?
> Moneypenny: My problem is that you never do anything with me.

Meanwhile, Bond believes he has quit the secret service and reminisces on past adventures in his office. Honey's knife belt, Klebb's shoe, Grant's garrotting watch and the rebreather from *Thunderball* are accompanied by snatches of music from the relevant film. Lovely. Moneypenny changes Bond's resignation letter to a request for two weeks' leave and gets a kiss on the lips as a reward. These first thirty minutes establish George Lazenby as Bond and are very successful. The main plot, however, is yet to start.

A long, sentimental and unnecessary love scene montage, mostly filmed in Portugal, slows down the film before we finally get moving with a tense section not present in Fleming's original novel. Bond breaks into a Swiss law firm. He gets a lead on Blofeld and the February 1969 issue of *Playboy* with the help of an ACME safecracker/photocopier, and agent Shaun Campbell, played by Bernard Horsfall. The exterior scenes were filmed at the Hotel Schweizerhof in Bern. The editing and use of the score here are first class.

Following short, sharp scenes at M's house and the College of Arms, Bond travels to Switzerland, disguised as Sir Hilary Bray. He arrives by train at Lauterbrunnen, 70km south-west of Bern and is accompanied by Frau Bunt to Blofeld's hideout, filmed on location at Piz Gloria at the summit of Shilthorn. Here he finally meets Blofeld. In the books, Bond meets his nemesis face-to-face for the first time in *On Her Majesty's Secret Service*. This allows Bond to pose as Hilary Bray: Blofeld would not recognise the undercover spy. The books were filmed out of order. However: *You Only Live Twice* comes after *On Her Majesty's Secret Service* in the literary chronology. Bond meets Blofeld in the film version of *You Only Live Twice*, which makes the plot of Bond-as-undercover-genealogist in *On Her Majesty's Secret Service* simply nonsense. In truth, Savalas' Blofeld is so different to Donald Pleasance's that they could be separate characters. Savalas is physically powerful, arrogant yet cultured: a sophisticated but tough gangster rather than an evil genius with a nasty scar. This Blofeld is a living, breathing character. The Persian cat and Nehru jacket are in place, however.

Lazenby has been kitted out in a kilt, merely to allow Ruby to write her room number on his leg under the table:

> Bunt: Is anything the matter, Sir Hilary?
> Bond: Just a slight stiffness coming on... due to the altitude, no doubt.

He is also given the most ridiculous line of dialogue in the entire series: 'Call me Hilly.' As Bond uncovers Blofeld's latest plot, we stray dangerously to Austin Powers territory as Blofeld hypnotises his angels of death: 'do you remember how you hated chicken?'

But in the crucial scene with Bond – 'Merry Christmas, 007' – he simply dominates Lazenby. Savalas here is quite superb.

> Blofeld: In a few hours, the United Nations will receive a Yuletide greeting. The information that I now possess the scientific means to control, or to destroy, the economy of the whole world. People will have more important things to think about than you.

Savalas is given some corking lines and delivers them with a suave menace: 'Such a keen climber, such a brilliant conversationalist … before he left us', and 'I mean what I say, and I'll do what I claim'.

The next several minutes are pure action. Bond escapes from his prison, the cable car wheelhouse, and is followed down the mountain in a terrific ski chase. *On Her Majesty's Secret Service* was the first James Bond film with a set-piece ski chase. Two, in fact. In fact, skiing had hardly been seen on screen at all before 1969, and *On Her Majesty's Secret Service* set the bar with two brilliantly filmed and edited sequences, with the throbbing regal main theme being put to spectacular effect. Bond would return to the slopes in *The Spy Who Loved Me* (1977), *For Your Eyes Only* (1981), *A View to a Kill* (1985), *The Living Daylights* (1987) and *The World Is Not Enough* (1999). He re-visits the Alps in *Spectre* (2015).

An unlikely but life-saving meeting with Tracy – filmed at the Grand Regina Hotel in Bern, Bond's relief at seeing her is palpable – leads to an superfluous but spectacular stock car race and a second ski chase, culminating in an avalanche where Tracy is captured by Blofeld.

The avalanche was filmed by John Glen and the 2nd unit. Glen had been called to Switzerland in February 1969, four months into the Swiss shooting schedule. The avalanche, thousands of tons of snow set off by explosions dropped from a helicopter, was later enhanced by models at Pinewood. Look out for some tiny animated skiers being consumed by the pursuing avalanche. A specially constructed two-mile track had been constructed for the bob-sleight chase, but before Glen's arrival, only ten seconds of workable footage had been completed. Glen brought in Willy Bogner to operate the camera and doubles were used to replace George Lazenby and Telly Savalas. The resultant chase, cut with front-projected inserts from Pinewood, is supremely realistic. The producers would remember John Glen when it came time to shoot another spectacular sequence for *The Spy Who Loved Me*.

And then, the wedding, with a tearful Moneypenny, and M and Draco discussing 'the bullion job' from a few years before, a neat reference to *Goldfinger*. And, of course, the unexpected aftermath, on a mountain road in the Arrábida National Park near Setúbal. What a pity we get a blast of the James Bond theme over the credits instead of Louis Armstrong.

George Lazenby as James Bond is handsome, athletic, magnetic, charming and credible. His acting is pretty good for a novice – the skills of the director and editor no doubt helped here – and he showed the beginnings of a successful characterisation. In particular, the final scene, when he holds his dead wife in his arms and weeps, is perfectly executed. 'The decision to use Lazenby was not left in my hands,' notes Peter Hunt. 'But they did say to me, 'Can you do it with him?' And I said, 'Yes, I can.' I had a big job directing him, even though he seems to think he wasn't directed, and it was quite a job to make him Bond. It was a difficult job, but the answer for me was that it worked, and it worked for the producers as well. He was a great looking guy and he moved along very well. I think if things had gone the other way, he would have gone on to be a very good Bond.' [63] 'George had a nice personality', wrote John Glen, 'and he was willing to try anything'. [64]

Critic John Brosnan would write in 1972, 'When *OHMSS* was released, it was immediately apparent that a serious error in casting had been made. First, Lazenby was simply too young for the part, his face suggesting none of the necessary Bondian world-weariness or ruthlessness. Secondly, his voice, despite the crash elocution course, was totally wrong, particularly when his underlying Australian accent broke through as it frequently did. Thirdly, and most importantly, it was obvious that Lazenby lacked training as an actor. Putting it bluntly, his performance was both awkward and wooden, and whatever the certain 'something' was that Hunt claimed he saw in him, failed to make the transition to the screen...' [65]

George Lazenby was not, and never could be, an immediate replacement for Sean Connery. Who could? But, hindsight in place, I would argue that this one film shows George Lazenby as a far more credible version of Fleming's James Bond than, say, Roger Moore or Pierce Brosnan. But then, Moore and Brosnan were movie stars first, actors second, and Lazenby was neither. 'He was a beginner, walking in Sean Connery's shadow,' writes Cubby Broccoli. 'Lazenby, in my judgement, made a good James Bond.'

And who are we to disagree? But if Sean Connery had starred in *On Her Majesty's Secret Service* and toned down his cockiness to suit the plot then there's no doubt that the 1969 entry in the Bond canon would have been the best of the lot.

> *On Her Majesty's Secret Service* had a lot to live up to. As far as the entire world was concerned, Sean Connery was James Bond. And here was some impostor – worse, an impostor from the colonies, George Lazenby, whom nobody had heard of – waltzing in to take his place. It wasn't right. It wouldn't do. To rub everyone's noses in it even further, *On Her Majesty's Secret Service* deliberately stuck closely to the book, which meant no audience-pleasing whizz-bang gadgets. And what's with the bummer of an ending? No wonder the film only took half the amount of *You Only Live Twice* at the box office.
>
> And yet I will fight anyone who dares to tell me that they don't like *On Her Majesty's Secret Service*. Because they are flat out wrong. In the 45 years since it was released, it stands out as one of the best OO7 films ever. Possibly even the best. It has the best soundtrack. It pushes the character into difficult new places. And that ending: that's not just a great James Bond ending; it's probably in the top 10 film endings of all time. If you've never seen *On Her Majesty's Secret Service*, you should watch it. If you've seen *On Her Majesty's Secret Service* before, you should watch it again. And if you don't like it, I'm serious about fighting you.
>
> Stuart Heritage, *The Guardian*, 23 February 2014

Diamonds Are Forever

Harry Saltzman and Albert R Broccoli Present Sean Connery as James Bond OO7 in Ian Fleming's *Diamonds Are Forever*

Release date: 14 December 1971. Running time: 120 minutes. Distributed by United Artists. Producers: Harry Salzman (7 of 9), Albert R Broccoli (7 of 17).

James Bond: Sean Connery (6 of 7), M: Bernard Lee (7 of 11), Q: Desmond Llewelyn (6 of 17), Moneypenny: Lois Maxwell (7 of 14), Leiter: Norman Burton. And Charles Gray (Blofeld) with Jill St. John (Tiffany Case), Jimmy Dean (Willard Whyte), Bruce Glover (Mr. Wint) Putter Smith (Mr. Kidd), Joseph Furst (Professor Doctor Metz), Lana Wood (Plenty O'Toole), Bruce Cabot (Bert Saxby), Joe Robinson (Peter Franks), David Bauer (Morton Slumber), Leonard Barr (Shady Tree).
Director: Guy Hamilton (2 of 4). Screenplay: Richard Maibaum (6 of 13), Tom Mankiewicz (1 of 3). Production design: Ken Adam (5 of 7). Main titles: Maurice Binder (5 of 14). Music: John Barry (6 of 11). Theme song performed by Shirley Bassey. Cinematography: Ted Moore (5 of 7). Edited by Bert Bates (1 of 2), John Holmes.

Plot

James Bond follows the trail of a diamond smuggling operation and discovers that a wider plot to use diamonds to power a solar laser is headed by his old enemy Blofeld.

Cast

By the time that *On Her Majesty's Secret Service* was released, George Lazenby had chosen to step down from the role that was about to make him world-famous. As Lazenby told the *Los Angeles Times*, 'The producers made me feel like I was mindless. They disregarded everything I suggested simply because I hadn't been in the film business like them for about a thousand years.' [66]

Diana Rigg: 'I think it's a pretty foolish move. I think if he can bear to do an apprenticeship, which everybody in this business has to do – *has to do* – then he should do it quietly and with humility.' [67]

Cubby Broccoli:

> George ruled himself out of the reckoning by behaving like the star he wasn't. I find it incredible that a plum role can't be respected. We chose George because in his physique and his looks and his walk, he was the best of the candidates. He had the masculinity. Looking at the film, to put it in an old Spanish phrase, one could wish he had less cojones and more charm. Lazenby didn't get on too well with the director, Peter Hunt, nor, apparently, with Diana Rigg. In professional terms, he was sawing off the branch he was sitting on. [68]

In time, Lazenby would come to reflect on his behaviour:

> The trouble was, I lived Bond out of the studios as well as in. I had to have a Rolls-Royce to go around in and women just threw themselves at me if I stepped into a nightclub. I couldn't count the parade that passed through my bedroom. I became hot-headed, greedy and big-headed. [69]

With George Lazenby literally out of the picture, Eon once again needed a new Bond. Director Guy Hamilton, returning after *Goldfinger*, initially wanted Burt Reynolds. 'I was in America and I found the perfect Bond, who was Burt Reynolds. He had all Sean's qualities, a nice wit, a little short maybe, but he moved like a dream. But UA said, 'forget it, he's just a stunt man'.' Reynolds, at that time still best known for *Gunsmoke* on TV, said, 'I think I could have done it well. In my stupidity, I said, 'An American can't play James Bond, it has to be an Englishman... nah, I can't do it.' Oops. Yeah, I could have done it. For a long time afterward, I'd wake up in a cold sweat going 'Bond, James Bond'.' [70]

British actors Michael Gambon, Dumbledore in six of the Harry Potter films, and Jeremy Brett, who would become synonymous with TV's Sherlock Holmes, were also considered. Gambon: 'I said, I can't play James Bond, because I'm bald, I've got a double chin and I've got girl's tits,' he told RTE's Ryan Tubridy in 2016. 'So he said, 'well, so has Sean Connery, so we put a wig on him, and we put two big leather bags full of ice on his chest before the take. And then a man comes in just before the action and takes the bags off and then Connery has a beautiful flat chest and he has false teeth and all that.' He said, 'you could well do it.' But he didn't offer it to me!' 'It's the sort of role you cannot afford to turn down', says Brett, 'but I think if I had got it, it would have spoiled me.'

Eventually, Broccoli and Saltzman found their James Bond: American actor John Gavin. He had caught the producers' eye in the 1968 French spy film *OSS 117: Double Agent* opposite future Bond villain Curd Jürgens. 'Time was getting awfully short', Cubby Broccoli told the *Los Angeles Times* in 1971. 'We had to have someone in the bullpen.' Gavin was signed to the role and pre-production began.

United Artists had other ideas. 'It was David Picker, president of United Artists', writes critic Alexander Walker, 'who enticed Connery back into the films. After three days' haggling with lawyers and accountants, he laid the world (or what it was *then* worth) at his feet: a $1.2m cash fee, ten per cent of the gross ... and – most important to Connery's peace of mind – the right to pick two additional non-Bond projects which UA agreed to finance. It was a shrewd deal.' [71]

Gavin stepped aside; his contract paid in full. And so Sean Connery, starting to look his age but effortlessly charismatic, would play Bond once again. 'Connery clearly does not want to be there,' wrote Xan Brooks forty years later. 'He shuffles through the motions like some ageing heavyweight showboater, flirting with disaster, his toupee slipping. When Bond is not fighting for his life and banging his elbows inside a cramped Amsterdam elevator, he's being kicked to hell by a pair of self-regarding girl acrobats in the Nevada desert. He's knackered, out of shape, halfway through the exit door.' [72]

Charles Gray is a suave, aristocratically assured but weak Blofeld, a real let-down after Donald Pleasance and Telly Savalas. And didn't he already appear as another character in another Bond film? Bruce Glover and Putter Smith as Mr Wint and Mr Kidd are suitably unnerving–if most certainly un-PC to modern viewers – and Bambi (Lola Larson) and Thumper (Trina Parks) show great promise before being too easily dispatched by Bond in a swimming pool. Jill St. John, a working actor since the age of six and the first of eight American female leads in the next fourteen films, is unconvincing as the brash, self-made professional diamond smuggler Tiffany Case. Lana Wood plays Plenty O'Toole. Wood is the younger sister of Natalie Wood, one-time wife of Robert Wagner. Wagner later married Jill St. John.

Theme Song

Rather obviously harking back to *Goldfinger*, the theme song here is again sung by Shirley Bassey. Probably the best part of the film, the 'touch it, stroke it and undress it' lyrics offended co-producer Harry Salzman, but Cubby Broccoli held firm, for which we give thanks.

Production

Diamonds Are Forever was filmed between April and August 1971 at Pinewood Studios, Buckinghamshire and on location in France, the Netherlands, the United States and the United Kingdom.

Observations

Other than the characters of Tiffany Case, Shady Tree, Wint and Kidd, the screenplay for *Diamonds Are Forever* takes almost nothing from Fleming's novel, one of his weakest. With the director and theme tune chanteuse of *Goldfinger* returning to re-connect with the Bond series' finest hour, screenwriter Richard Maibaum's initial ideas included the return of Gert Fröbe as Auric Goldfinger's diamond-obsessed twin brother. Cubby Broccoli rejected the script, which was re-written by Tom Mankiewicz, the first of three Bond co-writes. Mankiewicz would later contribute to *Superman: The Movie* (1978) and the TV series *Hart to Hart* (1979-1984). As with many of the group-written Bond films, the basic plot idea for *Diamonds Are Forever* is very clever. Much more than 'Blofeld holds the world to ransom with a giant laser', the underlying premise sees Blofeld forcing the world's superpowers to participate in a bidding war, with an auction where only one nation will triumph, and the rest will be defenceless. And there's the unfinished business of the murder of Bond's wife. What should have been a striking vendetta story with a dramatic undercurrent of uncertain nuclear supremacy is turned into a film that is cartoonish, meandering and at times (whisper it) simply boring.

The very cheesy pre-credits sequence ('There's something I'd like you to get off your chest') was filmed in the grounds of the Hôtel du Cap Eden Roc, Antibes. Sean Connery looks much older and heavier than in *You Only Live Twice*, filmed five years before. Once again, Nikki van der Zyl provides a dubbed voice here. Charles Gray is a caddish, slightly smarmy Blofeld. The opening shot suggests that Blofeld has undergone plastic surgery, which might have been a plausible explanation of Gray not looking anything like Telly Savalas. Or Donald Pleasance. Instead, Blofeld is creating look-alikes. Bond shoots one, then drowns the other in a mud bath. This is, in part, taken from the original novel, when Bond witnesses a jockey being tortured in a bath of hot mud. The briefing scene features a very bad-tempered M. Bond admits his lack of diamonds-based knowledge and M retorts: 'Refreshing to hear that there is one subject you're not an expert on!' The obligatory scene with Q was filmed at the Aston Martin factory in Newport Pagnell.

The disconcertingly matter of fact and decidedly sinister hitmen, Mr Wint and Mr Kidd, seem to choose the most unlikely methods – dropping a scorpion down a contact's shirt, or leaving a drugged Bond in an unfinished pipeline. Importantly, Wint and Kidd are never played for laughs, like Jaws or Sheriff Pepper, and this makes them memorable as characters for all the right reasons.

For the scene at the port of Dover where Moneypenny gives Bond his travel documents, Lois Maxwell and Sean Connery filmed their lines separately. They did not act together for this short scene. The hovercraft Bond uses to travel to Amsterdam was *The Princess Margaret*, in service from 1968 until 2000 and, after many years in preservation, was broken up as recently as 2018. Bond meets flinty Tiffany Case in Amsterdam, driving over the De Zeven Bruggen on his way to Reguliersgracht 36 – Tiffany's flat. The chemistry between Sean Connery and Jill St. John is strong but this Bond is almost a parody of himself in places, notably after the claustrophobic and brutal lift fight with diamond-courier Peter Franks. 'Oh my God, you've killed James Bond!', Tiffany yells. 'Is that who it was?' Bond replies.

The action moves to Los Angeles for a scene with Felix Leiter ('alimentary Dr Leiter') then to Las Vegas. Many of the locations are identifiable. These include Los Angeles International Airport for Bond and Tiffany's arrival; McCarran International Airport where Bond tracks the toy stuffed with diamonds; Las Vegas Hotel and Casino doubling as the Whyte House; Circus Circus Hotel & Casino when Tiffany is tailed by the CIA; Pabco Gypsum, 8000 E Lake Mead Blvd is Willard Whyte Tectronics and Missile Laboratories; and the Landmark Hotel where Bond rides the elevator.

The diamonds pass to Shady Tree, a stand-up comedian, at the Slumber Inc. Memorial Home. This building still exists: it's the Palm Downtown Mortuary & Cemetery at 800 South Boulder Highway, Henderson, in the southwest outskirts of Las Vegas. While Bond retrieves the cash for the diamonds, he's knocked unconscious by Wint and Kidd, who put him in a coffin and then into the cremation oven. In a genuinely alarming and claustrophobic scene, Bond nearly burns alive. As the tension builds, the coffin is suddenly opened by Tree and Slumber. 'You dirty, double-crossin' limey fink!' Tree squeaks. 'Those goddamn diamonds are phonies!'

The action moves to the casino in the Whyte House hotel, filmed at the Riviera Hotel and Casino. Bond meets the opportunistic Plenty O'Toole ('But of course you are. Named after your father, perhaps?'). There follows a long, tedious section as Bond tracks Tiffany and the real diamonds through the casino, hotel, airport, a gas station ... and eventually to WW Tectronics, a research laboratory owned by reclusive Las Vegas millionaire Willard Whyte. Bond blags his way into the lab and escapes, yes, in a moon buggy. Laughable.

Las Vegas at night looks sumptuous, Ted Moore at his best. The car chase is terrific, despite the presence of a redneck cop who is not JW Pepper but is certainly a prototype. Amazingly, the car chase was filmed on Freemont Street at the heart of the Las Vegas strip. As Bond drives past the Golden Nugget in Tiffany's brand-new Ford Mustang Mach 1 hundreds of spectators line the streets. He escapes with a neat exit over a low-loader – and the infamous two-wheel stunt down an alley.

Bond determines to confront Whyte. The elaborate lift and piton gun sequence is classic Bond. Instead of Whyte, he meets two identical Blofelds. Parts of the plot here are simply illogical. An unconscious Bond is placed in a partially constructed pipeline, which is buried the next morning. He escapes, finding a convenient access hole, with the words: 'I was just out walking my rat and seemed to have lost my way'. This line is pure Roger Moore. But then, Connery's first return as James Bond enabled him not to take things too seriously. The nonsense continues as Bond uses a voice-altering device to gain access to Blofeld. He finds out Whyte's location – Elrod House in Palm Springs, all futuristic concrete domes, dynamic diagonals and circular furniture – and, after a brief fight with Bambi and Thumper, rescues Whyte. In the meantime, Blofeld escapes and abducts Tiffany. [73] Keeping up?

Finally, Bond meets the real Blofeld, or Charles Gray's portrayal of him. Their bonhomie is confusing: Bond, this man killed your wife! From here, we get Blofeld in drag, Q jiggering the slot machines, some very dodgy special effects and a drawn-out inconclusive finale on an oil rig, shot off the shore of Oceanside, near San Diego, California. 'Such pretty cheeks', says Blofeld as Tiffany is taken away by his guards, 'if only they were brains...'

Diamonds Are Forever is full of slightly smutty lines like this – 'As long as the collars and cuffs match...', 'Right idea ... wrong pussy', 'Is there anything I can do for you?' asks Thumper. 'I can think of several,' smarms Bond. We get a couple of unnecessary dick puns. Bond's line after he's held up at gunpoint in his hotel room with Plenty is: 'Well, I'm afraid you've caught me with more than my hands up.' And then Bond strips out of his tuxedo for Tiffany Case, who becomes aroused as she watches him undress. Once he is naked in front, she smiles, 'I'm very impressed. There's a lot more to you than I had expected.'

In the scriptwriters' favour, we do have the memorable 'If we destroy Kansas, the world may not hear about it for years', and 'Well, one of us smells like a tart's handkerchief. I'm afraid it's me. Sorry, old boy.' This sets the tone for the next seven Bond films.

Indeed, in many ways, *Diamonds Are Forever* is the first Bond film of the Roger Moore era.

After the minor debacle of George Lazenby's momentary tenure as 007, the Bond producers offered Sean Connery a hefty paycheck to return to the fold for one last hurrah. The result, while never losing Bond's populist streak (it was another big hit), reveals more cracks than it ought. Connery ageing quickly, his hairline indeterminately assisted, doesn't fully recapture the swagger of his halcyon adventures.

The plot, one of Ian Fleming's better, is effectively unusual for its first half – a genuine piece of global policing for the British agent as he traces the diamond-studded clues from Amsterdam to Las Vegas (this remains the most Americanised of all the films), but here it founders with the re-appearance of Charles Gray, the third and least of the actors to play Blofeld. He's too smug and comic, with none of the deep freeze of Donald Pleasance. The big finale, wastefully spilling about an oilrig off the Californian coast, is a washout compared to the glorious, Ken Adams-designed uber-bases we were accustomed to.

Cubby Broccoli and Harry Saltzman, Bond's guiding lights, were furiously trying to recapture the glory of *Goldfinger,* Bond's high-water mark, corralling its director Guy Hamilton, writer Richard Maibaum and Welsh diva Shirley Bassey for a second opportunity to roll her tonsils around a theme song (a good one). But it feels distant, an echo of the elegance and restraint of *Goldfinger*, with too much emphasis on action (a dumb moon buggy chase through the Nevada desert is a limp effort) and acute violence (Bambi and Thumper, two sexy acrobats, beat seven bells out of poor OO7 in a scene that slips dangerously outside of the fantasy milieu).

Only, the cool frisson in having Bond play the gaudy tables of Vegas, a reverse of the lavish world of Monte Carlo; Jill St John's sassy redhead and the camp duo of henchman, Mr. Kidd and Mr. Wint (Putter Smith and Bruce Glover), assassins with a horribly leery modus operandi, stand the test of time. The main-man Connery, is evidently back against his better judgement and no amount of John Barry scoring, and fierce pyrotechnics could finally reignite the lustre of his heyday.

Ian Nathan, *Empire*, 2015

[1] Copyright the Ian Fleming Estate.

[2] Jim Leach in *James Bond and the Female Authority*, included in *For His Eyes Only: The Women of James Bond* (2015).

[3] *Tall, Dark and Gruesome* (1997)

[4] Derek's fourth wife was Bo Derek (nee, Mary Cathleen Collins) whom he directed in the progressively awful films *10* (1979), *Tarzan the Ape Man* (1981), *Bolero* (1984) and *Ghosts Can't Do It* (1989).

[5] *People* (18 July 1983).

[6] Nikki van de Zyl redubbed some, not all, of Jane Seymour's lines in *Live and Let Die*.

[7] Quoted in *James Bond: A Celebration* (1987)

[8] *James Bond: A Celebration* (1987).

[9] *For Your Eyes Only: Ian Fleming and James Bond* (2009) – this line is reproduced on hundreds of websites. The original source is now obscured.

[10] *Retrovision* magazine (1997).

[11] Part of a lengthy interview published at jamesbondOO7.com
[12] *The Bond Affair* (1966). The exceptions are *Moonraker* – Bond does not get the girl – and *The Spy Who Loved Me* which is an anomaly in the Bond canon.
[13] *The Man Who Saved Britain: A Personal Journey into the Disturbing World of James Bond* (2006).
[14] *The Daily Telegraph* (August 2014).
[15] *Typical Men – The Representation of Masculinity in Popular British Cinema* (2003).
[16] Other than Roger Moore, future Bond actors would follow this trend – Lazenby is Australian, Dalton is Welsh-born but grew up in the East Midlands near Derby, Brosnan is Irish-born, Craig is from the provincial North West.
[17] *A Critical History of British Cinema* (1978).
[18] Ben McIntyre in *For Your Eyes Only: James Bond + Ian Fleming* (2009). It would take until 2021 for his love interest to appear in two consecutive films: Léa Seydoux as Dr. Madeleine Swann.
[19] Burgess wrote his own Fleming/Le Carre spy novel semi-spoof, *Tremor of Intent*, in 1966. Tread carefully.
[20] Fleming's book, *Dr. No*, would sell 1.5 million copies in the seven months after the release of the film. By the end of 1963, Bond books were selling at the rate of almost 4, 500,000 annually.
[21] Andrew Spicer in *Typical Men – The Representation of Masculinity in Popular British Cinema* (2003).
[22] Greek actor Katina Paxinou, Oscar-winner for *For Whom The Bell Tolls*, was originally considered but was not available.
[23] *From Russia With Love* by Ian Fleming, copyright the Ian Fleming Estate.
[24] *Catching Bullets* (2012).
[25] *White Heat: A History of Britain in the Swinging Sixties* (2006).
[26] *Pussy Galore – Women and Music in Goldfinger* by Catherine Howarth, included in *For His Eyes Only: The Women of James Bond* (2015),
[27] *James Bond: A Celebration* (1987).
[28] *Goldfinger* (2000). Dr Mabuse was the antagonist in the Norbert Jacques novel *Dr Mabuse Der Spieler* (1921) and its film version (1922).
[29] The first of several cringe-worthy one-liners. We can add 'I think he got the point' (*Thunderball*), 'He had lots of guts' (*On Her Majesty's Secret Service*), 'He always did have an inflated opinion of himself' (*Live and Let Die*), 'Take a giant step for man' (*Moonraker*). Stand up Richard Maibaum, Tom Mankiewicz and Christopher Wood.
[30] Quoted in *Martinis, Guns and Girls* (2003).
[31] *The Man Who Saved Britain: A Personal Journey into the Disturbing World of James Bond* (2006).
[32] Margaret Nolan, who played Dink, would appear as eye candy in six *Carry On* films, as well as featuring in the title sequence of *Goldfinger*, painted gold.
[33] *The Man Who Saved Britain: A Personal Journey into the Disturbing World of James Bond* (2006).
[34] Fleming describes Oddjob's hands at some length in the original novel of *Goldfinger*: 'The fingers all seemed to be the same length. They were very blunt at the tips and … glinted as if they were made of yellow bone. There were no fingernails. Instead, there was this same, yellowish carapace. Down each edge … was a hard ridge of the same bony substance.' In the same book, Fleming memorably describes Junius du Pont's hand as 'pulpy and unarticulated – like a hand-shaped mud pack, or an inflated rubber glove', and in a reflection on past events, Le Chiffre's hands as 'pink crab hands …

scuttling out for the cards'.

[35] Bond also drives Aston Martin cars in *On Her Majesty's Secret Service* (a DBS, Bond is driving it when Tracy is killed) and both *The Living Daylights* and *No Time To Die* (V8 Vantage Volante).

[36] In *For His Eyes Only: The Women of James Bond* (2015), Dr. Eileen Rositzka attempts to argue that the name 'Honey Ryder' is sexually suggestive: '[her] first name promises sexual lubrication, whereas her surname points to the fact that she is likely to take a superior position in this exchange.' Erm, OK, whatever you say.

[37] *The Man Who Saved Britain: A Personal Journey into the Disturbing World of James Bond* (2006).

[38] In Fleming's original novel of *Goldfinger* – the 7th Bond book – Solo is a representative of the Mafia: '[he] had a dark, heavy face, gloomy with the knowledge of much guilt and many sins.' Interestingly, the name of this character was re-used as one of the leads in the TV series *The Man from UNCLE* (1964-1968). Many of the concepts for the series were devised by Ian Fleming – indeed, the series was almost titled *Ian Fleming's Solo* until Eon caught wind and threatened legal action. Fleming died between the filming of the pilot and the series' debut. William Boyd's 2013 James Bond novel is called *Solo*.

[39] Reviewed 31 January 1999.

[40] *For Your Eyes Only: Ian Fleming and James Bond* (2009).

[41] For the record: a theatre goer in the pyramids son-et-lumiere in *The Spy Who Loved Me*; a passer-by outside Venini Glass, a tourist on a bridge behind Bond and M and a NASA technician in *Moonraker*; a Greek priest in *For Your Eyes Only*; a member of the Soviet Security council and one of the tourists that assist Bond after he escapes from Khan's compound in *Octopussy*; a patron at one of Kara Milovy's orchestra performances in *The Living Daylights*; a delegate of the Russian Security Council in *GoldenEye*; Elliot Carver's media friend in *Tomorrow Never Dies* ('Consider him slimed'); a man in Zukovsky's casino (he gives Electra something to sign) in *The World Is Not Enough*; a general and a bystander in *Die Another Day* ('mobilise the South Korean troops'); the Prague Chief of Police in *Casino Royale*; a man sitting in the lobby of the Hotel Dessalines in *Quantum of Solace*; a pallbearer in *Skyfall* (cut from the final edit), a man talking to C/Denbigh in *Spectre*; as a Spectre party member in *No Time To Die*. Nice work if you can get it.

[42] Fleming refused to alter his lifestyle to extend his lifespan.

[43] Reviewed 31 January 1999.

[44] The Double-0 agents known to be present are 002, 003, 004, 005, 006, 007 and 009. There are others who remain unidentified. 002 is later killed by Scaramaga in *The Man With the Golden Gun*. Another 002 takes part in the Gibraltar training exercise at the beginning of *The Living Daylights*, in which 004 is killed and his body is tagged with the label Smiert Spionam (death to spies). 003 is found dead in Siberia in *A View to a Kill*. 006 is the main antagonist in *GoldenEye* and is mentioned by Ian Fleming in his book *On Her Majesty's Secret Service*. 008 is referenced in the films *Goldfinger* and *The Living Daylights*, both times as a potential replacement for James Bond, and also in Fleming's books *Moonraker* ('the powder-vine says that 008's got out. He's in Berlin, resting.') and *Goldfinger* ('M would know that Goldfinger had killed Bond and he would probably give 008 licence to kill in return.'). 009 is killed in the first scene of *Octopussy*; a later 009 has put the bullet in Renard's head in *The World Is Not Enough* and 007 takes 009's new Aston Martin in *Spectre*. In addition, Fleming writes that 011 had vanished in Singapore during the opening chapter of *Moonraker*.

[45] *Playboy* (November 1965) and *Time* (11 June 1965).
[46] Charles Hawtrey's character is Charlie Bind, agent double-0 – ooh!
[47] Quoted in *The Making of Casino Royale,* on the 2011 BluRay release.
[48] '*Casino Royale*: discovering the lost script', in *The Daily Telegraph* (2 March 2011).
[49] *Rogue Royale – The Lost Bond Film by the Shakespeare of Hollywood* (2016).
[50] Quoted in *The Making of Casino Royale*, on the 2011 BluRay release.
[51] *Starlog* #169 (August 1991).
[52] *You Only Live Twice* was published on 26 March 1964. Ian Fleming died on 12 August 1964. *The Man With the Golden Gun* followed, posthumously, in 1965, and *Octopussy* and *The Living Daylights* in 1966.
[53] Quoted in *The Art of Bond* (2006).
[54] For the record, Graham Thomas identifies the wrestlers as Kotozakura Masakatsu (26 November 1940 – 14 August 2007, achieved Yokozuna, the highest rank in sumo wrestling in 1973) and Fujinishiki Takemitsu (18 March 1937 – 17 December 2003, achieved Komusubi, the fourth highest rank in sumo wrestling in 1960).
[55] *Starlog* #169 (August 1991).
[56] Roy Armes in *A Critical History of British Cinema* (1978).
[57] *National Heroes: British Cinema in the Seventies and Eighties* (1985).
[58] *Retrovision* magazine (1997).
[59] No fan of the Bond films should be without the wonderful book *The Making of On Her Majesty's Secret Service* by Charles Helfenstein published in 2009.
[60] All five men were pictured in *Life* magazine on 11 October 1968 in a feature confirming Lazenby's appointment. Other actors linked with the role in 1967-1968 include Michael Caine, who didn't want to be typecast, and French-Canadian Daniel Pilon.
[61] *People* (18 July 1983).
[62] *On Her Majesty's Secret Service* by Ian Fleming, copyright the Ian Fleming Estate.
[63] *Retrovision* magazine (1997).
[64] *For My Eyes Only* (2001).
[65] *James Bond in the Cinema* (1972).
[66] 24 November 1969.
[67] *Chicago Tribune* (3 December 1969)
[68] First and last sentence from Broccoli's memoirs. 'Plum role … charm' from *The Sunday Times,* 21 December 1969.
[69] From *James Bond: A Celebration* by Peter Haining (1987).
[70] First half from interview on *Good Morning America* in 2015. Final line from his memoirs, *But Enough About Me* (2015).
[71] *National Heroes: British Cinema in the Seventies and Eighties* (1985).
[72] *The Guardian* (27 September 2012).
[73] The scenes in Tiffany's house were filmed nearby, at 515 W Via Lola, Palm Springs.

1972 – 1985: Keeping the British end up

Live and Let Die

Harry Saltzman and Albert R Broccoli present Roger Moore as James Bond – 007 in Ian Fleming's *Live and Let Die*
Release date: 27 June 1973. Running time: 121 minutes. Distributed by United Artists. Producers: Harry Salzman (8 of 9), Albert R Broccoli (8 of 17).
James Bond: Roger Moore (1 of 7), M: Bernard Lee (8 of 11), Moneypenny: Lois Maxwell (8 of 14), Leiter: David Hedison (1 of 2).
And Yaphet Kotto (Mr. Big) with Jane Seymour (Solitaire), Julius Harris (Tee Hee Johnson), Gloria Hendry (Rosie Carver), Clifton James (Sheriff J.W. Pepper), Geoffrey Holder (Baron Samedi), Roy Stewart (Quarrel Jr.), Earl Jolly Brown (Whisper).
Director: Guy Hamilton (3 of 4). Screenplay: Tom Mankiewicz (2 of 3). Production design: Syd Cain (3 of 3). Main titles: Maurice Binder (6 of 14). Music by George Martin. Theme song performed by Paul McCartney and Wings. Cinematography: Ted Moore (6 of 7). Edited by Bert Bates (2 of 2), John Shirley (1 of 2), Raymond Poulton (1 of 2).

Plot

James Bond is sent to New Orleans to investigate the murders of three British agents. Here he encounters Mr. Big, a heroin magnate with a complex organisation, a psychic tarot card reader, and black magic and voodoo.

Cast

During pre-production for *Live and Let Die* in 1972, Sean Connery had been asked to appear in a seventh Bond film but declined. And so, the search for a new Bond began once again. Patrick McGoohan was once more considered for the role he'd turned down in 1961. Peter Anthony was screen-tested, as he had been for *Dr. No*, but was still considered unsuitable. American actors Burt Reynolds (again), Adam West and Clint Eastwood were approached, but all thought the role should be played by a Brit. When he appeared on *Top Gear* in 2010, Sir Ranulph Fiennes, the explorer, claimed he made it down to the final six to replace Connery but was rejected because he had 'hands like a farmer'. Michael Billington was also tested for *Live and Let Die* and, later, three other Bond films. He is best known for portraying Paul Foster in the 1970 science fiction TV series *UFO*, and Daniel Fogarty in the historical drama, *The Onedin Line* (1971-1974).

The new Bond would, of course, be Roger Moore (14 October 1927 – 23 May 2017).

> "Are you alone?' Harry [Saltzman] asked me when he called me long distance at my Denham home. 'You mustn't talk about this', he added, 'but Cubby

agrees with my thinking in terms of you for the next Bond.' I didn't say anything to anyone. Once bitten, twice shy.' [1]

Unlike Connery and Lazenby, Roger Moore was a known prospect. Like Connery, Moore was born into a less-than-affluent part of a national capital: Shoreditch in London. The son of a policeman, his acting career started in 1945 when he was hired as an extra on *Caesar and Cleopatra,* starring Claude Rains and Vivien Leigh. The film's director, Brian Desmond Hurst, paid for Moore to attend RADA, where he first met Lois Maxwell. He later worked as a model and took a number of uncredited film parts before heading to the US in 1953. He was signed by MGM in 1954 but released after two years. Turning to TV, Moore would find success in *Ivanhoe* (1958-59), *The Alaskans* (1959-60), *Maverick* (1960-1961), *The Saint* (1962-1969) and *The Persuaders!* (1971-1972) as well as a few films, most notably *The Man Who Haunted Himself* (1970).

Moore would be announced to the world at the Dorchester in London on 1 August 1972. His portrayal would be quite different to the Bonds of the sixties, as comical as it was action-packed. Even his name sounds like a Richard Maibaum pun. 'So, how do you follow someone as hugely popular as Sean?' Moore asked himself in 2012. 'Well, I was conscious I should at least not speak with a Scottish accent. I would never order a vodka martini, nor would I drive an Aston Martin. They were too closely associated with Sean. I had to be the same, but different.' [2]

'Roger Moore re-created Bond as an old-style, debonair hero, more polished and sophisticated than Connery's incarnation,' writes Andrew Spicer, 'using the mocking insouciance he had perfected in *The Saint*.' [3]

'Roger Moore is an excellent actor who has carried the part well and not allowed himself to be completely swamped by the gadgets,' says Terence Young. 'But I don't think it is Bond he plays – but *The Saint*. A Saint dressed up as Bond, a lamb disguised as a wolf!' [4]

'I played Bond with the reality, credibility, and hopefully still encompassing stunts and effects and what have you, and out of it some indigenous humour,' remarked Sean Connery in a TV interview in 1983. 'And anything that happens is possible. I feel that Roger–which I think he may have inherited in part from after *Diamonds Are Forever*, where they were already getting into that area of too much hardware–that that was more important. His is a sort of parody of the character, as it were, so you would go for the laugh or the humour at whatever the cost of the credibility or the reality. I think [Moore] took another direction with it that way and acquired an entirely different audience.' [5]

'First of all, my whole reaction was always – he is not a real spy,' Moore said in 2012. 'You can't be a real spy and have everybody in the world know who you are and what your drink is. That's just hysterically funny. I always felt you should let the audience share the joke.' [6]

An early indication of how Moore would play the role would be evident when he played James Bond in a seven-minute comedy sketch on the British TV show *Mainly Millicent* in 1964 ('Waiter, bring me another waiter!').

'It was the substitution of the head prefect for the school bully,' writes Alexander Walker. 'In short, Moore lightened the sexist element by adding his own alloy of jokey comedy.' [7]

'Roger played Bond in a different key,' says Richard Maibaum, who co-wrote six of Roger Moore's seven Bond films. 'He made Bond more sophisticated: he didn't project the innate toughness that Sean had, or the irony. Roger had cynicism – and there's a real difference between irony and cynicism.' [8]

Yaphet Kotto plays Mr Big in his first large film role. Kotto went on to portray Idi Amin in the 1977 television film *Raid on Entebbe* and Parker in *Alien* (1979). He played opposite Robert De Niro in the comedy thriller *Midnight Run* (1988) and featured in the NBC television series *Homicide: Life on the Street* (1993–99). Jane Seymour, Solitaire, was only twenty-one when filming began. Although not her first film role, it was her most prominent to date. She was perhaps best known to UK viewers at that time from *The Onedin Line*. Seymour has had a long career in film and TV, including Emmy and/or Golden Globe nominations for *Captains and the Kings* (1976), *East of Eden* (1981), *Onassis: The Richest Man in the World* (1988), *War and Remembrance* (1988-1989) and *Dr Quinn Medicine Woman* (1993-1998), also winning a Golden Globe for the latter. Julius Harris portrays voluble Tee Hee. Harris was a familiar face in the 'blaxploitation' genre, appearing in films such as *Super Fly*, *Trouble Man* (playing a character called Mr. Big), *Black Caesar* and its sequel *Hell Up in Harlem* in 1972-73. Earl Jolly Brown portrays portly, rasping Whisper and Clifton James plays JW Pepper, a role he revisited (or reworked) in *The Man With the Golden Gun* (1974), *Silver Streak* (1976) and *Superman II* (1980). James had small but memorable, more serious, roles in *Cool Hand Luke* (1967), *The Untouchables* (1987) and *Bonfire of the Vanities* (1990). But it's Geoffrey Holder who steals the film as Baron Samedi. Holder was a polymath with much success on Broadway. He was a principal dancer with the Metropolitan Opera Ballet in New York City from 1955 to 1956 and also moved into film roles in 1962. The producers presumably saw him as the sorcerer in Woody Allen's *Everything You Always Wanted to Know About Sex but Were Afraid to Ask* (1972). Holder won two Tony Awards in 1975 for direction and costume design of *The Wiz*, the all-black musical version of *The Wizard of Oz*. Finally, we have yet another actor playing Felix Leiter. 'It's nice to have David Hedison as Bond's CIA buddy Felix Leiter,' wrote Roger Moore in 1972. 'We met in Hollywood years ago when he was making *The Fly* with Vincent Price [1958]. It was a science-fiction story about a fly with a man's head and David, in the title role, had a last line of 'Help me, help me' delivered in a squeaky, high-pitched voice. I always greet him with my own falsetto version of this line. We'd worked together on *The Saint* and when ideas were passed around about casting, I suggested David. He went to see the casting director and the rest is history.' [9]

Bernard Lee appears as M for the eighth time. There was initially some doubt whether Lee would be available, and Kenneth Moore was lined up to replace him. Lois Maxwell is in place as Moneypenny; Desmond Llewelyn's Q was not included in the script and he therefore misses his only Bond film between 1963 and 1999.

Theme Song

Surely the best of all of the Bond themes, 'Live and Let Die' was written to order by Paul and Linda McCartney and provided a much-needed hit single for their band Wings in summer 1973. The first rock song used to open a Bond film, McCartney has performed it on all of his concert tours since 1973. The song was nominated for the Academy Award for Best Original Song in 1974.

Production

Live and Let Die was filmed between October 1972 and March 1973 at Pinewood Studios, Buckinghamshire and on location in the United States and Jamaica. [10]

Observations

Roger Moore's debut James Bond film was released in June 1973. [11] It's a loose adaptation of Fleming's second Bond novel published nineteen years before: Bond's pursues Mr Big, a criminal with links to voodoo. In the book, Mr Big smuggles 17th-century gold coins from British territories in the Caribbean. In the film, he plans to distribute heroin for free to put rival drug barons out of business.

It's one of Moore's best entries in the series: he looks young, fit, handsome – effortlessly confident and poised. Here we see almost thirty years of acting chops on display: experience on which neither Connery nor Lazenby could draw. In his debut film, Moore hasn't yet started to parody himself too much. There are questionable racial politics, but *Live and Let Die* has some genuinely exciting sequences.

The opening gun barrel now has a hatless Bond for the first time. The pre-titles sequence does not feature Roger Moore at all. Three British agents are killed in New York, New Orleans ('Who's funeral is it?' 'Yours') and the fictional Caribbean nation of San Monique. That banging theme tune leads to our first view of the new James Bond. In bed. M and Moneypenny arrive to brief Bond, who emerges in a monogrammed dressing gown.

> Bond: Insomnia, sir?
> M: Instructions.

Moneypenny colludes with Bond to spare M the vision of Bond's naked female companion, the kind of in-joke-at-the-expense-of-logic that litters Moore's tenure. Bond uses an espresso machine, hardly a fixture of everyday life in the era of the three-day week. Compare this to *Dr. No*'s casino scene or *On Her Majesty's Secret Service*'s south-of-France car chase: it's clear that this Bond, Moore's Bond, will be a different beast to Connery's or Lazenby's. As Bond presses levers and generates steam, M asks dryly, 'Is that all that it does?' We also have a good pun as Bond uses his new watch to unzip his companion's dress. 'Sheer magnetism, darling,' he drawls. As with most things cinematic, the truth is more prosaic. 'It may seem like money for jam pressed close to the beautiful Madeline Smith and taking her clothes off into the bargain', wrote Moore in 1973. 'But on the twentieth take, your arm is aching, you've got cramp in your left foot and your right knee is going to sleep. When I arrived home ... the children asked me 'What did you do today, daddy?' I wasn't quite sure what to tell them. I could hardly say, 'I was in bed with a lady this morning and made twenty attempts to take her dress off this afternoon.'' [12]

Connections are made to Kananga, the dictator of the small Caribbean island of San Monique, and from there to New York City, where Kanaga is attending the United Nations. Bond is clocked as soon as he lands at JFK. As he is being driven along Franklin D. Roosevelt East River Drive (between NY-9A and Harlem River Drive) Bond's driver is killed with a poison dart shot from a wing mirror. Bond's car jumps the steps of 125 Broad Street. The driver's killer leads Bond to Mr. Big, a gangster who runs the chain of Fillet of Soul restaurants. Yaphet Kotto plays Kananga / Mr Big with quiet menace, charisma and zeal. Urbane and unflappable, Kotto and Geoffrey Holder are easily the best things about this film. These New York scenes were filmed at 35 E 69th St (the San Monique embassy), 144 E 74th St (Oh Cult Voodoo Shop) and 14-32 W 118th St (the back lot of Fillet of Soul). These busy streets, back alleys, basements and parking lots are in marked contrast to the plush hotel lobbies, ski slopes and seascapes of the Connery/Lazenby-era films. The city scenes are all shot in daylight – compare and contrast with the many neon-lit night-time scenes in the preceding film's Las Vegas.

Bond first meets Solitaire, a beautiful virgin tarot expert, and Tee Hee, whose arm has been replaced by an unconvincing steel claw.

> Mr Big: Is this the stupid mother that tailed you uptown?
> Bond: There seems to be some mistake. My name...
> Mr Big: Names is for tombstones, baby. Y'all take this honky out and waste him – now!

Bond dispatches Mr Big's henchmen by biffing them with a fire escape ladder. He travels to San Monique: the exterior scenes were filmed in Jamaica. At Bond's hotel, Sans Souci in Ocho Rios, the same location used for Miss Taro's bungalow in *Dr. No*, someone puts a snake in the bathroom, which Bond kills with the old aftershave and cigar trick. The inept double agent Rosie Carver, played by Gloria Hendry, a former *Playboy* bunny. 'It's just a hat, darling,' says Bond when she is spooked by a voodoo totem. 'Belonging to a small-headed man of limited means who lost a fight with a chicken.'

The line 'don't worry, darling, we'll soon lick you into shape' was ad-libbed by Roger Moore. As a side note, despite Moore's wife Luisa being told people wouldn't go to the film if it had an inter-racial sex scene, Moore said, to his credit, 'I personally don't give a damn, and it makes me all the more determined to play the scene'. [13]

A character called Quarrel Jr (Roy Stewart), presumably the son of the original Quarrel from *Dr. No*, takes Bond by boat to Solitaire's home. These scenes were filmed at River Bay Fishing Village, Montego Bay. We see the first of Moore's terrible casual outfits – a low cut white vest and light blue denim-on-denim suit. Rosie looks disconsolate when she is revealed as 'a lousy agent'. Bond reassures her with a pat on the bottom, 'Never mind, darling'. Different times. The character is swiftly killed off. Jane Seymour's Solitaire is little more than a cipher. What a pity the producers didn't cast a black actor as Solitaire: that would have been both bold and satisfying. Bond's doctored pack of tarot cards is decidedly creepy. 'The cards say we will be lovers', he says as a full pack of The Lover cards falls to the floor. But again, we have a classic double entendre from Moore, who unfailingly delivered the best of these with a straight face and a dry wit.

Bond: Lovers' lesson number one: We have no secrets. For example, I have a boat waiting. You can be on it. Lovers' lesson number two: Togetherness. Till death do us part, or thereabouts.
Solitaire: Is there time before we leave, for lesson number three?
Bond: Absolutely! No sense in going off half cocked.

Bond and Solitaire escape after a chase in an old London bus. 'If I never get another film role after *Live and Let Die*,' Moore wrote in his production diary, 'I can always get a job on the buses'. [14] 'I was the twit sitting in the back,' commented Jane Seymour. [15]

'Before we all left London for Jamaica,' wrote Moore years later, 'I was dispatched to Hammersmith Bus Garage in west London, where they had a huge skidpan, to drive a bus and then apply the brakes hard on the slippery surface – as I was to do in the film. I was terrified the bus would turn over, but such is their design, I discovered, that they rarely do.' [16]

The action moves to Louisiana for a pointless and tedious comedy flying lesson at the Lakefront Airport, New Orleans, doubling as the Bleeker Flying School. 'Let's just wing it, shall we, Mrs Bell?'

Bond is captured and the unnerving scene at the crocodile farm is the highlight of the film. For once, Bond's latest gadget, his magnetic watch, doesn't actually help him. The escape across the crocodiles' backs was done for real by Ross Kanaga, the owner of the crocodile farm where the scene was filmed, in Falmouth, Parish of Trelawney, Jamaica. The subsequent speed boat chase is very long – twelve minutes! – but includes two fabulous sight gags: one boat goes straight through a police car; another ends up in a swimming pool. These scenes, the first to be shot for *Live and Let Die*, were filmed in the bayous around Phoenix and Slidell, Louisiana, and at the Southern Yacht Club in New Orleans.

Boorish, loud, eternally irritating JW Pepper is a 'comic' version of Rod Steiger in *In the Heat of the Night*. This type of character became a staple of 1970s low-comedy film and TV – see also Rosco Coltrane in *Moonrunners* (1975) and *The Dukes of Hazzard* (1979-1985), Lyle 'Cottonmouth' Wallace in *Convoy* (1976) and Buford T. Justice in *Smokey and the Bandit* and two sequels (1977-1983). Pepper does get one half-decent line, though: 'I got me a regular Ben Hur.'

Part of the bayou chase was rehearsed a couple of days before shooting commenced. 'They say when death is imminent, your entire life flashes in front of your eyes,' Moore wrote in 1973. 'But the only thing flashing before my eyes was a large corrugated iron shed sticking up out of a Louisiana swamp which I was approaching at a fair old 60mph in an out-of-control boat. I was going to hit it – and there was simply nothing I could do about it. I ended up in a heap on the floor of the boat – my knee throbbing, my shoulder numb and my teeth feeling that they were being mangled one by one into little bits of gravel inside my mouth. Here I was, about to start playing James Bond for the first time, with no teeth.' [17]

Bond returns to San Monique to rescue Solitaire. He infiltrates Mr, Big's lair. Exterior scenes were filmed at Green Grotto Caves, Discovery Bay, Jamaica; interior sets were built at Pinewood. Like *You Only Live Twice*, it has a functioning monorail, seemingly a pre-requisite for Bond baddies' lairs. The payoff is limp, though. Bond uses a previously unseen rotary saw on his watch to cut the ropes that bind him and Solitaire, then despatches Mr. Big with a gas pellet that he has obtained using his watch's magnet, thus enabling him to tell Solitaire that her former employer had an inflated opinion of himself. The closing scene on the train is a reworking of the fight in *From Russia With Love*, if not quite so brutal. 'Just being disarming, darling.' Bond says.

With its seriously irritating comic redneck and a random martial arts movie pastiche, *Live and Let Die* moved Bond towards pure fantasy. *Live and Let Die* confirmed Roger Moore, for better or worse, as Connery's long-term successor. It was first shown on British TV on 20 January 1980 and drew in 23 million viewers.

> *Live and Let Die* is the ninth James Bond picture, and not exactly the best. It has all the necessary girls, gimmicks, subterranean control rooms, uniformed goons and magic wristwatches it can hold, but it doesn't have the wit and it doesn't have the style of the best Bond movies.
>
> This may have something to do with the substitution of Roger Moore for Sean Connery as 007. Moore has the superficial attributes for the job: The urbanity, the quizzically raised eyebrow, the calm under fire and in bed. But

Connery was always able to invest the role with a certain humour, a sense of its ridiculousness. Moore has been supplied with a lot of double entendres and double takes, but he doesn't seem to get the joke.

There are a few elements every Bond movie absolutely must have, and *Live and Let Die* has them. It opens, of course, with a meeting with M and the faithful Miss Moneypenny. It has Bond arriving at the Caribbean hideout by man-bearing kite. It has a spectacular chase (this one involves speedboats, but isn't as much fun as the great ski chase two Bonds ago). It has a spectacularly destroyed villain (he swallows a capsule of compressed air and explodes). It has the girls. And it has Bond exhibiting his mastery of the better things in life by asking room service for a bottle of Bollinger – not cold, but 'slightly chilled,' please.

And it does, to give it credit, have the one basic Bond scene that always seems copied from the previous Bond movie: The penetration of the underground citadel. This scene always begins with Bond pressing a hidden lever or discovering the secret door. Then there's a shot of a vast underground cavern, which is filled with uniformed functionaries who hurry about on mysterious scientific errands.

Bond slips unobserved from one hiding place to another; is discovered; eludes his pursuers; watches as six hired goons hurry past; and then goes through another door and unexpectedly finds the villain waiting there for him. The dialog here is always the same, something like 'Come in, Mr. Bond, we've been expecting you . . .' And then ... but do you get the same notion I do, that after nine of these we've just about had enough?

Roger Ebert, July 1973

The Man With the Golden Gun

Albert R Broccoli and Harry Salzman present Roger Moore as James Bond – OO7 in Ian Fleming's *The Man With the Golden Gun*

'He never misses his target, and now his target is OO7!'

Release Date: 19 December 1974. Running time: 125 minutes. Distributed by United Artists. Producers: Harry Salzman (9 of 9), Albert R Broccoli (9 of 17). James Bond: Roger Moore (2 of 7), M: Bernard Lee (9 of 11), Q: Desmond Llewelyn (7 of 17), Moneypenny: Lois Maxwell (9 of 14).

And Christopher Lee (Scaramanga) with Britt Ekland (Mary Goodnight), Maud Adams (Andrea Anders), Hervé Villechaize (Nick Nack), Richard Loo (Hai Fat), Soon-Tek Oh (Lieutenant Hip), Clifton James (Sheriff J.W. Pepper).

Director: Guy Hamilton (4 of 4). Screenplay: Richard Maibaum (7 of 13), Tom Mankiewicz (3 of 3). Production design: Peter Murton. Main titles: Maurice Binder (7 of 14). Music: John Barry (7 of 11). Theme song performed by Lulu. Cinematography: Ted Moore (7 of 7), Oswald Harris. Edited by John Shirley (2 of 2), Raymond Poulton (2 of 2).

Plot

James Bond searches for a stolen invention that can turn the sun's heat into a destructive weapon. He crosses paths with Francisco Scaramanga, a hit man with a seven-figure fee. Bond joins forces with Mary Goodnight and they track Scaramanga to a tropical isle hideout where the killer-for-hire lures Bond into a deadly maze for a final duel

Cast

Christopher Lee. Scaramanga. One of the best Bond actors and classiest Bond villains, without question. Lee, a remarkable man, was active in films for nearly seventy years, from 1947 to 2015. He is perhaps best remembered for his work with Hammer from 1957 to 1976 but made over two hundred film appearances, perhaps most notably in *The Wicker Man* (1973) and the *Lord of the Rings* series (2001-2003). Lee is utterly compelling in *Golden Gun*.

> His silent, post-kill gun stroking of Andrea is deliciously creepy; the gleam as he describes his first kill more eloquent than any mad cackle or subordinate execution. Scaramanga clearly derives sexual satisfaction from the act of killing – but then sex and death are the twin hearts of Bond, both franchise and character.
>
> Max Williams, *Revisiting The Man With the Golden Gun*, 2016

Lee, a screen legend in anyone's book, had worked with Roger Moore as early as 1949 in a film called *Trottie True*. They also appeared together in an episode of *Ivanhoe* in the 1950s. Lee died aged 93 in June 2015. The producers initially approached two-time Oscar nominee Jack Palance (*Sudden Fear*, 1952 and *Shane*, 1953) but this intriguing idea didn't take hold.

The radiant, Swedish Maud Adams achieved initially fame as a model. *The Man With the Golden Gun* was her first major role. Her screen time is far too short. Hervé Villechaize was born in France and was an accomplished artist. Like Maud Adams, this was his breakthrough role. He was working at that time as a rat catcher in Los Angeles. Roger Moore used to tell a wicked story about Maud Adams and Hervé Villechaize. 'He trotted up to Maud Adams in the lobby of the Peninsula Hotel in Hong Kong one morning, tugged on her knee-length skirt and looked up to say, 'Maud tonight I am going to creep into your room, climb under the duvet and make mad passionate love to you.' Unfazed, Maud replied, 'And if I found out you have, I'll be very cross.'' [18]

Britt Ekland plays the hapless and helpless Mary Goodnight who spends most of the film in a bikini. 'To do a Bond film had been a dream for me,' Ekland said later.' It was the most glamorous and exciting time I have ever had on a movie. [But] it does not make any difference whether you are a good actress.' [19]

Clifton James reprises the awful JW Pepper.

Theme Song

Lulu's powerful theme, the first of five consecutive themes by solo female singers, is Bond-by-numbers with barely concealed double entendres.

Production

The Man With the Golden Gun was filmed between November 1973 and August 1974 at Pinewood Studios, Buckinghamshire and on location in the UK, Hong Kong, Thailand and Macau.

Observations

The Man With the Golden Gun is a pretty bad film, all told, with unlikely set-piece following unlikely set-piece. More than any previous Bond film, the script is very silly indeed: an unhappy and awkward trade-off between Tom Mankiewicz's assassin vs assassin show-down and Richard Maibaum's then-topical energy crisis story. The pre-credits scene is one of the best, however. Christopher Lee manages to look menacing in a blue tracksuit. 'In 1973 the pool of really offensive heavies must have been low,' Lee wrote in his splendid memoirs. 'It was the director Guy Hamilton who gave me the invitation to play Scaramanga. Naturally, I said I'd be delighted. It was fun, and for me, the winds blew kindly than for any other Bond heavy bar Goldfinger. They replaced the lurid thug [in the book] with a more diverse character, some ambivalence about his own compulsive sexuality, an edge of humour and a sense that he is indulging himself in a great game.' [20]

Maud Adams is quite stunning if seemingly bored and unfulfilled – there's a definite nod to impotency when Nick Nack pops the champagne cork. We meet a stock American gangster, Rodney, played by Marc Lawrence, an actor with a seventy-year career in films. Lawrence had appeared in an unnamed role in *Diamonds Are Forever*, when Plenty O'Toole is thrown out of Bond's room into the hotel swimming pool. It's nice to think there's some continuity to the Connery era here. As the tense scene plays out, kudos as usual to the score and cinematography, we see that this is all a game for Scaramanga as he teases Rodney with a series of tasks. Look closely and you can see the Al Capone mannequin blink as he shoots his machine gun. You can see Moore as the Bond mannequin wobble as Scaramanga declares 'you'll be the death of me yet, Nick Nack'. Wait. Scaramanga has a Bond mannequin? Isn't Bond a secret agent? Who made the model of Bond and how is it so accurate? Let's suspend disbelief and go with it.

The plot hinges on someone wanting Bond dead. This gives us some of the best Bond / M dialogue.

> Bond: I mean sir, who would pay a million dollars to have me killed?
> M: Jealous husbands. Outraged chefs. Humiliated tailors. The list is endless.

Bond travels to Beirut to track down the bullet that killed OO2.

> Moore acquits himself well in a tightly edited fight scene. Ultimately, he swallows the bullet, enabling us to cut to the Q lab for the cringe-worthy line 'you have no idea what it went through to get here'. The trail leads to Macau, a former Portuguese enclave across the Zhujiang River estuary, about thirty miles west of Hong Kong.
>
> The soft-spoken gunsmith Lazar is a wonderfully creepy figure: one of those memorable minor roles Bond does so well.
>
> **Max Williams, *Revisiting The Man With the Golden Gun*, 2016**

'My favourite line is in *The Man With the Golden Gun*,' Roger Moore told *GQ* in 2012. 'I point the rifle at the gun maker's crotch and say, 'Speak now or forever hold your piece.' I was watching it on American television recently and the line was cut out!'

The obligatory casino scene, filmed at the Macau Palace, introduces the quite gorgeous Maud Adams as the doomed Andrea Anders. He follows her to Hong Kong with establishing shots of the ferry terminal and the RMS Queen Elizabeth. As in the early part of *Goldfinger*, Bond blags his way into a hotel room by charming a maid. A line is crossed as he bullies and threatens Andrea, twisting her arm and slapping her face. Despite the much-needed edge that this scene gives the film, it sits uneasily with Moore's portrayal of Bond. This Bond was not the single-minded killer of early Connery or Craig. 'Guy wanted to toughen up my Bond a little,' Moore wrote in 2008. 'I think it's most evident in the scenes I had with Maud Adams, where I twisted her arm and threatened – rather coldly – to break it unless she told me what I wanted to know. That sort of characterisation didn't sit easily with me. I suggested my Bond would have charmed the information out of her by bedding her first. My Bond was a lover and a giggler. However, Guy was keen to make my Bond a little more ruthless, as Fleming's original had been. I went along with him – his instincts were always very good.' [21]

A visit to the Bottoms Up Club, filmed in Tsim Sha Tsui shopping district of Kowloon City, Thailand, invites us to 'tour the world of Suzie Wong'. Bond witnesses a murder and is picked up by the police, or so it seems, until he is taken to M's office within the heavily-listing, semi-sunken Queen Elizabeth. That's not Roger Moore embarking, by the way. Here we are introduced to poor Mary Goodnight.

> Britt Ekland is charming in the role, but she fights a losing battle with the script. Indignity upon indignity is poured upon Goodnight's pretty blonde head. She's infatuated with Bond, while he treats her like a woodlouse in a burger.
>
> **Max Williams, *Revisiting The Man With the Golden Gun*, 2016**

And so to Bangkok to track down a wealthy Siamese entrepreneur suspected of arranging the murder in Macau: Hai Fat. Apparently, Lo Fat was removed from the script at the last minute. Hai Fat's mansion sees skinny-dipping Chew Me and, on a second visit with Bond sporting a fake third nipple, Nick Nack dressed as a Mexican wrestler wielding a pitchfork. Bond fights two sumo wrestlers, one of whom is defeated by wedgie. A tiresome kung fu sequence follows ('take Mr Bond to school'), also filmed in Bangkok. Ludicrously, two schoolgirls then beat up an entire kung fu class. If the last twenty minutes of nonsense hasn't made you switch off, then here comes Bond in a boat. Again. This boat chase, filmed at Damnoen Saduak floating market, leads to Bond finally meeting Scaramanga, and the dead Andrea, at Rajadamern Stadium in Bangkok.

Goodnight traps herself in the boot of Scaramanga's car, so Bond gives chase in a stolen AMC Hornet. Oh. God forbid. Here's JW Pepper.

> Pepper: I know you! You're that secret agent! That English secret agent! From England!

An amazing corkscrew jump over a broken bridge is elaborate and daring. It was conceived by stunt driver Jay Milligan, developed using computer simulation and performed in public (the 'Astro Spiral Jump') during a live event called the American Thrill Show, sponsored by the American Motors Corporation who provided most of the cars for *The Man With the Golden Gun*. For the film, the stunt was performed in a single take by uncredited British stuntman 'Bumps' Williard. It's almost ruined by the slide-whistle sound effect. And then Scaramanga's car converts to a model aeroplane flying over the fields of Bovington, Dorset.

We move to the third act at Scaramanga's island hideout, Koh Tapu in Thailand, for the long-awaited meeting of the protagonist and antagonist. As with the meeting between *Dr. No*, Bond and Honey Rider, Scaramanga, Bond and Mary Goodnight take lunch together. Roger Moore gets to exercise his acting skills with a genuinely great scene, as Bond and Scaramanga muse about the nature of their jobs, and the loneliness of their profession. Scaramanga argues that he and Bond are two sides of the same coin, but that Bond is not well paid for it. OO7 says he only kills on the orders of his government. Nice stuff. We also get a neat dig on Scaramanga's choice of wine. 'Slightly reminiscent of a 34 Mouton', Bond drawls. Possibly apropos of this slur, Scaramanga proposes a duel.

> Scaramanga: Like every great artist I want to create an indisputable masterpiece once in my lifetime. The death of OO7, mano-a-mano, face-to-face, will be mine.
> Bond: There's a useful four-letter word and you're full of it.
> Scaramanga: The English don't consider it sporting to kill in cold blood, do they?
> Bond: Don't count on it.

In a scene that was filmed but not included in the final cut, Bond fashions a Molotov cocktail, forcing Scaramanga to use his last bullet to shoot it from the air. He has a spare in his belt buckle.

The death of Scaramanga is tense but fun. Bond's waxwork turns out to be Bond himself and before Scaramanga realises, Bond turns and shoots him.

Nine years and six films after *Goldfinger*, the formula finally starts to look stale. Based only tangentially on Fleming's weakest novel, *The Man With the Golden Gun* is the first really poor Bond film. It is saved, in part, by some great acting from Roger Moore and Christopher Lee, the presence of Maud Adams and the usual craft of its technicians. But its low points – the script, the effects, Britt Ekland, the very unwelcome return of Sheriff JW Pepper – bring this ninth official Bond film to the level of desperate hackwork. Art, this ain't.

And, as a final nail, *The Man With the Golden Gun* includes what must the most sexist scene in the entire series. Bond is seduced by Andrea. 'Name your price,' she says. 'Anything, I'll pay it. You can have me too if you like. I'm not unattractive.' Meanwhile, Mary Goodnight is unceremoniously pushed into a wardrobe. Some time later, Bond lets her out and drawls, 'Forgive me darling. Your time will come, I promise.' That was beyond the pale, even in 1974.

The throbbing information that 'the energy crisis is still with us' isn't what you need or want to learn from a James Bond picture. But that poverty of invention and excitement characterizes Guy Hamilton's *The Man With the Golden Gun,* which opened yesterday at neighbourhood theatres. The movie, which also explains that 'coal and oil will soon be depleted', sets Bond in pursuit of a missing device that converts solar energy into electricity Bored already? That was predictable. Even Kingsley Amis, a great admirer of the late Ian Fleming, spoke of 'the over-all inferiority' of the writer's last novel, and this movie is doggishly faithful to its model. There's a male villain with three nipples, but you can't milk much plot out of that – or them. Amid the general lack of gumption, Roger Moore's large rigid figure appears to be wheeled about on tiny casters I always have a soft spot for statues that turn out to be alive, and there are a couple in this film. But an actor who appears to have been cast in clay is another matter, and Mr. Moore functions like a vast garden ornament. Pedantic, sluggish on the uptake, incapable of even swaggering, he's also clumsy at innuendo. (While Sean Connery wasn't the wit of the century, he did manage to be impudent, and there were those pleasing moments of self-parody.) But whether Mr. Moore is twisting a woman's arm to discover a fact that he already knows, or nuzzling an abdomen without enthusiasm, he merely makes you miss his predecessor. The script trundles out such lines as 'Your steam bath is ready' or 'A mistress cannot serve two masters' between the dullest car chase of the decade and a very routine explosion. The only energetic moments are provided by Herve Villechaize, as a midget gifted with mocking authority, and Christopher Lee as the golden gunman – both have a sinister vitality that cuts through the narrative dough. The movie also includes

some beautiful glimpses of Thailand. But if you enjoyed the early Bond films as much as I did, you'd better skip this one.
Nora Sayre, *New York Times*, 19 December 1974

The Spy Who Loved Me

Albert R Broccoli presents Roger Moore as Ian Fleming's James Bond 007 in *The Spy Who Loved Me*
'It's the biggest. It's the best. It's Bond. And beyond.'
Release date: 7 July 1977. Running time: 125 minutes. Distributed by United Artists.
Producer: Albert R Broccoli (10 of 17).
James Bond: Roger Moore (3 of 7), M: Bernard Lee (10 of 11), Q: Desmond Llewelyn (8 of 17), Moneypenny: Lois Maxwell (10 of 14) with Walter Gotell (General Gogol) (1 of 6), Geoffrey Keen (Frederick Gray) (1 of 6), Richard Kiel (Jaws) (1 of 2).
And Curd Jürgens (Stromberg) with Barbara Bach (Anya Amasova/Agent Triple X), Caroline Munro (Naomi), Robert Brown (Vice-Admiral Hargreaves), George Baker (Captain Benson), Michael Billington (Sergei Barsov).
Director: Lewis Gilbert (2 of 3). Screenplay: Richard Maibaum (8 of 13), Christopher Wood (1 of 2). Production design: Ken Adam (6 of 7). Main titles: Maurice Binder (8 of 14). Music: Marvin Hamlisch. Theme song performed by Carly Simon. Cinematography: Claude Renoir. Edited by John Glen (2 of 3).

Plot

When British and Soviet nuclear submarines go missing, James Bond unites with Russian agent Anya Amasova to track down and defeat megalomaniac shipping magnate Karl Stromberg, who is threatening to destroy New York City with nuclear weapons.

Cast

With this, his third Bond film, Roger Moore hits his stride. We know by now that this Bond is not the ruthless assassin of Fleming's books, nor even the poised, confident, tough Bond of Sean Connery.

Barbara Bach is cast as Anya Amasova, partially through the recommendation of her then-boyfriend, an executive at United Artists. Initially coming to prominence as a model in the 1960s, *The Spy Who Loved Me* was her first major film role. '[Bond is] a chauvinist pig who uses girls to shield him against bullets,' she told *People* in 1983. John Simon in *The New York Times* described her as 'the most beautiful woman to ever enter the Bondian universe', and 5-times Bond director John Glen said, 'she was one of the best leading ladies in the whole series'. [22]

Bernard Lee, Lois Maxwell and Desmond Llewelyn are present and correct. We also have three actors who debut recurring roles in *The Spy Who Loved Me*. Water Gotell plays General Alexis Gogol as a kind of friendly KGB chief in the first of six appearances. [23] Gotell had a major role as a different character in *From Russia With Love*. Experienced British character actor Geoffrey Keen (in dozens of films since 1943) plays Frederick Gray, also his first of six Bond films. Robert Brown portrays Vice-Admiral Hargreaves. Brown, Roger Moore's *Ivanhoe* co-star, would play M in the four films from *Octopussy* to *Licence To Kill*. Although never explicitly stated, we can assume that Hargreaves and M are the same character, with a new M replacing Bernard Lee's.

Seven-feet tall Richard Kiel as Jaws was spotted by the James Bond film producers in *Barbary Coast*, an American TV series starting William Shatner, which ran for thirteen episodes in 1975-1976. Austrian actress and model Eva Reuber-Staier – Miss World 1969 – plays Gogol's assistant Miss Rubelvitch. The character's name is a wry wordplay on 'Moneypenny'. Reuber-Staier would reprise the role in *For Your Eyes Only* and *Octopussy*.

And then we have Curd Jürgens as Stromberg – Blofeld with a new name – who exudes a quiet menace. Jürgens, a German-Austrian stage and film actor, active since 1935, appeared in dozens of films, including *The Longest Day* (1962, with Sean Connery, Gert Fröbe and Walter Gotell) and later the TV series *Smiley's People* (1982).

The British and American submarine captains are played by character actors Bryan Marshall and Shane Rimmer. Marshall was familiar to British TV viewers in dramas such as *The Forsyte Saga*, *Dixon of Dock Green*, *Z-Cars*, *The Saint* (with Roger Moore) and *The Onedin Line*. British domiciled Canadian Shane Rimmer, the voice of Scott Tracy in *Thunderbirds* (1965-1966), gets a plum role in his fourth Bond film after uncredited appearances in *You Only Live Twice* (as a radio control technician seen at the end of the film declaring that SPECTRE's rocket has exploded), *Live and Let Die* and *Diamonds Are Forever*. Rimmer can also be seen in *Star Wars* (1977), *Ghandi* (1982), *Out of Africa* (1985), *Batman Begins* (2005) and many other films and TV shows. George Baker, Sir Hilary Bray in *On Her Majesty's Secret Service*, is cast as Captain Benson, one of the naval officers in the briefing at the Royal Navy's Faslane Naval Base in Scotland.

Theme Song

Seemingly out of nowhere, 'Nobody Does It Better' is a wistful piano-based ballad beautifully performed by Carly Simon and classily produced by Richard Perry. It was rightfully a major hit all over the world.

Production

The Spy Who Loved Me was filmed between August and December 1976 at Pinewood Studios, Buckinghamshire and on location in Sardinia, Egypt, Russia, Scotland, Bahamas and Canada.

Observations

The Man With the Golden Gun was the last James Bond film to be co-produced by Harry Saltzman, who sold his shares in Eon to United Artists in December

1975. In an interview with the Daily Mail in 1973, Harry admitted that with only five more Fleming stories left he had every intention of getting out when the going was good. In March 1974, the Los Angeles Times reported that Saltzman was attempting to sell his stake in Danjaq to Paramount and the following year, after the disappointing box office performance of *The Man With the Golden Gun*, United Artists bought Saltzman's interest in the James Bond films.

Cubby Broccoli and Eon now had everything to prove.

'Cubby Broccoli was nothing if not a shrewd gambler,' write Martin Sterling and Gary Morecambe, 'and he gambled everything on his belief that the way to challenge the relative failure of *The Man With the Golden Gun* was not to pull in his horns, to think smaller, but to think big, to be bold. He was determined to make [the next Bond film] the most lavish and outrageous yet.' [24]

United Artists showed their support, and put faith in their investment, by doubling Broccoli's production budget to $13.5million. The resulting film, *The Spy Who Loved Me* is, by some margin, Roger Moore's best entry in the Bond canon.

'1977 was the year of the silver jubilee and punk, Britain fractured and filled with self-hate,' writes Andrew Pulver, 'This smirking Bond was fully at ease with its own lameness: he couldn't be serious because no one would take him seriously. In this, Moore was the perfect Bond at the perfect time; and almost entirely antithetical to the spirit of Fleming's original. Instead, *The Spy Who Loved Me* exemplifies Britain's conflicted internal battles: a nagging patriotism alongside a smuttiness that might have been lifted from the sex comedies that, other than Bond itself, were pretty much keeping British cinema afloat.' [25]

It was the third James Bond film to take almost nothing from the books. Both *You Only Live Twice* took only the main characters and locations, and *The Man With the Golden Gun* was a very loose adaptation of Fleming's last and weakest novel. The original novel of *The Spy Who Loved Me* was an anomaly in the canon. James Bond does not appear until three-quarters into the book, so the producers needed to create a completely new story. Screenwriter Christopher Wood, author of the *Confessions* series of erotic comic novels and their film adaptations, wrote a first draft, Anthony Barwick (*Captain Scarlet*, *Terrahawks*) re-modelled it, and several other writers contributed: Sterling Silliphant (*In the Heat of the Night*, *The Towering Inferno*, *The Poseidon Adventure*), John Landis (yet to achieve fame with *The Blues Brothers*), Anthony Burgess (*A Clockwork Orange*, *Jesus of Nazareth*) and long-time Bond screenwriter Richard Maibaum. In the end, Cubby Broccoli's wife Dana retooled a total of twelve scripts into a workable shooting script. The final credit was given to Wood and Maibaum. It's full of activity moving from Austria to Canada, Scotland, Egypt, Russia, the Bahamas, Italy, Spain, Sardinia and Switzerland.

Apart from Bond, only two characters from the novel appear in the film. 'Sluggsy' Morant and Sol 'Horror' Horowitz in the book become, Sandor and Jaws in the film. [26] The cinematographer, Claude Renoir, was the grandson of painter Pierre-August Renoir. Director Lewis Gilbert returned for his second Bond film.

The producer and director laid out their stall with a simultaneously audacious and hugely entertaining pre-titles sequence: 'the defining moment of all the films' suggests Matthew Parker.

> Roger Moore, in an outrageous yellow 'onesie', is being chased on skis by a host of villains. Bond is hopelessly outnumbered. The music rises in pitch then abruptly cuts off as Bond skis over a cliff and hangs in the sky, tumbling downwards in slow motion. Seconds pass. Then, suddenly, a parachute opens. A Union Jack parachute. And the theme music roars back in celebration. [27]

The scene was filmed by John Glen, who returned to the series as 2nd unit director and editor after a seven-year absence. In the interim, he had worked with Roger Moore on *Gold* (1974) and *Shout at the Devil* (1976), both directed by long-time Bond associate Peter Hunt, and on *Seven Nights in Japan* (1976) with Lewis Gilbert.

'Michael [G Wilson] and I got the idea for this sequence from a TV ad,' writes Cubby Broccoli. 'In the commercial, this genius of a ski-jumper [Rick Sylvester] is supposedly doing this spectacular leap off the ridge of the three-thousand-foot Asgard Peak in the Auquittug National Park, Baffin Island, Canada. In reality, he took his leap off the El Capitan peak in the Yosemite Valley, California; but it didn't matter to me where he did it. It was outrageous, took staggering courage and would obviously be a sensational curtain-raiser to the film.'

'I remember so vividly attending the premiere in London's Odeon Leicester Square,' wrote Roger Moore. 'And the deadly hush that descended over the audience as Bond skied off the edge of the cliff. You could hear the proverbial pin drop. Then, as the Union Flag parachute opened and the Bond theme roared to a crescendo, the audience stood to offer an ovation.' [28]

Spielberg's *Jaws* (1975) is recognised as the first modern blockbuster, and it's notable that in response, *The Spy Who Loved Me* was the biggest Bond film so far. For sheer spectacle, *The Spy Who Loved Me* opens with that difficult and remarkable ski jump stunt. We have the famous Lotus Esprit transforming into a submarine. And the interior of the supertanker, designed by Ken Adam, is quite awe-inspiring – it almost steals the show from Bond himself. The set was constructed on a purpose-built stage at Pinewood, the 007 Stage, opened by former Prime Minister Harold Wilson in December 1976.

The story is thin but busy and buzzes with tension. It's little more than a rewrite of *You Only Live Twice*: in both a criminal mastermind steals high-grade weaponry from rival super-powers (nuclear submarines, in this case) and hides then in a technically advanced, custom-built lair with a monorail (of course) and a control room with steel shutters. The baddie, the intriguing Karl Stromberg, is a rich industrialist and megalomaniac. In another throwback to *You Only Live Twice* he kills his secretary by feeding her to his shark. Soon, he blows up a helicopter with the two scientists who have designed an advanced submarine tracking system – the source of the disappearance of Russian and American submarines.

The trail starts in Egypt as Bond, a very assured Roger Moore, tracks down a microfilm that contains details of the tracking system. Both the KGB and a huge henchman also want the microfilm. There is an intimidating and exciting son-et-lumiere scene where these three characters dodge and weave to the backdrop of the pyramids. The almost expressionless but very attractive Barbara Bach as Russian agent Anya Amasova is a great match for Roger Moore – both are as wooden as deck chairs.

> OO7 will have to spend a good deal of the time rescuing the one person in the movie who most wants to get rid of him (though hardly the only), a terrific subtext to the main plot and about as complex a human relationship as we ever got in the dozen years of the Moore Bonds. [29]

Their verbal sparring – Bond in a tuxedo, Anya in the lowest of low-cut dresses – is a delight, however, despite the stilted acting. Bond's discomfort when cutting off Anya's reference to his wife is neatly done. The scene where nightclub owner Max Kalba is killed is a reworking of Fiona Volpe's death in *Thunderball* – but no less tense for that. Bond and Anya follow Kalba's killer – Jaws – and jump into his van. Anya falls asleep on Bond's shoulder and Roger Moore brings out his best 'smug' expression. For no logical reason, Jaws takes them to the temples at Karnak. The subsequent fight, in which Jaws is buried in masonry after almost pulling apart his van, is beautifully filmed and tightly directed. According to Roger Moore, Bond's final line 'Egyptian builders' was dubbed later. Egyptian censors had already approved the script and wouldn't allow variations. Moore mouthed the line on set and added the line afterwards.

Roger Moore: 'The sound man said, 'I wasn't able to hear his line with all the bloody scaffolding falling down; Lewis, you're going to have to do it again.' Lewis just said, 'Shut up.' And my friends in Egypt said 'Egyptian builders' got the biggest laugh of the movie.' [30]

Jaws is buried under masonry but survives: the first of a series of escalating sight gags. We'll quickly pass over the decidedly sexist scene where Bond mutters some nonsense about women drivers. A puff from a gadget cigarette renders him unconscious.

A briefing scene with a twist is held inside an Egyptian temple. M, Bond and Moneypenny are joined by Anya and her boss, Alexis Gogol. After Bond finds a clue to Stromberg's base in Sardinia, the agencies agree to work together. Bond and Anya travel from Egypt to Sardinia by train, just an excuse to re-work the Bond vs. baddy fights from in *From Russia With Love* and *Live and Let Die*. Jaws makes us jump as he emerges from a wardrobe and literally chews the scenery.

The check-in clerk at Bond's hotel is played by Valerie Leon. Leon appeared in many of the *Carry On* films, *The Italian Job* and the seventies TV ad for Hai Karate after shave.

Bond meets Q in Sardinia, who hands over the silliest gadget yet – a Lotus Esprit S1 which converts into a submarine. Bond poses as a marine biologist, Robert Sterling (Anya is Mrs Bond, of course, not a marine biologist in her own right). They meet Stromberg, who 'prefers not to shake hands'. Bond also, handily, sees a model of the *Liparus* super-tanker which has 'unusually shaped bows'. I suppose Bond is an ex-sailor and would know these things. Stromberg orders Bond to be killed and we have a long and excellent car chase as a motorcycle with rocket-launching sidecar, a high-powered car with gun-toting Jaws and an armed helicopter take on Bond in quick succession.

Bond asks, 'Ever get the feeling someone doesn't like you?'

The underwater scenes with the Lotus submarine are hilarious. A full-size submarine was constructed from an actual Esprit body shell – operated by scuba divers – along with smaller several models for the stages of conversion. In a remarkable side-story, the original submarine was put into storage for ten years after filming was completed and remained unclaimed when the lease expired. A buyer bought the contents at auction, unseen, for $100, restored the car's exterior and sold it to Elon Musk for $550,000. You can't make this up.

And, of course, we have one of the cheesiest moments of all, as the car emerges from the sea onto the beach and Bond opens the window and drops a fish with a classic raise of the eyebrow. You cannot fail to smile.

The underwater battles revisit *Thunderball*. Bond and Anya board an American submarine, which is then swallowed by Stromberg's ship. Stromberg (calling Moore's character 'Mr Bundt') tells Bond that he dreams of establishing an Atlantean paradise by triggering a global nuclear war. In a big shoot-em-up battle Bond blows everything up using a detonator from a nuclear missile. He was unable to deactivate Goldfinger's bomb twelve years before …

Bond then resets the coordinates of two nuclear submarines by *reading a manual*!

In a thrilling final scene, Bond rescues Anya – Stromberg has kidnapped her for unexplained nefarious purposes but is able to provide her with a tight-fitting dress. Bond shoots Stromberg four times, possibly irritated that Stromberg is eating oysters with Tabasco sauce – the same dastardly menu choice of Scaramanga in *The Man With the Golden Gun*.

Bond flees with Anya in an underwater version of the droid's escape pod spaceship in *Star Wars*. All hopes of a new feminism in Bond are dashed when Anya fails to carry out her threat to exact revenge on Bond but takes him to bed instead.

The Spy Who Loved Me, which premiered on 7/7/77, is light-hearted, frothy and funny. But, most importantly, it was cleverly made. By now, the writers and director are playing to Roger Moore's unique Bond persona. There are also glimpses of the path not taken. In a scene where the henchman Sandor clutches Bond's tie to keep from falling the edge of a roof, Bond presses him for information then knocks his hand away, sending the baddie to his death. This is worthy of Daniel Craig's Bond and indeed, this same moment will reappear in *Quantum of Solace*. But then again, only Roger Moore could get away with putting Bond in a ghutra, sitting on a camel and uttering a line like: 'When one is in Egypt, one must delve deeply into its treasures.'

Let's leave the final word to Andrew Pulver:

> In the end, *The Spy Who Loved Me's* real strength is that it's pure cheese – full fat, 100% proof – and knows it, but never makes the mistake of trying to outsmart itself. Unlike later editions, it doesn't try too hard to undermine proceedings. Current Bonds are desperately trying to play catch-up with the incarnation of the 100bpm action thriller, but *Spy* led the way in its own time, at its own pace. [31]

The Spy Who Loved Me is among the most outlandish James Bond movies, not exactly a staple of cinema realism to begin with. None of its characters can be described as three-dimensional, nor their relationships particularly meaningful. It also happens to be a rather dated Bond entry, with the 1970s hairdos, fads and the Marvin Hamlisch soundtrack that's more than a bit on the side of disco. The film stars Roger Moore who's hardly anyone's idea of a ruthless assassin and it was directed by Lewis Gilbert whose two other 007 entries are among the series' bottom-dwellers (*You Only Live Twice* and *Moonraker*) and yet, the end result is unquestionably one of the Bond series' brightest spots, and includes a good deal of its finest moments.

What *The Spy Who Loved Me* lacks when it comes to establishing the atmosphere of danger present in some the best Bond movies it makes up in spades in the creation of one apparently-impossible situation for the protagonist after the other, the kind that other entries would have been lucky to include a single example. The Moore Bonds often went overboard when aiming to thrill their audience. *The Spy Who Loved Me* took as many chances as any Bond film in memory and still has one of the series' highest batting averages, so to speak. It includes one of the all-time great car chases, starting on dry ground and ending with 007's Lotus Esprit submerged in the water, the only other Bond vehicle that gives the Aston Martin DB5 a run for its money. This scene perfectly illustrates its knack for progressively escalating the fun in the action scenes and pushing them further just when one would expect them to be winding down, facing Bond against a motorcycle with a rocket passenger annex a car with a shooting giant and a helicopter piloted by the very bombshell who just managed to infuriate Amasova by flirting blatantly with her undercover 'husband' a few minutes before.

The Moore Bonds always focused more on their plot's proceedings than on any kind of character development. They were filled with juvenile humour, which was fine when the jokes actually worked as they do in here when 007 smilingly nods to the gorgeous helicopter pilot while she's trying to blow him away or when he's seen activating his car's blinkers, underwater! During his tenure as Bond, Moore sometimes went into auto-pilot and let his performance be dictated solely by the movement of his eyebrows, but, curiously enough, when he was pressed to show a rougher side here (as when he rewards a henchman's confession by releasing him from the roof of a building), he came out remarkably well.

The Spy Who Loved Me [gives] Moore one of the top five James Bond movies and a good deal of validation for his often-maligned era of the series.
Gerardo Valero, *rogerebert.com,* 22 December 2014

Moonraker

Albert R Broccoli presents Roger Moore as James Bond OO7 in Ian Fleming's *Moonraker*
'Where all the other Bonds end… this one begins!'
Release date: 26 June 1979. Running time: 126 minutes. Distributed by United Artists. Producer: Albert R Broccoli (11 of 17).
James Bond: Roger Moore (4 of 7), M: Bernard Lee (11 of 11), Q: Desmond Llewelyn (9 of 17), Moneypenny: Lois Maxwell (11 of 14) with Geoffrey Keen (Frederick Gray) (2 of 6), Walter Gotell (General Gogol) (2 of 6), Richard Kiel (Jaws) (2 of 2).
And Michael Lonsdale (Hugo Drax) with Lois Chiles (Holly Goodhead), Corinne Cléry (Corinne Dufour).
Director: Lewis Gilbert (3 of 3). Screenplay: Christopher Wood (2 of 2). Production design: Ken Adam (7 of 7). Main titles: Maurice Binder (9 of 14). Music: John Barry (8 of 11). Theme song performed by Shirley Bassey. Cinematography: Jean Tournier. Edited by John Glen (3 of 3).

Plot

James Bond investigates the hijacking of an American space shuttle. As the trail leads to Venice and Rio De Janeiro, he confronts Hugo Drax, a power-mad industrialist who has a scheme to destroy all human life on earth. Bond and scientist Goodhead escape and pose as pilots on Moonraker 6 to destroy nerve gas capsules heading to Earth.

Cast

Roger Moore's contract for three films was now concluded. For the next several years, Moore was content to engage in brinksmanship with Broccoli, film by film. The name of Michael Billington once again enters the picture. Despite being killed off as a Russian agent in *The Spy Who Loved Me*, Billington would screen test for *Moonraker*, *For Your Eyes Only* and *Octopussy*. But he was never more than a pawn between Moore and Broccoli's contract re-sign negotiations.

Richard Kiel, Bernard Lee, Lois Maxwell, Desmond Llewelyn and Walter Gotell reprise their roles from *The Spy Who Loved Me*. Many of the other main

characters are played by French actors. Drax is memorably portrayed by bi-lingual Anglo-French actor Michael Lonsdale in his second major British film. You might recognise him as Deputy Commissioner Claude Lebel in 1973's *Day of the Jackal*. Originally, James Mason – the UK's top box office attraction in the 1940s – was cast as Drax but was replaced when the film's co-backers wanted a French actor. Corinne Cléry plays Corinne Dufour. Cléry had turned heads in *The Story of O* (1975) and appeared with Richard Kiel and Barbara Bach in Italian *Star Wars* rip off *The Humanoid*, released a few months before *Moonraker*.

Female lead Holly Goodhead is played with a determined lack of expression by Texas-born former fashion model Lois Chiles. Chiles described her character as 'a one-dimensional dingbat. There is an equal kind of thing between Bond and myself. I'm not a sex kitten.' Even so, Holly's name raised eyebrows. 'I thought that name was kind of a compliment. I think my parents thought it meant I was kind of smart.' [32] Prior to *Moonraker* she was perhaps most familiar as Robert Redford's college sweetheart in *The Way We Were* (1973). Chiles had been offered the role of Anya Amasova in *The Spy Who Loved Me* but had turned down the part, but two years later, she lobbied for Holly Goodhead when by chance, she was given the seat next to director Lewis Gilbert on a flight. 'Bland' is being kind. *Charlie's Angels* star Jaclyn Smith was originally offered the role had dropped out due to scheduling conflicts.

Theme Song

Shirley Bassey's third Bond film theme song is a forgettable ballad, pleasant enough but hardly in the same league as 'Goldfinger' or 'Diamonds Are Forever'.

Production

Filming of *Moonraker* commenced in August 1978 at Pinewood Studios, Buckinghamshire, at film studios in Épinay and Boulogne-Billancourt, France and on location in the US, France, Brazil, Italy and Guatemala.

Observations

Two words: hovercraft gondola. The next six years would see the rot setting in and give us three of the worst Bond films as the series lurched in self-parody. 'Filmed on location in Outer Space', the credits claim. Yeah, right. *Moonraker*, the film, takes almost nothing from *Moonraker*, the book, other than the name of the villain, a space theme and a single scene when Bond escapes through a ventilation shaft. This is perhaps a good thing as over one-quarter of the book is devoted to the description of a single game of bridge. In the book, the demented, power-mad billionaire Hugo Drax, wants to drop a missile with a nuclear warhead on London. In the film, Drax is head of a company that is building space shuttles for NASA. The plane carrying the shuttle crashes during a heist, but no trace of the shuttle's wreckage is found. This sets up a frankly unbelievable and rather tired plot. Bond's first move is to visit Drax in California. Drax tries to kill Bond twice within twenty-four hours, while simultaneously allowing him the freedom to break into his office to find a clue in a safe. The trail leads to Venice, and that inflatable gondola, then to Rio de Janeiro for a fight on a cable car and, inevitably, into space.

There are one or two good moments. The pre credits scene when Bond is thrown out of an aeroplane without a parachute is strikingly shot and brilliantly edited: John Glen's work one again. 'You missed, Mr. Bond.' 'Did I?' is a classic Bond exchange, and much of the last twenty minutes is spectacular, including that iconic line from Q: 'I think he's attempting re-entry, sir!'. And, of course, Ken Adams' sets – his last for the Bond series – are fabulous. Likewise, *Moonraker* is crisply filmed by Jean Tournier. There's no doubt that every scene in *Moonraker* looks amazing, no matter how ludicrous the plot becomes.

There are, however, some very cringe-worthy moments. A double-taking pigeon. And Dolly. And some shocking dialogue. An example:

> Bond: I'm looking for Dr. Goodhead.
> Goodhead: You just found her.

Bond smiles, raises an eyebrow, and says, 'A woman?' Ouch. At least she gets a good jab back, with the hugely sarcastic 'Your powers of observation do you credit, Mr. Bond.'

The film opens with that fabulous pre-credits sequence, an elaborate and memorable scene in which Bond is finishing up an assignment (or 'on his last leg' as Moneypenny explains) and is pushed out of an aeroplane without a parachute. The scene took weeks of planning and preparation and required a bespoke, lightweight, helmet-mounted camera for a startling eighty-eight separate jumps, each providing between three seconds of film. It was shot above Lake Berryessa in northern California under the supervision of second unit director John Glen.

> The sequence had been drawn up as a storyboard. Each particular shot was rehearsed on the ground and I watched while they crawled around, devising a way to get the parachute off the pilot and onto Bond. [33]

Stuntman Jake Lombard plays Bond in the scene, Ron Luginbill doubles for Jaws and twenty-five-year-old skydiving champion Bruce Jeffrey 'BJ' Worth portrays the unfortunate pilot. Lombard and Worth would help create a second pre-credits sky-diving sequence ten years later for *The Living Daylights* (also directed by Glen) and Worth would also appear in *Octopussy*, *A View to A Kill*, *GoldenEye* and *Tomorrow Never Dies*. We'll skip over Jaws flapping his arms when he loses his parachute.

After the fairly tame title sequence and less-than-classic theme song, we have the standard briefing scene, this time with M, Q and the Minister of Defence,

Frederick Gray. Q issues Bond with a dart gun operated by nerve impulse, so we know we'll see that later. They very quickly deduce that Hugo Drax is mixed up somehow. Bond is sent to Drax's mansion in California, 'every stone brought from France'. Not really: these scenes were filmed at Château de Vaux-le-Vicomte, Maincy (exterior) and Château de Guermantes (interior) both in Île-de-France. Lois Maxwell's daughter makes a cameo as one of Hugo Drax's 'super humans'.

Once again, we have the trope of the not-so-secret secret agent: 'Your reputation precedes you,' drawls Drax. You'll recall that Tiffany Case (*Diamonds Are Forever*), Lazar (*The Man With the Golden Gun*), Stromberg (*The Spy Who Loved Me*) and Valentin Zukovsky (*GoldenEye*) also know who he is. And, sigh, we have another oriental henchman, Chang – Toshir Suga, Michael G. Wilson's French-domiciled Japanese aikido teacher. Drax does get some droll, very dry lines, though, delivered perfectly deadpan.

> James Bond. You appear with the tedious inevitability of an unloved season.
> Mr. Bond, you defy all my attempts to plan an amusing death for you.
> Look after Mr. Bond. See that some harm comes to him.
> At least I shall have the pleasure of putting you out of my misery, Mr. Bond.

The scenes with Lois Chiles rival those with Barbara Bach for wooden acting. Bond mansplains with evident relish after being surprised that Dr. Goodhead is 'a woman'. Different times, still inexcusable. These scenes in Holly's office were filmed in the Pompidou Centre, Paris. We have a repeat of the spinal traction machine scene from *Thunderball*, this time set inside a centrifuge chamber. This results in the unusual spectacle of a dishevelled Roger Moore with ruffled hair and a sweaty shine. Bond breaks into Drax's safe (wearing black flares, an outrageous wide-collared shirt and perfectly coiffured barnet), utilising a safe-cracking cigarette case and a OO7 mini-camera. His unwitting accomplice is chased to death by Dobermans. This beautifully filmed scene verges on horror. Bond follows up a clue from Drax's safe; a glass-making company in Venice. There he meets Dr. Goodhead again and comments, very creepily 'I keep forgetting that you are more than just a beautiful woman'. And then the film takes a major dip, with a random knife-tossing corpse, yet another boat chase, the souped-up gondola/hovercraft and Victor Tourjansky's second cameo as a tipsy tourist. All highly illogical.

The next several minutes are very tedious, as Bond carries out some sleuthing and witnesses the death of some of Drax's lab technicians who are manufacturing orchid-based poison. There is a typical Moore/Bond moment as the password to a door lock is revealed to be the 5-note theme from *Close Encounters of the Third Kind*. A shouty but satisfying fight with Chang leads to another clue: boxes labelled Rio de Janeiro. Bernard Lee's final scene by the canals of Venice ('I play bridge with that Drax fellow' is a nifty reference to Fleming's original novel) leads to a short scene with Holly

Goodhead revealed as a CIA agent, complete with gadgets. An establishing shot of Concorde – Air France product placement, no less – and Bond is in Rio, with Roger Moore in an ill-judged white suit. He soon switches this for a debonair tuxedo for a great scene at the carnival, with Jaws frustrated by the revellers. New shots with seven hundred extras were cut into previously shot footage of the previous summer's carnival. There are obvious comparisons here with the junkanoo in *Thunderball* and the Carnival of the Dead in *Spectre*. A night-time raid on an empty warehouse provides a Drax Airfreight shipping label and a slim excuse for Bond to go to Sugarloaf Mountain to watch aeroplanes take off from Galeão International Airport. He meets up once again with Holly Goodhead and Jaws for an entertaining fight on a cable car, although none of the three actors went anywhere near an actual cable car for this sequence. Bond and Goodhead are captured and taken in an ambulance past billboards for 7 Up, Seiko and British Airways. Bond escapes, and without warning, is suddenly and nonsensically dressed as a cowboy and riding a horse into the Largo do Boticário in Rio to the theme of *The Magnificent Seven*. Another sigh. After yet another boat chase, this time through the Amazon (the '007 Theme' makes a welcome appearance), followed by a frankly ridiculous hang-glider escape from a waterfall, Bond ends up in an ancient temple. These scenes were filmed in the Tikal National Park, Guatemala and the Iguazú National Park, Brazil. Bizarrely he is at once surrounded by scantily clad lovelies with come-hither smiles. This is Drax's secret hideout: another fabulous Ken Adam set. No monorail. Bond is tipped into a pool where a rubber python tries to squeeze the life out of him. Luckily he has borrowed Holly's CIA pen-cum-poison-dispenser. If you watch closely, when Drax asks Bond, 'Why did you break off the encounter with my pet python?', his lips are saying 'boa constrictor'.

Rather than killing Bond directly, who has been a major thorn in his side in three countries, Drax explains his plot (of course), then places Bond and Dr. Holly in an exhaust duct to be fried by one of the Moonrakers as it takes off into space. There is a similar scene in the Fleming novel. We have another classic Ken Adam set here, then a not-so-classic escape as Bond uses a previously unseen explosive concealed in his watch. Bond and Holly escape through some tunnels, filmed in the Paris catacombs, and replace the astronauts in Moonraker 6.

And so we come to the space-bound finale: the raison d'etre for the existence of the film. Once they arrive at Drax's secret space station ('he must have a radar jamming system', Bond declares), the extent of Drax's plan is revealed.

Drax: First there was the dream, now there is reality. Here in the untainted cradle of the heavens will be created a new super race, a race of perfect physical specimens. You have been selected as its progenitors. Like gods, your offspring will return to Earth and shape it in their image. You have all served in public capacities in my terrestrial empire. Your seed, like yourselves, will pay deference to the ultimate dynasty which I alone have created. From their first day on Earth, they will be able to look up and know that there is law and order in the heavens.

Crikey.

Bond and Goodhead disable the radar jamming system, the US are able to immediately deploy a shuttle of their own, and we have a space battle to rival *The Black Hole*, *Buck Rogers in the 25th Century*, *Battlestar Galactica* and *Star Trek: The Motion Picture*. Not really: it's all uninspiring stuff by today's action film standards. Jaws teams up with Bond when he realises that he and his new girlfriend Dolly are not perfect specimens (John Glen: 'Jaws' romance ... on the space station was a bit much'). The US space marines arrive and battle Drax's minions with lasers. Bond shoots Drax with his wrist dart gun, and ejects him from an airlock, telling Goodhead, 'He had to fly'.

And then the final scene: Bond and Goodhead copulate in space. 'All that floating around, when you're hanging there, and you feel the blood rushing, your nose getting bigger, and it hurts', Roger Moore said many years later. 'It's painful. When Holly Goodhead says, 'Take me around the world one more time.' I'm like, 'Oh God I can't do this any more.'' [34]

Moonraker is an energetic romp, which cannot and should not be taken seriously for a second. The film marked the last contributions to the series from Ken Adam, Bernard Lee, Lewis Gilbert and Shirley Bassey: four key names in the enduring success in the first fifteen years of the Bond films.

Too bad that, as *Moonraker* appears, Ian Fleming is no longer with us. Too bad at any time, but particularly now when the narrative invention of his tales, extravagant from the start, has been allowed to get completely out of hand ... at his best, he always related the extravagance to some sort of reality. Bond survived partly, it is true, by the use of gadgets, but basically by courage and wit; and the films followed the same line. Little by little, the gadgets have been winning. With *Moonraker,* they have taken over; *Moonraker* is the adventure not of Agent OO7 but of rear-activated speedboat torpedoes and a handy little wrist-attached exterminator. Most of the action depends upon the impossible. The audience doesn't believe that James Bond can float to earth without a parachute and laughs because it doesn't have to believe. And the impossible comes every ten minutes. It was startling, therefore, to find myself, towards the end, reflecting that something was a bit tedious. I know why. The last part ... is a space adventure. The insecure assembly of wire and what-not assumed by sci-fi to be capable of whizzing through space, the long bare corridors which make up the architecture of a sci-fi metropolis – it's all here, and once too often. Sci-fi repeats itself, feeds on itself ... the sameness of these eternal spaceships is driving me nuts. Return Bond to earth!
Dily Powell, *Punch*, 4 July 1979

For Your Eyes Only

Albert R Broccoli presents Roger Moore as Ian Fleming's James Bond 007 in *For Your Eyes Only*

Release date: 24 June 1981. Running time: 127 minutes. Distributed by United Artists. Producer: Albert R Broccoli (12 of 17)

James Bond: Roger Moore (5 of 7), Q: Desmond Llewelyn (10 of 17), Moneypenny: Lois Maxwell (12 of 14) with Geoffrey Keen (Sir Frederick Gray) (3 of 6), James Villiers (Bill Tanner), Walter Gotell (General Gogol) (3 of 6).

And Julian Glover (Aristotle Kristatos) with Carole Bouquet (Melina Havelock), Chaim Topol (Milos Columbo), Lynn-Holly Johnson (Bibi Dahl), Michael Gothard (Emile Leopold Locque), Cassandra Harris (Countess Lisl von Schlaf), Jill Bennett (Jacoba Brink).

Director: John Glen (1 of 5). Screenplay by Richard Maibaum (9 of 13), Michael G. Wilson (1 of 5). Production design: Peter Lamont (1 of 9). Main titles: Maurice Binder (10 of 14). Music: Bill Conti. Theme song performed by Sheena Easton. Cinematography: Alan Hume (1 of 3). Edited by John Grover (1 of 3).

Plot

When the secret device that controls Britain's Polaris submarines goes missing after the spy ship carrying it sinks, James Bond joins forces with a vengeful woman and a hero of the Greek resistance movement to find the equipment.

Cast

'The cast came together over Summer 1980,' wrote director John Glen. 'But as the shooting date loomed, there was still one question that remained unanswered: Who would play James Bond? I had been told categorically that Roger Moore was out of the picture. I spent two or three days shooting screen tests at Pinewood.'

Michael Billington was once again in the running: his test for *For Your Eyes Only* was one of the four occasions he auditioned for the role of Bond. There was also support for Lewis Collins, Bodie in *The Professionals* (1977-1983).

> Film fans are clamouring for him to play secret agent James Bond on the big screen. But Lewis feared he will never land the plum 007 role. He reckoned the man behind the money-spinning Bond movies – Albert 'Cubby' Broccoli – didn't like him. 'I was in his office for five minutes, but it was really over for me in seconds. I have heard since that he doesn't like me. That is unfair. He is expecting another Connery to walk through the door and there are few of them around. I think he has really shut the door on me. He found me too aggressive. I knew it all – that kind of attitude. Two or three years ago, that would be the case, purely because I was nervous and defensive. The number of people who have suggested me as a candidate amazes me – and Cubby hasn't given me another shot. I would even screen test and all that. [35]

Other names put forward include Ian Ogilvy (Simon Templar in ***Return of The Saint***, 1978-1979), Michael Jayston (the eponymous spy in the British spy series *Quiller*, 1975, and Peter Guillam in *Tinker, Sailor, Soldier, Spy*, 1979) and Timothy Dalton who had recently appeared with Topol in *Flash Gordon* (1980). Julian Glover, already cast as Kristatos, wrote to Cubby Broccoli nominating himself. [36]

All of the speculation came to nothing as Roger Moore agreed to play Bond once again. The expectation of Sean Connery returning to the role for a rival production company no doubt forced their hand. Broccoli and Wilson cannot have been delighted, however, that Moore played a self-parody of his role as James Bond in *The Cannonball Run*, released a week ahead of *For Your Eyes Only*. Moore, as Seymour Goldfarb, Jr., a would-be actor who believes he's Roger Moore and drives an Aston Martin DB5 with the registration plate 6633 PP ... the same as the in *Goldfinger* and *Thunderball*.

Bernard Lee does not appear in *For Your Eyes Only*. Lee, the only actor to have appeared in every Bond film so far, died on 16 January 1981, mid-way through production but before his scenes were filmed. The script was reworked so that M is on leave. His lines are given to Sir Frederick Gray, played by Geoffrey Keen in his third of six appearances. Israeli Chaim Topol is cleverly cast as the mysterious, intense Milos Columbo. Topol came to greatest prominence in his portrayal of Tevye in *Fiddler on the Roof* on stage over 3,500 times between 1966 and 2009 and on-screen (1971). Also appearing are French fashion model Carole Bouquet, the face of Chanel in the 1980s and 1990s, as the enigmatic, resourceful Melina Havelock; professional figure skater Lynn-Holly Johnson as Bibi Dahl; and British actor Michael Gothard as non-speaking villain Emile Leopold Locque. The hugely experienced Julian Glover (Aristotle Kristatos) has appeared on stage, on TV and in films since the 1950s. He has taken roles in the *Star Wars*, *Indiana Jones* and *Harry Potter* series, as well as portraying Grand Maester Pycelle in *Game of Thrones* between 2011 and 2016.

Theme Song

Sheena Easton's reedy vocal provides a melancholy, reflective ballad. Blondie's rejected submission, can be found on their 1982 album, *The Hunter*.

Production

For Your Eyes Only was filmed between September 1980 and February 1981 at Pinewood Studios, Buckinghamshire and on location in the UK, Corfu, Italy and Greece.

Observations

Moonraker had used the last available title of a full-length Ian Fleming novel: the next four films used titles, some plot devices and character names from short stories published between 1959 and 1965. Fleming's eighth book, *For Your Eyes Only*, subtitled *Five Secret Occasions in the Life of James Bond*, collected four stories based on plots written for a CBS television series. These were adapted into short story form in Jamaica in January and February 1959 and a fifth from the previous year was added when the hardback was published in April 1960. For the film version, Richard Maibaum and new co-writer Michael G. Wilson stitched together two of these short stories. The killing of the Havelocks and revenge story of their daughter Melina (Judy in the original book) is the basis of the short story *For Your Eyes Only*, and the drug smuggling story *Risisco* provided the characters Kristatos and Columbo and the shoot-out in the warehouse.

Richard Maibaum: '[Michael and I] work together like two collaborators always work. We argue a lot! We had a problem in that *For Your Eyes Only* was a collection of five short stories and there wasn't much of a plot to any of them. I tried to use as much of [Fleming's] original dialogue as possible, but in the end, there were only about twenty-five lines left!' [37]

For Your Eyes Only, the cuckoo in the nest of Moore's Bond films, was back-to-basics after the excesses of *Moonraker* – just as *On Her Majesty's Secret Service* was considerably and deliberately more earthbound than *You Only Live Twice* and the hard-edged realism of *Casino Royale* was the polar opposite of *Die Another Day*'s silly fantasy. Unfortunately, *For Your Eyes Only* is way down the 'best of' list in comparison to those series' highlights.

Interestingly, as Mark O'Connell points out, the film's theme of a daughter protecting her dead father's interests would reoccur in both *Octopussy* and *A View to A Kill*. 'How fitting for a decade where many critics slated Moore's Bond for looking older than their fathers, most of his 1980s heroines couldn't stop talking about theirs.' [38] Twenty-three-year-old Carole Bouquet seemed to agree when she spoke about Moore, then 55, to *People* in 1983: 'He's very nice. He reminds me of my father.'

Terence Young, director of *Dr. No*, *From Russia With Love* and *Thunderball*, was invited to take charge of *For Your Eyes Only*. 'They asked me to do it because they said it was going to be the last in the series,' he said a few years later. 'I liked the idea because as I had made the first film I thought 'why not make the last?' When I introduced the condition that if ever Bond re-appeared part of the profits should go to the Red Cross, I heard no more!' [39]

For Your Eyes Only is directed by John Glen. Glen had edited and directed the 2nd unit on three previous Bond films, including the excellent action sequences in *On Her Majesty's Secret Service*, *The Spy Who Loved Me* and *Moonraker*. 'When my work on *The Sea Wolves* was complete,' Glen wrote, 'I was invited to Pinewood Studios to lunch with Cubby Broccoli. Following a very pleasant meal, someone mentioned Roger Moore's intimation that *Moonraker* would be his final Bond picture. The identity of the new Bond was not the only subject of speculation. Three or four days later, I received another invitation to have lunch with Cubby at Pinewood. 'What would you say to directing the next Bond film?' I sat in a stunned silence. 'That would be fantastic.' I left his office walking on air.' [40]

Glen would not only direct *For Your Eyes Only*, but also the next four films. Glen's action scenes were always impeccable. His decision to 'decorate' his films with 'beautiful girls', perhaps not. 'We were blessed with the best crop of girls we ever had,' he writes in his memoirs. 'I started off with a shot of the lovely Alison Worth or rather the lovely Alison Worth's bottom.' He goes on. We'll leave it there. His second unit director, Arthur Wooster, would work on eight of the next nine Bond films; Tom Pevesner has the first of six credits as either associate producer or executive producer, effectively line-managing the productions through to *GoldenEye*.

For Your Eyes Only succeeds with a harder-edged story and some genuine tension, book-ended by a pointless and very silly opening and a ridiculous ending. The pre-titles sequence sees Bond visiting the grave of his ex-wife, filmed at St. Giles' Church, Stoke Poges a few miles from Pinewood Studios. The stone reads: 'We have all the time in the world'.

> Unnamed Vicar: Mr. Bond, Mr. Bond, I'm so glad I caught you. Your office called. They're sending a helicopter to pick you up. Some sort of emergency.
> Bond: It usually is.

And then, a white Persian cat, a Nehru jacket, a bald head and a neck brace. It's Blofeld! Except, it's not. The unnamed, uncredited character could not be identified as Blofeld because of the hangover of Kevin McClory claiming sole rights to the character, a claim disputed by Eon. This whole scene is simply cocking a snook at McClory who was actively pulling together a team for his own film. The character is voiced by Robert Rietti, who had dubbed Strangways in *Dr. No*, Tanaka in *You Only Live Twice* and Largo in *Thunderball*. Blofeld, as we shall call him, takes control of the Universal Exports helicopter, seemingly passing through an empty depot, cleverly filmed with a foreground miniature. Kudos here to stuntman Martin Grace, who doubles for Roger Moore clinging to the outside of the helicopter. Bond prevails (a funky Bond theme plays), picks up Blofeld and drops him down a chimney at the Beckton gasworks in east London. Just before Blofeld is killed, he offers Bond a delicatessen in stainless steel. Apparently, this line had been added by Cubby Broccoli as a reference to his early years as a second-generation Italian immigrant in New York. It's a metaphor for offering something without a hidden agenda.

In his autobiography, *For My Eyes Only*, director John Glen talks about how the film's London premiere was for the benefit of the Royal Association for Disability and Rehabilitation. 'One or two critics had pointed out that to kick off the film by scuppering a villain in a wheelchair showed rather poor taste,' he writes.' Of course, that was never intentional and the fact that we had a villain in a wheelchair was just an unfortunate coincidence. There were 30 or 40 disabled guests at the premiere who watched the film from the first two rows in the stalls. I was glad that when that sequence came on, they were the ones who laughed loudest.'

After the title sequence, the action switches to the British spy vessel the St Georges, which is sunk after accidentally trawling an old naval mine in the Ionian Sea, off the coast of Corfu. St George was carrying an Automatic Targeting Attack Communicator (ATAC), the system which is used coordinate the Royal Navy's fleet of Polaris submarines, and therefore of great value to the British. James Bond is assigned to retrieve the ATAC. In Corfu, Kalami Bay to be precise, an underwater archaeologist, Sir Timothy Havelock, has been asked to help find the St. Georges. He is gunned down with his wife. His daughter, Melina, survives.

For Your Eyes Only presents a very different female lead in Melina Havelock, played with chilly class by Carole Bouquet. Havelock is a woman of action, if rather cool. Her primary motivation is a desire for revenge. Bond says, somewhat patronisingly: 'Before setting out on revenge, you first dig two graves.' And she shuts him down with, 'I don't expect you to understand. You're English, but I'm half Greek. And Greek women, like Electra… always avenge their loved ones. I must go.' She twice saves Bond: once as he escapes from Gonzales' villa, and again during the monastery raid. And she shows no sexual desire for Bond until the very last scene and even then, their interaction is unconvincing.

Bond is told by Chief of Staff Bill Tanner (James Villiers) that the Havelocks' assassin was a Cuban, Hector Gonzales. Bond flies to Madrid to find out who hired him. All of the 'Spanish' scenes were filmed in Corfu. At Gonzales' villa, Bond is captured but escapes with the help of an umbrella. In a scene taken from Fleming's book, Gonzales is shot with a crossbow by Melina Havelock. They escape together, but Bond's booby-trapped Lotus explodes when the anti-burglar system is triggered. A chase in Melina's clapped out Citroen 2CV – Bond's dirty look when he first sees it is laugh-out-loud funny – is a terrific sequence and a highlight of the film. The car chase was put together by Rémy Julienne, veteran of *The Italian Job* and well over 1,000 other films. *For Your Eyes Only* was the first of six Bond engagements for Julienne and his team.

Back in London, Bond and Q use Identigraph facial identification technology to determine who Bond saw speaking to Gonzales: the unsmiling, silent Emile Leopold Locque. It's nice to see Desmond Llewelyn get a few more lines than usual here, and to see the warmth in his relationship with Roger Moore. We have a classic retort when Bond sees a spiked umbrella in Q's lab. 'Stinging in the rain?' Bond quips. Q says, 'That's not funny, OO7.' He's right.

Bond flies to Cortina d'Ampezzo in the Italian Dolomites to track down Locque. His contact and informant is Aristotle Kristatos, a well-connected Greek businessman but a rather limp villain, almost peripheral to the story. Kristatos has an ice-skating protégé sexpot, Bibi Dahl, who is never anything less than irritating and is surely in the wrong film. There is an underused Irma Bunt/ Helga Brandt character played by English actor Jill Bennett, former wife of the playwright John Osbourne.

Kristatos tells Bond that Locque was hired by Milos Columbo. This is, of course, a bluff. There is more skiing. The ski chase through the bob-sleigh track, absurd as it is, is very good and up to John Glen's high standards of action. Unfortunately, this scene caused the death of an Italian crew member.

Back in his hotel room, Bond finds Bibi wearing just a towel.

Bond: How did you get in here?
Bibi: One of the porters is a fan. He'll do anything for me, and I'll do anything for you.
Bond: Well, I'm exceedingly flattered, Bibi... but you're in training.
Bibi: That's a laugh. Everybody knows it builds up muscle tone.
Bond: I think you're wonderful, Bibi, but I don't think your Uncle Ari would approve.
Bibi: Him? He thinks I'm still a virgin.
Bond: Yes, well, you get your clothes on, and I'll buy you an ice cream.

Bond flies to Corfu in pursuit of Columbo. He meets Kristatos in a casino, filmed at the Achillion Palace Hotel. Kristatos tells more tall tales about Columbo. Bond meets Columbo's mistress Countess Lisl von Schlaf. They go back to her place. Cassandra Harris, Mrs P. Brosnan, easily steals the scene here.

Lisl: Me nightie's slipping.
Bond: So is your accent, Countess. Manchester?
Lisl: Close. Liverpool.

In the morning, Lisl and Bond are ambushed by Locque and a young Charles Dance. Lisl is killed. Bond meets Columbo, wonderfully and roguishly portrayed by the charismatic Topol, who tells him that Kristatos is working with the KGB to retrieve the ATAC. Bond accompanies Columbo on a raid on one of Kristatos' opium-processing warehouses in Albania, just across the Adriatic Sea from Corfu but filmed in Agiou Spyridonos. Bond chases Locque. There is a minor continuity error here. The Mercedes-Benz that Locque drives is an S-Class that becomes a newer model after it enters a tunnel. In a memorable scene, Bond kicks Locque and his car over a cliff.

'The script said that Bond was to 'toss [a] dove pin at Locque and then kick the car hard to force it over the cliff'', wrote Roger Moore in his memoirs. 'I said that my Bond wouldn't do that. It would be far better, I reasoned, if in tossing the badge in I caused Locque to move, thus unsettling the balance of the car, and sending him over that way. John Glen was adamant that this man had killed my friend and now I should show my anger and a more ruthless side to my character. It didn't sit happily with me, so we compromised – I tossed the badge in and gave the car a not-so-hard kick to topple it.' [41]

'I set out to make *For Your Eyes Only* a turning point in the Bond series,' said John Glen. 'It was time to get back to the spirit of Ian Fleming's books and time to make Bond seem a little harsher than he had been in the previous few films. *For Your Eyes Only* was a story with a harder edge and I felt Bond had to respond to these situations in an appropriate way.' [42]

Bond and Melina dive to the St. Georges to retrieve the ATAC but are captured by Kristatos. These underwater scenes are a combination of stand-ins filmed in the Bahamas, an underwater set at Pinewood and an ingenious effect where Roger Moore and Carole Bouquet were filmed at high-speed with a wind machine to blow their hair and air bubbles cleverly added to the negative in post-production. But how did Melina know to leave the diving tank at the underwater ruins? There follows a tense, unused action sequence from the original novel of *Live and Let Die*, when Bond and Melina are dragged over a coral reef and make use of the scuba tank Melina had deposited earlier. Handy. And it's clearly not Roger Moore diving down to retrieve the spare tank but a stuntman with long, blond hair. And, in a plot development that must annoy screenwriters everywhere, the crucial clue is given by a talking parrot called Krone.

Melina: Kristatos is still alive.
Bond: And probably headed to Moscow or Havana by now.
Melina: We'll never get him.
Bond: Or the ATAC.
Parrot: ATAC to St. Cyril's.

Bond relays this to Whitehall via a confession booth. 'Forgive me, Father, for I have sinned.' Q's classic response: 'That's putting it mildly, 007.'

In the film's excellent climax, Bond has to scale an enormous cliff-face so that he, Melina and Colombo's men can storm Kristatos' monastery stronghold, filmed at the Holy Trinity in Meteora, Greece, and also at a replica nearby. This is a classic John Glen set-piece, genuinely tense, and has a bum-clenching one-take stunt by Rick Sylvester – the same guy that skied off a cliff at the beginning of *The Spy Who Loved Me*. Watch for when Bond's team surprises the room of off-duty guards. A blond man seen rising from a bed on the left is the same actor seen a few minutes earlier, tied up and gagged after being shot with an arrow. Having overcome Kristatos' men and retrieved the ATAC, Bond is confronted by General Gogol. Bond coolly destroys the ATAC. 'That's detente, comrade.'

All this good work is almost thrown away with a final scene gag. 'Having opened with a random cameo from a power-crazed megalomaniac,' sniggers Max Williams, 'the film closes by wheeling out Margaret Thatcher.' [43] It was almost a Prince Charles lookalike until the actor booked to play him was arrested for 'something unseemly'. [44]

So, *For Your Eyes Only* is a pretty solid entry in the series, Roger Moore's second or third best Bond film and his last half-decent outing.

FORGET about the relationship of this planet to the sun. Whenever possible, summer officially begins with the release of a new James Bond film – that is, today, with the opening of *For Your Eyes Only.*

Nothing else in our popular culture has endured with such élan as Agent OO7, whether played by Sean Connery, by George Lazenby or by the incumbent, Roger Moore. Not the least of the feats of the Bond films is their having outlived all the imitations, particularly the Matt Helm and Flint pictures. *For Your Eyes Only* is not the best of the series by a long shot – that would be a choice between *Goldfinger* and *Moonraker*–but it's far from the worst. It has a structural problem in that it opens with a precredit helicopter chase – in, over, around and through London – which is so lunatic and inventive that the rest of the movie is hard-put to achieve such a fever-pitch again. Though Mr. Moore shows no sign of tiring – his Bond retains an ageless cool that remains outside of time – the screenplay by Richard Maibaum and Michael Wilson is occasionally lazy, allowing us fleeting moments of introspection when logic raises its boring head. One of the secrets of the best of the Bonds is the manner in which we, in the audience, are made willing accomplices to illogic.
Vincent Canby, *New York Times*, 26 June 1981

Octopussy

Albert R Broccoli presents Roger Moore as Ian Fleming's James Bond OO7 in *Octopussy*
'James Bond's all time high!'
Release date: 6 June 1983. Running time: 131 minutes. Distributed by MGM / United International. Producer: Albert R Broccoli (13 of 17).
James Bond: Roger Moore (6 of 7), M: Robert Brown (1 of 4), Q: Desmond Llewelyn (11 of 17), Moneypenny: Lois Maxwell (13 of 14) with Walter Gotell (General Gogol) (4 of 6), Geoffrey Keen (Fredrick Gray) (4 of 6).
And Louis Jourdan (Kamal Khan) with Maud Adams (Octopussy), Kristina Wayborn (Magda), Kabir Bedi (Gobinda), Steven Berkoff (General Orlov), David Meyer (Mischka), Anthony Meyer (Grischka), Vijay Amritraj (Vijay).
Director: John Glen (2 of 5). Screenplay: Richard Maibaum (10 of 13), Michael G. Wilson (2 of 5), George MacDonald Fraser. Production design: Peter Lamont (2 of 9). Main titles: Maurice Binder (11 of 14). Music: John Barry (9 of 11). Theme song performed by Rita Coolidge. Cinematography: Alan Hume (2 of 3). Edited by Peter Davies (1 of 3), Henry Richardson.

Plot

James Bond is assigned to solve the murder of agent OO9, killed in East Germany, clutching a fake Fabergé egg. The trail leads to India, where the enigmatic Octopussy operates a smuggling ring under the cover of a travelling circus. Bond uncovers a plot to expand Soviet control into West-Central Europe.

Cast

Roger Moore was reluctant to commit to *Octopussy*. As a result, Michael Billington was again tested, along with James Brolin (from *Marcus Welby MD*, 1969-1976). Brolin played a scene from *From Russia With Love* with Maud Adams as Tatiana. 'It was an excellent test,' noted director John Glen. Brolin was hired. And then Roger Moore decided that he would play Bond again after all.

Maud Adams returns to the series as the titular co-lead, after roles in *Rollerball* (1975), *Tattoo* (1981) and the TV drama *Playing for Time* (1980). She was cast after Sybil Danning, Faye Dunaway, Barbara Carrera, Persis Khambatta and Barbara Parkins were deemed unsuitable, too expensive or simply turned Eon down. What a shame that the hugely talented character actor Steven Berkoff, playing the scheming KGB throwback General Orlov, decides to ham it up: yet another top-class actor trying too hard as a Bond villain, shouting at everyone in a bad Russian accent. This fab-actor-overdoing-the-Bond-villain issue would occur again. See Christopher Walken, Joe Don Baker, Jonathan Pryce, Robert Carlyle, Toby Stephens and Christoph Waltz in films to come.

French actor Louis Jourdan plays suave, glowering Kamal Khan, an exiled Afghan prince and jewellery smuggler. Active in Hollywood from 1946, he retired in 1992 and lived to be 93. Kristina Wayborn, another Swede, was cast as Magda, in a twist to the usual henchman character: a dominant, strong woman. With Maud Adams' sharp, tough title character, these are welcome developments in what has been, at times, a very misogynistic film series.

Desmond Llewelyn, Robert Brown, Lois Maxwell, Walter Gotell and Geoffrey Keen reprise their roles from earlier films. In a bit of stunt casting, Indian tennis player Vijay Amritraj plays Bond's cheerful and charming MI6 allay, Vijay.

Theme Song

Lyricist Tim Rice wisely avoids using the film's title. 'All Time High' is a mid-tempo torch ballad and perennial pub quiz question sung by Rita Coolidge.

Production

Filming for *Octopussy* commenced in August 1982 and took place at Pinewood Studios, Buckinghamshire and on location in the UK, the United States, Germany and India.

Observations

Ian Fleming's short story *Octopussy* was posthumously serialised in *The Daily Express* in October 1965, then published in book form in 1966, initially with one other story (*The Living Daylights*, first published in *The Sunday Times* in 1962), subsequently with a third added when published in paperback (*The Property of a Lady)* and a fourth when reprinted some years later (*007 in New York*). The film owes very little to one of Fleming's most memorable stories: only a passing reference to Major Dexter Smyth and the title of the story are utilised. Elements of *The Property of a Lady* are also used, specifically the auction scene and the Macguffin of the Fabergé egg.

Whilst not even close to being a Bond classic, *Octopussy* – in which Roger Moore turns James Bond into a clown both figuratively and literally – is a good-natured, routine yet utterly ridiculous film. It certainly has its moments. In its favour, we have: a decent plot; some great action, including one of the best pre-title sequences; a fabulous fight on a train; a very creepy hunt for OO9-as-a-clown; a couple of decent jokes; and the Swedish double whammy of Maud Adams and Kristina Wayborn. The case against: Roger Moore swinging on a vine yodelling like Tarzan; a gorilla suit; a crocodile submarine; a killer yo-yo; the TV wristwatch that Bond uses to look at breasts; 'sit!'; 'hiss off'; Q in a hot air balloon; Q saying 'perhaps later'; an adolescent erection sight gag; Bond saying, 'Gracias, querida' (Spanish for 'Thank you, darling'); the casual racism; and a 56-year-old clown trying to disarm a nuclear bomb.

Octopussy was released in June 1983, four months before *Never Say Never Again*, an unofficial (i.e., not Eon-produced) remake of *Thunderball* starring a certain S. Connery. Both films were made concurrently at Pinewood and Elstree, twenty miles apart. 'I don't think there was any competition between Sean and I,' said Roger Moore. 'We'd meet occasionally and discuss how they had tried to kill us. We'd always believed that the producers tried to kill you, to get the insurance, and they'd get somebody that looked like you to finish off the scene.' [45]

The first version of the screenplay was written by George MacDonald Fraser, author of twelve Flashman adventure novels (1966-2005) and the films *The Three Musketeers* (1973) and *The Four Musketeers* (1974). This was reworked by Richard Maibaum and Michael G. Wilson but retained some of Fraser's ideas, giving him his only Bond screenwriting credit. As with *Diamonds Are Forever*, the basic plot is very good, just indifferently executed: A Soviet general plans to fake a nuclear accident at a US airbase in West Germany. This will force the Americans out of Europe, leaving the Russians free to roll in their tanks. Unlike Stromberg or Drax, Steven Berkoff's General Orlov is a realistic megalomaniac.

The pre-credit sequence is a classic. Bond is undercover in Latin America (aka RAF Northolt with added palm trees) on a mission to blow up a plane with a new radar system. He arrives in a convertible Range Rover and ingeniously reverses his jacket and flat cap to turn his outfit into that of a military officer. Bond is captured when the officer he's impersonating makes an appearance. The look-a-like General Toro ('Well, small world. You're a Toro, too') is played by Ken Norris, Roger Moore's double from his days on *The Saint*. Fortunately, Bond has an ally: Bianca, played by seventeen-year-old model Tina Hudson ('Chems, please be careful'). She drives the Range Rover alongside the truck where Bond is being held and flirts with two soldiers causing a distraction so that OO7 Bond can escape. This same unlikely ploy was used in *Moonraker*. Bond detaches the horsebox and opens it to reveal an Acrostar micro-jet. And off he flies, calling 'see you in Miami'. The action here is a smartly edited combination of the micro-jet, a larger Hawker Siddley 127 for long shots, model work, foreground miniatures, a Moore-piloted cockpit at Pinewood, Moore in the hanger at Northolt, footage from the Hurricane Arch Bridge, Utah and a 60mph car-mounted model aircraft. The rocket that follows the aircraft was, amazingly, a firework tied to the back. All very satisfying. Bond then lands by a fuel station and says, with an oily grin, 'Fill her up, please'. This provides a nice titter as the titles kick-in.

Cut to East Berlin, as agent 009 is fatally wounded, dressed as a circus clown and carrying a fake Fabergé egg. Scenes here were filmed in Black Park, next to Pinewood and at Heatherden Hall on the Pinewood site. The 'Residence of the British Ambassador' in *Octopussy* is the same place where Oddjob knocks the head off the statue in *Goldfinger*. Bond arrives at Moneypenny's office, and meets fawning Penelope Smallbone, Moneypenny's new assistant, played by Michaela Clavell, daughter of author James Clavell. The new M, Bond and Fredrick Gray meet MI6 art expert Jim Fanning who identify the 009 egg as a fake. The real thing is due to be auctioned at Sotheby's later that afternoon. Bond agrees to accompany Fanning to Sotherby's to see who bids on the real Fabergé egg.

Meanwhile, in a scene worthy of the Connery era, the KGB high command meet in a cavernous conference room – Peter Lamont's set paying worthy tribute to Ken Adam's classic designs of the 1960s. Steven Berkoff's Orlov is simply bonkers, whereas Gogol is the voice of reason.

> Orlov: General Gogol is presumptuous. He speaks for himself and others who cling to timid, outdated and unrealistic policies. Must I remind you, the committee, of our overwhelming superiority over NATO forces before we give it away?
> Gogol: This is absolute madness. We know where it will end. NATO will counterattack with nuclear weapons.
> Orlov: Never. The West is decadent and divided. It has no stomach to risk our atomic reprisals. Throughout Europe, daily demonstrations demand unilateral nuclear disarmament.
> Gogol: I see no reason to risk war to satisfy your personal paranoia and thirst for conquest.

We then learn that Orlov has been 'borrowing' art treasures to create fakes. The 'Kremlin National Fine Art Museum' is in fact, the National Maritime Museum in Greenwich. Back in London, at Sotheby's, Bond turn on his full smarm as he spots the elegant Magda across the auction room. 'Now there is a lady,' he murmurs. Magda is played by Swedish actor Kristina Wayborn. This fascinating character is unfortunately underdeveloped. Magda is accompanied by Kamal Khan. 'Usually a seller,' explains Fanning. 'Marginal quality from dubious sources.' Bond switches the real egg for the fake egg and forces Khan into a bidding war.

Auctioneer: Yours, sir, for £500,000.
Fanning: We could have been stuck with it.
Bond: I doubt it. He had to buy it.
Fanning: But why?
Bond: That's what I intend to find out.

Bond following Kamal Khan to India. A rather obvious establishing shots of the Taj Mahal, Ãgra (400 miles from where *Octopussy* was filmed) sets the scene for Bond to meet his Indian liaison, Vijay, identified as a snake charmer playing 'a charming tune' – the 'James Bond Theme'. They travel to Bond's hotel, the Shiv Niwas Palace in Udaipur, and exchange witty dialogue.

Vijay: I've got a part-time job at Kamal's tennis club.
Bond: What have you learned so far?
Vijay: Well, my backhand's improved.

Bond meets Khan and defeats him in a game of backgammon. This is a reworking of the Goldfinger/Simmons gin rummy card game. Bond requiring double six to win the game and using Khan's loaded dice is very contrived, but the scene ends with a classic line 'Spend the money quickly, Mr Bond', taken from the novel *Moonraker*.

Drax turned to the table. 'Good night, gentlemen,' he said, looking at each of them with the same oddly scornful expression. 'I owe about £15,000.' He leant forward and picked up his cigarette case and lighter. Then he looked again at Bond and spoke very quietly, the red moustache lifting slowly from the splayed upper teeth. 'I should spend the money quickly, Commander Bond,' he said. Then he turned away from the table and walked swiftly out of the room.
From Ian Fleming's *Moonraker*. [46]

And, thirty minutes in, *Octopussy* has shown us everything it has to offer. The rest is nonsense, leavened by a few good lines and a couple of excellent action sequences.

A Tuk-Tuk chase features Vijay Amritraj deploying his tennis racquet, to twanging sound effects and a double-taking camel. Sight gags include Bond using torches from a fire juggler, a sword pulled from the mouth of a sword swallower and a judicious use of a bed of nails. Cultural stereotypes? Bond visits Q in a field lab and asks him to stitch a hole in his dinner jacket where an assailant tried to stab him. Q says, 'They missed you. What a pity.' Ah, Desmond Llewelyn. Wonderful. Q becomes directly involved in Bond's mission in *Octopussy*, one of only two occasions where this happens – the other is *Licence to Kill* after Bond resigns from the service to avenge Felix Leiter. Q's assistant here, Smithers, is played by British actor Jeremy Bulloch who famously portrayed Boba Fett in *The Empire Strikes Back* (1980) and

Return of the Jedi (1983). Two other *Star Wars* alumni will appear later in *Octopussy*, as we shall see.

Bond meets Magda again in the hotel casino. Bond recognises her from the Sotheby's auction from earlier in the film.

Magda: You have a very good memory for faces.
Bond: And figures.

She has an ulterior motive. After spending the night with him, ('I need refilling'), Bond allows her to steal the real Fabergé egg, which has been fitted with listening and tracking devices by Q. Magda memorably falls backwards out of the window and spins gracefully, sari unfurling. Khan waits in a car and Gobinda (Kabir Bedi) captures Bond.

After dinner with Khan at his winter palace – establishing shots show the spectacular nineteenth-century Monsoon Palace, overlooking Udaipur – Bond unsuccessfully attempts another congress with Magda ('I could come in for a night cap.'), then burns through the bars on the window of his room with an acid-filled Mont Blanc pen. He climbs onto the ledge, and shimmies along to the next window. Here he sees Magda in her underwear, the first of two Peeping Tom episodes in this film. Bond learns that Khan is working with Orlov, along with the name of the East German town Karl Marz Stadt (now called Chemnitz). Bond escapes from Khan's palace. The Tarzan yodel is a series low point that brings the film down to mere slapstick. Compare this with the tension of the crocodile escape in *Live and Let Die*. Bond's encounter with tiger is still an embarrassment. His safari suit more so.

Magda's octopus tattoo gives a clue to 'a wealthy woman who lives on the floating palace. No one knows her real name, but she's known as Octopussy.' Vijay tells Bond that only women are allowed in Octopussy's palace. 'Sexual discrimination,' Bond says, 'I'll definitely have to pay it a visit.' Exterior scenes for Octopussy's palace were filmed at the spectacular Taj Lake Palace on Lake Pichola, Udaipur.

Finally, over an hour in, we get to see Maud Adams. Like Pam Bouvier in the forthcoming *Licence To Kill*, she is a tough cookie. 'There are vast rewards for a man of your talents, willing to take risks,' she purrs. 'I am not for hire,' Bond replies. 'Naturally, you do it for Queen and Country', she says. 'I don't have a country, no price on my head. I don't have to answer to you, a paid assassin, for what I am.' Delicious. We know who's in charge here.

In a nod to Fleming's original short story, Octopussy has a personal connection with Bond. She is the daughter of the late Major Dexter-Smythe, whom Bond was assigned to arrest for treason. Bond allowed him to commit suicide rather than face trial for murder. In the 2015 film *Spectre*, Dexter-Smythe's victim is the father of the protagonist, both films taking elements from the same Ian Fleming short story.

Octopussy invites Bond to 'stay on as my guest'. He then forces himself on her (she resists, then relents), snoops around and finds a circus programme in a desk, then despatches three assassins, one of whom has a killer yo-yo and another ends up with an octopus on his face. Zzzzzz.

Into the third act. Bond travels to East Germany via Checkpoint Charlie and infiltrates Octopussy's circus. He discovers that Orlov has replaced the Soviet treasures with a 100-megaton nuclear warhead, primed to explode during a show at a US Air Force base in West Germany. The next several minutes are Bond action at its best. Starting with Bond stealing Orlov's car, with the jewellery in the boot, soldiers shoot out his tyres, so he simply runs the empty wheel rims onto the railway tracks and pursues the train. A fortunate points change puts him alongside the train and he manages to board with a handy umbrella and a convenient sunroof. He is spotted and chased along the roof and between the carriages. Martin Grace, Roger Moore's stunt double, was severely injured on the train stunt, filmed at the Nene Valley Railway near Peterborough. In his memoirs, John Glen says: 'Unfortunately, the train's designated stopping point was missed, and it headed straight for a nasty obstruction – a piece of protruding pipe hit Martin when he was still outside the carriage. He suffered a bad groin injury during the collision, but it's indicative of the man's enormous strength that he managed to hang on until the train stopped. If he had fallen off at the time of impact, he would probably have ended up under the wheels of the train.' [47]

The action scenes in John Glen's Bond films are always good value: it seems like Bond is in real danger. We'll skip over the part where Bond disguises himself in a gorilla suit, shall we? Bond's fight with Gobinda on the train, though filmed in the studio, used clever techniques such as a moving horizontal canvas backdrop, Roger Moore suspended on thin wires, sparks flying from rigged sword and bursts of CO_2 in place of steam. This is all very effective. Despite falling from the train, Bond avenges 009 and makes it to the circus (filmed at RAF Upper Heyford in Oxfordshire) by hitch-hiking with a stereotypical German beer-drinking, sausage-scoffing couple. They might even have been wearing Lederhosen. Bond sneaks into a caravan and changes into a clown costume. There are five minutes left on the bomb countdown at this point, plenty of time to put on the make-up and find those oversized boots.

'It was a bit of a struggle to get Roger to dress up and wear the garish face paint,' noted John Glen. [48]

Khan is seated with two US servicemen. The one on the right is played by Richard LeParmentier, who portrayed Admiral Motti in the original *Star Wars*. Darth Vader found his lack of faith disturbing. On the left, it's Bruce Boa, Rebel Force General Rieekan in *The Empire Strikes Back* ('You're a good fighter, Solo. I hate to lose you.')

Bond finds Octopussy and convinces her that Khan has double-crossed her. There is a tense moment when Bond is trying to get to the bomb hidden in the cannon but is constantly blocked by clowns performing their acts. Back in

India, Octopussy and her circus acts are infiltrating Khan's palace when a hot air balloon appears, resplendent in Union Jack livery. Bond is aboard and the vessel is piloted by Q. The hot air balloon was a remote-control model in front of a photographed backdrop. Octopussy attempts to kill Khan but is captured by Gobinda and they prepare to fly away in Khan's aircraft. Bond pursues them on horseback as they attempt to escape in their plane – the jump from the horse onto the tail of plane was done for real. There is a moment of delicious humour when Kamal turns to his henchman Gobinda and hisses 'Go out and get him!'. 'Out there?' 'Go!' 'Yes, excellence.'

Whilst spectacular, the fight on the roof of the plane is very silly – no one, not even Roger Moore, can cling to outside of an upside-down aircraft by their fingertips. And Bond despatching Gobinda by flicking him in the face with an aerial is outrageous. Bond and Octopussy jump out of the aircraft seconds before it dives into a mountain, killing Khan. The crashing plane was a model at Pinewood after an attempt to film another model aircraft tipping off a cliff didn't work when it righted itself and flew out of range of the cameras. M and General Gogol discuss the fate of the jewellery, whilst Bond recuperates with Octopussy aboard her private barge in India.

'*Octopussy* is an unusually timeless Bond film,' suggests Mark O'Connell. [49]
He's right. But there are several uncomfortable moments. The final scene is cringingly sexist and the line, 'that'll keep you in curry for a while', was unacceptable even in 1983.

> Let's face it: the sensationally successful and long-lived James Bond films will not quit, and for good reason. They are *Star Wars* fantasies for the middle-aged of all ages. *Octopussy*, the 13th in the series, is actually better than most.
>
> The film makes no pretence of being based on anything except the Ian Fleming character and the high good humour and wit of the film makers. Agent OO7 faces a succession of unspeakable dangers and obliging women with the absurdly overstated, indefatigable waggishness that has outlived all imitations. Roger Moore, who plays Bond yet again, is not getting any younger, but neither is the character. The two have grown gracefully indivisible.
>
> Much of the story is incomprehensible, but I'm sure that the characters include a crazy Soviet general (Steven Berkoff), who is as feared by the Russians as by the Allies; a decadent Afghan prince (Louis Jourdan), who gambles with loaded dice and would not hesitate to blow up the world for personal profit, and the glamorous tycoon of the film's title (Maud Adams), who lives in a lake palace in Udaipur, India, from which she runs an international business empire of hotels, airlines and an East German circus.
>
> The point of any Bond adventure is its incredible gadgets – this film includes a virtually pocket-size jet plane – and the variations worked on the chases, sequences that, like great vaudeville gags, build from one surprise to the next to discover the unexpected topper. In *Octopussy* the best of these are a hilarious, precredit sequence in which Bond flees Cuba, another in India

where Bond finds himself in league with a tiger in the course of an unusual 'shoot' and one across East Germany involving an automobile, a circus train and an atomic bomb. *Octopussy* includes a lot of low-voltage sexual hanky-panky and some scenes of mayhem that are more picturesque than realistically violent.
Vincent Canby, *New York Times*, 10 June 1983

Never Say Never Again

Jack Schwartzmann & Kevin McClory present a Taliafilm Production, An Irvin Kirschner Film – Sean Connery – *Never Say Never Again*
Release date: 7 October 1983. Running time: 134 minutes. Distributed by Warner Brothers. Producer: Jack Schwartzman.
James Bond: Sean Connery (7 of 7), M: Edward Fox, Q: Alec McCowen, Moneypenny: Pamela Salem, Felix Leiter: Bernie Casey.
With Klaus Maria Brandauer (Largo), Max von Sydow (Blofeld), Barbara Carrera (Fatima Blush), Kim Basinger (Domino Petachi), Rowan Atkinson (Nigel Small-Fawcett), Gavan O'Herlihy (Jack Petachi).
Director: Irvin Kershner. Screenplay: Lorenzo Semple Jr. Music: Michel Legrand. Theme song by Lani Hall. Cinematography by Douglas Slocombe. Edited by Ian Crafford.

Observations

We're tempted to pretend that this film simply doesn't exist. But, amid the limp script, workmanlike delivery, insipid music, dull female lead, lack of 'James Bond Theme', missing pre-credits sequence, and no John Barry or Ken Adam, we have a gratifying number of positives. The final product, not surprisingly, feels like a Bond film from a parallel universe: M, Q, Moneypenny and Blofeld are there but played by new actors. And Bond? Well ...

1966's *Thunderball* had been co-produced by Kevin McClory with Albert Broccoli and Harry Saltzman. Robert Sellers' *The Battle for Bond* (2007) details the lengthy, complex gestation of McClory's remake of the fourth James Bond film. The rights to the story of *Thunderball* reverted McClory in 1976. '[That year] McClory tried to make a movie titled *James Bond of the Secret Service*,' podcaster Chris Wright told *Variety* in 2015. 'The first draft shared some remarkable similarities with Eon's *The Spy Who Loved Me*, including an underwater base and an invulnerable henchman.'

Sean Connery himself contributed material to the script, which was soon reworked into a new project called *Warhead*. '*Warhead* would have featured SPECTRE using The Statue of Liberty as their base and included robot sharks armed with explosives swimming around the New York sewer system!' says Wright. Press reports named Orson Welles as Blofeld and Trevor Howard as M. The lead female would have been called Justine Lovesit. Described as '*Star*

Wars underwater,' the project fell apart when Connery, frustrated by McClory's continued legal wranglings, pulled out. Eventually, McClory and Connery found common ground and Connery committed to returning to Bond and play the part for the seventh and final time. But that didn't stop Eon taking them to court. 'We sought an injunction against them,' wrote Cubby Broccoli, 'claiming, amongst other things, that they would be trading on our success, that they had milked idea from previous Bonds, and by remaking *Thunderball* would be using more of our material than their own. We lost, not because of the weakness of our claim, but because it was held they were so far advanced on the production it would be unfair to pull the switch.'

'There was no animosity between Sean and me,' claimed Roger Moore, then filming his fifth Bond, *Octopussy*. 'We often had dinner together and compared notes. I never actually saw Sean's film.' [50]

Sean Connery approached Terence Young to direct *Never Say Never Again*. This idea was rejected by Kevin McClory. Peter Hunt and Richard Donner were also asked but declined. The substitute, Irvin Kershner fresh from *The Empire Strikes Back*, was an inspired choice, giving the film a crisp finish and a pace that hid Connery's less-than-youthful physicality. He had previously directed Connery in the forgotten 1966 comedy *A Fine Madness*. Kershner brings out an excellent performance from Connery. It might conceivably be his best acting performance as 007.

Barbara Carrera, Klaus Maria Brandauer, Kim Basinger and Max von Sydow play Fatima Blush, Maximillian Largo, Domino Petachi and Ernst Stavro Blofeld, a decent cast hand-picked by Sean Connery. Carrera turned down a major role in *Octopussy* to play opposite Connery. 'That was true,' she told *The New York Times* in 2012. 'I grew up with him, you know? He was my big hero. He was *the* Bond. When the first Bond came out, that was my timeout from the world. And of course, when I found out later that they wanted me for the role of Octopussy, with Roger Moore as Bond, I thought about it. But then Irvin Kershner, the director, told me that he was doing this film where Sean Connery was returning, and he asked me if I wanted to be in it. I said yes, yes, absolutely, without even seeing the script or anything. I was still new at the time, and I knew if I did this for him, it would put me on the map around the world. Everyone would know who I was.'

Austrian actor Klaus Maria Brandauer had come to prominence as a self-absorbed actor in *Mephisto* (1981). *Never Say Never Again* was a breakthrough role for Kim Basinger, leading to *The Natural* (1984), *9½ Weeks* (1986), *Batman* (1989) and ultimately to an Oscar for *LA Confidential* (1997). Swedish film legend Max von Sydow has made eleven films with Ingmar Bergman, as well as *Flash Gordon* with Timothy Dalton (1980) and many others since including Oscar nominations for *Pelle the Conqueror* (1987) and *Extremely Loud & Incredibly Close* (2011).

Comedy writer Dick Clement provided some re-writes to the script. 'The script was a terrible mess,' he told *The Independent* in 1997. 'For example, the scene moves from the south of France to the Bahamas, and we looked and looked and looked and said, 'There isn't one line in this script to actually suggest why they've gone to the Bahamas.' I went to the producer and said, 'Why are they in the Bahamas? And he said, 'That's a very good question. Mostly because there's a film unit already shooting sharks there.' I said, 'I think we can improve on that'.' [51]

And in *The Battle for Bond* he's quoted saying: 'I remember saying to Sean once, 'In the script you have a bonk in the morning, then you've got this whole underwater sequence where you wrestle with sharks, and you come out and you have another bonk in the afternoon. That proves something.' 'Yeah,' he said. 'That proves it's a movie.''

Without the gun barrel sequence, the pre-credits scene is really an under-the-credits scene, as we see an energetic James Bond failing a routine training exercise. The theme song, by Lani Hall (remember her? thought not) is insipid. After a short scene introducing Blofeld, who appears for only about five minutes in this film, M orders Bond to a health clinic to get back into shape. The nurse at Shrublands is called Patricia, as in *Thunderball*. She avoids Bond's advances. But shortly afterwards, she knocks on his bedroom door with a tray of lentil delight, dandelion salad and goats' cheese. Bond opens his suitcase to reveal some beluga caviar, quail's eggs, vodka and foie gras, surely a Moore/Bond move? Meanwhile, Jack Petachi, of the US Airforce has checked into Shrublands with his 'nurse', the totally bonkers Fatima Blush, actually SPECTRE No. 12. He's had a replica of the President's eye implanted. She beats him up for smoking a cigarette. Having been spotted spying on Blush and Petachi, Bond is attacked in the gym later on by Bomber from *Auf Wiedersehn, Pet*. A fight rages through the building, until Bond throws his urine sample into Lippe's eyes and he backs into a shelf of glass that impales him.

SPECTRE's plan to steal nuclear missiles goes ahead. Fatima kills Jack by throwing a snake into his car, causing him to crash. In London, under orders from the Foreign Secretary, M reactivates the double-0 section and Bond is assigned the task of tracking down the missing weapons. There is a humorous scene with Q, which includes the best line of the film ('Good to see you Mr. Bond. Things've been awfully dull 'round here. I hope we're going to see some gratuitous sex and violence.'). Bond picks up a white, cylindrical device.

Bond: What is this for?
Q: I'll show you. You unscrew it, then stick it up your nose. It's for my sinus.

In the Bahamas, OO7 meets his contact, Nigel Small-Fawcett, in an embarrassingly unfunny cameo by pre-Bean Rowan Atkinson. Bond sees Fatima Blush water-skiing while he has a drink. She skis up a ramp to the bar, and lands in Bond's arms. 'Oh, how reckless of me. I've made you all wet,' she apologises. 'Yes, but my martini is still dry,' quips OO7. He meets Domino Petachi, the pilot's sister, and her wealthy lover, the nerdy Maximillian Largo,

SPECTRE's highest-ranking agent. Largo is an intriguing villain, nicely played, with surface geniality but Fleming's hint of madness within.

> The pale eyes swivelled to meet his. There was a quick red glare in them. It was as if the safety door of a furnace had swung open. The blaze died. The door to the inside of the man was banged shut. Now the eyes were opaque again – the eyes of an introvert, of a man who rarely looks out into the world but is for ever surveying the scene inside him.
> From Ian Fleming's James Bond novel, *From Russia With Love.* [53]

Blush and Largo are by far the best bits of *Never Say Never Again*. Blush and Bond make love to a saxophone musical backdrop and then go diving. She sticks something on his oxygen tank. Whatever it is attracts some radio-controlled sharks.

Small-Fawcett confirms that Largo's yacht is now heading for Nice, France. There, Bond joins forces with his French contact Nicole, and his CIA counterpart and friend, Felix Leiter. Bond goes poses as a masseur in a health centre (Connery in grey sweatpants) and learns that Largo is hosting an event at a casino that evening. Largo asserts his superiority by inviting Bond to play a 3-D video game called Domination. The loser receives a series of electric shocks or pays a corresponding cash bet. Bond ultimately wins through skill and simply being tougher than Largo. Instead of taking the cash prize, Bond asks to dance with Domino. And so, here's a first. James Bond dancing the tango. Add this to Bond in dungarees, Bond on a bicycle, Bond in a V-neck sweater, Bond eating an apple and Bond on a motorcycle. [53]

Bond tells Domino that her brother had been killed on Largo's orders. He returns to his villa to find Nicole drowned. After a vehicle chase on his Q-branch motorbike, Blush captures Bond. In the best scene of the film, a taut, watchful, probably insane Fatima holds Bond at gunpoint. We get this wonderful dialogue.

> Blush: You're quite a man, Mr James Bond. But I am a superior woman. [She lowers her gun towards his crotch] Guess where you get the first one.
> Bond: Well, in view of your hatred of men...
> Blush: Liar! You know that making love to Fatima was the greatest pleasure of your life.
> Bond: Well, to be perfectly honest, there was this girl in Philadelphia...
> Blush: Shut up! I am the best.
> Bond: Yes. Yes, you're right. In fact, I was going to put you in my memoirs as number one.
> Blush: All right. [She throws him a newspaper] Write! Now write this... The greatest rapture in my life was afforded me in a boat in Nassau by Fatima Blush. Signed, James Bond, OO7.
> Bond: I just remembered. It's against service policy for agents to give out endorsements.

Disappointingly, he kills her with a Q-branch-issue fountain pen.

'I worked on the character for about a month', said Barbara Carrera, 'and then finally one day it came to me, the idea of Kali, the Hindu goddess. People think of Kali as very bad, she comes and she destroys things. But what Kali actually does is she destroys negativity. Wherever there is negativity, she comes in as a storm, or fire, or pestilence. And then another thought came to me – black widow spiders. A black widow spider will always make love to its prey before it kills it. So I thought, Kali, black widow spider, what a good combination for this character, because Fatima makes love to her prey and then annihilates them, she takes them to the heights of ecstasy and takes away their bad life and gives them a new life, a rebirth.' [54]

The film never quite recovers from this moment on.

Bond and Leiter attempt to board Largo's motor yacht, the Flying Saucer, in search of the missing nuclear warheads. Bond finds Domino in see-through gym wear. He attempts to make Largo jealous by kissing her in front of a two-way mirror. In another key scene, Largo becomes enraged and sets to with an axe. Largo traps Bond and takes him and Domino, somewhat randomly, to Palmyra, his base of operations in North Africa. Largo punishes Domino for her betrayal by selling her to some passing Arabs. Yep, misogyny at its worst. Not good. Bond subsequently escapes from his prison with a watch-mounted laser and rescues Domino on horseback.

We stumble to the studio-bound, by-the-numbers finale. Bond reunites with Felix Leiter on a US Navy submarine and with the help of Domino's pendant, they track Largo to a location known as the Tears of Allah on the Ethiopian coast. Bond and Leiter infiltrate the facility and a gun battle ensues. Bond fights Largo in an underwater scene that is mercifully much shorter than those in *Thunderball*. Just as Largo tries to use a spear gun to shoot Bond, he is shot by Domino, taking revenge for her brother's death. It's not at all clear how she came to be in that precise place at that precise moment.

Bond returns to the Bahamas with Domino:

Domino: You'll never give up your old habits, James.
Bond: No, you're wrong. Those days are over. [Small-Fawcett appears]
Small-Fawcett: I'm sorry, Mr Bond. Obviously caught you at a bad moment.
Bond: M sent you!
Small-Fawcett: Only to plead for your return, sir. M says without you in the service he fears for the security of the civilised world.
Bond: Never again.
Domino: Never?

Connery finally exits his most famous role with a smile and a wink.

Kevin McClory died in November 2006. He never abandoned the idea of remaking *Thunderball* for a second time, including a late-80s plan to recycle an early version of *Never Say Never Again* as a projected film called *Atomic Warfare* (his choice for James Bond: Pierce Brosnan) and a late-90s plan to produce *Doomsday 2000*, which would have opened on 31 December 1999 in direct competition with *The World Is Not Enough*. Largo would be played by Wesley Snipes, M by Geoffrey Palmer, Gwyneth Paltrow would appear as Domino and, wait for it, 68-year old Sean Connery would return as James Bond. Danjaq – Eon's parent company and owners of the Bond screen rights – acquired all rights and interests of Kevin McClory's estate in 2013. MGM, Danjaq and the McClory estate issued a statement saying that they had brought to an 'amicable conclusion the legal and business disputes that have arisen periodically for over 50 years.'

Should you watch *Never Say Never Again*? Well, yes. Connery, Carrera and Brandauer are worth a look for sure. But sit through at least twenty of the twenty-five Eon films first, please.

Ah, yes, James, it is good to have you back again. It is good to see the way you smile from under lowered eyebrows, and the way you bark commands in a sudden emergency, and it is good to see the way you look at women. Other secret agents may undress women with their eyes. You are more gallant. You undress them, and then thoughtfully dress them again. You are a rogue with the instincts of a gentleman.

It has been 12 years since Sean Connery hung it up as James Bond, 12 years since *Diamonds Are Forever*, and Connery's announcement that he would 'never again' play special agent OO7. What complex instincts caused him to have one more fling at the role, I cannot guess. Perhaps it was one morning in front of the mirror, as he pulled in his gut and reflected that he was in pretty damn fine shape for 53. And then, with a bow in the direction of his friend Roger Moore, who has made his own niche as a different kind of Bond, Sean Connery went back on assignment again.

There's more of a human element in the movie, and it comes from Klaus Maria Brandauer, as Largo. Brandauer is a wonderful actor, and he chooses not to play the villain as a cliché. Instead, he brings a certain poignancy and charm to Largo, and since Connery always has been a particularly human James Bond, the emotional stakes are more convincing this time.

Sean Connery says he'll never make another James Bond movie, and maybe I believe him. But the fact that he made this one, so many years later, is one of those small show-business miracles that never happen. There was never a Beatles reunion. Bob Dylan and Joan Baez don't appear on the same stage anymore. But here, by God, is Sean Connery as Sir James Bond. Good work, OO7.

Roger Ebert, October 1983

A View to A Kill

Albert R Broccoli presents Roger Moore as Ian Fleming's James Bond OO7 in *A View to A Kill*

'Has James Bond finally met his match?'

Release Date: 22 May 1985. Running time: 131 minutes. Distributed by MGM / United International. Producers: Albert R Broccoli (14 of 17), Michael G. Wilson (1 of 12)
James Bond: Roger Moore (7 of 7), M: Robert Brown (2 of 4), Q: Desmond Llewelyn (12 of 17), Moneypenny: Lois Maxwell (14 of 14) with Geoffrey Keen (Fredrick Gray) (5 of 6), Walter Gotell (General Gogol) (5 of 6).
And Christopher Walken (Max Zorin) with Tanya Roberts (Stacey Sutton), Grace Jones (May Day), Patrick Macnee (Sir Godfrey Tibbett), Patrick Bauchau (Scarpine), David Yip (Chuck Lee), Willoughby Gray (Dr. Carl Mortner).
Director: John Glen (3 of 5). Screenplay by Richard Maibaum (11 of 13), Michael G. Wilson (3 of 5). Production design: Peter Lamont (3 of 9). Main titles: Maurice Binder (12 of 14). Music: John Barry (10 of 11). Theme song performed by Duran Duran. Cinematography: Alan Hume (3 of 3). Edited by Peter Davies (2 of 3).

Plot

James Bond recovers a microchip from the body of a deceased colleague in Siberia. Investigations lead to Max Zorin and his bodyguard, May Day, who are scheming to cause massive destruction in Silicon Valley and give him a monopoly over the microchip industry.

Cast

John Glen's most commercially successful Bond film, *Octopussy*, ensured that Roger Moore would return one last time. 'MGM/UA put pressure on Cubby to do another Bond with Roger,' John Glen writes. 'I think that everyone knew that Roger was nearing the end of his Bond career but the temptation to safeguard the elements that had made *Octopussy* such as success was too great to resist. There was an understanding that *A View to A Kill* would be his farewell performance and he entered into it with great enthusiasm.' [55]

On paper, the supporting cast was terrific – Christopher Walken, Grace Jones, Patrick Macnee. On film, however, these three are less than stellar. Christopher Walken – a fine actor and first Oscar winner to take on the Bond villain role – goes over the top as the over-zealous, psychopathic megalomaniac Max Zorin. Reined in, or perhaps played against a livelier, younger lead, his performance would have been mesmerising.

'Walken's performance slyly destabilises some formulaic tropes of the Bond film series to notable effect,' writes Andrew McNess. 'For instance, while Zorin is disconcerted by the possibility that Bond will uncover his various schemes, he would not appear especially threatened by Bond as a personal rival. When Bond beds May Day, Zorin registers faint bemusement rather than aggravation.' [56]

Astonishingly David Bowie met the producers before Walken was cast but was unable to commit to several months' shooting.

Patrick Macnee, despite being less agile than Roger Moore, has lots of fun, matching Moore's levity with tongue firmly in cheek: a Persuader and an Avenger reprising their joint lead in 1976's forgettable *Sherlock Holmes in New York*. [57]

The model and singer Grace Jones, hot from her success as Zula the Amazonian in *Conan the Destroyer*, is wasted in a badly written role: a stalking presence in the first half of the film but ultimately just another baddy-who-turns-good-to-assist-Bond. See also Pussy Galore and Jaws. As a female henchman (henchperson?) she's way, way out of the league of the likes of Rosa Klebb, Irma Bunt, Fiona Volpe and Helga Brandt. Then again, Jones wasn't necessarily cast for her acting skills. She always looks amazing in *View to a Kill*. And seriously intimidating.

> *Starlog:* It must be fun working with Grace Jones.
> Roger Moore: Well, if you keep out of the way of her feet and her handbag, yes. [58]

Tanya Roberts was cast as Stacey Sutton after Priscilla Presley turned Eon down. Roberts played one of *Charlie's Angels* in the fifth season of the ABC crime drama (1980-1981) and the title role in *Sheena: Queen of the Jungle* (1984) for which she was nominated for a Golden Raspberry as worst actress of 1984 – a feat she repeated in 1985 for *View to a Kill*. [59] David Yip as Bond's American contact was familiar to UK TV viewers as *The Chinese Detective* (1981-1982). Robert Brown, Geoffrey Keen, Walter Gotell, Desmond Llewelyn and Lois Maxwell all appear again.

Theme Song

A powerful and exciting pop song by 80s popsters Duran Duran, entertaining and fit-for-purpose, despite Simon Le Bon's verging-on-flat vocals.

Production

A View to A Kill was filmed between June 1984 and spring 1985 at Pinewood Studios, Buckinghamshire and on location in the United Kingdom, Iceland, Switzerland, France and the United States.

Observations

Roger Moore's final Bond is, I'm afraid, the worst of the lot. Shame. It's difficult to find anything positive to write about this confused, dull, dreadful film. At 57, Roger Moore looks like he's still having a fabulous time. 'I felt a little long in the tooth,' he wrote thirty years later. 'But I was pretty fit and still able to remember lines. I slipped into the tuxedo – it had been let out a bit since my first film – one last time.' [60]

The twinkle in his eye is there and Moore clearly revels in the deep irony in playing a wrinkled, bouffant-haired, globe-trotting, secret agent grandfather who awkwardly jogs through action scenes. But his age? It shows, it really does.

A metaphor for the film as a whole might be inferred from the disaster that burned down the OO7 Stage at Pinewood in June 1984, during pre-production.

Above: Daniel Craig makes his final appearance in the long-delayed *A Time To Die* in 2021.

Below: *No Time to Die*. Daniel Craig and Léa Seydoux on set in Matera, Italy, August 2019.

Left: 'Bond, James Bond' – Sean Connery in the opening scene of *Dr. No*.

Right: George Lazenby was a bold choice to play James Bond in the sixth official film: *On Her Majesty's Secret Service*.

Left: The man who saved Bond. Roger Moore takes James Bond into the 1970s.

Right: Timothy Dalton. The connoisseur's Bond?

Left: Pierce Brosnan – a Bond for the 1990s.

Right: Daniel Craig as the sixth official Bond, whose five-film tenure lasted from 2006 to 2021.

Above: Ursula Andress as Honey Rider emerges from the sea. 'Are you looking for shells?' she asks Bond. 'No,' he replies, 'just looking.'

Below: Lois Maxwell (Moneypenny), Bernard Lee (M) and Sean Connery in *From Russia With Love.*

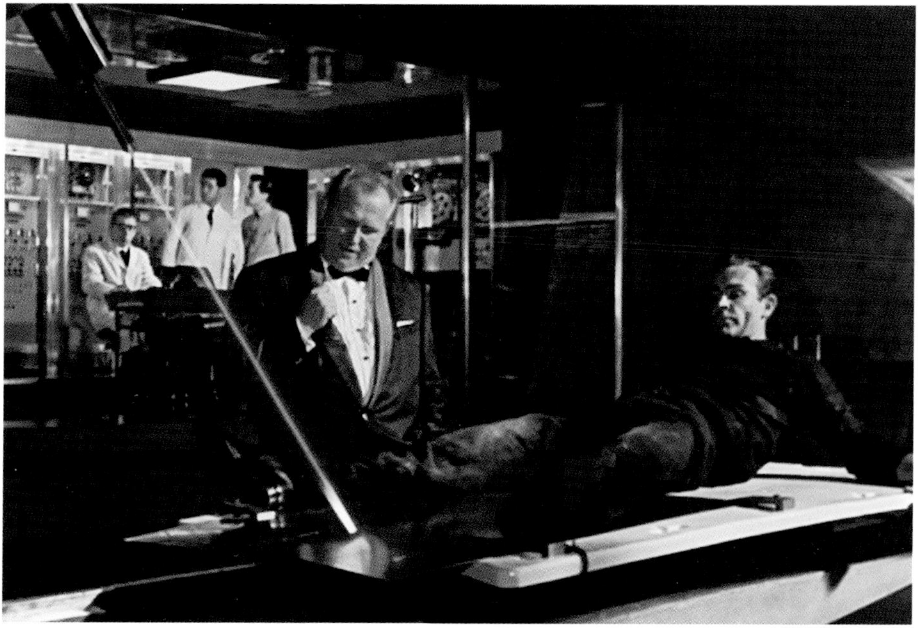

Above: 'No, Mr Bond, I expect you to die!' Sean Connery and Gert Fröbe in *Goldfinger*. Never bettered.

Below: Luciana Paluzzi as Fiona Volpe in *Thunderball.*

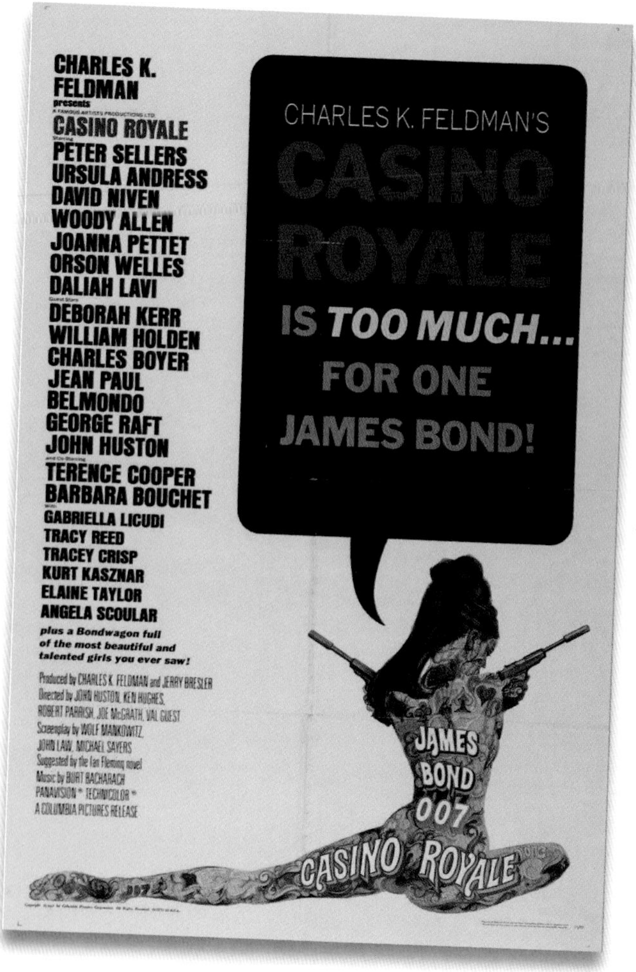

Above: The rogue version of *Casino Royale*. Tread carefully.

Below: Donald Pleasance initiates a million parodies as Blofeld in *You Only Live Twice.*

Above: Diana Rigg as Contessa Teresa di Vicenzo, briefly Mrs Tracy Bond in *On Her Majesty's Secret Service.*

Below: Sean Connery returns in *Diamonds are Forever*, with the gold-digger Plenty O'Toole, played by Lana Wood.

Above: Roger Moore's first scene as OO7, here with Bernard Lee as M, in *Live and Let Die*.

Below: Maud Adams, Hervé Villechaize and the incomparable Christopher Lee in *The Man with the Golden Gun.*

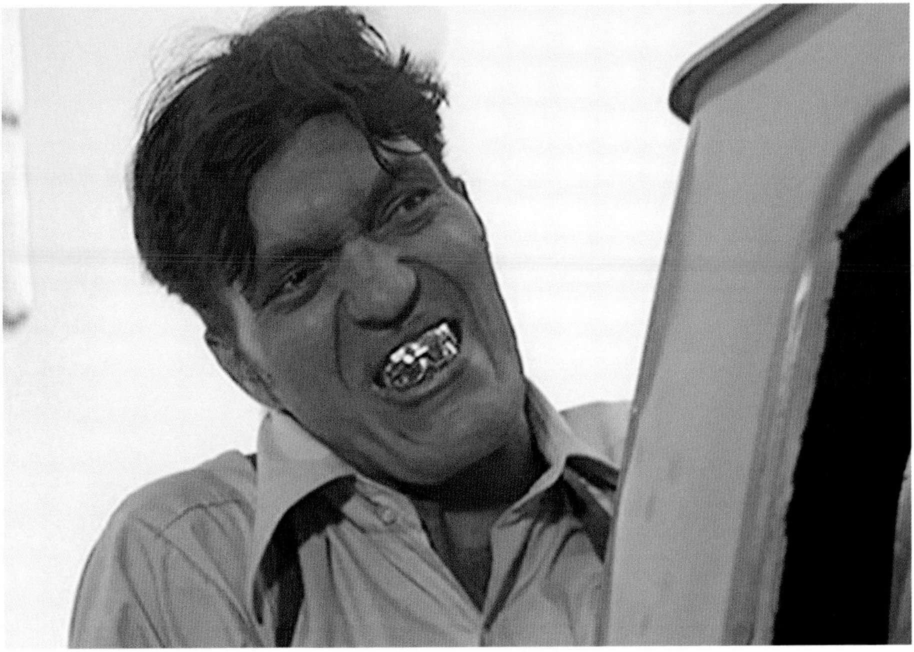

Above: Richard Kiel as Jaws, one of the great Bond villains, in *The Spy Who Loved Me*.

Below: One of the series' low-points: the hover-gondola in *Moonraker.*

Above: Roger Moore in a genuinely tense scene in *For Your Eyes Only*.

Below: 1983 saw two Bond films released; the 'official' one was the flawed *Octopussy* with Roger Moore.

Left: The other film from 1983 saw Sean Connery return in *Never Say Never Again*. It's also flawed, but better than you might recall.

Above: Christopher Walken and Grace Jones in *A View to a Kill*.

Above: Olivia D'Abo and Timothy Dalton in *The Living Daylights*. She's forgotten her cello. He's not happy.

Below: Robert Davi, award-winning actor, screenwriter, director, producer and jazz vocalist. Perfectly cast as Sanchez in *Licence to Kill*.

Above: The wonderful Judi Dench as M in *GoldenEye*, the first of her eight appearances.

Below: Pierce Brosnan in his second film as Bond, and Michelle Yeoh in *Tomorrow Never Dies*.

Above: Was Sophie Marceau as Elektra King in *Tomorrow Never Dies* the best female lead of all? Perhaps.

Below: Haile Berry as Jinx in *Die Another Day*. The worst female lead of all? Perhaps.

Above: Daniel Craig as the sixth official James Bond in *Casino Royale.*

Below: The poster for *Quantum of Solace*, the first direct Bond sequel.

Above: Javier Bardem is scintillating as Raoul Silva in *Skyfall*, especially the 'Now they only eat rat' scene.

Below: Bond and Dr Madeline Swann in the closing moments of *Spectre*.

A View to A Kill takes its title and French setting from a fabulous Ian Fleming short story published in 1960. Well, most of its title, as the original story is called *From A View to A Kill*, and this was the original title for this film in which the basic premise of *Goldfinger* is updated to 1980s Silicon Valley. But it's not quite business as usual. This was always going to be Moore's last outing and is simultaneously silly and empty, despite the high levels of craft. Perhaps the lack of emotional heart of the film is made obvious in the opening moments of the credits – a woman unzips her jacket and the numbers OO7 are projected on her breasts in neon.

A View to A Kill opens with a forgettable pre-titles sequence as Bond recovers a microchip from OO3's body in Siberia. This sequence was filmed on the Jökulsárlón glacier lagoon in Iceland and on Piz Bernina in Switzerland. It re-hashes the ski-ing scenes from *The Spy Who Loved Me* and *For Your Eyes Only*, two of the last three Bond films. The stunts, filmed again by Willy Bogner, are undoubtedly spectacular but offer nothing new. Unless we include Bond inventing snowboarding with the broken runner from a snowmobile. Regrettably the soundtrack cuts to 'California Girls', not by The Beach Boys whose publisher would not release the rights of the original, but by a soundalike band. This is not so much a wink at the audience but a gurn.

In a trope we've seen once too often, OO7 makes a rendezvous with a submarine disguised as an iceberg. It is being piloted by Agent Jones, a lady submariner played by former Miss World Mary Stävin.

> 'Be a good girl, would you, and put it on automatic. And call me James, it's five days to Alaska.' [61]

Whatever did they do? Jigsaw puzzles? Crochet? Browse the walk-in bath catalogues?

After the opening titles, we have the customary briefing in M's office. It's all very familiar and a little too cosy. Q gives Bond several gadgets – polarising sunglasses, a miniature camera in a ring, a billfold with an ultraviolet light, a bug detector in an electric razor, a credit card for opening windows ... need we go on? Roger Moore clearly has no idea what he's saying as he explains the plot ('Until recently, all microchips were susceptible to damage from the intense magnetic pulse of a nuclear explosion. One burst in outer space over the UK and everything with a microchip in it, from the modern toaster to sophisticated computers and our defence systems, would be rendered useless'). Poor Desmond Llewelyn stumbles over the phrase 'silicon integrated circuit'. Bond, M, Moneypenny and Q go to Ascot races to get a look at Max Zorin, the owner of the company which manufactured the microchip found with OO3, and his striking bodyguard May Day. Patrick Macnee, in a warm performance, is introduced as Sir Godfrey Tibbett ('Our department'). The contrast between the youthful, vigorous Christopher Walden (41) and Grace Jones (36) contrasts markedly with the ageing MI6 team: Moore (56), Maxwell (57), Macnee (62),

Brown (62) and Llewelyn (69). These scenes were filmed at Royal Ascot in summer 1984 during an actual racing event, with some close-ups and inserts at Pinewood.

Bond travels to the Eiffel Tower in Paris to meet his contact, the sleazy Achille Aubergine (Jean Rougerie), a detective hired by the French Jockey Club. Aubergine is killed by a butterfly on a fishing rod. Bond pursues his murderer, May Day, but his shooting skills have dropped off alarmingly since he pinged Drax's hidden assassin a few years before. May Day parachutes from the Eiffel Tower. Once again, stunt jumper BJ Worth performed this for real: you can see a diving board added to the tower to give him the lateral distance needed to clear the superstructure. Bond commandeers a car and gives chase. Again, this sequence was supervised by Rémy Julienne and involved driving down the steps Pont d'Léna and speeding along the Port de la Bourdonnais towards the Pont Alexandre III. During the chase Bond's car loses both its roof and its back half. By now, James Bond is surely the world's least discrete secret agent. May Day escapes with Zorin on a speedboat, the Pont des Invalides is visible behind. So far, *A View to A Kill* has been fast-moving with tight, short scenes. The rest of the film moves from boring to ludicrous, from silly to merely awkward.

Bond and Tibbett go undercover as James St. John Smythe at Zorin's house, the magnificent Château de Chantilly in Picardie. Their interplay is warm and witty. Jenny Flex (18-year-old Alison Doody in her first major film role) tells Bond that she 'loves an early morning ride'. During a lengthy garden party scene, Bond spots Stacey Sutton – the sexy saxophone on the soundtrack alerts Bond that here's one of his future conquests – and smarmily suggests that 'she'd certainly bear closer inspection'. In close succession, we get two unlikely gadgets, anti-glare sunglasses and a cheque-book reader. I know we're supposed to suspend disbelief, but when the development of the plot hangs on Bond having just the right gadget in his pocket then we are allowed to shout 'lazy writing' or 'formulaic', or both.

After one of the horses vanishes, Bond does some snooping with Tibbett. Zorin's lab yields a clue ('these microchips are programmed to control an injection of additional natural horse steroids'), then Bond and Tibbett despatch some heavies in packing crates. Part of this was filmed at the Renault Building in very un-French Swindon. 'It's all wrapped up,' quips 007.

In one of the best scenes in the film, Zorin, usually detached and dismissive, practices judo with May Day. The sexual tension is palpable in this erotically charged scene. As Bond races to get back, May Day recalls seeing him in Paris. Bond is unable to get back to his own room, so sneaks into May Day's. Rather than throwing him out, she climbs into bed with him: this is on her terms, not his. According to Charles Burnetts, this scene is 'an over-determined conquest between historic colonizer and oppressed … her dominance of him redressing the historical corollary; she … sits astride a surprised yet happily resigned Bond'. [62]

May Day kills Tibbett in a car wash, and Zorin challenges Bond to a booby-trapped steeplechase race and we get thirty seconds of decent action and a nice exchange of words.

Bond: Killing Tibbett was a mistake.
Zorin: I'm about to make the same one twice.
Bond: My department know I'm here. They'll retaliate.
Zorin: If you're the best they have, they'll more likely try to cover up your incompetence.
Bond: Don't count on it, Zorin.
Zorin: You amuse me, Mr Bond.
Bond: Well, it's not mutual.

Imagine these lines being spoken by Connery or Craig, Dalton or Brosnan. Delicious.

An unconscious Bond, the expired Tibbett and their Rolls-Royce are pushed into a lake at Wraysbury in Surrey, a few miles from Pinewood. Bond escapes. The next five minutes lift the film slightly as an unexpected visit from General Gogol sees Zorin ticked off ('No-one ever leaves the KGB'). One of Gogol's attendants is Dolph Lundgren in his screen debut.

A reworking of the cabal planning scene from *Goldfinger* provides some much-needed exposition. This film's Mr Solo, the one dissenting voice, the sacrificial lamb, is thrown from an airship. The rejoinder 'does anyone else want to drop out?' doesn't have quite the same ring as 'he had a pressing engagement', although Walken skilfully underplays the delivery.

And so, to San Francisco. Bond meets his CIA contact Chuck Lee (David Yip) at Fisherman's Wharf. Felix Leiter must have been on leave. Maud Adams makes a fleeting appearance in her third Bond film in the background of one of the crowd scenes. Spying on Zorin in his oil pumping station, Bond hears the phrase 'main strike'. He encounters two Soviet agents sent by Gogol to snoop on Zorin, a man and a woman: one is shredded by a water turbine, the other is an old flame of Bond's, Pola Ivanova (Fiona Fullerton), who helps him escape. How convenient. They share a hot tub at the Nippon Relaxation Spa, aka 1705 Buchanan St, San Francisco and we have this excruciating dialogue:

Pola [as Bond massages her shoulders]: That feels wonderful.
Bond: Feels even better from where I'm sitting. Would you like it harder?
Pola: James, you haven't changed. Let's put on something more ... inspirational.
Bond: Why not?
[He gets out to change the cassette tape. She switches on the hot tub water jets.]
Pola: Oh!
Bond: Are you all right?
Pola: The bubbles tickle my ... Tchaikovsky!

Going undercover as journalist James Stock, Bond interviews a state official at the City Hall, sees Stacey Sutton once again, and follows her home. The shots of the Sutton estate were filmed at Dunsmuir Hellman Historic Estate in Oakland, across the bay from San Francisco.

Bond offers to cook her dinner after a shoot-out with some baddies. Stacey explains that she's only got leftovers, but Bond manages to whip up a quiche. Yep, quiche. Easier for Roger to chew? Or just a wry nod to future Bond scriptwriter Bruce Feirstein's best-selling tongue-in-cheek look at contemporary masculinity, *Real Men Don't Each Quiche*, that sold millions of copies in 1982-1983?

We get some light flirtation and an intriguing back story about Stacy's family, but Moore and Roberts are very much going through the motions as actors. Dull isn't the word. Well, yes it is, in fact. Bond and Stacey go to City Hall and break in to find out what Zorin is up to. But Zorin and May Day are already there. They kill Howe, the mayor, after some splendid expository dialogue.

Howe: What's going on?
Zorin: Tell them... there's been a break-in. Ask them to get here as soon as possible. You're being used, Mr Howe.
Howe: What have they done?
Zorin: You discharged her. So she and her accomplice came here to kill you. Then they set fire to the office to conceal the crime, but they were trapped in the elevator. And perished in the flames.
Howe: But that means I would have to be...
Zorin: Dead. That's rather neat. Don't you think?

As promised, Zorin and May Day trap Bond and Stacey in a lift which they set on fire. Bond climbs out into the lift shaft, while Stacey hangs on and screams for Bond not to leave her. She does this a lot.

'Diane Feinstein, the Mayor of San Francisco, gave us permission to stage a fire at City Hall, which is a beautiful building that filmmakers often use to double for the White House. [Special effects supervisor] John Richardson put down big steel sheets to protect the roof during the fire, then set light to butane jets to give the impression of a roaring blaze.' [63]

Bond and Stacey make it to the roof, and he carries her down a ladder. He nearly slips at one point. That's about as tense as this film gets. They steal a fire truck – a forced sequel to previous chases in a moon buggy, tuk-tuk and a double-decker bus. The hapless cops follow them. This is mere slapstick. The scene at Lefty O'Doul 3rd Street Bridge is so cliched as to be simply laughable (but not funny).

The exterior scenes at the abandoned Main Strike silver mine were filmed at the Amberley Chalk Pits in Surrey, with an enormous interior set built at Pinewood that echoes the previous year's *Indiana Jones and the Temple of Doom*. This entire section of the film is dreary, risible and tasteless, as though

Glen and his team were intent on remaking the 1974 Charlton Heston / Ava Gardner disaster film *Earthquake*. The wild-eyed Zorin machine guns as many of his men as he can and makes his escape in an airship.

Roger Moore:

> I did not go to 'rushes' every day … to see what we shot the day before, which I normally did. So it came as a surprise to me when I saw the premiere … to see so much violence. It seemed to me a much more violent film than any of the Bonds I'd done up till then. I preferred the old-style Bond – not so many people were killed at the one time.

For the finale, Bond heads for a showdown with Zorin on the Golden Gate Bridge. These scenes were completed on three sets at Pinewood, including a full-size replica of some of the bridge on the back lot and parts filmed in the studio with front projection of the roadway and bay below. 'Most of what is shot on the Bond films is real,' writes John Glen. 'There is very little fakery. The 'secret', if there is one, is to cut-together footage from numerous different sources in such a way that the audience is given as strong a perception as possible that what they're watching is really happening. In this instance, the combination of studio, location and model shots was very successful.' [64] No amount of dramatic John Barry music can lift this above tedium, however. Bond prevails and we head to the closing scene. Q's spy robot is making its way through Stacey's house. M asks Q, 'What's the position?'. 'Oh, James,' sighs Stacy. End credits, at last.

There's so little to enjoy in *A View to A Kill* that it makes *Octopussy* look like a lost masterpiece. Who can forget Bond escaping certain drowning by sucking the air out of a car's tyre? Or Christopher Walken attempting to out-ham Grace Jones? Or the lines 'I've been waiting for you. To take care of me personally' and 'That's not the soap'.

If not for the Bond connection, *A View to A Kill* would have been long forgotten, like, say, *Into the Night*, *Remo Williams*, *Spies Like Us* and *Malibu Express*, all released that same year. Its accident of birth guarantees regular Sunday tea-time TV slots for this turgid, exhausted film in perpetuity.

So farewell then Roger Moore as OO7. Without Moore, without an actor who could carry the role after Sean Connery and the series' upheavals of 1967 to 1971, the Bond films would have ended in 1973. For this, we give thanks. In hindsight, there are many flaws with Moore's portrayal of James Bond, but his amiability, charm, wit and sense of fun shine out in every scene. His chemistry with other actors and his dry delivery of totally ridiculous lines are moments to cherish. Each of his seven films has at least something to recommend it. Even, just, *A View to A Kill*.

> The last hurrah for Roger Moore as OO7, and that nagging sense that retirement was long overdue is transformed into blatant evidence. No matter

how hard they try, the difference between a podgy 58-year-old Moore and his stunt stand-ins was clear as day, and the love scenes with beaming but bland blonde Tanya Roberts is really quite yucky. The jib was up, he'd paid his dues, but this creaking Bond adventure is beyond redemption.

The plot is a failed attempt to rewire *Goldfinger's* global market meltdown strategy for the microchip business – relevant, perhaps, at the time but, frankly, boring in concept. Christopher Walken sleepwalks his way through playing smarmy Nazi geneticist Zorin, where you would think he would have a ball hamming it up as a Bond villain. Indeed, it is a rare moment when Grace Jones makes the biggest impression as an Amazonian (naturally) henchman called May Day. She gets to parachute off the Eiffel Tower; that's cool.

Director John Glen, with master stunt co-ordinator Vic Armstrong, strain every sinew to make the action exciting with fire-engine chase sequences in San Francisco and a grand finale on the Golden Gate Bridge, but no amount of smoke and mirrors can enable us to believe that Roger the Codger is really doing his bit for Queen and country. Although, you have to admit, Duran Duran wrote a cracking theme song.

Ian Nathan, *Empire*, August 2006

[1] *Bond on Bond* (2012).
[2] *Bond on Bond* (2012).
[3] *Typical Men – The Representation of Masculinity in Popular British Cinema* (2003).
[4] *James Bond: A Celebration* (1987).
[5] *Film '83*.
[6] *Roger Moore and the Lighter Side of Bond*, The New Yorker (8 November 2012).
[7] *National Heroes: British Cinema in the Seventies and Eighties* (1985)
[8] *James Bond: A Celebration* (1987).
[9] *Roger Moore as James Bond* (1973). Last two sentences from *Bond on Bond* (2012).
[10] The March 1973 end date is extrapolated from Moore's filming diaries. Explicit dates are not included, but on the last day of shooting Moore mentions that he is immediately heading to California to present an Oscar. The ceremony was held on 27 March 1973.
[11] Seven of the next eight Bond films would be released every other May, June or July through to 1989 – the exception was *The Man With the Golden Gun* which was brought forward six months.
[12] *Roger Moore as James Bond* (1973).
[13] *Roger Moore as James Bond* (1973).
[14] *Roger Moore as James Bond* (1973).
[15] *People* (18 July 1983).
[16] *My Word Is My Bond* (2008).
[17] *Roger Moore as James Bond* (1973).
[18] *Bond on Bond* (2012).
[19] *People* (18 July 1983).
[20] *Tall, Dark and Gruesome* (1997).
[21] *My Word Is My Bond* (2008).
[22] *The New York Times* (22 August 1977) and *For My Eyes Only* (2001).
[23] In *The Living Daylights*, Gogol's first name is Anatol and he has retired from the KGB to become a representative of the Soviet Ministry of Foreign Affairs.

[24] *Martinis, Girls and Guns* (2003).
[25] *The Guardian* (28 September 2012).
[26] Horror has steel-capped teeth. In *The Daily Express* comic strip adaptation (1967-1968), artist Yaroslav Horak's representation of Sluggsy looks very much like Milton Reid, who would appear as Sandor in film version *The Spy Who Loved Me*. This might simply be co-incidence. Reid can be seen as a guard in both *Dr. No* and the 1967 version of *Casino Royale*. He and auditioned for Oddjob in *Goldfinger*.
[27] *GoldenEye – Where Born Was Born: Ian Fleming's Jamaica* (2014).
[28] *My Word Is My Bond* (2008).
[29] Gerardo Valero at rogerebert.com (22 December 2014).
[30] *Roger Moore and the Lighter Side of Bond*, The New Yorker (8 November 2012).
[31] *The Guardian* (28 September 2012).
[32] *People* (18 July 1983).
[33] *For My Eyes Only* (2001).
[34] *GQ* (2012).
[35] *The Daily Star* (26 August 1982).
[36] During discussions, according to John Glen, Glover mentioned a young Irish actor called Pierce Brosnan. This sounds unlikely, as Brosnan had made only a handful of TV and film appearances thus far: his breakout role in the mini-series *Manions of America* was still a year away.
[37] *James Bond: A Celebration* (1987).
[38] *Catching Bullets* (2012).
[39] *James Bond: A Celebration* (1987).
[40] *For My Eyes Only* (2001).
[41] *My Word Is My Bond* (2008).
[42] *For My Eyes Only* (2001).
[43] at denofgeek.com (2016).
[44] John Glen in *For My Eyes Only* (2001).
[45] *GQ* (2012).
[46] Copyright the Ian Fleming Estate.
[47] *For My Eyes Only* (2001).
[48] *For My Eyes Only* (2001).
[49] In *Catching Bullets* (2012).
[50] *My Word Is My Bond* (2008).
[51] *The Independent* (30 November 1997).
[52] Copyright the Ian Fleming Estate.
[53] Pierce Brosnan's Bond has a long motorcycle chase, handcuffed to Michelle Yeoh, in *Tomorrow Never Dies*. Daniel Craig's Bond would ride a motorcycle briefly in *Quantum of Solace* and, thrillingly and at length, in the pre-titles scenes in both *Skyfall* and *No Time To Die*.
[54] *The Battle for Bond* (2007).
[55] *For My Eyes Only* (2001).
[56] *A Close Look at A View to A Kill* (2015), an ambitious but flawed attempt to over-analyse the film and 'illuminate an underrated classic'.
[57] MacNee would reprise his role as Watson in two 1991 films, both with Christopher Lee as Holmes.
[58] *Starlog #96* (July 1985).
[59] Madonna has won the award five times, although not for *Die Another Day*.
[60] *My Word Is My Bond* (2008).

[61] Perhaps co-incidentally, this echoes a line from Fleming's short story: 'Now, be a good girl and do as you're told. Just put my report on the printer to M. He'll see the point of me cleaning this thing up. He won't object.'
[62] *Bond's Bit on the Side – Race, Exoticism and the Bond 'Fluffer' Character*, in *For His Eyes Only: The Women of James Bond* (2015). In the same book, Travis L Wagner suggests that the final scene in *Die Another Day* – when Bond drops diamonds onto Jinx's stomach as foreplay – has 'implications [that] are troubling, especially in the light of the fact that the blood diamond trade in Africa is rooted in colonialism, violence and genocide. Jinx becomes not a point of challenge to Bond as a patriarchal coloniser, but another body to exploit, making the ... scene ... one of the most problematic in the entire [series].' I wonder if someone is taking this all just a little too seriously.
[63] *For My Eyes Only* (2001).
[64] *For My Eyes Only* (2001).

1986–1993: Watch the birdie, you bastard

The Living Daylights

Albert R Broccoli presents Timothy Dalton as Ian Fleming's James Bond 007 in *The Living Daylights*
'The New James Bond… Living on thc Edge'.
Release date: 29 June 1987. Running time: 130 minutes. Distributed by MGM / United International. Producers: Albert R Broccoli (15 of 17), Michael G. Wilson (2 of 12). James Bond: Timothy Dalton (1 of 2), M: Robert Brown (3 of 4), Q: Desmond Llewelyn (13 of 17), Moneypenny: Caroline Bliss (1 of 2), Leiter: John Terry with Geoffrey Keen (Frederick Gray) (6 of 6), Walter Gotell (General Gogol) (6 of 6). And Joe Don Baker (Brad Whitaker) with Maryam d'Abo (Kara Milovy), Jeroen Krabbé (General Georgi Koskov), John Rhys-Davies (General Leonid Pushkin), Art Malik (Kamran Shah), Andreas Wisniewski (Necros, dubbed by Kerry Shale), Thomas Wheatley (Saunders).
Director: John Glen (4 of 5). Screenplay by Richard Maibaum (12 of 13), Michael G. Wilson (4 of 5). Production design: Peter Lamont (4 of 9). Main titles: Maurice Binder (13 of 14). Music: John Barry (11 of 11). Theme song performed by A-Ha. Cinematography: Alec Mills (1 of 2). Edited by John Grover (2 of 3), Peter Davies (3 of 3).

Plot

James Bond assists in the defection of a highly ranked Soviet general who reveals that the new head of the KGB, General Pushkin, is starting up a counterintelligence operation. During the operation, Bond uncovers a plot involving a crooked American arms dealer, the war in Afghanistan and a drug-smuggling ring.

Cast

Roger Moore hung up his Walther PPK for the final time following *A View to A Kill*. 'It was inevitable that we would have to make changes,' said Cubby Broccoli. 'Nothing lasts for ever. We all grow older. [Roger] looked good for his age, but obviously, he couldn't move the way he used to. And the camera kept reminding us of it.'

Initially, the fifteenth Bond film was to have been a full reboot, exploring 007's first mission. Barbara Broccoli went to Australia to look for possible Bonds and brought back videos of twelve actors. These included Andrew Clarke, Sam Neill and Antony Hamilton.

'Andrew Clarke was a front runner for quite some time,' says John Glen. 'But after a while, he had enough and left.' Clarke was very popular in his native Australia in the 1980s and 1990s, appearing in the soap *Sons and Daughters* (1982-1983) and the mini-series *Anzacs* (1985). He would later play The Saint in the television pilot for a new series.

Sam Neill had appeared in films since 1977, most notably in *Omen III: The Final Conflict* (1981). He was perhaps best known for the ITV series *Reilly Ace of Spies*, which was broadcast between September and November 1983.

'Sam Neill was one of the last actors I tested,' said Glen, 'and I remember thinking he was very good indeed.' [1]

Despite being favoured by Michael Wilson and Barbara Broccoli, Neill has subsequently described the audition as a 'bad dream'.

'The lesson I learnt that day,' he told *The Daily Telegraph* in 2018, 'was never be bullied by your agent into going along to something you don't want to do ever again. That was the last time.'

Anthony Hamilton had appeared in the 1984 television film *Samson and Delilah* and the American TV series *Cover Up* (1984-1985). Cubby Broccoli favoured Lambert Wilson, a young, handsome, 28-year old French actor and singer who would later appear in two of *The Matrix* films. Mel Gibson asked for too much money. *Shoestring* star Trevor Eve was tested and names such as Tom Selleck, Anthony Andrews, Nigel Havers and Bryan Brown were mentioned in the press. John James, Jeff Colby in *Dynasty* and *The Colbys*, was hammered by Jean Rook in *The Daily Express*: 'think of him mouthing 'My name is Barned' through that expensive bridgework'.

Meanwhile, another contender caught the eyes of the producers: Irish-born Pierce Brosnan. Brosnan was married to Cassandra Harris, who had portrayed Countess Lisl von Schlaf in *For Your Eyes Only*. [2] Brosnan had visited the set in 1981 and had taken lunch with Cubby Broccoli. His name was linked to the James Bond series as early as mid-1985, with *A View to A Kill* still in the cinemas. Interviewed by Terry Wogan on BBC TV, an almost scarily handsome Brosnan smiled and said, 'it's a wicked rumour, really – fabrication by the press in the US.' Nevertheless, Brosnan was offered the part of James Bond in *The Living Daylights* a few months later, after a three-day screen test. At that time, he was the titular star of the lightweight US TV show *Remington Steele*. The publicity of his Bond audition prompted the show's producers to take up an option to make a new series on the day before Brosnan's contract expired. For now, Brosnan was out of the running.

Broccoli turned again to Timothy Dalton. Dalton had, of course, been approached to play James Bond in 1968. 'It just seemed like a ridiculous notion!' he told Will Harris in 2014. 'I mean, I was very flattered that someone should even think that I should, but I don't know, I was in my early 20s, I think, and… hey, look, on an intelligent level, it just seemed idiotic to take over from Sean Connery. I mean, if I was perfect for it, if I thought I'd be brilliant in it, if I'd loved the idea of taking over, I would've still said no. It is idiotic to take over from Sean Connery at the time when those movies were… I can remember as a kid going to see them. Not a child, but I was a teenager. I mean, you can't take over for Sean Connery in that series at its height! After *Dr. No*, after *From Russia With Love*, after *Goldfinger*… I don't know how many more he did, but to me, those were always the three great ones. You don't take over. So, of course, I said no.' [3]

Forward to 1986, and Dalton, by now 40 years old and the producers' preferred choice, was still unwilling to commit. Broccoli and Wilson auditioned Robert Bathurst, later to find fame on British TV's *Cold Feet*. 'Oh, that was such a ludicrous audition,' Bathurst told *The Scotsman* in 2003. 'I could never have done it – Bond actors are always very different to me. But some casting director persuaded me to go. The thing was, they already had Timothy Dalton. But I think he hadn't signed yet, so they wanted to tell him, 'They're still seeing people, you know,' to put pressure on him to sign. I was just an arm-twisting exercise.'

The tactic paid off. Timothy Dalton's James Bond brought a rough-hewn, harder-edged but more human sensibility to his two films. '[Dalton was] a rare sample of a vanishing breed,' notes Cubby Broccoli. 'A gentleman actor with a tolerable ego.'

'His Bond was dark, morally ambiguous, self-critical and modern,' writes Andrew Spicer. 'Without Connery's leavening humour, the result was a claustrophobic intensity that failed to win over the public.' [4]

Though largely unappreciated in the late 80s, Dalton's gritty portrayal anticipated today's more character-driven Bond: a combination of the power of Daniel Craig with some of the arrogance of Sean Connery. Dalton's take on Bond is terrific and his debut film is very good indeed. What's more, Dalton arguably fits Ian Fleming's description of his hero more than any other actor who had or has played the role.

'I felt it would be wrong to pluck the character out of thin air, or to base him on any of my predecessors' interpretations,' Dalton told *The New York Times* in 1987. 'Instead, I went to the man who created him, and I was astonished. I'd read a couple of the books years ago, and I thought I'd find them trivial now, but I thoroughly enjoyed every one. It's not just that they've a terrific sense of adventure and you get very involved. On those pages, I discovered a Bond I'd never seen on the screen, a quite extraordinary man, a man I really wanted to play, a man of contradictions and opposites.'

'I definitely wanted to recapture the essence and flavour of the books, and play it less flippantly,' he said in 1987. 'After all, Bond's essential quality is that he's a man who lives on the edge. He could get killed at any moment, and that stress and danger factor is reflected in the way he lives, chain-smoking, drinking, fast cars and fast women.' [5]

'Connery was very tough,' he said many years later. 'And I think Moore, when he first took it over was tough, as well, but then he moved into that area that he was probably most comfortable with, having done *The Saint*. We wanted to take it back to that earlier toughness. But, of course, it's got to be funny. It should be funny. Out of great danger often comes great humour.' [6]

Dalton was introduced as the new James Bond in a press conference in Vienna on 5 October 1986. Timothy Leonard Dalton Leggett was born in Colwyn Bay, Wales, on 21 March 1946 and grew up in Belper, Derbyshire. He left school in 1964 to enrol in the Royal Academy of Dramatic Arts, twenty years behind his predecessor Roger Moore, and to tour with the National Youth Theatre. For the next several years, Dalton concentrated on a theatre career, initially with the Birmingham Repertory Theatre (1966), the Prospect Theatre Company (1972-1974) and the Royal Shakespeare Company (1973-1982). He made his film debut as Philip II of France in *The Lion in Winter* (1968), the performance which first attracted the attention of the Bond producers. Dalton returned to cinema in 1978 as the husband of 85-year-old Mae West in *Sextette*. He worked mainly in American television in the early 1980s – *Antony and Cleopatra*, *Mistral's Daughter*, *Sins*. He played Prince Barin in *Flash Gordon* (1980) and Mr. Rochester in a BBC adaptation of *Jane Eyre* (1983).

In a strong supporting cast, the female lead, British former model Maryam D'Abo plays a Czech cellist called Kara Milovy. D'Abo had auditioned for the part of Pola Ivanova in *A View to A Kill*, a role that went eventually to Fiona Fullerton. She had been hired to help during the auditions for the new Bond, recreating the scene in *From Russia With Love* when Bond finds Titania in his bed. American actor Joe Don Baker plays Brad Whitaker, an arms dealer, self-styled general and rare American villain. Baker had made a big impression in the BBC-TV series *Edge of Darkness* (1985) and the film *Lethal Weapon* (1987). Dutch actor Jeroen Krabbé plays General Georgi Koskov, Whitaker's ally and a renegade Soviet general. His most recent success outside his native country had been in the films *Jumping Jack Flash* and *No Mercy* (both 1986). Welsh character actor John Rhys-Davies, a familiar face on British TV in the 1970s and 1980s, appears as General Leonid Pushkin, the new head of the KGB, replacing General Gogol. Pakistani-English actor Art Malik plays Kamran Shah, a leader in the Afghan Mujahideen. Malik's breakthrough roles were *The Jewel in the Crown*, *A Passage to India* and *The Far Pavilions*, all in 1984.

Moneypenny and Leiter were re-cast. British actor, twenty-five-year-old Caroline Bliss was the second Miss Moneypenny and American John Terry (Lockhart in *Full Metal Jacket*) was the sixth Felix Leiter.

Theme Song

A-ha's theme tune is catchy Scandi-pop. John Barry is co-credited as composer. The promo video features various scenes from the film projected on to the band as they perform on the empty 007 Stage. The song was a top ten hit across Europe and a number one in the band's native Norway.

Production

The Living Daylights was filmed between September 1986 and February 1987 at Pinewood Studios, Buckinghamshire and on location in the United Kingdom, Gibraltar, Austria and Morocco.

Observations

Despite Dalton's Bond being the antithesis of Roger Moore's, almost everything else in the film series remains the same – producers, director, screenwriter, M and Q, John Barry, Maurice Binder. What seemed ground-breaking in 1985 now comes across as just more of the same, with a new face, a harder attitude and an unexpected air of romance.

The film opens in Gibraltar, with a thrilling action sequence, typical of fourth-time director John Glen. For once, the pre-titles scene has a direct bearing on the rest of the film. M is briefing OO2, OO4 and OO7, who are about to parachute out of a plane. They must take on the SAS in a paintball match to capture radar installations. 'They put me on the Rock of Gibraltar, on the top of a cliff,' Dalton said in 2010. 'A 700-foot sheer, damned cliff, and I hate heights!' [7]

OO4 is killed when his climbing rope is cut. A message is clipped to his corpse: Smiert Spionam. We see Dalton's face when Bond reacts to OO4's death scream. Already, Dalton's Bond is depicted as a man of action – Connery's Bond was first seen in a casino, Lazenby's hidden behind a hat and glasses and Moore's in a monogrammed silk dressing gown. A fabulous chase across Gibraltar, with Dalton visibly hanging onto the roof of a Jeep, leads to Bond parachuting onto a yacht.

Bond: I need to use your phone.
Linda: Who are you?
Bond: Bond. James Bond. Exercise control, OO7 here. I'll report in an hour.
Linda [offering Bond a glass of champagne]: Won't you join me?
Bond: Better make that two.

Boom!

The next five minutes or so are based on Ian Fleming's 1962 short story, reset from Germany to Slovakia. It provides some undeniably tense moments. Bond is in Bratislava helping Soviet General Koskov defect to Britain. He is to watch for a KGB sniper assigned to shoot the Russian as he escapes from a concert hall during the interval. The exterior was filmed at the Volksopera on Währingerstrasse, in the northwest suburbs of Vienna – the safe house is about 200 metres away – and the interior at the Sofiensäle concert hall in central Vienna. Head of station, Saunders (Thomas Wheatley), calls Bond 'old man'. He'd obviously not seen *From Russia With Love* recently. Bond notices that the sniper is a female cellist from the orchestra. Seeing that she isn't a professional killer, and that they are being played for fools, he disobeys his orders to kill her and shoots the rifle out of her hands. Here is a spy with a conscience.

Saunders: I'm telling M you deliberately missed. Your orders were to kill that sniper.
Bond: Stuff my orders. I only kill professionals. That girl didn't know one end of a rifle from the other. Go ahead. Tell M what you want. If he fires me, I'll thank him for it. Whoever she was, I must have scared The Living Daylights out of her.

Koskov is smuggled in an oil pipeline to Austria. Julie T Wallace has a delightful cameo as an inside aid. Koskov departs to the UK in a Harrier jet from the roof of the Wiener Gasometer.

Back at Universal Exports, we meet the new Miss Moneypenny played by Caroline Bliss. She likes Barry Manilow. Koskov is being debriefed at a safe house, filmed at Stonor Park, Surrey, when Bond arrives with a hamper from Harrod's. There is a sweet moment when M clocks the price of the champagne and raises his eyebrows. 'The brand on the list was questionable, sir,' Bond explains, 'so I chose something else.'

A muscular, blond man, Necros, breaks in dressed as a milkman. Never wanting to pass an opportunity for sponsorship, the milk float has the Unigate logo, the dairy producer active from 1959 to 2000. Apropos of nothing, Unigate's slogan in the Seventies was 'Watch out, there's a Humphrey about'.

Koskov is abducted and is assumed to have been taken back to Moscow. Meanwhile, in a bit of plot exposition, KGB General Pushkin is in Tangier meeting crooked arms dealer Brad Whitaker the Forbes Museum, doubling for Whitaker's house.

> Whitaker: How do you like my personal pantheon of great commanders?
> Pushkin: Butchers.
> Whitaker: Surgeons. They cut away society's dead flesh.

More of them later. At Q's lab ('pay attention, OO7'), Bond is given a key ring with a stun feature, built-in explosive and a skeleton key that can open ninety percent of the world's locks. More of that later, too.

Bond returns to Bratislava to track down Kara Milovy. As with Koskov, we are not quite sure whether Kara is 'good' or 'bad'. He follows her onto a tram and sees her being arrested by the KGB. He recovers her cello case at the tram depot on Kreutzgasse to find her rifle loaded with blanks. In Kara's flat, 92 Antonigasse, he learns that Kara is Koskov's girlfriend and deduces that Koskov's entire defection was staged. Like Kara, Koskov is a sympathetic character, not obviously allied to Bond or to the KGB. After the megalomaniac baddies of the Moore-era Bond, we have, finally, simple espionage: 'a maelstrom of Fleming-friendly paranoia and distracting stalemates in which to toss Bond around.' [8]

Bond convinces her that he is a friend of Koskov's and persuades her to accompany him to Vienna. They trick the KGB and escape in Bond's Aston Martin V8 Vantage, the first time that the iconic car brand has been since *On Her Majesty's Secret Service*. Of course, the car has a few 'optional extras'. The first of these is an update of the wheel-borne tyre shedders from *Goldfinger*, now a laser that Bond uses to cut a police car's body from the chassis. 'Salt corrosion,' Bond remarks drily. He then blows up a roadblock with a missile and deploys at outrigger and wheel spikes for driving on snow. The car is destroyed, so the escape into Austria using Kara's cello case as a sledge. 'We've nothing to declare!' Bond shouts. Despite revisiting some Bond tropes of the past, this sequence feels fresh and is very entertaining.

Bond checks into a hotel with Kara, filmed at Schönbrunn Palace (exterior) and Im Palais Schwarzenberg (interior) in Vienna. The concierge asks if he'd like his usual suite, a conceit that always raises a smile. In an unusual touch, Bond romances Kara at the Wiener Riesenrad ferris wheel at the Prater amusement park, forever linked to the classic Carol Reed film *The Third Man* (1949). Saunders discovers a history of financial dealings between Koskov and Whitaker but is killed by Necros, who again leaves the message 'Smiert Spionam'.

Bond and Pushkin conspire to fake Pushkin's assassination filmed at Elveden Hall, an 18th-century stately hall in Suffolk, later used as Lara Croft's home in the first *Tomb Raider* film. In an unlikely touch, Bond is picked up by two women and is duped by a drugged drink. Koskov shows his true colours.

> Koskov: I'm sorry, James. I have been on a secret mission for General Pushkin to disinform British Intelligence. For you, I have great affection, but we have an old saying: 'Duty has no sweethearts'.
> Bond: We have an old saying, too, Georgi. And you're full of it!

This last line is a slight rewrite of Bond's encounter with Scaramanga in *The Man With the Golden Gun*.

Koskov, Necros, Kara, and the captive Bond fly to a Soviet air base in Afghanistan, filmed at Ouarzazate Airport in Tangier. Koskov betrays Kara and imprisons her and Bond. They escape and free a condemned prisoner, Kamran Shah (Art Malik), leader of the local Mujahideen. We have a classic dry comment from Bond.

> Kara: We're free!
> Bond: Kara, we're in a Russian airbase in the middle of Afghanistan.

Bond discovers Koskov is using Soviet money to buy opium from the Mujahideen to make a quick profit. After visiting the Mujahideen hideout, filmed at the magnificent stronghold of Aït-Ben-Haddou in Morocco, he plants a bomb on board the cargo plane carrying the opium. He is seen by the Soviets and prepares to take off. Meanwhile, in a trademark John Glen action sequence, the Mujahideen attack the air base on horseback. The long shot of the bridge spanning a gorge was achieved with the careful use of a foreground miniature: a five-feet high model placed in front of the camera to force the perspective of the real bridge in the distance and allow director John Glen to zoom and pan. Kara drives a jeep into the cargo hold of the plane as Bond takes off.

Necros also jumps aboard, setting up a thrilling action climax, one of the most spectacular stunts in any Bond film. As Bond and Necros fight as they cling to a cargo net hanging from the back of the plane. This scene was played for real by BJ Worth and Jake Lombard, two of the stunt performers from the opening skydiving sequence in *Moonraker*. It is not for the acrophobic. Eventually, with Necros hanging onto Bond's shoe, Bond cuts the laces and deadpans 'He got the boot.' Perhaps it's not the wittiest or even cheesiest of one-liners, but it is apt for this more serious take on Bond. The interior of the plane was built on a hydraulic rig at Pinewood, allowing pitch and yaw to be controlled. The mountain scenery below was painted by Jaqueline Stears of the Pinewood art department. It's all very impressive.

In a double-whammy postscript, Bond returns to Tangier to kill Whittaker and Pushkin arrests Koskov. Meanwhile, in London, Kara is giving a performance attended by M, Freddie Gray and General Gogol, Walter Gotell in his final scene, his sixth Bond film. The conductor is played by John Barry. *The Living Daylights* was Barry's last score for the Bond series and this neat cameo paid due tribute to his immeasurable contribution across twenty-five years.

Bond surprises Kara in her dressing room, and they embrace.

All in all, *The Living Daylights* is a refreshing and entertaining film – whilst not (yet) a wholesale reinvention of the Bond formula, the script, direction and in particular Timothy Dalton's performance give us much to enjoy. In 1987, Roger Ebert wrote that a combination of a female lead without 'the charisma or the mystique to hold the screen with Bond' and 'a hero with a sense of humour' put *The Living Daylights* 'somewhere on the lower rungs of the Bond ladder'. Thirty-plus years on from Ebert's review, it's clear that *The Living Daylights* is a film of its time. It's a very enjoyable watch and yet a curio. Dalton is terrific with a palpable magnetism as James Bond, the plot is complex but not impenetrable, the stunts and cinematography are impeccable. Despite some failings, it was certainly the best Bond film for ten years, perhaps even since *On Her Majesty's Secret Service*.

If the only thing left of *The Living Daylights* was Maryam d'Abo's smile and the taut early sequence that culminates with Timothy Dalton's 007 deliberately missing a shot at cellist turned sniper Kara Milovy, it would still be my favourite Bond film.

Dalton, the antithesis of his wisecracking predecessor Roger Moore, promised on taking up the tux to approach Bond with 'a sense of responsibility to the work of Ian Fleming'. It was a comment that said much about how far the series had strayed from its roots. Happily, though, Dalton was true to his word; a few almost unbearably tense minutes, based on the short story from which *The Living Daylights* takes its title, was all it took to reassure my teenage self that Bond was in safe hands. Entrusted to Moore, it would have been all over in a quick flurry of one-liners and raised eyebrows. But Dalton draws on Fleming's narrative to convey a sense of Bond's interior life.

Even so, he's not everyone's cup of tea. 'As entertaining as root canal work,' suggested one appraisal of his Bond legacy. And it's true that Dalton's 007, so ruthless and intense – although less so here than in his second outing, *Licence to Kill* – is probably the darkest of the lot. But such comments go too far; Dalton is a Bond way more sinned against than sinning. As with England football managers, so with Bonds: whenever there's a new one, we want him to be the polar opposite of the last bloke. Dalton ticks this box, but that's not to say he's devoid of humour; it's just that the wit is drier and more deadpan. 'We have an old saying too, Georgi – and you're full of it,' he tells Koskov; later – after killing the villainous, military-obsessed arms dealer Brad Whitaker – he quips: 'He met his Waterloo.'

Dalton's more nuanced and complex interpretation came at a time when 007 was in mortal danger. With each film from *Moonraker* on, Moore had become less. Dalton's debut marked a fresh start for a series that – after 25 years of Martinis, Girls and Guns – many felt had shifted irrevocably towards self-parody. It's just a pity that his stay was so brief, because his approach allows Bond's relationships to evolve in ways rarely seen in the earlier films.

This much-maligned film has wheedled its way irrevocably into my affections: uniquely in the world of Bond, it allows a vein of romantic adventure to develop that's real, not illusory. In theory, it's a quality all the Bond films should have, what with their beautiful settings and beautiful people, their idealised tales of good triumphing over evil. In practice, though, they're often a bit of an embarrassment – an antediluvian catalogue of Honeys, Pussys and Plentys. *The Living Daylights* is different; even from a quarter of a century away, there's nothing to sully the romantic air. It's no coincidence that the most recent Bond films are the closest in tone.

Les Roopanarine, *The Guardian*, October 2012

Licence To Kill

Albert R Broccoli presents Timothy Dalton as Ian Fleming's James Bond 007 in *Licence To Kill*

'James Bond is out on his own and out for revenge.'

Release date: 13 June 1989. Running time: 133 minutes. Distributed by MGM/United International. Producers: Albert R Broccoli (16 of 17), Michael G. Wilson (3 of 12)

James Bond: Timothy Dalton (2 of 2), M: Robert Brown (4 of 4), Q: Desmond Llewelyn (14 of 17), Moneypenny: Caroline Bliss (2 of 2), Leiter: David Hedison (2 of 2)

And Robert Davi (Franz Sanchez) with Carey Lowell (Pam Bouvier), Talisa Soto (Lupe Lamora), Anthony Zerbe (Milton Krest), Benicio del Toro (Dario), Pedro Armendáriz Jr. (President Hector Lopez), Priscilla Barnes (Della Churchill). Director: John Glen (5 of 5). Screenplay by Richard Maibaum (13 of 13), Michael G. Wilson (5 of 5). Production design: Peter Lamont (5 of 9). Main titles: Maurice Binder (14 of 14). Music: Michael Kamen. Theme song performed by Gladys Knight. Cinematography: Alec Mills (2 of 2). Edited by John Grover (3 of 3).

Plot

James Bond resigns his post in MI6 and goes rogue on a mission of revenge after a Latin American drug lord maims his close friend Felix Leiter.

Cast

Casting for *Licence to Kill* was particularly strong, with no weak links, even in the minor characters. Timothy Dalton returned as James Bond. Carey Lowell plays Pam Bouvier, an ex-Army pilot, and CIA informant. Bouvier had auditioned for the role after Sharon Stone had been inexplicably passed over. Charismatic and compelling Robert Davi is Franz Sanchez, the most powerful drugs lord in Latin America. For arguably the first time since *The Man With the Golden Gun*, here is a villain that is the protagonist's physical equal and, like Scaramanga, a corrupt mirror image of Bond himself. Davi had most recently appeared in *The Goonies* and *Die Hard*. American former model Talisa Soto is Lupe Lamora, Sanchez's damaged but resourceful girlfriend. Timothy Dalton was unavailable for Talisa Soto's screentest, so Robert Davi filled the role of Bond, and proved, according to John Glen, to be excellent in the part. Anthony Zerbe (Trench in *Harry O*) plays Milton Krest, Sanchez's partner. The name of this character (and that of his boat) comes from Ian Fleming's short story *The Hildebrand Rarity*. There is also an early role for Benicio del Toro as Dario, Sanchez's personal henchman. David Lynch luminary Everett McGill plays corrupt DEA agent Killifer, the hugely experienced Don Stroud is Sanchez' head of security Heller, Las Vegas entertainer Wayne Newton has a lovely cameo as the TV evangelist Professor Joe Butcher, and Frank McRea (*48 Hrs*, *Rocky II*) plays Quarrel III, erm, Sharky. In a neat casting tribute, Pedro Armendáriz Jr. son of Pedro Armendáriz (Kerim Bey in *From Russia With Love*) plays Hector Lopez, the president of Isthmus. Desmond Llewelyn, David Hedison, Robert Brown and Caroline Bliss reprise roles from previous films.

Theme Song

The riff from 'Goldfinger' colours this soulful and sexy Gladys Knight song.

Production

Licence To Kill was filmed between July and November 1988 at Estudios Churubusco, Mexico City and on location in the United States and Mexico.

Observations

Licence To Kill is the fastest-paced and most violent of the Bond series so far: the influence of successful and very American films such as the *Indiana Jones* series (1981, 1984), the first three *Rambo* films (1982-1988), *The Terminator* (1984), *Beverley Hills Cop* and its first sequel (1984-1987), *Lethal Weapon* (1987), *Robocop* (1987) and *Die Hard* (1988) no doubt coloured the producer's visions for this, the 16th film in the series. The violence is never excused away with a quip. At times this film feels like an extended episode of *Miami Vice*. John Glen referenced the original source material. 'In trying to be true to the violent nature of the Fleming stories,' he suggested, 'we had clearly overstepped the mark.' [9]

A lean, sometimes over-earnest film, it was awarded a 15 certificate, but only after several edits. It is saved by the action sequences, John Glen's tight direction, an economical script, Michael Kamen's omnipresent score and the acting performances of Timothy Dalton, Robert Davi, Carey Lowell, Talisa Soto and Desmond Llewelyn.

Licence To Kill is a revenge story with no hint of a super-baddy wanting world domination. This takes the film away from 'action-adventure' and towards pure 'action'. 'The action film is built around a three-act structure centred on survival, resistance and revenge,' writes Harvey O'Brien. 'It is a narrative of social and personal redemption in which the act of will is embodied in the physical body of the hero – tested, traumatised and triumphant.' [10]

This theme of vengeance is a central element of each of Daniel Craig's five Bond films.

A very moody, short-tempered film, *Licence To Kill* was the first Bond picture to be filmed entirely outside of the United Kingdom. After plans to film in China fell through, exterior scenes were mostly filmed in Mexico City and Key West, Florida. Internal sets were built at Estudios Churubusco in Mexico City, mostly for financial reasons. *Conan the Destroyer*, *Dune*, *Rambo: First Blood Part II* and *Romancing the Stone* had been produced at the studios between 1984 and 1986; *Total Recall*, *Honey, I Shrunk the Kids* and *The Hunt for Red October* (with Sean Connery) would be filmed there in 1988-1989. There are no Ken Adam-style huge sets in *Licence To Kill*. Some elements of the script were taken from Ian Fleming's second novel *Live and Let Die*: Felix Leiter being fed to a shark and the shoot-out in the warehouse.

The opening ten minutes set up the entire film. Bond, his old friend Felix Leiter and their pal Sharky are driving through the Florida Keys on the way to Leiter's wedding. A helicopter intercepts them: Leiter's DEA colleagues have news that drugs baron Franz Sanchez is making a rare visit to Crab Key. Sanchez finds his girlfriend, Lupe, with an unlucky suitor ('what did he promise you, his heart?) and whips her with a stingray tail. [11] Lupe is an update of Domino in *Thunderball*: a kept woman who helps Bond, sleeps with Bond and is ultimately freed by him from her bondage. Sorry. Bond and Leiter board the helicopter to arrest Sanchez and there is a shoot-out as they try to take him. Sanchez escapes in a plane. Bond has the helicopter chase him and, in a remarkable stunt performed by BJ Worth and Jake Lombard, Bond lassos the plane's tail and the helicopter lifts it away ('let's go fishing'). Bond and Leiter parachute to the church, the St Mary Star of The Sea Catholic Church, Key West. Cue opening titles. So far, so good.

Back in Key West, the wedding breakfast is in full swing at the Leiter residence, 707 South Street, Key West. Bond sees Leiter with CIA informant

Pam Bouvier in his study. This is a low-key introduction to one of the film's major characters. As Bond prepares to leave, there is a rare reference to Bond's dead wife.

> Della: Oh, James, I wanted you to have something. You know the tradition? The next one who catches this [she removes her garter] is the next one who...
> Bond: No. No. Thanks, Della. It's time I left. [Bond catches the garter and departs.]
> Della [to Leiter]: Did I say something wrong?
> Leiter: He was married once. But it was a long time ago.

Is Della a proxy-Tracy? Perhaps.

Sanchez is in custody. He bribes DEA agent Ed Killifer and escapes in an audacious rescue plan which involves driving off the Seven Mile Bridge and being picked up by divers. Dario kidnaps Leiter and he is taken to an aquarium owned by one of Sanchez's accomplices, Milton Krest. Leiter shouts, 'Where's my wife?', and Dario mocks him by saying, 'Don't worry. We gave her a nice honeymoon.' In a horrifying scene, taken from the original novel *Live and Let Die*, Sanchez has Leiter lowered into a tank holding a tiger shark.

Bond is at the airport and is alarmed when the check-in clerk tells him that a major drug dealer has escaped from custody. He goes immediately to the Leiters' house and finds Della's body and Leiter comatose on the sofa, with a note that reads, 'He disagreed with something that ate him'. Della has been murdered – and by implication, raped. Sharky identifies Leiter's injury as a shark bite, so he and Bond proceed to check out nearby aquariums. The last place they visit is Milton Krest's fish supplies and marine research centre. Bond talks his way in and sees Leiter's buttonhole on the floor. Returning later that night, Bond discovers hidden cocaine in the tanks of fish feed. He is interrupted and there is a terrific, tense shoot out, typical of John Glen's skills as an action director. One of his adversaries swims with an electric eel. Bond resists the opportunity to say 'simply shocking'. Bond kills Killifer, the corrupt DEA agent, by suspending him over the same shark tank used for Leiter and throwing a suitcase of money at him.

Bond is picked up by the DEA and taken to Key West's Hemingway House. Here he meets M. Timothy Dalton proves his acting skills in a terrific scene with Robert Brown. Bond can hardly suppress his anger and frustration.

> M: You were supposed to be in Istanbul last night. I'm afraid this unfortunate Leiter business has... clouded your judgment. You have a job to do. I expect you on a plane this afternoon.
> Bond [through gritted teeth]: I haven't finished here, sir.
> M: Leave it to the Americans. It's their mess. Let them clear it up.
> Bond: Sir, they're not going to do anything. I owe it to Leiter. He's put his life on the line for me many times.

M: Oh, spare me this sentimental rubbish! He knew the risks.
Bond: And his wife?
M: This private vendetta of yours could easily compromise Her Majesty's Government. You have an assignment. I expect you to carry it out objectively and professionally.
Bond: Then you have my resignation, sir.
M: We're not a country club! Effective immediately, your licence to kill is revoked and I require you to hand over your weapon. Now. I need hardly remind you that you're still bound by the Official Secrets Act.
Bond: Well, I guess it's, er... a farewell to arms.

That closing Hemingway reference is especially neat. Bond escapes under fire from his former colleagues and seeks revenge: a course of action he had advised against in *For Your Eyes Only*. He follows his only lead to Krest's research vessel, the Wavekrest, using manta ray camouflage. He meets Lupe again ('make a sound and you're dead'), foils Sanchez' latest drug shipment and discovers that Sharky has been killed. Bond escapes in spectacular fashion in a memorable scene where he uses a harpoon gun to hang onto a sea plane, then water-skis behind it, climbs on board, ejects the pilots and flies away, laughing as he discovers bags full of money. 'It was the best kind of action scene a director could have,' wrote John Glen. 'It solved a narrative and gave the audience something they'd never seen before.' [12] On paper this is as ludicrous as anything from Moore's tenure, but on film it's hugely enjoyable.

Bond returns to Leiter's house, hacks into his computer – a desktop with a CD player, state-of-the-art in 1989 – and discovers that Leiter's next meeting with Pam Bouvier would be at the Barrelhead Bar in Bimini, supposedly an island seventy kilometres east of Florida but actually filmed at Harbour Lights Bar in Key West. In a brawl worthy of *The Dukes of Hazzard* or the first *Casino Royale*, Bouvier blows a hole in the wall and tells Bond that 'if it wasn't for me your ass would be nailed to the wall'. They agree to work together and travel to the Republic of Isthmus. Bouvier is a sassy, tough woman who wears her hair short, hides a gun up her evening dresses and downs a vodka martini in one. She's a refreshing change after several limp American female leads since *Diamonds Are Forever*.

Hotel manager: If I could ask you to sign the registration cards?
Bond: No. My executive secretary, Miss Kennedy, will take care of that.
Hotel manager: Miss Kennedy. Right here, please. Gracias. Your key. Enjoy your stay.
Bouvier [to Bond]: It's *Ms* Kennedy. And why can't *you* be *my* executive secretary?

'I portrayed Pam as gritty and tough,' Lowell told *Classiq* in 2018. 'When she meets Bond at the bar, she's wearing a black leather vest and pants, and carrying a sawn-off shotgun. She's flinging men over her shoulder and smashing bottles on their heads. Quite different from other Bond girls.'

Bond uses his stolen money to pose as a high-roller in Sanchez' casino, in scenes filmed in Mexico City at the former Casino Español and inside the Teatro de la Ciudad. Bond successfully gains the drug dealer's attention and gets a meeting so that he can scope out the villain's office for an assassination. This is the first face-to-face encounter between Bond and his main antagonist. Once again, the dialogue is top-notch.

> Sanchez: It's a wise gambler who knows when his luck has run out. [he indicates Bond's gun] Why this?
> Bond: In my business, you prepare for the unexpected.
> Sanchez: And what business is that?
> Bond: I help people with problems.
> Sanchez: Problem solver.
> Bond: More of a problem eliminator.
> Sanchez: And are you here on business?
> Bond: No, temporarily unemployed. I thought I might find work here.
> Sanchez: Senor Bond, you've got big cojones. You come here, to my place, without references, carrying a piece, throwing around a lot of money. But you should know something. Nobody saw you come in, so nobody has to see you go out.

In a clever touch, after Bond has his Walther PPK taken from him by Sanchez, he takes a Beretta from Pam Bouvier – his original brand of firearm which has been replaced by the Walther in the first Bond film. Bond returns with Bouvier to his hotel – filmed at Gran Hotel Ciudad de México in Mexico City, a location re-used in *Spectre* – and is on his guard when the hotel receptionist informs that his uncle has arrived and is waiting for him. And here's Q in his finest appearance in a Bond film. The dialogue between Timothy Dalton and Desmond Llewelyn sparkles.

> Bond: Q! What the hell are you doing here? I might have killed you!
> Q: Well, I'm on leave. Thought I'd pop round and see how you were getting on.
> Bond: This is no place for you, Q. Go home.
> Q: Don't be an idiot. I know exactly what you're up to and you're going to need my help. Remember, if it hadn't been for Q Branch, you'd have been dead long ago. [he opens his case] Everything for a man on holiday. Explosive alarm clock guaranteed never to wake up anybody who uses it. Dentonite toothpaste. To be used sparingly. It's the latest in plastic explosive.
> Bond: Pam, this is Q, my uncle. Uncle, this is Miss Kennedy, my cousin.
> Q: Ah! We must be related!

Q provides Bond with the equipment to assassinate Sanchez. We get some genuine secret agent work as Bond disguises himself as a waiter, makes his way to the roof of Sanchez' bank on the top of a lift (*à la Diamonds Are Forever*) – in reality, the splendid Palacio Postal in Mexico City – then abseils to a window ledge to place his plastic explosives. From across the street, he gets ready to blow out the window and shoot Sanchez: 'watch the birdy, you bastard.' He is foiled by representatives from Hong Kong narcotics who have been planning a deep-cover case for several years. Sanchez arrives with his army and Bond is injured. He wakes in Sanchez' villa, the Villa Arabesque in Acapulco. 'You were just in time,' says Dalton in his best Derbyshire accent. 'Things were about to turn nasty.' Lupe helps Bond escape as Sanchez heads to the Wavekrest for a meeting with Krest.

Robert Davi is truly menacing here. Krest attempts to explain to Sanchez how Bond escaped from the Wavekrest. 'Do I have this right?' Sanchez asks. 'He water-skied behind the plane, jumps on it...' 'Well, yeah,' insists Krest. 'He threw the pilots out and flew away.' 'Like a little bird,' purrs Sanchez. Gulp.

'We see here how Sanchez develops,' suggests Cary Edwards. 'As his empire crumbles so does his moral code.' [13]

Meanwhile, Q, Pam and Bond have planted the stolen money in the boat's decompression chamber. Sanchez thinks he has been double-crossed. 'That's not my money!' Krest stutters. 'That's right, amigo: it's mine!' And, in a shot that upset the censors and needed to be edited, Krest's head explodes inside the decompression chamber. Nice.

Sanchez takes Bond to his refining plant, disguised as the headquarters of a religious cult. The amazing set is a genuine location, the Centro Ceremonial Otomí in Temoaya, Mexico. '[It was] an imposing and abstract structure that one could have been forgiven for thinking had been constructed by Ken Adam,' wrote John Glen. 'This magnificent place was the answer to our prayers.' [14]

Here, Bond learns that Sanchez's scientists can dissolve cocaine in petrol to be sold as fuel. During Sanchez's tour of the plant, Dario recognises Bond ('Who's the new guy?'). Sanchez ties Bond up and puts him on a conveyor belt that leads to some whirling blades. Sanchez has a classic line here: 'Put him in the conveyor. When you're up to your ankles, you'll beg to tell me everything. When you're up to your knees, you'll kiss my ass to kill you.'

Pam arrives just in time to save Bond and kill Dario. Roger Moore might have dropped a witty quip here. Dalton simply snarls 'Switch the bloody machine off!'

In a full-on action finale, the highlight of the film, Sanchez takes four tankers full of the cocaine/petrol mixture and Bond and Pam pursue them by plane. Bond is dropped onto a tanker and takes them out, one by one. This sequence took seven weeks and ten trucks to film on a closed road near La Rumorosa, Baja California, between Mexicali and Tecate. Once again, Rémy Julienne and his team were in charge of the stunt driving. Only James Bond could pull a wheelie with a tanker or tilt it on its side to avoid an incoming missile. There is some self-reverence when Bond is crawling around the truck. Sanchez shoots at him and the 'James Bond Theme' is heard in the sound of the ricocheting bullets. Sanchez attacks Bond with a machete aboard the final remaining tanker, breaking the brake cables. The tanker crashes, Sanchez, soaked in petrol, attempts to kill Bond. 'You could have had everything,' he hisses, preparing to deliver the death blow. 'Don't you want to know why?' asks a bloody and beaten Bond, who reveals his cigarette lighter – the Leiters' gift for being the best man at their wedding – and sets Sanchez on fire.

The closing scene, an unexplained party at Sanchez's former residence, resolves the threads of the plot. Bond gets his job back. Lupe thanks him for freeing her from Sanchez. Bouvier and Bond share a kiss. The bizarre winking fish is utterly at odds with the overall tone of this brutal revenge tale.

Licence to Kill was released on 14 July 1989 in the US, in the wake of *Indiana Jones and the Final Crusade*, featuring Sean Connery. It was up against *Lethal Weapon 2* (7 July 1989) and the all-conquering *Batman* (23 June 1989). Box office takings suffered accordingly: *Licence to Kill* was the 36th highest-grossing film in the US that year, behind forgotten films such as *Fletch Lives*, *K-9*, *Black Rain* and *Major League*. 'The film just didn't seem to go right,' says Cubby Broccoli. '*Batman* was hyped like no other movie in my experience. In making Bond an altogether tougher character, we had lost some of the original sophistication and wry humour. That is the way the public want him, and we had to get back onto that track. Back to a lighter touch, with more fun and capers like we had on the earlier Bonds.'

On reflection, *The Living Daylights* and *Licence To Kill* have aged rather well and deserve recognition of a genuine attempt to take James Bond into new territory. Perhaps it was all a few years too soon. Dalton, though, is never less than excellent in the lead role. It's a shame he didn't make a third entry in the Bond canon.

'*Licence to Kill* broke the mould in important ways,' suggests Cary Edwards. 'Relationships were redefined, signifiers were ignored or reinvented, and a more grounded Bond film emerged. Dalton brought layers of self-loathing and anti-authoritarianism to the role at odds to his predecessors.' [15]

As it was, *Licence To Kill* was the last James Bond film for six years. This protracted delay represents a changing of the guard: it was not only Dalton's final film, but also the last to feature Robert Hedison as M and Caroline Bliss as Moneypenny. It would be the final to include contributions from title designer Maurice Binder (who died 9 April 1991), screenwriters Richard Maibaum (who died 4 January 1991) and Michael G. Wilson, director John Glen, cinematographer Alec Mills, editor John Grover and the last with active involvement from producer Cubby Broccoli.

The Brosnan era was on the horizon, but we remain thankful for Timothy Dalton, the connoisseur's screen Bond.

> On the basis of this second performance as Bond, Timothy Dalton can have the role as long as he enjoys it. He makes an effective Bond – lacking Sean

Connery's grace and humour, and Roger Moore's suave self-mockery, but with a lean tension and a toughness that is possibly more contemporary. The major difference between Dalton and the earlier Bonds is that he seems to prefer action to sex. But then so do movie audiences, these days.
Roger Ebert, 14 July 1989

Dalton's second and final outing delivered his vision of Bond, perfectly. Perhaps you buy into this vision, perhaps you don't. But *Licence To Kill* is unflinchingly Dalton: a Bond only he could have made. Many fans bemoan the shortness of Tim's tenure – yet Dalton doesn't need to be mourned. He made his Bond. Few have made a better one.
Max Williams, *Revisiting Licence To Kill*, 2016

[1] This and the previous quote from *For My Eyes Only* (2001).
[2] Harris had died of ovarian cancer in December 1991, aged 43.
[3] *Timothy Dalton on Penny Dreadful, serenading Mae West, and being James Bond* – avclub.com (2014).
[4] *Typical Men – The Representation of Masculinity in Popular British Cinema* (2003).
[5] *Playgirl* (1987).
[6] *Entertainment Weekly* (November 2010).
[7] *Entertainment Weekly* (November 2010).
[8] Mark O'Connell in *Catching Bullets* (2012).
[9] *For My Eyes Only* (2001).
[10] *Action Movies: The Cinema of Striking Back* (2012).
[11] The whip is taken from Fleming's short story *The Hildebrand Rarity*.
[12] *For My Eyes Only* (2001).
[13] *He Disagreed With Something That Ate Him* (2018).
[14] *For My Eyes Only* (2001).
[15] *He Disagreed with Something That Ate Him* (2018).

1994-2004: I know the rules, and number one is 'no deals'

GoldenEye

Albert R Broccoli presents Pierce Brosnan as Ian Fleming's James Bond 007 in *GoldenEye*.
'No limits. No fears. No substitutes.'
Release date: 13 November 1995. Running time: 130 minutes. Distributed by MGM/ United International. Producers: Albert R Broccoli (17 of 17), Michael G. Wilson (4 of 12), Barbara Broccoli (1 of 9).
James Bond: Pierce Brosnan (1 of 4), M: Judi Dench (1 of 8), Q: Desmond Llewelyn (15 of 17), Moneypenny: Samantha Bond (1 of 4) with Michael Kitchen (Bill Tanner) (1 of 2), Robbie Coltrane (Valentin Dmitrovich Zukovsky) (1 of 2), Joe Don Baker (Jack Wade) (1 of 2).
And Sean Bean (Alec Trevelyan) with Izabella Scorupco (Natalya Simonova), Famke Janssen (Xenia Onatopp), Gottfried John (General Arkady Grigorovich Ourumov), Alan Cumming (Boris Grishenko), Tchéky Karyo (Dmitri Mishkin).
Director: Martin Campbell (1 of 2). Screenplay by Michael France, Bruce Feirstein (1 of 2), Jeffrey Caine, Kevin Wade (uncredited). Production design: Peter Lamont (6 of 9). Main titles by Daniel Kleinman (1 of 7). Music by Éric Serra. Theme song performed by Tina Turner. Cinematography: Phil Méheux (1 of 2). Edited by Terry Rawlings.

Plot

In 1986, MI6 agents James Bond and Alec Trevelyan infiltrate a Soviet chemical weapons facility and plant explosives. Trevelyan is captured and executed, but Bond escapes. Nine years later, a powerful clandestine satellite system falls into the hands of the Janus crime syndicate and Bond must confront his past to prevent Janus from using the satellite's pulse weaponry.

Cast

Pre-production for the seventeenth Eon Bond film began in May 1990. Again, Timothy Dalton was due to appear as Bond, fulfilling his three-film contract. The script, by Michael G. Wilson and *Miami Vice* screenwriter Alfonse Ruggiero Jr. was due to start production in Hong Kong later in 1990 for a release in late 1991.

Ruggiero was, much later, interviewed by author Mark Edlitz.

Edlitz: Do you recall discussing possible film titles?
Ruggiero: Yes, we were discussing film titles. *GoldenEye* was a possibility. I don't remember how it was brought up. I think Michael just said, 'I think *GoldenEye* would be a good title for this'. Of course, GoldenEye is where

Fleming's home was in Jamaica. It's where he lived and wrote. When Michael came up with the name I thought, That's cool. That's James Bond. We thought about *Colonel Sun,* which is also good. But once we had *GoldenEye*, I thought, we're off.
Edlitz: One of the rumours is that *The Property of a Lady,* the Fleming short story, was in consideration.
Ruggiero: I do not remember it, but it does not sound like a good idea. It feels like it should be an English drama and not a Bond film.
Edlitz: Did you speak to Dalton about his ideas?
Ruggiero: Yes. Dalton came in. I'm not sure exactly what the problem was but I felt like he wasn't happy being Bond at that moment.

'I think I was starting what would have been my third Bond film in '89 or '90,' Dalton told *Entertainment Weekly* in 2010. 'It had been written, we were talking directors, and then the lawsuit came.'

In March 1990, the Bond series' distributors, MGM/UA, were bought by the owners of the French production company Pathé. The deal included international broadcasting rights to the Eon back catalogue. Danjaq, Eon's parent company, alleged that this deal violated the distribution agreements the company had made with United Artists back in 1962. The subsequent lawsuits were not settled until 1992, by which time it seems that the Wilson/Ruggiero idea had been scrapped. In mid-1993, Danjaq hired *Cliffhanger* writer co-scripter Michael France to develop *Bond 17*. At the same time writers Richard Smith and John Cork were taken on to develop outlines for two further Bond films, potentially Dalton's fourth and fifth, as detailed in *Variety*, 26 May 1993.

Danjaq Inc. has hired Richard Smith and John Cork to pen separate scripts for Agent 007, raising to three the James Bond movies in development. Michael France is now penning 17th in the series. He has not been pitted in a script race with Smith or Cork, Danjaq spokesman Charles Juroe told *Daily Variety*. 'There is no question about it: France is writing *Bond 17.* These other two gentlemen are writing for future Bonds down the line, assuming (the revived series is) a success,' said Juroe. The Bond veteran said having one or two Bond scripts was routine for a company used to producing a sequel every other year. 'When you get up to 17 in one series, you do things differently. You don't wait until 17 is a success to say, 'Oh, we better do another one,' Juroe quipped. 'This two-year cycle does not give Danjaq the luxury to wait 10 or 11 months down the line to get started on the next one. They've learned they have to be ahead of the game.' And are they writing for thesp Timothy Dalton? 'Dalton is the Bond of record, ' Juroe said.
Suzan Ayscough, *Variety*, 26 May 1993

The working title for the proposed eighteenth Bond film was *Reunion with Death*.

The as-yet-unnamed *Bond 17*, meanwhile, was scheduled for a summer 1994 release. But, having read the script whilst shooting the mini-series *Scarlett*, Dalton, his contract now expired, decided that he would not return for a third Bond film; he officially resigned in April 1994.

> We have been advised by Timothy Dalton that after starring successfully in two James Bond films he had decided that he does not wish to return as the star of the next film of the series. Over the past eight years we have enjoyed a very happy personal and professional relationship with Timothy. In his portrayal of the James Bond character, he made the role his own by bringing Bond back to the hard-edged style of the early Ian Fleming novels to delight audiences around the world. We regret Timothy's decision. We have never thought of anyone but Timothy as the star of the seventeenth James Bond film. We understand his reasons and will honour his decision. We look forward to announcing plans for the seventeenth James Bond film in the near future. [1]

'By the time the lawsuit that stopped the last Bond movie that I was going to make was resolved', Dalton said in 2010, 'five years had passed. I certainly didn't want to carry on after having been associated with Bond for almost ten years at that point. It brings a big hole into that universe.' [2]

Once again, the James Bond production team was looking for a new lead actor. Both Kenneth Branagh and Hugh Grant were mentioned. Liam Neeson was heavily courted, but he turned it down on the instructions of his future wife, the late Natasha Richardson. 'My wife-to-be said, 'If you play James Bond, we're not getting married''. And I had to take that on board because I did want to marry her. Women, foreign countries ... it's understandable,' Neeson told *Men's Journal*.

During an interview with *The Daily Telegraph* in 2014, future M actor Ralph Fiennes let slip that he also had been in talks with Bond producers to star in *GoldenEye*. 'There was a conversation that was great and a meeting with Cubby Broccoli, that was terrific,' he said. 'I think that's all I can say, except that it didn't lead to anything on both sides. I don't think I felt ready to commit and I think they were looking at Pierce [Brosnan].'

Ah yes, Pierce Brosnan, the man who had been offered the role seven years before. 'That it didn't happen was shocking,' he said in 1991. 'Welcome to the world of business and cold-deal Hollywood. I was devastated. I bore it philosophically for a while. Then about six months later, it got to me. I was driving down Pacific Highway and I had to pull over to the kerb, get out of the car and bellow at the ocean.' [3]

Brosnan was 41 in 1994. Since 1987 he had broken out of TV roles with *The Fourth Protocol* (1987), *The Lawnmower Man* (1992) and *Mrs Doubtfire* (1993), his reputation growing with each film. He has also nursed his wife Cassandra through her fatal ovarian cancer.

Eon returned to screenwriter Michael France. 'I wanted to bring out a little more of the darker stuff,' France told bondfanevents.com in 2017, 'and some of the Bond we know from the Fleming novels, and present a Bond that is like the Bond of *Goldfinger*. You`re entering a fantasy world, but while you`re watching the movie it seems real. Two hours after you watch *Goldfinger*, you think there`s no way any of that can happen, but when you`re watching it, you believe it – you want to believe it.'

Jeffrey Caine, creator and writer of the British TV drama series *The Chief*, polished the story, specifically the focus on character relationships. Dialogue was refined by ex-journalist Bruce Feirstein.

Eon put together a brilliant trailer to tease their new star. 'It's a new world with new enemies and new threats, but you can still depend on one man.' 'Were you expecting someone else?' grins the next James Bond – a throwback to several Bond films of the past and perhaps a wry reference to Timothy Dalton. [4]

So, here was a handsome man of action, a combination of Connery's grace and virility, Dalton's grit and Moore's tongue-in-cheek glee. But, crucially, this Bond is more sensitive, more vulnerable. Brosnan's portrayal, sometimes cold, often flawed, is a major stepping stone to the wholesale re-invention of the Daniel Craig era. 'Brosnan's Bond is characteristically attractive and debonair,' writes Peter C. Kunze. 'And his humour is suggestive, even crass, and delivered with a cheeky overtone that showcases his playful nature'. [5] 'His lithe, sinuous athleticism', argues Andrew Spicer, 'is well-suited to the fast-paced action and state-of-the-art gadgetry that retain the series' core appeal.' [6]

> There was a lot at stake. I didn't want to be the man who put the final nail in the coffin. If I screwed up and it hadn't worked, I don't know if the series had gone on. Tim gave a wonderful performance, a performance which was very true to what Fleming had put down. But the world, the punters, the audience had been conditioned and primed with humour. If you're going to play it dead straight and on the nose, then it had better be rich in many varying aspects of the character. The audience want to have fun.
>
> Pierce Brosnan [7]... in 1999

Professional Yorkshireman Sean Bean plays Alec Trevelyan, the double-crossing OO6 with an unconvincing posh accent. Familiar as TV's *Sharpe* (1993-1997) and Mellors in a BBC adaptation of *Lady Chatterley* (1992), he had also turned heads with a scintillating turn in *Patriot Games* (1992). This was many years before he appeared as Boromir in *Lord of the Rings* (2001-2003) and Eddard 'Ned' Stark in the first season of *Game of Thrones* (2011). Michael Kitchen (*Brimstone and Treacle*, 1976; *Out of Africa*, 1985 and many others) plays Bill Tanner. The new Miss Moneypenny, Samantha Bond, an alumnus of the Royal Shakespeare Company (1987-1993) is sparkier, sassier and more sarcastic than Caroline Bliss from the Dalton films.

Other significant cast members include Polish-Swedish model and singer Izabella Scorupco (Natalya Simonova), Dutch former fashion model Famke Janssen (Xenia Onatopp), a new role for Joe Don Baker (Jack Wade), Fassbinder alumnus Gottfried John (General Arkady Grigorovich Ourumov), and Scottish actors Robbie Coltrane (Valentin Dmitrovich Zukovsky, six years before the first Harry Potter film) and Alan Cumming (Boris Grishenko). Desmond Llewelyn is in place as Q, the only actor to remain in character across the Dalton to Brosnan eras.

And, significantly, M is played with vim and brio by the wonderful Judi Dench. Dench was not yet screen-acting royalty (*Mrs Brown* was released in 1996, and her Oscar-winning turn for *Shakespeare in Love* would follow in 1998) but a much-admired and very busy stage actor notably with the Royal Shakespeare Company (1969-1985) and the National Theatre (1982-1998). Dench's astute casting as Bond's boss – a woman, much older than him, a 'bean-counting evil queen of numbers' – finally marked the end of the misogyny that beset the films in the 1970s and 1980s. It also opened up future opportunities for above-the-marquee names such as Halle Barry (*Die Another Day*), Michael Masden (underused in *Die Another Day*), Ralph Fiennes (*Skyfall*, *Spectre*, *No Time To Die*), Albert Finney (*Skyfall*), Javier Bardem (*Skyfall*), Christoph Waltz (*Spectre, No Time To Die*) and Rami Malek (*No Time To Die*). Credit here to director Martin Campbell who suggested the significant change of gender for the new M.

Max Williams:

> The casting of Dench was arguably the first step on the road to *Skyfall*. A hugely respected actor taking a role in a James Bond utterly seriously, while also extending the limits of what the series could be. Now Oscar winners such as Ralph Fiennes, Javier Bardem and Christoph Waltz pop up and nobody bats an eyelid. Now we can enjoy a youthful Q, a black Moneypenny, an actual M transition, rather than a new face behind the desk pretending to have sat there forever. Dame Judi is responsible for all that – but her biggest contribution is on-screen, not off it. Throughout her time I can't remember a scene she didn't steal. [8]

Theme Song

Slow and brooding, this Tina Turner song written by members of U2 harks back to the sixties but sounds very 1995.

Production

GoldenEye was filmed between January and June 1995 at Leavesden Studios, Hertfordshire, and on location in Switzerland, France, the United States, Monaco, Russia and the United Kingdom.

Observations

And so, a new James Bond played by an actor 25 years younger than Roger Moore. Is this the same Bond, we ask?

'The Bond films' evasion of the issue of the lead actor can be interpreted as part of a wider policy within the series to avoid, as far as possible, the incorporation of historical or political developments,' suggests Martin Flanagan. 'When such references do come, as in the storyline of *GoldenEye* which draws upon the dissolution of the Soviet Union, they invariably represent a shallow co-opting of historical signifiers designed to give audiences a ready-made reference point that can be quickly assimilated and forgotten, enabling them to return to the basic business of attending to the action.' [9]

This is not the same character as the Roger Moore Bond – these are two different secret agents who happen to share the same name. And, following a conceit evident in comic books, the Bond series now adopted a floating timeline allowing Bond to be, in effect, timeless. *GoldenEye* eschews camp excess and brings back Cold War villains, impressive stunts, smart gadgets and lots of fighting. This film had a lot riding on it. As in 1973, a misstep might have ended the series there and then.

The 17th James Bond film was directed by New Zealander Martin Campbell. The previous sixteen has been helmed by only five men: Terence Young (3 films), Guy Hamilton (4), Lewis Gilbert (3), Peter Hunt (1) and John Glen (5). Campbell had established his craft on British tea-time TV shows such as *The Professionals*, *Shoestring* and *Reilly: The Ace of Spies*, each of which had leading actors who were in the frame to play James Bond at one time or another. It was the six-part BBC mini-series *Edge of Darkness* that allowed him to move into films. He was by no means a proven director of high profile, big-budget action films, but the producers' choice was shrewd as *GoldenEye* re-invented and probably saved the Bond series, just as *Casino Royale*, again directed by Campbell, would do the same a decade later. This would be the last James Bond film to be produced by Albert R 'Cubby' Broccoli, who died aged 87 in Beverley Hills on 27 June 1996. Every Bond film since has opened with the line 'Albert R Broccoli's Eon Productions presents ...'

GoldenEye's great opening sequence is set in Arkhangel, in what was then the USSR, in 1986. It includes two very cool stunts which approach the opening moments of *The Spy Who Loved Me* for sheer audacity: a bungee jump from the top of a dam (filmed at the Contra Dam in Ticino, Switzerland) and a motorcycle leap off a cliff into a falling plane. We see a light aircraft approaching a huge dam, man sprints across it, we don't see his face. He attached a rope to the fence and his feet. And jumps. This was done for real, with no CGI, by Wayne Michaels and was at the time the highest ever jump from a fixed object. With milliseconds to spare, James Bond, for it is he, fires a piton into the ground and lowers himself the rest of the way. We see eyes, and a silhouette but not his face up until he appears hanging upside down in a toilet stall, interrupting a man reading the paper. 'Beg your pardon, forgot to knock.' He makes his way through the facility until he is held at gunpoint by a figure in the shadows. 'Ni odnoho vyzdoha,' he shouts. 'Gdye vashy?' It's OO6, Alec Trevelyan (who must have used the back door). What an opening! But if that wasn't enough, Trevelyan is shot by Ouromov and Bond flees, chasing down an aeroplane on a motorcycle and sky-dives after it. Once again, BJ Worth performs the sky-dive. There's more action in the first nine minutes of *GoldenEye* than in most of, to pick any film at random, *A View to a Kill*.

After the titles sequence, the first by Daniel Kleinman, we have skipped forward nine years and in a scene replayed from *On Her Majesty's Secret Service*, Bond is driving along the French coast – in this case, the Route de Gentelly on the Côte d'Azur and the Route Grande Corniche, Roquebrune-Cap-Martin overlooking Monte Carlo – when his eye is caught by a female driving a red Ferrari. This is Xenia Onatopp, a member of a crime syndicate called Janus.

> Women are often meticulous and safe drivers, but they are very seldom first-class. In general, Bond regarded them as a mild hazard and he always gave them plenty of road and was ready for the unpredictable.
> From Ian Fleming's *Thunderball.* [10]

The funky music sounds like an outtake from *Starsky & Hutch*. Director Martin Campbell has a cameo as one of the cyclists. Bond, in a tuxedo, meets Elektra in the Casino de Monte-Carlo. After a game of Baccarat, Bond introduces himself in Brosnan's mid-Atlantic drawl ('Barnd. James Barnd.') and order his favourite drink. So, within the first twenty minutes of *GoldenEye*, we have seen Bond's trademark drink, the requisite casino scene and the return of the Aston Martin DB5 tying the series with the Connery era – the DB5 had not been seen in the Lazenby, Moore or Dalton films. These explicit references signalled a mini-wave of 1960s nostalgia in 1996-1998, with film versions of *Mission: Impossible*, *The Saint* and *The Avengers* debuting to varied acclaim.

The Bond/Onatopp dialogue here goes straight for the double entendre.

> Bond: It appears we share the same passions. Three, anyway.
> Onatopp: I count two – motoring and baccarat. I hope the third is where your real talent lies.
> Bond: One rises to meet a challenge.

At Port Hercule de Monaco, Onatopp and Russian general Ouromov steal a prototype EuroCopter Tiger, a helicopter that is impervious to electronic interference. She flies it to the GoldenEye facility in Siberia, the 'perfect getaway vehicle'. The exterior scenes were filmed in Switzerland, not far from Piz Gloria (Blofeld's mountain hideaway in *On Her Majesty's Secret Service*). Here we meet computer programmers Natalya Simonova, resourceful and intelligent, and Boris Grishenko, seriously irritating. Onatopp massacres the staff and steals the control discs for two electro-magnetic pulse weapons, the GoldenEye satellites, which they use to destroy the facility. Simonova and Grishenko are the only survivors.

Bond arrives at MI6 headquarters and is greeted by the new Moneypenny, this time played by Samantha Bond.

Moneypenny: I know you'll find this crushing but I don't sit at home praying for an international incident so I can run down here all dressed up to impress James Bond. I was on a date with a gentleman. We went to the theatre.
Bond: Moneypenny, I'm devastated. What would I ever do without you?
Moneypenny: As far as I can remember, James, you've never had me.
Bond: Hope springs eternal.
Moneypenny: This sort of behaviour could qualify as sexual harassment.
Bond: Really? What's the penalty for that?
Moneypenny: Someday you have to make good on your innuendos.

Ker-ching!

And, of course, the new M, in the form of Judi Dench. Dench's presence makes an immediate impact and unsettles the basic formula. The scenes between M and Bond show conflict from the beginning.

M: You don't like me, Bond. You don't like my methods. You think I'm an accountant, a bean counter more interested in my numbers than your instincts.
Bond: The thought had occurred to me.
M: Good, because I think you're a sexist, misogynist dinosaur. A relic of the Cold War, whose boyish charms, though wasted on me, obviously appealed to that young woman I sent out to evaluate you.
Bond: Point taken.
M: Not quite. If you think I don't have the balls to send a man out to die, your instincts are dead wrong. I've no compunction about sending you to your death. But I won't do it on a whim, even with your cavalier attitude towards life.

'I don't think I realised at first what a huge responsibility I had in playing M,' Dench says in her memoirs. 'I was just really excited about it. Pierce and I got on very well indeed.' [11] The producers soon realised what a coup they had made in securing Dench. Her parts would get bigger in subsequent films and M's relationship with Bond would develop more oedipal overtones during Daniel Craig's tenure. Dench's M would eventually die in the arms of Craig's Bond.

The Q laboratory scene is a witty as ever, as Bond gets a new BMW, a leather belt and a pen with an in-built explosive. He also inspects a sandwich. 'Don't touch that,' Q exclaims. 'That's my lunch!'

Bond travels to St. Petersburg, Russia and meets with new CIA contact, Jack Wade. Felix Leiter, for now, is no more. Wade puts him in touch with Valentin Zukovsky, a charming rogue in the Dikko Henderson mould, a former KGB agent-turned-gangster played with real relish and a nod to Sydney Greenstreet by Robbie Coltrane, triple BAFTA award-winner for *Cracker*. Coltrane has a classic line: 'Walther PPK. Only three men I know use such a gun. I believe I've killed two of them.' Zukovsky agrees to set up a meeting between Bond and Janus.

Bond encounters Onatopp in the swimming pool of the Grand Hotel and she tries to kill him by squeezing him between her thighs. This is a wonderfully saucy scene. 'No, no, no,' Bond says, 'No more foreplay.' She takes him to Janus, who reveals himself as Trevelyan in a graveyard of statues. There is more charged dialogue.

Bond: Alec?
Trevelyan: What's the matter, James? No glib remark? No pithy comeback?
Bond: Why?
Trevelyan: Hilarious question. Particularly from you. Did you ever ask why we toppled all those dictators and regimes, only to come home – 'Well done. Good job, but sorry, old boy. Everything you risked your life for has changed.'
Bond: It was the job we were chosen for.
Trevelyan: Of course you'd say that. James Bond, Her Majesty's loyal terrier, defender of the so-called faith.

Bond is shot unconscious with a tranquilizer dart and wakes up with Natalya aboard the stolen helicopter. From here, it's non-stop action as Bond headbutts the control panel and hits the eject button, only to be arrested by the KGB. Bond and Natalya escape in a terrific scene shooting their way out of the KGB archive. Then, in one of the film's most spectacular sequences, Bond steals a tank and chases Ouromov through the streets of St. Petersburg. The chase passes St Isaac's Cathedral, along Galernaya Ulitsa and Moshkov Pereulok and over the Pevchesky Bridge. Other scenes set in the city were filmed in London at St. Pancras station, in the Somerset House courtyard, at the Brompton Cemetery ('Our Lady of Smolensk', exterior), the Greek Orthodox Cathedral of the Divine Wisdom ('Our Lady of Smolensk', interior) and at the Langham Hotel in Mayfair. The James Bond theme blasts out as Brosnan straightens his tie, drops a statue on two pursuing police cars and, product placement alert, drives through a truck of Perrier.

He follows Trevelyan to his armoured train, with the Bond series once again filming at the Nene Valley Railway in Peterborough. He kills Ourumov, but Trevelyan and Onatopp escape in a hidden helicopter. Bond cuts through the floor with his laser watch, Natalya triangulates Grishenko's satellite dish to Cuba. They escape just before the train explodes.

Natalya: Do you destroy every vehicle you get into?
Bond: Standard operating procedure.
Natalya: Boys with toys.

We move into the final act. Firstly, Bond and Natalya meet Wade in the Florida Keys and borrow his plane for the flight to Cuba. Searching for *GoldenEye*'s satellite dish, they are shot down and captured. Onatopp drops from a helicopter and attacks Bond, but he shoots the helicopter pilot, sending the vehicle into a spin that pulls Onatopp between two trees. 'She always did enjoy a good squeeze,' Bond deadpans.

Bond and Natalya see water draining from a lake, uncovering the satellite dish. This is not a set – it's an actual observatory, the Arecibo Radio Telescope in Puerto Rico. They infiltrate the control station, but Bond is captured and Trevelyan reveals his plan. Natalya re-programmes the satellite's guidance system to initiate atmospheric re-entry and it destroy itself. Boris unwittingly triggers an explosion with Bond's pen grenade. 007 sabotages the antenna and he and Trevelyan fight hand-to-hand, until Bond allows Trevelyan to fall to the ground. The dish explodes, killing Trevelyan. Natalya commandeers a helicopter and rescues Bond. It drops them in a field, where they are rescued by Wade and a team of US Marines.

The last forty minutes or so of *GoldenEye* are as good as any Bond film before or since. This was truly satisfying opening of the Brosnan-era Bond, reinvigorating rather than re-inventing the series. The law of diminishing returns would henceforth apply.

GoldenEye was a smasher, and for me, a franchise peak. It introduced us to a new James Bond, the fifth, first met wearing a baggy black playsuit and running along the top of a dam. Where were we? Hundreds of feet above a Soviet munitions factory. A swan dive, a bungee rope, and a grappling-hook gun with laser cutter attachment got our agent inside. We didn't get a good look at him until he crawled into a communal toilet to waylay a henchman. 'Sorry,' he purred, the accent faintly Irish, a tanned and leathery face coming into view. It was Pierce Brosnan! Only just holding back a smile and quipping while he clobbered enemies exactly as Bond should.

GoldenEye's pre-credit sequence never let up. The film was only minutes old, and already there were so many outrageous action scenes to deconstruct with friends. The big-casino voice of Tina Turner sung over the credits. There'd been one-liners, gadgets, wasted vehicles, inept communists ...

And this is how we're best off rating Bond films, I think – by check-box. Does this or that instalment have a cool pre-credit sequence? Are you able to give the theme song a passable rendering in the shower without re-Googling the lyrics? Does the baddie have a lair? Is there a memorable assistant villain? How plausible is Bond's feature-length pairing with an attractive female civilian? How shocking the inevitable moment of his betrayal? Does he do something strenuous, dirty or violent and still remain immaculate in a suit? Does he notch more air miles than a golf pro, and desecrate the local architecture in at least one famous city?

By these major criteria and by many other minor ones – the sort that operate on an almost subliminal level of Bond-movie gratification – *GoldenEye* was immediately a winner for me.

The film is not perfect. Product placement reached unprecedentedly squalid levels, with Bond regularly brandishing his Omega Seamaster to no purpose, and in the chase scene driving his tank through a branded stack of mineral water. But I can forgive it. *GoldenEye* is the best Bond, confirmed by its superiority in the most important category of all, the lavishness of the villain's execution. Sean Connery ensured that Auric Goldfinger, in 1964, got sucked out of an aeroplane window. Roger Moore condemned Hugo Drax, in 1979's *Moonraker,* to a lonely death in space. In *GoldenEye*, Brosnan's Bond dropped Bean's Trevelyan many hundred feet on to concrete. The fall was not quite fatal for the villain – until a satellite the size of a tennis court landed on him. Pointy-end first. Aflame.

Within the limits of the Bond universe, this was actual poetry.

Tom Lamont, *The Guardian*, 26 September 2012

Tomorrow Never Dies

Albert R Broccoli's Eon Productions Limited presents Pierce Brosnan as Ian Fleming's James Bond OO7 in *Tomorrow Never Dies*

Release date: 9 December 1997. Running time: 119 minutes. Distributed by MGM / United International. Producers: Michael G. Wilson (5 of 12), Barbara Broccoli (2 of 9).

James Bond: Pierce Brosnan (2 of 4), M: Judi Dench (2 of 8), Q: Desmond Llewelyn (16 of 17), Moneypenny: Samantha Bond (2 of 4) with Joe Don Baker (Jack Wade) (2 of 2), Colin Salmon (Charles Robinson) (1 of 3).

And Jonathan Pryce (Elliot Carver) with Michelle Yeoh (Colonel Wai Lin), Teri Hatcher (Paris Carver), Götz Otto (Richard Stamper), Ricky Jay (Henry Gupta), Vincent Schiavelli (Dr. Kaufman), Geoffrey Palmer (Rear Admiral Roebuck), Julian Fellowes (Minister of Defence).

Director: Roger Spottiswoode. Screenplay by Bruce Feirstein (2 of 2). Production design: Allen Cameron. Main titles: Daniel Kleinman (2 of 7). Music: David Arnold (1 of 5). Theme song performed by Sheryl Crow. Cinematography: Robert Elswit. Edited by Michel Arcand, Dominique Fortin.

Plot

Media mogul Elliot Carver wants his news empire to be dominant worldwide, but the Chinese government will not allow him broadcast rights. Carver plans to use his media empire initiate war between China and the West. James Bond travels to China to stop him with the help of Chinese secret agent Wai Lin.

Cast

Malay actor Michelle Yeoh acquits herself admirably – she was an established performer in Hong Kong action films – but British stage actor Jonathan Pryce as gleefully deranged media mogul Elliot Carver thinks he's been cast in an Austin Powers film. One wonders how Anthony Hopkins would have played the role: Hopkins was cast and spent three days on set before quitting.

Italian actor Monica Bellucci read for the role of Paris Carver. 'There was a beautiful woman up for the part of Paris', Brosnan said later, 'a really lovely movie star who I spoke out loud and hard for. But it was not meant to be.' Bellucci would later be cast in *Spectre* (2015) and the part of Paris went to Teri Hatcher, then best-known for her portrayal of Lois Lane in *Lois & Clark: The New Adventures of Superman* (1993–97).

The officious Admiral Roebuck is played by British character actor Geoffrey Palmer, a familiar face on TV and films since 1958. Colin Salmon plays M's deputy chief-of-staff Charles Robinson, the first of three appearances in the series. Salmon had been a busy actor since his impressive turn in *Prime Suspect 2* in 1992. There are also early appearances for Gerard Butler (King Leonidis in *300* and many others), Julian Rhind-Tutt (Mac in *The Green Wing*), Jason Watkins (Mr Shakespeare in *Nativity*) and Hugh Bonneville (Robert, Earl of Grantham in the tedious *Downton Abbey*). Judi Dench, Samantha Bond and Desmond Llewelyn are present and correct.

Theme Song

KD Lang's terrific theme song ('Surrender'), heard over the end titles, was passed over for a forgettable Sheryl Crow waltz.

Production

Tomorrow Never Dies was filmed between April and autumn 1997 at Eon Studios, Hertfordshire, at Pinewood Studios, Buckinghamshire and on location in France, the United Kingdom, Germany and Thailand.

Observations

Glossy and formulaic but lots of fun, *Tomorrow Never Dies* has some tremendous set pieces, including a terrific car chase and some classic lines in a tight, funny and sarcastic script credited to Bruce Feirstein, co-writer of *GoldenEye*. As with many Bond films, several others contributed to the script after a brainstorming session with director Roger Spottiswoode and seven leading screenwriters. Nicholas Meyer, Oscar-nominated for his script for *The Seven Per Cent Solution*, performed some re-writes. Both Daniel Petrie, Jr (*Beverley Hills Cop*, *Turner & Hootch*) and David C. Wilson (*The Perfect Weapon*, *Supernova*) added their ideas before a final polish by Feirstein.

The result included some classic lines:

Just brushing up on a little Danish.

Bond: With all due respect M, sometimes I don't think you have the balls for this job.
M: Perhaps. The advantage is I don't have to think with them all the time.

Call the president – tell him if he doesn't sign the bill lowering the cable rates, we will release the video of him with the cheerleader.

It's mostly dull routine, but every now and then, you get to sail on a beautiful evening like this – and sometimes work with the decadent agent of a corrupt Western power.

And best of all:

You always were a cunning linguist, James.

The plot premise is good – a sly dig at media moguls such as Robert Maxwell and Rupert Murdoch. Jonathan Pryce, as Elliot Carver, decides to go full ham, which is a pity, as, like Christopher Walken in *A View to a Kill*, he's a very good actor indeed. His henchmen include the brainless Stamper (another blond muscle man) and the stereotypical fastidious, evil Doctor Kaufman.

The pre-titles scene is excellent. In a joint UK/Russia operation, James Bond has infiltrated a terrorist arms bazaar on the Russian border. This scene was filmed at the Altiport de Peyresourde in Loudervielle, nor far from the Spanish border. Watching live footage are M, Chief of Staff Charles Robinson, Admiral Roebuck from the Royal Navy and the Russian General Bukharin.

Our man's in position on the centre camera. It's like a terrorist supermarket. Chinese Long March Scud, Panther AS-565 attack helicopter, a pair of Russian mortars, and the crates look like American rifles. Chilean mines. German explosives. Fun for the whole family.

M insists on letting Bond finish his reconnaissance, but Roebuck orders the frigate HMS Chester to fire a missile at the bazaar. Bond discovers two nuclear torpedoes mounted on a high-performance jet trainer and is forced to pilot the plane away seconds before the bazaar is destroyed, with bursts of the '007 Theme' powering the action. Meanwhile, media baron Elliot Carver plans to use an encoder obtained at the bazaar to provoke a Sino-British conflict. Cyberterrorist Henry Gupta uses the decoder to send HMS Devonshire off-course into Chinese-held waters in the South China Sea. Carver's stealth ship ambushes it, steals one of its missiles and shoots down a Chinese fighter jet. Carver's men kill the Devonshire's survivors with Chinese weaponry. The British Minister of Defence orders Roebuck to deploy the fleet to recover the frigate. M is given 48 hours to investigate and avert a war.

In a scene filmed at Brasenose College and New College, James Bond is in Oxford with Professor Inga Bergstrom. 'I've always enjoyed studying a new tongue,' he drawls. Called back to action, M briefs him in the back of her Daimler as it races across London, adding a real urgency to this stock element of the Bond films. Bond flies to Hamburg and is greeted at the airport by his Avis representative. It's Q who gives Bond a new car, a BMW which can be controlled by his mobile phone. These scenes, with Q demonstrating the car, were filmed at Flughafen Hamburg and Stansted Airport, Essex and are Desmond Llewelyn's last hurrah as Q bar a brief emotional farewell in *The World Is Not Enough*. Bond goes undercover at the launch of Elliot Carver's new network, filmed at IBM's HQ in London. Paris Carver, played by Teri Hatcher, is unusual for a female lead in that she is a grown-up; she and Bond have a history. M drops out of character momentarily and suggests Bond should seduce his old flame. 'Use your relationship with Mrs. Carver if necessary', she says with a glimmer of a smirk. 'Remind her. Then pump her for information.'

When Bond says to Paris 'I always wondered how I'd feel if I ever saw you again' sound genuine. Paris, however, responds with a slap to the face and some sharp words. 'Tell me, James, do you still sleep with a gun under your pillow?'

And, later:

Paris: I used to look in the papers every day for your obituary.
Bond: Sorry to disappoint.

Bond shuts down the broadcast, then goes back to his hotel room. He gets his gun ready and drinks vodka in a scene reminiscent of Sean Connery's Bond waiting for Dent in *Dr. No*. Remarkably, this scene was filmed at Stoke Park Country Club in Buckingham, the location for the iconic golf match in *Goldfinger*. Bond's and Paris's reconciliation is passionate, but we know what will happen next. Carver phones Bond, who tells him that he knows Paris has been in his room. Bond finds her dead. She has been killed by Doctor Kaufman in a delicious cameo by the wonderful American character actor Vincent Schiavelli sporting a thick Cherman accent. 'I am a professor of forensic medicine,' he grunts. 'Believe me, Mr. Bond, I could shoot you from Stuttgart unt still create the proper effect. I am just a professional, doing my job.' Bond, of course, turns the tables with a cool 'me too'. Bond uses his car's remote control to escape Carver's men in a fun scene filmed in a multi-storey car park at Brent Cross Shopping Centre in London, above the Parkhaus Saturn on Steinstraße, Hamburg and a jump across the Mönckebergstrasse in Hamburg. This is classic Bond.

Bond's spectacular freefall into water was conducted by BJ Worth, his sixth flying stunt for the Bond series. Eighty jumps in total were needed to complete the sequence. OO7 finds the wreck of the Devonshire and discover that one of its cruise missiles missing. He also encounters Wai Lin, a Chinese agent on the same case. Bond's relationship with Wai Lin, played with verve and nerve by Jackie Chan protégé Michelle Yeoh, mirrors that with Anya Amasova in *The Spy Who Loved Me*. They are separated by geography, ideology and gender but work together to defeat a common threat.

> Wai Lin becomes the first 'Bond girl' to function more as a partner for 007 than as a love interest, someone to be rescued, or both. Played by Hong Kong star Michelle Yeoh, this character is just as physical and lethal as Bond, and she never screams for help. Brosnan and Yeoh click, and if there was ever a Bond girl worth considering for an encore, Wai Lin is it. [12]

Yeoh is terrific. They are captured by Carver's men and are taken to Carver's Vietnamese office, actually the Westin Banyan Tree Hotel in Bangkok and escape by sliding down huge Elliot Carver portrait. Bond quips, 'Next time, I'll take the elevator.' He means 'lift', of course. Bond and Wai-Lin, handcuffed together, take a motorbike to escape Carver's men. This is a fabulous action scene, with some very clever effects – they escape using their wits and a handy crowbar. The two agents have a shower in the street and they agree to work together. Bond volunteers to send a message on her communications array, then looks baffled at the Chinese characters on the keyboard – he had told Moneypenny in *You Only Live Twice* that he has a first-class degree in Oriental languages, the rascal.

They contact the Royal Navy and the People's Liberation Army Air Force to explain Carver's scheme. They find Carver's stealth ship, a conceit surely worthy of the Moore era, to prevent him from firing a missile at Beijing. The routine, noisy, over-explosive finale includes Bond killing Carver with a sea drill. Original, I guess, if little more than empty spectacular. The film ends with Bond and Lin kissing on a piece of seaborne debris.

The production had its challenges. Judi Dench: 'I got on very well with Martin Campbell, who directed *GoldenEye*, but less so with Roger Spottiswoode, the director of *Tomorrow Never Dies*. When we started to loop it [re-record dialogue], he said to me, in a very surprised tone of voice, 'You're very good at this'. This really was the last straw and then I said to him, 'You know, it was very off-putting indeed to have learnt the script and at quarter to ten the night before to get a loud knocking on the door by the courier with a new script. That's not fair.' 'Well, we didn't start with the right script in the first place.' 'Well that's hardly my fault. Did you see me the other day at Streatham? I nearly ran you over.' And Barbara Broccoli said, 'Pity you didn't accelerate and do the job for all of us.'' [13]

Tomorrow Never Dies is handsome, stylish and overblown, but lacks a distinctive personality – much like Pierce Brosnan's portrayal of the lead character in this film. As Brosnan himself said in 2014, 'I felt I was caught in a time warp between Roger and Sean. It was a very hard one to grasp the

meaning of, for me. The violence was never real, the brute force of the man was never palpable. It was quite tame, and the characterisation didn't have a follow-through of reality, it was surface. But then that might have had to do with my own insecurities in playing him as well.' [14]

Simon Winder:

No matter how long [Brosnan] may be on screen, you are simply too aware that his core competency is to model risibly clunky, expensive watches of a kind that could only appeal to people who think of Monaco as glamorous. [15]

The scrutiny surrounding *Tomorrow Never Dies* isn't as intense as it was around *GoldenEye*, but the attendant hype is, if anything, even more severe. Product tie-ins are everywhere. With *GoldenEye*, producers Barbara Broccoli and Michael G. Wilson successfully re-invented 007 for the '90s and proved that the venerable action hero could still be a viable box office draw. Now, with *Tomorrow Never Dies*, it's back to business as usual.

Tomorrow Never Dies is a better film than *GoldenEye*. In fact, it's the best Bond film in many years. For the first time since Sean Connery left the part, this movie feels like a Connery Bond adventure. Pierce Brosnan, having left behind the jitters he occasionally exhibited during *GoldenEye*, now inhabits his character with a suave confidence that is very like Connery's. The villain of the piece, Elliot Carver, is cut from the Blofeld/Goldfinger mould – sinister, cunning, and charismatic.

While the script isn't as openly jokey as some of the Roger Moore screenplays, it contains a fair number of one-liners. While some of these are predictable, several of them are unforgettably witty. M makes an acid comment about the roles of men and women in the politics of war, and Moneypenny offers a pun about Bond's canny knowledge of different languages (surely the best line of the film).

Bond fans will likely love this movie. Detractors will yawn it away as 'more of the same'.

James Berardinelli, *ReelViews*, 1997

The World Is Not Enough

Release date: 8 November 1999. Running time: 128 minutes. Distributed by MGM/ United International. Producers: Michael G. Wilson (6 of 12), Barbara Broccoli (3 of 9).

James Bond: Pierce Brosnan (3 of 4), M: Judi Dench (3 of 8), Q: Desmond Llewelyn (17 of 17), Moneypenny: Samantha Bond (3 of 4) with Robbie Coltrane (Valentin Zukovsky) (2 of 2), Michael Kitchen (Bill Tanner) (2 of 2), Colin Salmon (Charles Robinson) (2 of 3), John Cleese ('R') (1 of 2).

With Robert Carlyle (Victor 'Renard' Zokas) and Sophie Marceau (Elektra King), Denise Richards (Dr. Christmas Jones).

Director: Michael Apted. Screenplay: Neal Purvis (1 of 7), Robert Wade (1 of 7). Production design: Peter Lamont (7 of 9). Main titles: Daniel Kleinman (3 of 7). Music: David Arnold (2 of 5). Theme song performed by Garbage. Cinematography: Adrian Biddle. Edited by Jim Clark.

Plot

James Bond is tasked by M to protect Elektra King, who is seemingly being targeted by Renard, the world's most wanted terrorist.

Cast

French actor Sophie Marceau plays ruthless, narcissistic Elektra King as a female character who provides much more than mere decoration. She is the series' first and only female arch-villain. When she straps Bond into a torture chair, she takes perverse glee in tightening the screws. The relationship between Bond and Elektra is the key dynamic in the film. MGM's preference was for Sharon Stone, but Sophie Marceau is very watchable: vulnerable, sexy, fascinating, deadly, and utterly nuts.

Robert Carlyle chews the scenery as the tortured Renard in true baddie style. Producer Michael G Wilson had seen Carlyle in an extraordinary performance in an episode of *Cracker*, alongside Robbie Coltrane. *To Be a Somebody*, written by Jimmy McGovern, was first broadcast in 1994, two years before Carlyle's big-screen breakthrough in *Trainspotting*, and three before *The Full Monty*. His character is at least three-dimensional and less of a caricature than some previous Bond villains. 'This type of work is entirely different from what I've been involved in,' Carlyle said at the time. 'It's a wonderful, wonderful fantasy. OK, this guy feels no pain. How far does this go? Is this emotional? If you don't feel any physical or emotional pain then you don't feel anything – you're a complete vacuum, you're nothing. The only feelings he has are for this woman. He is completely obsessed with her.' [16]

Denise Richards, who had played a gutsy pilot in *Starship Troopers* (1997), is badly miscast as Dr. Christmas Jones. She received a Golden Raspberry in 1999 for 'Worst Supporting Actress' for *The World Is Not Enough*. Italian film actor and model Maria Grazia Cucinotta plays Giuleitta da Vinci, the 'Cigar Girl'. [17] Cucinotta played a striking role in the warm, gentle and thoroughly lovely film *Il Postino* (1995). She had auditioned for the part of Elektra King, but director Michael Apted didn't think her English was good enough.

Several actors reprise their roles from earlier films: Judi Dench, Desmond Llewelyn, Samantha Bond, Robbie Coltrane, Michael Kitchen and Colin Salmon.

Newspaper reports during the production of the film suggested that the film would feature cameos by many previous Bond leads, including Ursula Andress, Diana Rigg, Famke Janssen and Barbara Bach. This might have been little more than a trumped-up media rumour. But look closely in Zukovsky's warehouse: the girlie pictures on the walls are of former Bond female leads.

Theme Song

Rock band Garbage provide all the Bond theme tropes without offering anything new. Scott Walker's thrilling and melancholic 'Only Myself to Blame' was intended to play out over the end titles, but director Michael Apted vetoed it. Bonkers.

Production

The World Is Not Enough was filmed between January and June 1999 at Pinewood Studios, Buckinghamshire (the first since *The Living Daylights* in 1986-1987), and on location in Spain, the United Kingdom, Azerbaijan, France and Turkey.

Observations

There's a theory that the third outing is where any Bond actor nails it. *Goldfinger*, *The Spy Who Loved Me* and *Skyfall* lend credence to this. After the terrific, very lengthy pre-credits sequence, however, *The World Is Not Enough* is a failure.

The film's plot is quite interesting. It's the debut Bond script for Neal Purvis and Robert Wade, authors of the taut British crime thriller *Let Him Have It* (1991) and *Plunkett & Macleane* (1999), an action comedy set in 1748 which also features Robert Carlyle. Purvis and Wade have written each of the subsequent six Bond films, sometimes with contributions from others. Dana Stevens made uncredited refinements to the script, in particular the Bond–Electra dynamic, and Bruce Feirstein provided a final polish.

For *The World Is Not Enough*, Purvis and Wade rewrite the basic premise of *Goldfinger*. In both, the villains plan the nuclear destruction of a massive store of a precious resource to drive up the prices and allowing them to become the wealthiest people in the world. The basic premise was inspired by a segment on ABC News' *Nightline,* which was seen by producer Barbara Broccoli on a flight to Miami in November 1997. The report detailed how oil reserves in the region of the Caspian Sea – the world's largest inland body of water bounded by Kazakhstan, Russia, Azerbaijan, Iran and Turkmenistan – were now an opportunity for the western world to capitalise. Broccoli hypothesised how a Bond villain might want to create a monopoly by removing all competitors and owning the only pipeline in the region. This is overlaid with a dual kidnapping: first of Elektra King, who has a fascinating back story and turns out to be the real villain, and then M, who is captured by Robert Carlyle, hamming it up as a man who feels no pain.

The World Is Not Enough is director Michael Apted's only Bond credit. Very prolific, Apted had previously directed several British documentaries and TV series (most notably *Coronation Street* and *Play for Today*) and such varied films as *Coal Miner's Daughter* (1980), *Gorky Park* (1983) and *Gorillas in the Mist* (1988). He worked on the *Up* series broadcast every seven years on British TV since 1964, initially as a researcher, latterly as director. He died in January

2021. Intriguingly, Barbara Broccoli was a big fan of Peter Jackson's *Heavenly Creatures* (1994) and was interested in Jackson directing *The World Is Not Enough*. A Jackson-directed Bond film remains on every cinema fan's bucket list, I'd expect.

Where this film falls down is in the casting of Denise Richards as Christmas Jones, a nuclear scientist who dresses in 'cleavage-touting *Tomb Raider* combats' and 'delivers her jargon-heavy speeches with the glassy-eyed peppiness of a lobotomised cheerleader'. [18] We shouldn't blame Denise Richards. we should point the finger straight at the scriptwriters. The character is surely named purely for some shocking one-liners. Firstly, the barely acceptable 'I thought Christmas comes only once a year'. Secondly, 'isn't it time you unwrapped your present'. And, worse of all, 'I always wanted to have Christmas in Turkey'. [19] Furthermore, there is no chemistry between Bond and Jones whatsoever, whereas the electricity sparks between Bond and Elektra King. Perhaps that's the point.

The film opens with a bespectacled Bond in Bilbao, Spain. An establishing shot frames the Guggenheim Museum, and the bank itself, 'La Banque Suisse de L'Industrie', is a law office just across the river. Bond is meeting Swiss bankers in a scene initially planned to be set in Cuba, and then in Switzerland. He is offered a cigar by Maria Grazia Cucinotta, the 'cigar girl', and she offers to let Bond check her figures. 'I'm sure they're perfectly rounded,' he replies in perfect Mooreese.

Bond asks for the name of the killer of a fellow MI6 agent, but the banker is killed before he can reveal it. Bond escapes from the office with the money across the Puente de La Salve. Back in London, foam on Bond's fingers alerts him that the money is booby-trapped. Sir Robert King is killed when the cash explodes. A lengthy and witty boat chase was filmed for real over seven weeks through London. Many locations are identifiable, including Lambeth Bridge, Vauxhall Bridge, Westminster Bridge, Tower Bridge, St. Saviour's Dock, Clippers Quay, Millwall Docks, Royal Victoria Dock, Spirit Quay, Tobacco Dock and Chatham Docks.

In a subtle in-joke, the bespectacled wheel clamper soaked by Bond is played by Ray Brown, the most prominent star of a BBC fly-on-the-wall docusoap series called *The Clampers*, where Brown's zealous behaviour had made him a figure of popular distain. The chase ends at the Millennium Dome, still under construction, where the cigar girl attempts to escape by hot air balloon. Bond offers her protection, but she blows herself up rather than reveal to OO7 who she is working for. Fourteen minutes in, we cut to titles.

M and Bond attend Robert King's funeral in Scotland, filmed at Stowe Gardens in Buckinghamshire. At MI6's Scottish HQ, Eilean Donan – the same castle used in *Highlander* (1986) – Bond has been placed on the inactive roster due to a shoulder injury suffered in London. In what must surely cross doctor/patient boundaries, he seduces his physician, the delightfully named Molly Warmflash, played by Serena Scott Thomas. [20]

And we have the sauciest Bond/Moneypenny dialogue to date:

Ms. Moneypenny: James! Have you brought me a souvenir from your trip? Chocolates? An engagement ring?
James Bond: I thought you might enjoy one of these. [gives her a phallic cigar tube]
Ms. Moneypenny: How romantic. I know exactly where to put that. [she throws it in the waste bin]
James Bond: Oh Moneypenny, the story of our relationship: close, but no cigar.

At a briefing – sharp-eyed viewers will spot a portrait of original M actor Bernard Lee hanging behind the current M's desk – we are told that Robert King's daughter Elektra has previously been kidnapped by a terrorist called Renard, who has been shot in the head by OO9. Because all Bond villains need a deformity of some kind, poor Judi Dench does her best with some awful dialogue. '[The bullet is] moving through the medulla oblongata, killing off his senses: touch, smell; he feels no pain. He can push himself harder and longer than any normal man. The bullet will kill him, but he'll grow stronger every day until the day he dies.' Physically pain-free, perhaps. But his emotional pain through his complex relationship with Elektra is only hinted at and is a missed opportunity.

In the meantime, Bond visits Q's lab. We'll skip over the flame-throwing bagpipes. Q admonishes Bond for destroying his 'fishing boat'.

Q: For my retirement. Away from you. Now, I want to introduce you to the young fellow I'm grooming to follow me. [R (John Cleese) appears from beneath a trick pool table, with Bond's new BMW. His lab coat is caught…]
Bond: Helps if you open the door.
R: And you might be…?
Q: This is OO7!
Bond: If you're Q, does that make him R?
R: Ah yes, the legendary OO7 wit. Or at least half of it.

Basil Fawlty, for it is he, demonstrates the BMW with 'the very latest in interception counter-measures. Titanium armour. A multi-tasking heads up display. And six beverage cup holders.'
Plus a jacket that inflates into a big protective ball. We feel that this might come in handy later.

Ian Johnstone:

The scene in which Bond is given the latest MI6 gadgetry which will save him in his hour of need, is always put at the end of the shooting schedule. The reason is simple. During the film, Bond may have used many devices, some of which will have landed up on the cutting room floor because they don't prove wholly effective or for reasons of length. So the meeting in which Bond is instructed in and equipped with his invaluable lifesavers is logically shot when the filmmakers already know which ones he is going to use. [21]

'You're not planning on retiring any time soon, are you?' Bond asks. 'Now pay attention, 007,' Q replies. 'I've always tried to teach you two things. First, never let them see you bleed.' 'And the second?' 'Always have an escape plan.' Q, and his reassuring presence, exits as he holds Bond's gaze. Sob. This was the last scene shot for the film on 25 June 1999. Sadly, the wonderful Desmond Llewelyn died in car accident aged 85, soon after the release of *The World Is Not Enough*. 'I will be in the Bond films as long as the producers want me and the Almighty doesn't,' he said shortly before his death. [22]

Bond flies to Turkey, where Elektra King is overseeing the construction of her family's oil pipeline. Her oil terminal, with the oil pipeline on its roof, is the former Motorola building in Swindon, with the pipeline created using CGI.

The World Is Not Enough is the second Bond film to use Turkey as a location – much of *From Russia With Love* was filmed in Istanbul. A car chase through Istanbul was planned but not developed further: this idea was reused for the opening scene in *Skyfall*. None of the cast travelled to Istanbul for *The World Is Not Enough*. Interiors were shot at Pinewood, and the shots of Renard and his men getting off the boat on the jetty were shot in the tank at Pinewood against a bluescreen.

In one of the film's best scenes, the sexual tension between Bond and Elektra is palpable. According to writer Iain Johnstone, Elektra is based on Tracy Bond. '[Screenwriter Robert] Wade said she was a very strong inspiration for the character of Elektra in *The World Is Not Enough*, because she is a rich man's daughter who is out to prove herself and Bond is on a mission to look after this girl, whom he at first finds vulnerable and then not so vulnerable.' [23]

Elektra asks Bond if he ever lost a loved one. Bond looks uncomfortable and doesn't answer. The reference to his dead wife is implicit. This is followed by scenes of Bond and Elektra skiing together that surely evoke memories of Bond and Tracy escaping Blofeld in *On Her Majesty's Secret Service*. What's more, the phrase *The World Is Not Enough* comes from the novel and film of *On Her Majesty's Secret Service* when Hilary Bray tells Bond that the family motto is Orbis non sufficit. As Barbara Broccoli once said, 'Bond thinks he's found Tracy, but he's really found Blofeld.' [24]

The skiing scenes were filmed in France, in Chamonix-Mont-Blanc. Bond and Elektra are attacked by armed, paraglider-equipped snowmobiles. Bond, unarmed, uses the terrain to his advantage. Bond and Elektra are caught in an avalanche, again a possible reference to *On Her Majesty's Secret Service*. 007 handily activates his inflatable jacket.

Bond visits Valentin Zukovsky at his Baku casino to gain information about Elektra's attackers. The exterior is Halton House in Buckinghamshire, about twenty miles north of Pinewood. Once again, Robbie Coltrane steals every scene in which he appears.

The plot now gets convoluted, so pay attention. In quick order, Bond uses x-ray glasses; deduces that Elektra's head of security, Davidov, is secretly in league with Renard; witnesses Elektra losing $1 million a game of single-card draw, another reference to *On Her Majesty's Secret Service*; beds Elektra (her villa in Baku is, in reality, Küçüksu Kasrı, a summer palace in Istanbul with interiors filmed at Luton Hoo in Bedfordshire – Shrublands in *Never Say Never Again*); kills Davidov and takes his place in a trip to a Russian missile base in Kazakhstan which is being decommissioned by Doctor Christmas Jones, a physicist who dresses like Lara Croft. Bond poses as a Russian scientist before entering the silo and encountering Renard, fresh from a cheesy scene about 'flames that never die', who is removing the GPS locator card and weapons-grade plutonium from a nuclear bomb. Keeping up? Or just bored?

And is this exchange simply creepy?

> Jones: The world's greatest terrorist running around with six kilos of weapons-grade plutonium can't be good. I gotta get it back, or someone's gonna have my ass.
> Bond: First things first.

From here, the film just seems to fizzle out, with set pieces that just exist without any real reason other than to be spectacular. These include two scenes that look like extracts from a computer game as firstly Bond and Jones deactivate a bomb in an oil pipe (he must be getting better at this, by now, surely?), and secondly, Zukovsky's caviar factory in the Caspian Sea – a huge set at Pinewood – is destroyed by helicopters with enormous buzz saws.

M is kidnapped and imprisoned in the Kız Kulesi, the Maiden's Tower in Istanbul harbour. Bond is taken their and Elektra tortures him with a garrotte. Zukovsky and his men arrive and seize the tower, but Zukovsky is shot by Elektra. Although dying, he frees Bond with a gun in his cane. Bond frees M and kills Elektra after a steely exchange.

> Bond: I won't ask again. Call him off. Call him off!
> Elektra: You wouldn't kill me. You'd miss me.
> Bond: [shooting Elektra in the chest] I never miss.

The regret, fatigue and sadness in that last line is palpable. Bond stroking Elektra's forehead is a lovely moment.

The lacklustre, flaccid finale sees Bond diving down to board Renard's stolen Russian nuclear submarine and rescue Jones. We've seen it all before and it's all very 'ho-hum'.

The World Is Not Enough has its moments – sometimes you just have to be in the mood for a bit of bonkers Bond. But it feels like Bond-by-numbers outside the first fifteen minutes and the Bond/Elektra dynamic. Three films in and the

Brosnan formula is already starting to go stale. *The World Is Not Enough* is by no means a classic or even particularly memorable. Close but, well, no cigar.

Inherent in the notion of a film sequel is the lure of an intensified repetition of previous pleasures. After close to four decades of changing socio-sexual mores, competition from satires and rip-offs such as the Austin Powers and Matt Helm films, and the obvious difficulty of engaging the public with five different incarnations of an iconic character, the very existence of *The World Is Not Enough*, the nineteenth official Bond movie, is proof that Bond's makers have mostly been delivering the goods. James Bond is the icon other icons look up to.

Bond films are formula film-making, and the production machinery behind them is so extensive and expert the movies are almost director-proof. *The World Is Not Enough* duly follows the traditional blueprint with nifty gadgets and cars, beautiful and available women and a couple of superb set pieces (the pre-credit sequence and the skiing scene). However, an equally important part of the Bond formula is cartoonish style, a light tone and two-dimensional characterisation. Many of us like it that way – we care more about what Bond wears and drives than what he feels.

The makers of *The World Is Not Enough* have attempted to depict all-too fleshy characters who desire, lack and feel. It's what is valued in a Ken Loach film, but it acts as an explosive and unsettling expulsion from the fantasies Bond films invite us to. One can't name a patricidal character Elektra and then expect the audience not to giggle at the film's attempts to psychologise her; one can't have Denise Richards play a nuclear physicist and make any claims to conventional believability. Robert Carlyle striving to imbue a character with truth and depth is almost always a good thing, but when that character is a Bond villain who wants to conquer the world, one has to ask what the director was thinking of. Worst of all, they've done the same to Bond, not understanding that deep feelings don't go easily with nonchalance, suavity, elegance or cool, much less with killing people as a profession.

Intending to turn Bond and his world into what they can't be, these attempts to create emotional depth reveal an underlying contempt for what the Bond movies actually are. They imply realism is not just one mode among many but the superior, most culturally worthy and difficult mode. By that logic, of course, to make Bond films better is to make them more –realistic'. Thank God for action, production values and the second unit. They're what make *The World Is Not Enough* still worth watching.

Jos Arroyo, *Sight + Sound*, January 2000

Die Another Day

Albert R Broccoli's Eon Productions Limited presents Pierce Brosnan as Ian Fleming's James Bond OO7 in *Die Another Day*

Release date: 20 November 2002. Running time: 133 minutes. Distributed by MGM / 20th Century Fox. Producers: Michael G. Wilson (7 of 12), Barbara Broccoli (4 of 9). James Bond: Pierce Brosnan (4 of 4), M: Judi Dench (4 of 8), Q: John Cleese (2 of 2), Moneypenny: Samantha Bond (4 of 4) with Colin Salmon (Charles Robinson) (3 of 3).

With Toby Stephens (Gustav Graves) and Halle Berry (Giacinta 'Jinx' Johnson), Rosamund Pike (Miranda Frost), Rick Yune (Zao), Will Yun Lee (Colonel Tan-Sun Moon), Kenneth Tsang (General Moon), Michael Madsen (Damian Falco), Madonna (Verity).

Director: Lee Tamahori. Screenplay: Neal Purvis (2 of 7), Robert Wade (2 of 7). Production design: Peter Lamont (8 of 9). Main titles: Daniel Kleinman (4 of 7). Music: David Arnold (3 of 5). Theme song performed by Madonna. Cinematography: David Tattersall. Edited by Christopher Wagner.

Plot

James Bond is captured by North Korean agents. After fourteen months he is traded as part of a prisoner exchange. Bond is convinced that he has been set up by a double agent in the British government. The trail leads to British billionaire businessman Gustav Graves who is launching a satellite to focus solar energy. Graves intends to use the satellite as a weapon to destabilise North and South Korea.

Cast

Stage and film actor Toby Stephens plays Gustav Graves. By 2002 his film career had included adaptations of works by Virginia Woolf, William Shakespeare, Honoré de Balzac, Alexander Pushkin and AS Byatt. American film star, Oscar winner and X-person Halle Berry is cast as Giacinta 'Jinx' Johnson. Her most acclaimed role at that time was for *Monster's Ball*, and she became the first and, as of 2021, only African-American woman to win the Academy Award for Best Actress, presented to her mid-way through the production schedule for *Die Another Day*.

Chinese actor Kenneth Tsang, veteran of dozens of Hong Kong, plays General Moon with genuine humility. Emilio Echevarría appears as Raoul, an MI6 agent in Havana. Rosamund Pike makes her film debut as Miranda Frost and Michael Madsen from *The Doors*, *Thelma and Louise*, *Reservoir Dogs*, *Donnie Brasco* and many others, has a regrettably tiny role. Roger Moore's daughter has a cameo as an air steward.

Theme Song

The forgettable theme song is by Madonna. The film's producers decided to employ a more well-known name after Garbage's previous theme song had failed to find commercial success. One assumes that Madonna's contribution to the soundtrack of *Austin Powers: The Spy Who Shagged Me* was not a deciding factor.

Production

Die Another Day was filmed between December 2001 and mid-2002 at Pinewood Studios, Buckinghamshire and on location in the United Kingdom, the United States, Spain and Iceland.

Observations

Lest we forget, this is the Bond film when our hero kitesurfs along a glacier being melted by a laser beam from space. And drives an invisible car, an idea even more silly than a hover-gondola.

Die Another Day is dafter than most of the Roger Moore films, and Pierce Brosnan sleepwalks through much of his final outing as James Bond. Likewise, Halle Berry looks great as Jinx but, uncharacteristically, gives a very poor acting performance. Bond bleeds for the first time. We have a fabulous car chase on a frozen lake, and the delightful Rosamund Pike as the spiky Miranda Frost, and, well, that's about it. Can anyone actually remember the story?

The 12-minute pre-title sequence is generally very good, with Brosnan as charismatic as usual, even the dialogue is decidedly clunky. Bond has landed in a North Korean compound (he arrives by surfboard: 'Pukch'ong Coast, North Korea' is the very British Holywell Bay beach in Cornwall, the surfing itself was filmed at Pe'ahi in Hawaii) where petulant Colonel Moon is waiting to trade conflict diamonds for weapons. [25] The US DMZ scenes were filmed at RAF Odiham in Hampshire and Hankley Common in Surrey. Moon's second-in-command, Zao, learns from a contact that Bond is an MI6 agent ('Moon got a call exposing me. He had a partner in the West. Even his father knew about it.'). Bond faces a firing squad but detonates an explosive device in a case of diamonds. He chases Moon across a minefield in a hovercraft – the 'James Bond Theme' sounds like it's playing in the next room – ultimately sending the rogue Korean over a model unit waterfall, while he grabs a bell at the last second. 'Saved by the bell,' he quips, as he is captured and tortured. For the first time the credits tell a story as we see what is happening to Bond.

After fourteen months Bond is traded for Zao in a prisoner exchange in a scene filmed at Hawley Common in Hampshire, a location later used for scenes in *Johnny English Reborn* (2011), *Avengers: Age of Ultron* (2015) and *Jurassic World, Fallen Kingdom* (2018).

Bond is taken to meet M, who tersely informs him that he is under suspicion of having leaked information under duress.

> M: Double-O status rescinded. You're no use to anyone now.

And then Bond slows his heartbeat through sheer force of will to simulating a cardiac arrest. I'm sorry? Run that past me again. As medical staff rush to his assistance, Bond comes back to life. 'I'm checkin' out, thanks for the kiss of life', he tells a nurse as he leaves.

In a humorous sequence, Bond swims across the harbour, and strolls into the Hong Kong Yacht Club.

Chang: Mr Bond, so good to see you. It's been a long time.
Bond: Could you send up my tailor and some food?
Chang: The lobster's good, with quails' eggs and sliced seaweed.
Bond: And if there's any left, a '61 Bollinger.
Chang: Been busy, have we, Mr Bond?
Bond: Just surviving, Mr Chang. Just surviving.

A haircut and a shave, his tuxedo, and a masseuse called Peaceful Fountains of Desire ('compliments of the management') complete his transformation to Roger Moore.

Bond learns from Chang that Zao is in Cuba. Chang provides Bond with a passport and tickets to Cuba. In a Havana cigar factory, in reality, a former clothing factory and tailors at 92-100 Stoke Newington Road in Hackney Downs, London, Bond meets Raoul, an MI6 sleeper agent. Raoul has strong echoes of Kerim Bay from *From Russia With Love*. Like Michael Masden's Falco, this character is criminally underused. Raoul traces Zao to 'a strange clinic run by Doctor Alvarez. He leads the field in gene therapy. Increasing the life expectancy of our beloved leaders. And, of course, the richest Westerners. We may have lost our freedom in the revolution, but we have a health system second to none.'

Before you can say 'Honey Ryder', Halle Berry's sparky Jinx emerges from the sea in a bikini. Bond claims to be an ornithologist. Jinx eyes Brosnan's crotch while delivering the single entendre 'wow, now there's a mouthful'.

This and most of the other Cuban scenes were filmed in and around Cádiz, Spain, with Playa de La Caleta providing the setting for Bond's first encounter with Jinx. Both the Calle Campo del Sur and the Mercado Central de Abastos are easily identifiable. Bond meets Raoul at the Torre del Sagrario, checks into the 'El Palacio Hotel', in reality a health spa called Balneario de Nuestra de la Palma y del Real, and drives along the Carretera de la Playa del Castillo, a few miles south of Cádiz.

After an in-silhouette sex scene, *Die Another Day* gets silly (or sillier) as Bond follows Jinx to a gene therapy clinic – the Castillo de San Sebastián in Cádiz. Alvarez, the latest in a long line of unhinged doctors, explains how patients can have their appearances altered through DNA restructuring ('I like to think of myself as an artist'). Bond locates Zao, who drops a pendant that contains a cache of diamonds bearing the crest of the British billionaire businessman Gustav Graves. Graves had discovered a vein of diamonds in Iceland, leading to his wealth and celebrity.

On a flight back to the UK, Bond is served a vodka martini by Roger Moore's daughter. Nepotism? And 'London Calling' on the soundtrack? Seriously? Self-publicising adrenalin junkie Gustave Graves parachutes into a press conference just opposite Buckingham Palace. Arrogant and smug might best describe his character. Bond meets Graves and his publicist Miranda Frost, who is an undercover MI6 agent, at Blades club. Blades, a fictional gentlemen's club, is a key location in Ian Fleming's novel *Moonraker*, where Bond catches Drax cheating at bridge. These scenes were filmed at the Reform Club on Pall Mall, London, ten minutes' walk from the imaginary location of Blades. The film's best action sequence follows as Bond and Graves move from a fencing 'cock fight' to a full-on hand-to-hand swordfight.

Toby Stephens, the son of the irrepressible Maggie Smith, is a terrific actor who played James Bond in a splendid series of radio adaptations of Fleming's original novels. He curls his lip and gives a good sneer as Gustave Graves in this film but beyond that is a thinly drawn cartoon baddie – 'a dapper splice of Richard Branson and Hugh Grant's evil twin' as Ian Nathan would have it. [26] The singer-cum-very-bad-actor Madonna plays Verity, a fencing teacher. Her scene with Bond is stiff and awkward. 'Do you handle your weapon well?', she asks. 'I've been known to keep my tip up', he responds. Chemistry, nil.

In one of those unlikely Bond plot twists, 007 is invited by Graves, for no obvious reason, to a scientific demonstration in Iceland. In a disused London Underground station, M tells Bond of MI6's doubts about Graves and restores his Double-O status – 'Well, it seems you've become useful again'. At MI6 HQ, the new Q, or just Quartermaster as Bond calls him, gives 007 an invisible car, 'the ultimate in British engineering'. 'You must be joking,' Bond asks. Sadly not.

'The invisible car was a turning point in Bond history,' writes Robbie Collin. 'It was the moment at which the trajectory of the Brosnan films, then in their eighth year, became unsustainable. $50 million of the feeblest special effects money can buy doesn't beat the timeless simplicity of Pierce Brosnan doing his best to look impressed while staring at an empty plinth.' [27]

Moving swiftly on, the second act is set in Iceland, a combination of elaborate Pinewood set location work at the Eden Project in Cornwall and RAF Little Rissington in Gloucestershire, genuine Icelandic grandeur and shabby CGI. Establishing shots show Bond driving along the Suðurlandsvegur, the main road east out of Reykjavík.

It's all downhill from here, as Graves arrives in a jet-powered ski-car and unveils a new orbital mirror satellite, Icarus (does this sound familiar to anyone who has watched *Diamonds Are Forever*?). Icarus can focus solar energy on a small area (does this sound familiar to anyone who has watched *The Man With the Golden Gun*?). Jinx is also in Iceland under cover as a journalist.

> Graves: As you know, I try to give the planet something in return for what it`s given me. Those little shards of heaven known as diamonds. Now, diamonds aren`t just expensive stones. They are the stuff of dreams. And the means to make dreams real. Imagine being able to bring light and warmth to the darkest parts of the world. Imagine being able to grow crops the year round, bringing an end to hunger. Imagine a second sun, shining like a diamond in the sky.

> Let there be light. I give you Icarus! Icarus is unique. Its miraculous silver skin will inhale the sun`s light and breathe it gently upon the earth`s surface. You have no idea how much Icarus is about to change your world. And now, let us brighten this night with our inner radiance.

Bond snoops around and defrosts Frost as Jinx in a red leather catsuit gets zapped by Graves' electronic glove and is captured. 'Who sent you?' she is asked. 'Yo mamma,' she responds. I'm not making this up. Bond rescues her, CGI lasers everywhere, and discovers Gustav Graves is Colonel Moon, who has, wait for it, changed his physical appearance with DNA treatment. Frost is exposed as a double agent.

And so, naturally, we need some action before we can think too much about what we've just seen. Bond escapes using his glass-shattering ring, steals Graves' jet-car and skids around the Jökurlsárlón glacier lagoon. Gustav tries to zap him with his satellite, but the ever-resourceful Bond, who deploys an anchor, flies over a cliff as his car jerks mechanically from the horizontal to the vertical. He recommissions a parachute and kitesurfs over a tsunami. This scene deploys heavy use of clunky computer-generated imagery. Whereas in the past, the Bond stunts were done for real, in *Die Another Day,* the green screen work takes much of the thrill out of one of the core foundations of this series. Bond riding a tidal wave on the remains of his jet-ski is one of the series' low points.

By now weary of all of this nonsense, let's simply list the film's remaining plot points: Bond and Zao face-off in a lengthy car chase across an ice lake and through the ice palace; Bond rescues Jinx from drowning; Bond and Jinx follow Graves and Frost to the Korean peninsula; Graves reveals to his father the true purpose of the Icarus satellite, helping to reunify North Korean and South Korea by force; in Graves' command aircraft, Bond and Graves fight as Frost attacks Jinx – director Lee Tamahori employs frequent bursts of slo-mo; Bond opens Graves' parachute, causing him to be pulled out of the plane and into one of its engines; Bond and Jinx escape in a helicopter from the cargo hold, carrying away Graves' stash of diamonds in the process; Moneypenny pretends to snog Bond in a computer simulator. In the final scene, Bond and Jinx have sex amidst the diamonds in a Buddhist temple. The exterior was shot at Penbyrn in rural Wales. Sample dialogue: 'Wait. Don't pull it out. I'm not finished with it yet.'

Die Another Day heavy-handedly references all of the nineteen previous Bond films at the expense of a cohesive plot, notably when Halle Barry reprises the scene from *Dr. No* when Honey Ryder emerges from the sea. We also see the shoe with the poison-tipped blade in Q's station laboratory (*From Russia With Love*), Bond's Aston Martin with a passenger ejector seat (*Goldfinger*), the underwater rebreather (*Thunderball*), the line '*Diamonds Are Forever*, but life isn't' in a magazine article, Bond retrieving a diamond from a woman's navel (*Live and Let Die*), a hall of mirrors (*The Man With the Golden Gun*), a

Union Jack parachute (*The Spy Who Loved Me*), a facial recognition programme (*For Your Eyes Only*), and Bond being betrayed by a fellow agent (*GoldenEye*), amongst many others. There are also some more subtle allusions to previous films. When Bond first meets Jinx, she tells him her name, and adds, 'My friends call me Jinx.' Bond replies, 'Mine call me James Bond.' In *From Russia With Love*, Tatiana Romanova says 'My friends call me Tania', and Bond gives the same reply. In *Die Another Day* Bond says to Jinx 'the cold must have kept you alive'. This references *GoldenEye* when Bond tells Natalya Simonova that being cold is what keeps him alive. Bond says, 'From nothing to everything in no time at all', a clear nod to Eon, the Bond production company. Brosnan's Bond disguises himself as an ornithologist and brandishes a copy of *Field Guide to the Birds of the West Indies* – a tip of the hat to Ian Fleming's inspiration for the name of his most famous character. [28] And, best of all, after Brosnan comes through the window of the medical facility in Cuba, he grabs a few grapes, as Connery did before making his exit from a room in the medical centre in *Thunderball*.

Die Another Day set a record for product placement in cinema with 24 tie-ins worth $120 million, including four vehicles and five drinks companies. This, along with the comic-book gene replacement therapy plot, typifies the shallowness of the Brosnan era.

Die Another Day was Pierce Brosnan's final Bond film, despite the expectation when it was released that he would return for a fifth. When asked if he had ever re-watched the films, Brosnan simply said: 'I have no desire to watch myself as James Bond. 'Cause it's just never good enough. It's a horrible feeling.' [29] Brosnan is being harsh on himself. His portrayal of James Bond was charismatic, funny, and tongue-in-cheek but with a conscience. The wordless scene in *Tomorrow Never Dies* when he mourns Paris Carver, for example, shows a genuine depth of characterisation that neither Roger Moore nor George Lazenby could have pulled off.

> Brosnan carried his films in a way no other Bond has had to do. With a weak Bond, none of his films, including *GoldenEye*, are strong enough to work regardless – in the way *On Her Majesty's Secret Service* transcends the game but miscast George Lazenby. Meanwhile, both Dalton and Moore required scripts that played to their very different strengths. In some ways, Brosnan was too good a fit. The writers could shun Bond the character and focus on the fripperies because they knew Brosnan would shine regardless.
> Max Williams, *Revisiting Die Another Day*, 2016.

Other than reference-spotting and laughing out loud for all the wrong reasons, the only genuinely positive aspect to *Die Another Day* is that it forced a series reboot that gave us one of the very best James Bond films.

As a postscript, word of a spin-off series involving Halle Berry's character Jinx began circulating in 2002. 'Bond screenwriters Neal Purvis and Robert Wade

were hired to write the script and, though it was never officially announced, Stephen Frears was on board to direct,' said Chris Wright, host of the James Bond Radio podcast. 'But in late October of the following year, MGM pulled the plug.' 'Not a lot is known about the script itself,' said Tom Sears, Wright's co-host. 'But Purvis and Wade have suggested that their idea was to involve Jinx in a story that would've been a lot less excessive than *Die Another Day*.'

Finally, students of the small print at the end of this film might have spotted Gregg Wilson, credited as 'development executive'. Gregg is Michael G Wilson's son, and has worked on each subsequent Bond film as associate producer, as well as taking uncredited acting cameos, just like his father. Here is the first of the third generation of Bond producers.

This is a strange and unfulfilling beast, neither a reinvention nor a celebration of the dutiful gadgets/girls/cars/fruitcake-billionaire-imperils-the-world formula, but an intermittently entertaining patchwork of both. The plot-line undoubtedly sounded hip and risky at brain-storming meetings: adding a detective element, being daring enough to lock Bond up over the opening credits, making Halle Berry a partner for the leading man rather than a simpering bed-fellow. However, there are just too many twists and extraneous strands for the running time to cope with. It's not a lack of effort but a lack of restraint that makes it such a muddle. The blunted, hectic editing leaves the film agitated and graceless. The execution is so complex, so riddled with afterthought, it makes a mess of the clean linear lines that made the formula so successful. And CGI this poor is embarrassing.

But before you lose faith and head for your *Dr. No* special edition, the grand traditions and great scenes emerge. Bond duels with Graves in a posturing fencing match, crashing through a starchy gentlemen's club with magnificent gusto. Leering henchman Rick Yune has diamonds embedded in his scarred mug, and multiple *Goldfinger*-style laser beams turn a punch-up into a freaky dance number. They make you want to cheer with relief.

Die Another Day is also very sexy. Berry, restricted by a one-dimensional character, makes no bones about which gadgets she has at her disposal. All told, the camera spends more time perusing her chest than it does the sleek bonnet of the new Aston Martin, while Pike makes for an enticing contrast, an ice-cold MI6 agent throwing frosty barbs in the direction of Bond's libido. In fact, all the cast more than pass muster.

Toby Stephens proves the most buoyant and happily hammy of all Brosnan's foes, recast by a madcap gene therapy into a dapper splice of Richard Branson and Hugh Grant's evil twin. Although, when you boil down his motive, he is a tad conflicted as to whether capitalism or communism is the raw material for his devilry.

And throughout it all, Brosnan is the glue that keeps the film from descending into parody. He is now so confident flipping from gritty determination to louche chauvinism, you can feel him slip nuances beneath

his director's nose. Not quite the birthday party we were expecting, but it's a diverting enough spectacle. The character and his careful owner are just too good to let the evident wobbles founder this universal export. You just wish the producers would learn to stop worrying.
Ian Nathan, *Empire*, November 2002

[1] Eon's press release, 1994. Sourced from *Martinis, Girls and Guns* (2003).
[2] *Entertainment Weekly* (October 2010).
[3] *LA Times*, 'Pierce Brosnan Bonds With 'Mister Johnson' (9 April 1991).
[4] In *Dr. No*, Bond, Honey and Quarrel are told by a henchman: 'We know you're there. We've been expecting you'; in *Diamonds Are Forever*, Bond sneaks into Whyte's penthouse and Blofeld says 'We've been expecting you'; in *Live and Let Die* Bond says 'Good evening. The name's Bond. I have a reservation' and the response is 'Mr Bond. Of course. Mrs Bond's been expecting you.'; later in the same film Kananga says, 'Mr Bond! There you are! And Miss Solitaire as well. Hardly unexpected but most welcome.'; in *The Man With the Golden Gun* Scaramanga has a phone conversation before Bond arrives on his island: 'Yes, it's a... guest I'm expecting. No, he won't be leaving.'; in *The Spy Who Loved Me*, Stromberg says 'Good evening Mr Bond, I've been expecting you.'; in *Octopussy* the Delhi hotel receptionist welcomes him by saying 'We've been expecting you'. There was once a cartoon in *Private Eye* that showed Blofeld coming out of the shower wearing a towel and holding a rubber duck. 'Ah, Mr Bond,' he exclaims. 'I wasn't expecting you.'
[5] *From Masculine Mastermind to Maternal Martyr – Judi Dench's M, Skyfall and the Patriarchal Logic of the James Bond Films*, in *For His Eyes Only: The Women of James Bond* (2015).
[6] *Typical Men – The Representation of Masculinity in Popular British Cinema* (2003).
[7] *The World Is Not Enough: A Companion* (1999).
[8] *Revisiting Skyfall* (2016).
[9] *The Chronotype in Action, from Action and Adventure Cinema*, edited by Yvonne Tasker (2004).
[10] Copyright the Ian Fleming Estate.
[11] *And Furthermore* (2010).
[12] James Berardinelli, *ReelViews* (1997)
[13] *And Furthermore* (2010).
[14] 'Pierce Brosnan: 'I was never good enough as Bond'', *The Daily Telegraph* (12 April 2014).
[15] Winder's almost unreadable *The Man Who Saved Britain: A Personal Journey into the Disturbing World of James Bond* (2006) is full of waspish comments such as this. It's a very funny book, but perhaps not for reasons the author intended.
[16] *The World Is Not Enough: A Companion* (1999).
[17] Cucinotta's character is listed as simply 'Cigar Girl' in the film's credits,
[18] Mark O'Connell in *Catching Bullets* and Jessica Kiang in *IndieWire* (both 2012).
[19] We should note that a character called Christmas Humphreys appears in screenwriters Purvis and Wade's *Let Him Have It* (1991).
[20] Scott Thomas has managed a unique double whammy of portraying the mothers of both the Duke and Duchess of Cambridge–Diana, Princess of Wales, in the television mini-series *Diana: Her True Story* (1993), and Carole Middleton in *William & Kate: The Movie* (2011). She is the younger sister of Kirsten Scott Thomas.
[21] *The World Is Not Enough: A Companion* (1999).

[22] *The World Is Not Enough: A Companion* (1999).
[23] *The World Is Not Enough: A Companion* (1999).
[24] *Bond Girls* (2010).
[25] And every Bond fan asks "Colonel Moon'? Why not 'Colonel Sun'?'
[26] *Empire* (November 2002).
[27] *The Daily Telegraph* (10 October 2015).
[28] Peter Haining notes that a character called James Bond appears in Agatha Christie's *The Listerdale Mystery* (1934). He concedes that this is an intriguing coincidence.
[29] 'Pierce Brosnan: 'I was never good enough as Bond', *The Daily Telegraph* (12 April 2014).

2005–2021: I've got a little itch, down there. Would you mind?

Casino Royale

Albert R Broccoli's Eon Productions Ltd presents Daniel Craig as Ian Fleming's James Bond 007 in *Casino Royale*
Release date: 14 November 2006. Running time: 144 minutes. Distributed by MGM/Columbia. Producers: Michael G. Wilson (8 of 12), Barbara Broccoli (5 of 9).
James Bond: Daniel Craig (1 of 5), M: Judi Dench (5 of 8), Leiter: Jeffrey Wright (1 of 3) with Giancarlo Giannini (René Mathis) (1 of 2), Jesper Christensen (Mr. White) (1 of 3).
With Mads Mikkelsen (Le Chiffre) and Eva Green (Vesper Lynd), Simon Abkarian (Alex Dimitrios), Caterina Murino (Solange Dimitrios), Ivana Miličević (Valenka), Isaach de Bankolé (Steven Obanno), Sébastien Foucan (Mollaka), Tobias Menzies (Villiers), Ludger Pistor (Mendel), Claudio Santamaria (Carlos).
Director: Martin Campbell (2 of 2). Screenplay: Neal Purvis (3 of 7), Robert Wade (3 of 7), Paul Haggis (1 of 2). Production design: Peter Lamont (9 of 9). Main titles: Daniel Kleinman (5 of 7). Music: David Arnold (4 of 5). Theme song performed by Chris Cornell. Cinematography: Phil Méheux (2 of 2). Edited by Stuart Baird (1 of 2).

Plot

After receiving a license to kill, British Secret Service agent James Bond heads to Madagascar, where he uncovers a link to Le Chiffre, a financier for terrorist organizations. Learning that Le Chiffre plans to raise money in a high-stakes poker game, MI6 sends Bond to play against him.

Cast

Pierce Brosnan had signed a deal for four films when he was cast in the role of James Bond and this was fulfilled with *Die Another Day* in 2002.

'I went to them and asked about making *Casino Royale*, which is the first Ian Fleming book,' Brosnan told *The New York Times* in 2004. 'I had hooked up with Quentin Tarantino, who wanted to direct the movie. On the fifth apple martini one evening, he mentioned *Casino Royale*, which is the blueprint for the psyche of Bond, and I took that idea to the Broccoli family, who produce the Bond movies. They have a way of doing the films, and they are not open to discussion. They threw my idea out the window. But then, in the middle of negotiations, they changed their minds. They never offered a sound reason.' [1]

Some years later, in an interview with Matthew Field and Ajay Chowdhury, Brosnan said: 'I was in the Bahamas working on a movie called *After the Sunset*, and my agents called me up and said, 'Negotiations have stopped. They are not quite sure what they want to do. They'll call you next Thursday.' I sat in Richard Harris' house in the Bahamas and Barbara [Broccoli] and Michael

[Wilson] were on the line. 'We're so sorry.' She was crying. Michael was more stoic and he said, 'You were a great James Bond. Thank you very much,' and I said 'Thank you very much. Goodbye.' That was it. I was utterly shocked.' [2]

The frontrunner to replace Brosnan was Clive Owen, the winner of a 2005 public poll for who should star as Bond. He was familiar from the TV series *Chancer* and *Lorna Doone* and for his acclaimed performances in *Close My Eyes* (1991), *Croupier* (1998), *King Arthur* (2004) and Oscar-nominated *Closer* (2004). He appeared as an assassin in the 2002 film *The Bourne Identity*. But Owen too walked away from James Bond over a contract disagreement: an article in *Variety* from 2005 alleged that Owen was approached but turned the part down because he was refused 'gross profit points' on his contract – meaning he'd receive a percentage of the profits from each new Bond film. 'Playing James Bond would have been like entering a golden prison', Owen told *Glamour* magazine in 2007, 'and I doubt that would have suited me. I may be the only actor who consistently said, 'No, no and no'. I never understood what I would have been able to add to the role, or how I could play a character who has already been defined in the past. For me, Sean Connery is the real James Bond.'

Michael G. Wilson has suggested that he had a list of two hundred actors, with names ranging from Sam Worthington, Dominic West and Hugh Jackman to Jason Statham and Colin Firth. Known quantities Ewan McGregor, Julian McMahon and Karl Urban each of whom met either the casting directors or producers. Rupert Friend, then hot property after his appearances in *The Libertine* (2004) and *Pride and Prejudice* (2005) took part in a full day's screen test. Casting director Debbie McWilliams later told BBC Radio 4's *The Film Programme* that Friend turned down the part. Goran Visnjic (*ER*) and Antony Starr (hardly known outside New Zealand in 2005) are also said to have been tested, along with Henry Cavill, the preference of director Martin Campbell. At 22, it was felt Cavill was too young, even for a reboot. According to Cavill, the final decision was between him and the producers' final choice, Daniel Craig: 'I was going to be the very young, wet behind the ears secret agent,' Cavill said. 'He was the more traditional secret agent, and they made the right choice, I think.'

Producer Barbara Broccoli had seen and liked Craig's performance as a psychopathic priest in *Elizabeth* (1998). His character was an assassin, dispatched by Rome to kill the queen. In one scene, the priest has to kill an informant. 'I just remember getting chills all over my body,' Broccoli told *GQ* in 2020. 'I just thought, Oh, my God.'

Craig, born 2 March 1968, began his acting career after graduating from the Guildhall School of Music and Drama in 1991. One of his earliest theatre reviews said, 'Daniel Craig contains his violence like an unexploded mine'.[3] He made his theatre debut in 1993 as the conflicted legal clerk Joe in *Angels in America* at the National Theatre. His first big TV break was one of the scintillating cast in BBC's *Our Friends in the North*, broadcast in early 1996.

Our Friends in the North helped to establish the careers of its four lead actors, Daniel Craig, Christopher Eccleston, Gina McKee and Mark Strong. Internationally, Craig's rangy performances in *Road to Perdition* (2002), *The Mother* (2003), *Enduring Love* (2004) and especially the British gangster film *Layer Cake* (2005) caught the attention of both audiences and critics. This was followed by rock-solid turns as a Mossad agent in Steven Spielberg's *Munich* and in the TV film *Archangel*, both in 2005.

Director Martin Campbell notes:

> What happens in the casting process, you probably get fifty names which you all consider and talk about. None of the names stood out, and what you do is test, and we tested eight and I can't tell you who those eight were, but we did test them. Daniel flew over from I think, doing *The Visiting*, a remake of *Bodysnatchers.* And he literally got off the plane and ran over to the studio. I did his test and he was excellent on the test. Then the script came in and we had bits and pieces on the script, and of course, it just seemed to me that he was absolutely perfect for this part. It's very much as Fleming describes Bond. We all had to be unanimous and Daniel Craig got the part. And that's what happened. He is clearly the best actor ever in our Bond films. He's done a lot of stuff and he's always good. In *Road to Perdition*, I thought he did a wonderful job. Whatever he does, he's got this chameleon-like quality. Very committed actor, and whether he's playing Hamlet or Bond, he puts the same energy into the part. [4]

Craig's casting was confirmed on 14 October 2005. 'I only knew positively that I had got the part on Monday,' the actor insisted at the official announcement at a naval training centre in London. 'I had a couple of Martinis when I found out.' His inspiration for the character? Indiana Jones. 'What was brilliant was that he [Jones] was fallible, he bled,' Craig told the *New Zealand Herald* in 2015. 'It's never left me. If you do action, an audience has to feel jeopardy.'

'It wasn't just recasting the role,' Barbara Broccoli said. 'It was a new century and a new era. It felt like we had to redefine.'

Initially, the producers' choice of lead actor garnered controversy. Moments after the announcement, one fan wrote on the website Absolutely James Bond, 'My God, don't the producers have any brains? Craig is not Bond material. Bond must be tall, dark and handsome. Or at least two of the three, and he isn't even one!' 'Is the world ready for the first blond Bond?' asked the BBC news. 'The new James Bond is blond. Rough trade, with a pale, flattened face and large, fleshy ears. Accent: well, it ain't Oxbridge.' shouted *The New York Times*. 'The Name's Bland—James Bland,' ran the front page of the *Daily Mirror*. There is a website (look it up) that has fruitlessly pilloried the casting decision for years.

'I had prepared to a degree for a negative reaction [to my casting],' Craig commented at the time. 'It's something you can't plan for, or else you'd get paranoid very quickly.' [5]

When *Casino Royale* was released, Craig's intense, muscular, kinetic performance silenced all the critics. 'Craig reinvigorates a fagged-out franchise that's been laying on bigger stunts and sillier gadgets to disguise the fact that it's run out of ideas,' wrote Peter Travers in *Rolling Stone*, 17 November 2006. 'And he does it with an actor's skill, an athlete's grace and a dangerous glint that puts you on notice that Bond, James Bond, is back in business.'

Michael G. Wilson and Barbara Broccoli showed great wisdom in bringing in an actor who could do more than just throw a punch or deliver dialogue – they simply went for a very good actor. Daniel Craig brings an emotional depth to James Bond. He plays the role with a calm intensity. He has an edge, even when dressed in a tuxedo. Here was a Bond that could hurt, a Bond that could cry.

'I'd never copy somebody else', Craig once said, 'I would never do an impression of anybody else or try and improve on what they did. That would be a pointless exercise for me. I wouldn't have signed on unless I could strip the character back to basics. I wanted Bond to be somebody who was foul – someone who makes mistakes and gets involved in situations where things may go wrong. Dramatically, it's just more exciting.' [6]

Four former Bonds approved.

'I think Daniel Craig is a terrific choice,' said Sean Connery. 'I think they're going back to a more realistic type of Bond movie, as I don't think they could have gone much further with the special effects.' [7]

'Now they've found *the* Bond – Daniel Craig,' wrote Roger Moore. 'I always said Sean played Bond as a killer and I played Bond as a lover. I think that Daniel Craig is even more of a killer. He has this superb intensity; he's a glorious actor. My God, he did more action in the first half, in the first second, of the film, than I did in all the Bonds put together. He's brilliant.' [8]

'I thought the first 25 minutes of Daniel's first movie was the best 25 minutes I've seen in any Bond movie,' said Timothy Dalton. 'I thought it was a fantastic opening.' [9]

'Daniel Craig is a great actor and he's going to do a fantastic job,' noted Pierce Brosnan. [10]

'You just look in those eyes and you know he's capable of doing anything,' suggests Barbara Broccoli.

'What's extraordinary,' Craig said a few years later, 'is that at a point in my career when I was enjoying making movies and working with wonderful directors and just getting a big kick out of it, I was given this opportunity to do something for which I had no benchmark, no experience whatsoever. I threw myself into it full bore and it was a success. But I'm not quite sure how. Except that we had a good script and I committed to it, and we had a good cast, and Martin Campbell did a pretty good job of that film whichever way you look at it.' [11]

Judi Dench continued in her role as M. 'Daniel Craig is very different to Pierce Brosnan,' she wrote later. 'But both are very good actors with an enormous sense of humour.' [12] This raises a paradox, as the film is a reboot, and therefore the first Bond story. Not to worry. Judi Dench continues to be magnificent in the role. In the Craig films, however, Dench's portrayal of M is different. Through *Casino Royale*, *Quantum of Solace* and, in particular, *Skyfall* when she is practically co-lead with Craig, M is more motherly, more tender. The first time M and Bond meet in *Casino Royale* is when he breaks into her house to trace the bomb-maker's contact. Here, we see that M and Bond share a close, emotional relationship, but that there is an undercurrent of tension between them. She treats him like a wayward son; he responds with the blank look of an admonished teenager. Another time, she is interrupted by a call from the office when she is running a bath. This M has a life beyond MI6. Bernard Lee's M was hardly ever seen outside his office.

Eva Green, as the sensitive, sharp, conflicted, fragile Vesper Lynd is simply radiant. Green had made a huge impact in both *The Dreamers* (2003) and Ridley Scott's historical epic *Kingdom of Heaven* (2005). She initially turned down the role of Lynd but was approached once more when principal photography was already underway. In 2007, *Entertainment Weekly* named her the fourth-best Bond female lead behind Ursula Andress, Honor Blackman and Diana Rigg, 'embodying all the traits that characterize 007's most memorable minxes – the smarts of Pussy Galore, the drive of Melina Havelock, the sobriety of Anya Amasova, and the, ahem, jewels of Tiffany Case'. Green won a BAFTA and an Empire award for her performance. Noted Broadway actor Jeffrey Wright makes his first of three appearances as Felix Leiter.

Danish character actor Mads Mikkelsen plays Le Chiffre with a quiet, disquieting menace ('so I think ... I'll feed you what you seem not to value') and fellow Dane Jesper Christensen makes the first of three appearances as Mr. White. There is also a cameo from Tsai Chin as one of the gamblers – she played Ling, Bond's playmate in the pre-credit sequence of *You Only Live Twice*.

Theme Song

The tremendous theme song, 'You Know My Name', is written and sung by Soundgarden's Chris Cornell – his vocal power held in check until certain key moments. Wow.

Production

Casino Royale was filmed between January and July 2006 at Pinewood Studios, Buckinghamshire, at Barrandov Studios, Prague, and on location in the United Kingdom, the Czech Republic, the Bahamas and Italy.

Observations

The James Bond series needed more than just a new lead actor and the side-lining of Q and Moneypenny to freshen things up. With *Casino Royale*, we start again at the beginning. But there are some familiar foundations: director

Martin Campbell re-invents Bond for a second time after helming *GoldenEye*; production designer Peter Lamont contributes to his ninth (and final) Bond film; David Arnold scores his fourth soundtrack; Daniel Kleinman creates the main titles for the fifth time; Neal Purvis and Robert Wade provide their third script, this time with scintillating dialogue from Canadian screenwriter Paul Haggis, author of consecutive best picture Oscar-winning films *Million Dollar Baby* (2004) and *Crash* (2005). The opening titles read, again, at last, 'based on a novel by Ian Fleming'. What's more, Craig's performance matches Fleming's first description of OO7, at the end of chapter one of *Casino Royale*.

> For a few moments, Bond sat motionless, gazing out of the window across the dark sea; then he shoved the bundle of banknotes under the pillow of the ornate single bed, cleaned his teeth, turned out the lights and climbed with relief between the harsh French sheets. For ten minutes, he lay on his left side, reflecting on the events of the day. Then he turned over and focused his mind towards the tunnel of sleep. His last action was to slip his right hand under the pillow until it rested under the butt of the .38 Colt Police Positive with the sawn barrel. Then he slept, and with the warmth and humour of his eyes extinguished, his features relapsed into a taciturn mask, ironical, brutal, and cold.
> From Ian Fleming's *Casino Royale.* [13]

Over three distinct acts – the Miami bomb, the Montenegro poker game, the Venice payoff – *Casino Royale* reconstitutes Bond in a post-9/11 world. The story is a refreshingly faithful update of Fleming's first Bond novel but expands and extends the story to provide a multi-layered, modern and thoroughly satisfying thriller. The first third kicks off with a pig-headed and arrogant Bond earning his Double-O status. The film opens with a taut, grainy three-and-a-half-minute black and white pre-titles sequence set in Prague. Bond confronts Station Chief Dryden.

> M doesn't mind you earning a little money on the side, Dryden. She'd just prefer it if it wasn't selling secrets.

'The sequence's unusual visual style evokes the deep-focus, Techniscope compositions of the gritty British spy films of the Sixties, like *The Ipcress File* and *The Spy Who Came in From the Cold*', suggests Robbie Collin. 'Films that pushed back against the globe-trotting gloss of the early Connery Bond pictures. Small objects like desk lamps loom large in the frame, while faces are shunted to the sides and shrouded in shadow: just a bit of good old-fashioned Cold War paranoia.' [14]

Dryden asks Bond how his contact died. 'Not well', replies OO7, as we cut to Bond savagely beating a man to death in a bathroom. In the original script, this was set at a cricket match in Lahore, India. We don't see the bigger picture, so it could still be.

> An effective introduction to a gritty new era of Bond – a transition smoothly made, with the use of an old device: monochrome, which had not been used in a Bond film since *Diamonds Are Forever* in 1971. [15]

In Uganda (Black Park again), the mysterious Mr. White introduces Obanno, a member of a rebel group called 'the Lord's Resistance Army', to Le Chiffre, a private banker to terrorist groups, or 'freedom fighters' as he calls them. Obanno entrusts Le Chiffre with a large sum of money to invest safely for him and Le Chiffre uses it to buy options on the aerospace manufacturer Skyfleet, betting the money on the company's failure. Why he does that will become evident soon enough.

To Madagascar, 6 July 2006. These scenes were all filmed in the Bahamas, with the betting ring taking place at the Royal Bahamas Defence Force Base, and the parkour chase along Coral Harbour Road in New Providence. The 'Nambutu Embassy' is the former Buena Vista hotel on Delancy Street, Nassau, now a distillery. Bond gives chase, his quarry using athletic and gymnastic expertise to escape. Bond is less agile and precise, but he makes up for it with brute strength.

'It was important to me that I do as many of my own stunts as possible for authenticity,' Craig told the *Boston Globe* in 2006. 'Take the Madagascar sequence. I wanted to be seen jumping from crane to crane, physically exerting myself. [Stunt coordinator] Gary Powell and I wanted to get this as real as possible. I didn't get fit just to take my shirt off. Although that applies a little.'

The subsequent briefing scene sees a dressing down for Bond. The dialogue and acting is exquisite.

> M: How the hell did you find out where I lived?
> Bond: The same way I found out your name. I thought 'M' was a randomly assigned letter. I had no idea it stood for –
> M: Utter one more syllable and I'll have you killed.

Judi Dench, wonderful as always, is not playing the same character she did in the Pierce Brosnan films; this time, M is the relic of the Cold War, not Bond. 'In the old days', she complains, 'if an agent did something that embarrassing, he'd have the good sense to defect.'

A clue from the bomb-maker's phone ('ellipsis') points to Alex Dimitrios, a corrupt Greek official and middleman for Le Chiffre, based in the Bahamas. Bond travels there, ostensibly on leave. This is the Bahamas for real, the fifth time that an Eon Bond film had used the Caribbean island as a location after *Thunderball* and underwater scenes in *You Only Live Twice*, *The Spy Who Loved Me* and *For Your Eyes Only*. He identifies Dimitrios from the Ocean Club's CCTV footage.

On the beach, Bond emerges from the water in another homage to the Ursula Andress scene from *Dr. No*. If we're being pretentious, we can claim that this scene marked a Venus-like rebirth for James Bond. Daniel Craig later claimed that the iconic image was a fluke. 'It happened by accident. Where we were filming in the Bahamas, the beach has a very low shelf and the water is very narrow. I kind of swam underwater for a while and then came up, and of course, it's only up to my knees. So you saw more of me than we were expecting! But I didn't realise the repercussions of it. I had no idea I would be haunted by it for the rest of my life.' [16]

Bond attracts the attention of Dimitrios's wife, Solange, who is riding along the shore. The name of this character is taken from the short story *OO7 in New York*. Later, Bond beats Dimitrios at poker, winning an Aston Martin DB5, and is busy seducing Solange when she gets a phone call from her husband telling her he is flying to Miami.

> Bond: Good evening. Can I get a bottle of chilled Bollinger Grand Annće and the beluga caviar?
> Room service: And would that be for two, sir?
> Bond [irritated]: What?
> Room service: For two?
> Bond: No, for one.

Bond kills Dimitrios and follows his henchman Carlos to the airport. The 'Body World' scenes were filmed at the Ministry of Transport building in Prague, the rest of the Miami interior scenes are Václava Havla airport, also in Prague.

In a top-class, very entertaining action sequence, Bond halts the destruction of Skyfleet's airliner, costing Le Chiffre huge losses. The chase around Miami International Airport was shot in rural Surrey at the *Top Gear* test track at Dunsfold Aerodrome. The twinkling Floridian cityscape was digitally added to the background during post-production. Interestingly, the inclusion of the bomber blowing himself up is a development from a scene in Ian Fleming's original novel.

> Then with a blinding flash of white light, there was the ear-splitting crack of a monstrous explosion and Bond was slammed down to the pavement by a solid bolt of hot air which dented his cheeks and stomach as if they had been made of paper. He lay, gazing up at the sun, while the air (or so it seemed to him) went on twanging with the explosion as if someone had hit the bass register of a piano with a sledgehammer. When, dazed and half-conscious, he raised himself on one knee, a ghastly rain of pieces of flesh and shreds of blood-soaked clothing fell on him and around him, mingled with branches and gravel.
> From Ian Fleming's *Casino Royale.* [17]

In any other film, this would have been the climax. In *Casino Royale*, we're just getting going.

M provides some important exposition, setting up the high stakes poker game.

> M: We can't let him win this game. If he loses, he'll have nowhere to run. We'll give him sanctuary in return for everything he knows. I'm putting you in the game replacing someone who's playing for a syndicate. According to Villiers, you're the best player in the Service.
> Bond: Trust me, I wish it wasn't the case.
> M: I would ask you if you could remain emotionally detached but I don't think that's your problem, is it, Bond?
> Bond: No.

The second act, running for an exquisitely perfect fifty minutes, revisits the key beats of Fleming's debut novel: René Mathis, the card game, the CIA bail-out, the kidnapping of Vesper and the torture scene are all present and correct.

> The second section of *Casino Royale* is quite possibly the best Bond film ever made. From the shot of the train snaking through the forest to Le Chiffre falling lifeless to the floor, the quality is so high you practically get vertigo.
> **Max Williams, *Revisiting Casino Royale*, 2016**

Bond first meets Vesper Lynd, a British Treasury agent, on the train to Montenegro. The relationship between Bond and Vesper goes through several distinct phases. They get to know each other over dinner, deducing each other's backgrounds.

> Vesper: Now, having just met you, I wouldn't go as far as calling you a cold-hearted bastard...
> Bond: No, of course not.
> Vesper: But it wouldn't be a stretch to imagine. You think of women as disposable pleasures, rather than meaningful pursuits. So as charming as you are, Mr. Bond, I will be keeping my eye on our government's money – and off your perfectly formed arse.
> Bond: You noticed?
> Vesper: Even accountants have imagination. How was your lamb?
> Bond: Skewered. One sympathizes.

In Montenegro, they check into the Hotel Splendide, aka the Grand Hotel Pupp in Karlovy Vary, about 80 miles west of Prague, close to the German border. The fictional hotel name is a nod to the 2000 dark comedy of the same name which featured a certain D. Craig in a lead role.

A visit to the picturesque town of Loket, a fifteen-minute drive from Karlovy Vary, introduces René Mathis. When Bond finds a tuxedo in his hotel room, Lynd claims she was able to order it, tailor-made, by sizing him up – her eyes

slide from his head to his toes. Eva Green here is simply glowing. As with Bond's famous emergence from the sea in the Bahamas earlier in the film, this turns the objectification away from the female lead and towards Bond himself. This would have been unthinkable in any of the previous films.

The casino itself is the former Kaiserbad Spa in Karlovy Vary. The card game, Texas Hold 'Em poker in the film version, replaces baccarat from the book, re-introduces Le Chiffre, perfectly played by Mads Mikkelsen. The card game is broken up by two tense action sequences. Firstly, Obanno ambushes Le Chiffre in his suite but allows him to continue with his plan to win back the money. As Obanno leaves, Bond is spotted and a violent fight follows, with one man thrown down a stairwell. Bond strangles Obanno. Vesper has a Lady Macbeth moment in the shower ('It's like there's blood on my hands. It's not coming off'). This scene shows a marked development of emotional, not sexual, intimacy between Vesper and Bond. He simply holds her. This represents a key shift in their relationship... 'the moment when the masculinity of Connery, the vulnerability of Lazenby, the diplomacy of Moore, the instinct of Dalton and professionalism of Brosnan has now become the *conscience* of Craig.' [18]

As the tournament resumes, Bond loses his stake after Le Chiffre is tipped off to Bond seeing his 'tell'. Is it Vesper that is the leak, or Mathis? We are never quite certain, but later dialogue as Bond and Vesper talk on the beach gives us a clue.

> Vesper: Does everyone have a tell?
> Bond: Yes. Everyone. Everyone except you.

Vesper refuses to fund further playing, but Felix Leiter, a fellow player and 'brother from Langley', agrees to stake Bond to continue playing in exchange for allowing Le Chiffre to be taken into American custody.

A second key scene breaks up the card game when Le Chiffre has his girlfriend poison Bond to stop him winning the game. Bond contacts MI6 and their doctors talk him through a digitalis injection and DB9's in-built ECG – 'push the damn button'. Vesper arrives to rescue him and Bond returns to the game ('That last hand, it nearly killed me.'). Leiter is eliminated and the game culminates in a $115 million hand in which the remaining players go all-in. Le Chiffre trumps the other players, but Bond wins with a straight flush.

Vesper leaves after she gets a message from Mathis. Bond follows to see her kidnapped. He gives chase in his Aston DBS but flips his car to avoid Vesper. This sequence accidentally set a world record. Initially, an eight-inch ramp was built at Dunsfold Aerodrome to flip the car and when the test vehicles hit the ramp at 65mph, they barrel-rolled three or four times. Satisfied that the stunt would work, the Bond crew moved to the Hill Circuit at the Millbrook test track in Bedfordshire, doubling for the country roads of Montenegro. The ramp was raised to 18 inches but didn't flip the heavier DBS successfully, so the team fitted it with a gas cannon to punch a metal ram out into the ground and force a flip. Stunt driver Adam Kirley took the car to 75mph, pressed the trigger and established a new Guinness World Record for most cannon rolls in a car: seven complete turns.

Le Chiffre takes Bond and Vesper to an abandoned ship and tortures Bond in a scene taken directly from Fleming's novel that makes many men cross their legs in discomfort. Bond is stripped and whipped but remains defiant.

> Le Chiffre: You've taken good care of your body. Such a waste.
> Bond: You know... I never understood all these elaborate tortures.
> Le Chiffre: It's the simplest thing... to cause more pain than a man can possibly endure. And of course, it's not only the immediate agony, but the knowledge that if you do not yield soon enough, there will be little left to identify you as a man. The only question remains, will you yield in time?

'I was protected by fibreglass, thankfully,' Craig said at the time. 'Although at one point when Mads was hitting it with the whip, it cracked and I flew across to the other side of the room. We shot that entire scene in one day, and strangely enough, there were a lot more people on set that day.' [19]

As Le Chiffre prepares to castrate Bond, Mr. White enters and kills Le Chiffre and his associates.

Bond wakes in hospital, the Villa del Balbianello on Lake Como. This same villa was used as Padme's lakeside retreat in *Star Wars: Episode II Attack of the Clones* (2002), with computer-generated imagery replacing the building's true exterior. Mendel, the Swiss banker, transfers Bond's winnings. Vesper's and Bond's romance develops. 'You know James,' Vesper tells Bond, 'I just want you to know that if all that was left of you was your smile and your little finger, you'd still be more of a man than anyone I've ever met.' Bond replies, as Daniel Craig almost cracks that smile, 'That's because you know what I can do with my little finger.' Can you imagine Roger Moore saying that line and not making it sound smutty?

Bond tells Vesper that he loves her and wants to resign from MI6. They travel to Venice. The hotel interior scenes were filmed at the Národní Muzeum in Prague. When M calls Bond and tells him the money was never deposited, Bond realises Vesper has betrayed him and follows her from St. Marks's Square past the Sotoportego de le Colonne and the Conservatorio di Musica Benedetto Marcello to her secret meeting with her contact Gettler, based on a literary character who briefly appeared in the Fleming novel.

> [Bond] telephoned Mathis in Paris. The customer had had a Swiss triptique. His name was Adolph Gettler. He had given a bank in Zurich as his address. Gettler was understood to be connected with the watch industry. Inquiries could be pursued if there was a charge against him. Vesper had shrugged her shoulders at the information.
> From Ian Fleming's, *Casino Royale.* [20]

The sinking palazzo was created in the studio, a mix of CGI and model work, seamlessly added to shots of real buildings along the Canale Grande, close to the Rialto in the Cannaregio district of Venice. Vesper's death is genuinely poignant. White, watching nearby, walks away with the money. Crucially it's M who recognises Vesper's sacrifice. Bond's bitter line 'The job's done and the bitch is dead' is taken directly from Fleming, perhaps the most famous last line in a 20th-century thriller, with Bond telling headquarters: 'The bitch is dead now.'

The final scene breaks all conventions. For the first time, a Bond film does not end in an embrace between Bond and his female lead. Indeed, none of the Craig films does. At a grand estate on Lake Como, Villa la Gaeta, Mr. White receives a phone call. As he asks for the caller's identity, he is shot in the leg. The caller walks up and introduces himself: 'The name's Bond… James Bond.' Cue the James Bond Theme and a huge adrenalin rush for the viewer. Yippee!

Craig's dour, angry take on Bond gives us a recognisable human being, in vivid contrast to Moore's often limp comedy or Brosnan's sometimes cartoonish portrayal. Only the two Bond actors with the shortest tenures had previously allowed any humanity to colour James Bond: George Lazenby in the distinctly change-of-mood final moments of *On Her Majesty's Secret Service* and Timothy Dalton in the revenge plot of *Licence To Kill*. This film trumps both.

This has almost everything you could want from a Bond movie, plus qualities you didn't expect they'd even try for. It does all the location-hopping, eye-opening stunt stuff and lavish glamour expected of every big-screen Bond, but also delivers a surprisingly faithful adaptation of Fleming's short, sharp, cynical book with the post-WWII East-vs.-West backdrop persuasively upgraded to a post 9/11 War on Terror.

From *Goldfinger* on – especially in the Roger Moore and Pierce Brosnan films – the usual gambit has been to open with a pre-credits sequence highlighting amazing stunt work and a larger-than-life exploit. Here, with a new actor cast as a Bond only just issued with his license to kill, we get an intense, black and white scene set in an office in Prague.

For a few reels, *Casino Royale* lets the new boy settle into what could almost be a Brosnan or Dalton movie – hard-hitting, but tinged with the fantastical. Bond goes off the map to harry the organisation of 'banker to the world's terrorists' Le Chiffre, with a beddable beach beauty along the way, and a thwarted attack on a super-sized jet aeroplane which could have been the climax of any other adventure.

There are miscalculations (a collapsing building in Venice is a gimmick too many in an emotional finale which would play better without all the noise) and audiences who just want a handsome fantasy figure might find a muscular Bond with perpetually bruised knuckles and the beginnings of a drink problem too much of a stretch. But long-running series can only survive

through constant renewal. *Casino Royale* is the most exciting Bond film, in conventional action terms but also in dramatic meat, since *On Her Majesty's Secret Service*, with the added advantage of a star who finally delivers what the credits have always promised: 'Ian Fleming's James Bond'.
Kim Newman, *Empire*, 2006

Quantum of Solace

Albert R Broccoli's Eon Productions Limited presents Daniel Craig as Ian Fleming's James Bond 007 in *Quantum of Solace*
Release date: 20 October 2008. Running time: 106 minutes. Distributed by MGM/Columbia. Producers: Michael G. Wilson (9 of 12), Barbara Broccoli (6 of 9).
James Bond: Daniel Craig (2 of 5), M: Judi Dench (6 of 8), Leiter: Jeffrey Wright (2 of 3) with Jesper Christensen (Mr. White) (2 of 3), Giancarlo Giannini (René Mathis) (2 of 2), Rory Kinnear (Tanner) (1 of 4).
With Mathieu Amalric (Dominic Greene) and Olga Kurylenko (Camille Montes), Gemma Arterton (Strawberry Fields), Anatole Taubman (Elvis), David Harbour (Gregg Beam), Joaquín Cosío (General Medrano), Fernando Guillén Cuervo (Carlos).
Director: Marc Forster. Screenplay: Neal Purvis (4 of 7), Robert Wade (4 of 7), Paul Haggis (2 of 2). Production design: Dennis Gassner (1 of 3). Main titles: MK12. Music: David Arnold (5 of 5). Theme song performed by Alicia Keys and Jack White. Cinematography: Roberto Schaefer. Edited by Matt Cheese and Rick Pearson.

Plot

James Bond's hunt for those who blackmailed Vesper Lynd leads him to businessman Dominic Greene, a key player in the Quantum organization. Bond learns that Quantum intends to stage a coup d'état in Bolivia to seize control of the water supply.

Cast

Daniel Craig, Judi Dench, Jeffrey Wright, Giancarlo Giannini and Jesper Christensen reprise their roles from *Casino Royale*. Dominic Green is played by French actor Mathieu Amalric
French-Ukranian Olga Kurylenko plays the elegant but damaged Camille Montes. 'I saw hundreds of tapes and then from those hundreds of tapes I selected around twenty girls to come in and read for me,' says director Marc Forster. 'Out of those twenty, I selected four to read with Daniel Craig and just basically played the scene. And Olga just seemed to naturally connect with him ... there was something in her eyes where I felt like she has lived life. It was important for me in Camille's character that she was a fighter and she had this tragedy in her past and I thought when I met Olga that she had these sort of qualities about her.' [21]

Joaquín Cosío plays the very nasty General Medrano. He had been nominated for the 2005 Mexican Academy of Film Awards for his portrayal of Mascarita in the Mexican box office hit *Matando Cabos*. Bill Tanner, a character from the original books, is portrayed by English theatre actor and playwright Rory Kinnear. This character had previously been played by James Villiers (*A View to A Kill*) and Michael Kitchen (*GoldenEye*, *The World Is Not Enough*). Smaller roles are taken by Gemma Arterton (Strawberry Fields), Fernando Guillén Cuervo (Carlos), Anatole Taubman (Elvis) and David Harbour (Gregg Beam).

Theme Song

The second top-class theme in a row, a powerful dissonant duet by Alicia Keys and the White Stripes' Jack White. Amy Winehouse's unavailability is a missed opportunity, but what we have fits the bill perfectly.

Production

Quantum of Solace was filmed between August 2007 and June 2008 at Pinewood Studios, Buckinghamshire, and on location in Italy, the United Kingdom, Panama, Austria and Chile.

Observations

Whilst a jumble of a plot, often incoherent, parts of *Quantum of Solace* are classic Bond – the immediate energy of the opening seconds, the astonishing chase through Siena, the beauty of the opera scene, the shock of agent Fields' demise, the striking finale at the 'Perla de las Dunas' in Chile. The film picks up immediately where *Casino Royale* left off: it's the series' first straight-up sequel. The film was stylishly directed by Marc Foster, who had impressed many people with *Monsters Ball* (2001) and *The Kite Runner* (2007), and has a definite liking for overhead camera shots. It is again written by Purvis, Wade and Haggis.

There is no opening gun barrel. James Bond is driving along the shores of Lake Garda with the captured Mr. White in the boot of his Aston Martin DBS. A noisy, choppy and energetically cut car chase ends in Siena: both the Via Giovanni Dupre and the nearby Piazzetta della Paglietta are identifiable. Bond delivers White to M. 'It's time to get out,' he grunts at the end of a pre-titles sequence that lasts just four minutes.

As the famous palio horserace takes place nearby, White is interrogated.

> White: You really don't know anything about us. It's so amusing because we are on the other side, thinking, 'The MI6, the CIA, they're looking over our shoulders. They're listening to our conversations.' And the truth is you don't even know we exist.
>
> M: Well, we do now, Mr. White, and we're quick learners.
>
> White: Oh, really? Well, then, the first thing you should know about us is that we have people everywhere.

M's personal bodyguard, Mitchell, betrays them and tries to kill M. In a taut on-foot chase scene, Bond pursues Mitchell through the crowds attending the Palio and across the rooftops of Siena.

Director Marc Forster:

> They showed me the tunnels which the Roman's built under the city. And I thought it would be interesting to put the safe house underground … and then start the chase exactly when the horse race starts and have them intercut those two chases. He pops up in the middle and then he goes up to the roof and then crashes through the dome from the top. Originally in the script, it was to enter the dome from the ground and fight up some scaffolding. I thought it was more interesting and more spectacular to crash in from the top and have the intercutting between the race and them. Originally the rooftops were supposed to be built in Pinewood and we couldn't afford it. So I said, why don't we ask if we could shoot in the final location. So the city of Siena allowed us to shoot on real rooftops. [22]

Craig himself performed some of the stunts, including the leap across the balcony and the jump onto the roof of the bus. The sequence on the scaffolding, as Bond and Mitchell swing with their guns out of reach, has a genuine sense of danger and risk.

Back in the UK, M expresses anger that an organisation they don't even know about has managed to turn one of her agents. They discover through tagged bank notes (or 'bills' as M would have it) that Mitchell had a contact in Haiti, Edmund Slate. Bond travels there – these scenes were all filmed in Panama – and learns that Slate is a hitman sent to kill Camille Montes at the behest of her lover, the devious environmentalist entrepreneur Dominic Greene. Camille, however, has her own agenda.

Bond finds Slate and fights hand-to-hand in a scene straight from *The Bourne Identity*. It is while M and Tanner are walking across the square of the Frobisher Crescent within the Barbican Centre in London that Bond tells them that Slate was a 'dead end'. M responds, 'Damn him. He killed him.'

Bond cases Greene's warehouse. The card Bond hands to Greene's men says the name 'R Sterling'. Bond-nerd fact: this alias was last employed in *The Spy Who Loved Me* when Roger Moore's Bond poses as a marine biologist when meeting Stromberg. See if you can spot the extra sweeping up behind Daniel Craig but keeping the brush head several centimetres above the floor. Bond learns that Greene is helping exiled Bolivian General Medrano to overthrow the government and become the new president, in exchange for a seemingly barren piece of desert. This part of the film is quietly absorbing, as the plot unravels itself without offering any definite answers.

Camille has an ulterior motive: to kill Medrano in revenge for the death of her parents. Bond, misunderstanding the situation, rescues her, first with a neat motorbike jump, and then in a lively boat chase. MI6 track Greene to a private air flight heading for Bregenz, Austria. Felix Leiter and Gregg beam of the CIA are on board. Bond follows them: the Bregenz airport scenes were filmed at RAF Farnborough, twenty-five miles southwest of Pinewood.

In a delightful seven-minute sequence set at a performance of *Tosca*, Bond identifies members of Quantum's executive board. These scenes were filmed on a floating stage at the Festspielhaus in Bregenz: the 'eye' design was the actual set for Philipp Himmelmann's spectacular 2007 production. Bond listens in as Quantum discuss their business in plain sight, and then interrupts.

'Can I offer an opinion?' he asks. 'I really think you people should find a better place to meet. Where do you think you're going? Well, *Tosca* isn't for everyone.'

The members of Quantum are exposed one by one. White is present but plays it cool. The cinematography, editing and sound mix in the scene where Bond meets the Quantum officers in a corridor, but they are unable to pull their guns on each other is quite brilliant, mixing snippets from *Tosca* with absolute silence. This is almost art-house Bond. 'That sequence was set in the script in a UN type of setting with people over-hearing these conversations through different languages,' says Marc Forster. 'I thought it was interesting, but visually I couldn't get it in my head. I felt it looked a little familiar. And then I saw the opera set and the eye reminded me of Bond. I always loved the influence of Hitchcock on the Bond films – the early Bond films – *The Man Who Knew Too Much* certainly popped in my head. I thought *Tosca* was a parallel to our story, and so I could have the opera and him, and then go into this sort of Mexican standoff dream-like action sequence.' [23]

A Special Branch bodyguard working for one of the Quantum members is killed by Greene's men after Bond throws him off a roof. M assumes Bond killed him, and she has his passports and credit cards revoked. Bond heads to Italy and convinces his old ally René Mathis to accompany him to Bolivia. This scene was filmed at the Torre di Talamonaccio hotel in Orbetello on Italy's Mediterranean coast. The scene where Mathis joins Bond in the lounge bar of their flight to Bolivia was filmed at the Virgin Atlantic training facilities in Crawley: Bond drowns his sorrows with Vesper's photograph and necklace.

Bond and Mathis are met at the airport by the perky MI6 agent Fields (her first name is never mentioned in the film – according to the credits, it's 'Strawberry').

Fields: Mr. Bond, my name is Fields. I'm from the consulate.
Bond: Well, of course you are. And what do you do at the consulate, Fields?
Fields: That's not important. My orders are to turn you around and put you on the first plane back to London.
Bond: Do those orders include my friend Mathis?
Fields [to Mathis]: I'm sorry, I don't know who you are.
Bond: You see that? Gone such a short time and already forgotten.
Mathis: You're just saying that to hurt me.

Bond and Mathis share a knowing quip about handcuffs. The next flight isn't until the next day, so Bond checks into a hotel: 'We are teachers on sabbatical, and we have just won the lottery.' Fields, of course, finds Bond irresistible. At a fundraising event, Bond rescues Camille from Greene, but they are pulled over by Bolivian police who have been paid off by Greene and Medrano. They find a seriously injured Mathis in the boot of Bond's car. In an ensuing struggle, Mathis and the policemen are killed. Bond's response when dumping the dead Mathis in a roadside bin is the brutally honest: 'He wouldn't have cared.'

The following day, Bond and Camille survey Quantum's intended land acquisition by air. Their plane is shot down by a Bolivian fighter aircraft. This is perhaps too close to the air-bound finale of *Die Another Day*, and was included merely to link each of the four action sequences to one of the elements – earth (the car chase), water (the boat chase), air (the aeroplane sequence) and fire (the finale). We can question whether all of them are essential to the advancement of the plot. Bond and Camille skydive into a sinkhole and, with a large helping of random co-incidence, discover that Quantum is damming Bolivia's water supply to create a monopoly. It's not quite Hugo Drax's plan to breed a new race of super-humans.

Back in La Paz, Bond meets Felix Leiter, who tells him that Greene and Medrano will meet in the Atacama Desert to finalise their agreement. In a knowing homage to Shirley Eaton's demise in *Goldfinger*, Fields is found dead, covered in oil.

The finale at the eco-hotel in the Atacama Desert in Chile is striking, with just the right mixture of explosions and hand-to-hand (or axe-to-foot) violence to bring the film to a satisfactory conclusion. It was filmed at a hostel for astronomers at the European Organisation for Astronomical Research, fourteen hours' drive north of Santiago.

Bond avenges Mathis and Camille kills Medrano.

> Reality in violence is kept to the fore as, once again, we watch the bloodied 007 clean himself up in the mirror. But the standout in this area is Camille's reaction to the final battle, discovering Medrano in the middle of a sexual assault and finding herself trapped in a burning building. On its own, it's horrible – coupled with the character's back-story, it's deeply upsetting.
> **Andrew Ellard, *Noisetosignal.org,* November 2008**

Bond confronts and captures Greene and interrogates him about Quantum. He leaves him in the desert with only a can of engine oil, a measure of revenge for Fields. Bond and Camille say farewell. 'I don't think the dead care about vengeance.' He says. She looks at him and says, 'I wish I could set you free. But your prison is in there.'

In a nicely emotional epilogue, again with echoes of the final moments in *The Bourne Supremacy*, Bond travels to Kazan, Russia, where he finds Vesper Lynd's former lover, Yusef Kabira – Bond had pocketed a photograph earlier in the film. Kabira is with a Canadian Intelligence agent and warns her of Kabira's true intentions. Craig's acting here is outstanding: 'It's a beautiful necklace. Did he give it to you? I have one just like it. He gave it to a friend of mine, someone very close to me.' Kabira is arrested. Outside, M talks to Bond.

Bond: Congratulations. You were right.
M: About what?
Bond: About Vesper. [he moves to leave] Ma'am.
M: Bond, I need you back.
Bond: I never left.

As he walks away, he drops Vesper's necklace in the snow. Gunbarrel and credits.

Mark Harrison observes:

> *Quantum of Solace* feels as if it takes place in a much smaller world than its predecessor, with most of the surviving characters returning, as an emotionally wounded Bond single-mindedly pursues the truth behind Quantum. Whatever else the film got wrong as a result of a harried production schedule, the concluding scene in which Bond discovers Vesper's boyfriend trying the same move on a Canadian intelligence agent is very well executed. The necklace is dropped in the snow in the final shot of the movie and Bond gets his quantum of something or other.[24]

Given an inexplicably cool reception by the critics, *Quantum of Solace* is a good, if flawed, action film with a rather damp, weasel villain and some illogical plotting. Craig is terrific throughout. Remove that superfluous boat chase, or perhaps the aerial scenes, and it would be a tighter, better film. What we have, though, is much, much more than acceptable.

> He's back. Daniel Craig allays any fear that he was just a one-Martini Bond, with this, his second OO7 adventure, the perplexingly named *Quantum of Solace.*
>
> Craig [has] made the part his own, every inch the coolly ruthless agent-cum-killer, nursing a broken heart and coldly suppressed rage. If the Savile Row suit with the Beretta shoulder holster fits, wear it. And he's wearing it.
>
> In theory, he is out to nail a sinister international business type: Dominic Greene, played by French star Mathieu Amalric, who under a spurious ecological cover plans to buy up swaths of South American desert and a portfolio of Latin American governments to control the water supply of an entire continent. As Greene, Amalric has the maddest eyes, creepiest leer, and dodgiest teeth imaginable.
>
> Clearly, Bond has to take this fellow down. But he also wants to track down the man who took his beloved Vesper away from him: he is pathologically

seeking payback, and to the fury of his superiors, this is getting personal. Olga Kurylenko plays Camille, a mysterious, smouldering figure, out to wreak vengeance on the corrupt Bolivian dictators who killed her family.

Set against this is the cool, cruel presence of Craig – his lips perpetually semi-pursed, as if savouring some new nastiness his opponents intend to dish out to him, and the nastiness he intends to dish out in return. This film, unlike the last, doesn't show him in his powder-blue swimming trunks (the least heterosexual image in 007 history), but it's a very physical performance.

Quantum of Solace isn't as good as *Casino Royale*: the smart elegance of Craig's Bond debut has been toned down in favour of conventional action. But the man himself powers this movie; he carries the film: it's an indefinably difficult task for an actor. Craig measures up.

Peter Bradshaw, *The Guardian*, 18 October 2008

Skyfall

Albert R Broccoli's Eon Productions Ltd presents Daniel Craig as Ian Fleming's James Bond 007 in *Skyfall*.

Release date: 23 October 2012. Running time: 143 minutes. Distributed by MGM/Columbia. Producers: Michael G. Wilson (10 of 12), Barbara Broccoli (7 of 9).

James Bond: Daniel Craig (3 of 5), M: Judi Dench (7 of 8), Q: Ben Whishaw (1 of 3), Moneypenny: Naomie Harris (1 of 3) with Ralph Fiennes (Gareth Mallory/M) (1 of 3), Rory Kinnear (Tanner) (2 of 4).

With Javier Bardem (Raoul Silva), Bérénice Marlohe (Sévérine), Albert Finney (Kincade), Ola Rapace (Patrice).

Director: Sam Mendes (1 of 2). Screenplay: Neal Purvis (5 of 7), Robert Wade (5 of 7), John Logan (1 of 2). Production design: Dennis Gassner (2 of 3). Main titles: Daniel Kleinman (6 of 7). Music: Thomas Newman (1 of 2). Theme song performed by Adele. Cinematography: Roger Deakins. Edited by Stuart Baird (2 of 2), Kate Baird.

Plot

James Bond's latest assignment goes wrong and it leads to the exposure of undercover agents around the world. With MI6 now compromised inside and out, Bond follows a trail to Silva, a man from M's past who wants to settle an old score.

Cast

Daniel Craig as Bond and Judi Dench as M are joined by two actors taking on the iconic roles of Q and Moneypenny. Both characters had been absent in the first two Craig films. Ben Wishaw's casting in *Skyfall* was a cunning move by the producers. For the first time, Q is *younger* than Bond and is able to make a wry joke about hi-tech gadgets. 'Were you expecting an exploding pen?'

teases Q. 'We don't really go in for that sort of thing anymore.' 'Not exactly Christmas,' Bond responds. Wishaw made his reputation as a stage actor, notably as the lead in Trevor Nunn's 2004 production of *Hamlet* at the Old Vic, for which he was nominated for the Olivier Award for Best Actor, and as a drug dealer in Philip Ridley's controversial play *Mercury Fur* (2005). On TV, he won the British Academy Television Award for Leading Actor for Richard II in the hugely acclaimed *The Hollow Crown* (2012) and in film he played alongside Daniel Craig in *The Trench* (1999), *Enduring Love* (2004) and *Layer Cake* (2004). Naomie Harris plays Moneypenny with zest and verve. Harris had appeared in over twenty films in the ten years before *Skyfall*; she is probably most recognised as the voodoo witch Tia Dalma in the second and third *Pirates of the Caribbean* films.

Three Oscar nominees play major supporting roles. Javier Bardem, cold-eyed Raoul Silva, is an acclaimed Spanish actor who was nominated for the Academy Award for Best Actor for both *Before Night Falls* (2000) and *Biutiful* (2010) and won the Academy Award for Best Supporting Actor for his role as a psychopathic assassin in *No Country for Old Men* (2007). Ralph Fiennes as Gareth Mallory first achieved success onstage at the Royal National Theatre in London in the 1980s. His Oscar nominations came for *Schindler's List* (1994, best supporting actor) and *The English Patient* (1997, best actor). Veteran British actor Albert Finney plays Kincade. Over a long career, Finney made over 40 films and was nominated for an Oscar six times. His most famous films are *Saturday Night and Sunday Morning* (1960), *Tom Jones* (1963), *Two for the Road* (1967), *Scrooge* (1970), *Annie* (1982), *The Dresser* (1983), *Miller's Crossing* (1990), *A Man of No Importance* (1994), *Erin Brockovich* (2000), *Big Fish* (2003) and *The Bourne Ultimatum* (2007). He died in 2019.

French actor Bérénice Lim Marlohe plays the enigmatic, damaged Sévérine. Familiar from French TV from 2008, *Skyfall* was her first major film role. Swede Ola Rapace portrays the hitman Patrice.

Theme Song

A massive hit in autumn 2012, 'Skyfall' was written and sung by Adele. The dramatic opening major 9th chord is the same used at the end of the 'James Bond Theme', that huge Vic Flick final guitar strum from *Dr. No*. It won the Oscar for best original song in 2013.

Production

Skyfall was filmed between November 2011 and spring 2012 at Pinewood Studios, Buckinghamshire, and on location in Turkey, the United Kingdom, China and Japan.

Observations

It starts with the script. Despite some distant plotting similarities to *The Man With the Golden Gun* – Bond tracks down a rogue assassin living on a mysterious island off Macau; he has a woman who tries to free herself from him by seducing Bond, but gets killed in the process – *Skyfall* is rooted in a superb script. As with the previous four Bond films, the script is credited to Neil Purvis and Robert Wade. Added polish comes from the American playwright John Logan, who had been nominated for a screenwriting Oscar for *Gladiator* (2000), *The Aviator* (2004) and *Hugo* (2011), and for a Tony in 2010 for best play for *Red*.

'Sam Mendes and I have known each other for 15 years from theatre circles,' Logan told Steve 'Frosty' Weintraub in 2011. 'We ran into each other at Bar Centrale down on 46th, and he said, 'Can you have lunch tomorrow?' I said, 'Sure, let's have lunch, that's great.' He said there's this great script by Purvis and Wade, but he wanted me to come on board. And I did the ultimate thing you never do, which is I said 'Yes. I don't care what you pay me, I don't care what I have to do, yes!'.'

'There's a perfect Bond movie out there,' Daniel Craig told *GQ* in 2012. 'And I'm going to find it if it kills me. Which it might. I have to be that way about it. The script that we have at the moment – and this is not just actor hyperbole – I'm genuinely excited about it. There's a really good hook. In fact, we now have two or three really good hooks, two might work, and that's what you want. That's what we had in *Casino...* but ultimately, that's because it's based on source material, the book had those hooks. We've got those in this script, and as long as we hit those, the rest of it is hopefully going to come together.'

Tight direction and fabulous acting performances from everyone involved, push *Skyfall* towards the top of the 'best ever Bond' lists. Daniel Craig, Judi Dench and Ralph Fiennes are terrific. Both Moneypenny and Q return to the series, played with élan and wit by Naomie Harris and Ben Whishaw. But every great OO7 film has to have a great villain: Goldfinger, Le Chiffre, Blofeld, Rosa Klebb, Stromberg. Javier Bardem classily plays Raoul Silva as a charismatic, compellingly colourful, rage-fuelled psychopath intent on discrediting M. The one-on-one scenes with Craig are scintillating. We have stunning set-pieces in Istanbul, Shanghai and Macau. On its release, *Skyfall* was the highest revenue grossing UK film of all time, only overtaken since by *Star Wars: The Force Awakens*.

Charles Gant, film editor for *Heat* magazine, notes: '*Skyfall* was a brilliant strategic move. It was cleverly positioned as simultaneously modern and retro. It appealed as much to the Daniel Craig era fans, who are relative newcomers to the franchise, and by trading on the Bond is 50 moment, it managed to engage the older, more nostalgic elements of the audience, who may have lost interest over the previous few films.' [25]

For the first time, there is no juvenile female lead: the major female character is M, a complex and sympathetic character study by the writers and portrayed with much skill by Judi Dench. Eve Moneypenny, a trained agent, is not merely bikini-clad eye candy.

We should also offer a nod here to cinematographer Roger Deakins, who garnered the first-ever Oscar nomination for a cinematographer for a James

Bond film. Deakins' spectacular cinematography is evident from the opening shots.

The film opens mid-mission in Istanbul. The first shot mimics the familiar gun barrel sequence as Bond steps into a hallway backlit by warm, golden light. Bond finds a fellow MI6 agent, Ronson, who has just been shot. The hard drive from Ronson's laptop has been stolen, and this contains details of MI6's undercover operatives. Bond chases the baddy on a motorcycle from Eminönü Square and across the roof of the Grand Bazaar, ending up, in an outrageous sequence, on the roof of a train. The shot where Bond jumps onto the train was filmed at the Kasim Gülek Bridge in Adana, about 1,000km southeast of Istanbul. Moneypenny drives alongside in a Land Rover, describing the action to M back at base. Craig-as-Bond fixes his cufflinks, just as Connery does after his dockside fight in *You Only Live Twice*. As Bond and his adversary, Patrice, fight on top of the train, M orders Moneypenny to shoot Patrice, but she hits Bond, who, in a spectacular shot, falls off the Vardar Bridge into a river, presumed killed. Twelve minutes of taut action. Wow. Cue Adele's thrilling theme song and a massive burst of adrenalin.

Ben Radatz writes:

> The viewer is completely immersed within the mind of Bond as he sinks to the bottom of a riverbed after being shot by friendly fire during the film's climactic cold opening. Set in the depths and ruins of his own private thoughts and memories, the sequence is a combination of many analogies: his past and current emotional state, his uncertain future, his many indistinguishable misdeeds and duties flashing before his eyes. It is the first Bond sequence, and the first Bond film, to dig into 007's psychological past, both using his childhood home as an emotional safehouse and a prison, giving his character greater depth and a vulnerability more in step with creator Ian Fleming's incarnation of the gallant, yet flawed, superspy. [26]

Three months later, M composes Bond's obituary. A similar scene occurs at the beginning of Ian Fleming's book *You Only Live Twice*. Much of the detail drives the narrative of Daniel Craig's characterisation and gives colour to the events of both this film and *Spectre*.

> James Bond was born of a Scottish father, Andrew Bond of Glencoe, and a Swiss mother, Monique Delacroix, from the Canton de Vaud. His father being a foreign representative of the Vickers armaments firm, his early education, from which he inherited a first-class command of French and German, was entirely abroad. When he was eleven years of age, both his parents were killed in a climbing accident in the Aiguilles Rouges above Chamonix. [27]

M's authority and position is challenged by Gareth Mallory, the new chair of the Intelligence and Security Committee and a former SAS officer. This scene was filmed at the Reform Club in London, the venue for the Bond-Graves swordfight in *Die Another Day*.

> Mallory: I'm here to oversee the transition period leading to your voluntary retirement in two months time. Your successor has yet to be appointed, so we'll be asking you...
> M: I'm not an idiot, Mallory. I know I can't do this job forever, but I'll be damned if I'm going to leave the department in worse shape than I found it.
> Mallory: M, you've had a great run. You should leave with dignity.
> M: Oh, to hell with dignity. I'll leave when the job's done.

M is on her way back to MI6 HQ when she is stopped by police. She receives a taunting computer message – 'Think on your sins' – moments before the MI6 building explodes.

James Bond, meanwhile, has survived his tumble off the bridge in Turkey and has used his presumed death to retire. He is haggard and has gained a girlfriend, beard, drink problem and death wish. We are never told where, but the beach scenes were filmed at Çalığ beach at Muşla on Turkey's west coast and some of the crowd in the bar speak Turkish. Bond learns of the attack (by chance, watching CNN in a bar) and returns to London, where he once again breaks into M's house: she has evidently relocated since *Casino Royale*, and she is also now a widow.

'Where the hell have you been?' M demands. 'Enjoying death,' Bond replies. 'You'll have to be debriefed and declared fit for active service,' she replies. 'You can only return to duty when you've passed the tests, so take them seriously. And a shower might be in order.'

Bond fails this series of physical, medical and psychological examinations, but M approves his return to the field. Bond pulls some shrapnel out of his shoulder, lodged there during his gun battle with Patrice. The analysis of the metal leads Bond to Shanghai. A scene in London's National Gallery delivers a wry statement on Bond's age. As Q – young, smart, tech-savvy – and Bond study *The Fighting Temeraire* by William Turner, Q remarks on the painting's symbolism of an old ship being taken to be broken up. 'Always makes me feel a little melancholy,' Q says. 'A grand old warship being ignominiously hauled away for scrap. The inevitability of time, don't you think?' Bond is unimpressed and only sees 'a bloody big ship'.

Robbie Collin writes:

> Of all the things that Daniel Craig's Bond films have done right to date, the rightest is almost certainly this: they looked forward to where the Brosnan films were leading, and then ran, headlong and panting, in the opposite direction. The idea of an up-to-date Bond became an oxymoron. Now, his obsolescence was what would make him relevant. [29]

Other than a couple of establishing shots at Pudong International Airport and the Yan'An Elevated Expressway, none of *Skyfall* was filmed in Shanghai (or Macau). Bond's Shanghai hotel is the Virgin Active in Canary Wharf, London; the Shanghai tower block is Broadgate Tower on Primrose Street, London; Ascot racecourse is the setting for Shanghai airport.

The tower assassination scene is a direct lift from Ian Fleming's first book, *Casino Royale*:

> 'His bullet got deflected by the glass and went God knows where. But I shot immediately after him, through the hole he had made. I got the Jap in the mouth as he turned to gape at the broken window.' Bond smoked for a minute. 'It was a pretty sound job. Nice and clean too. Three hundred yards away. No personal contact.'
>
> From Ian Fleming's, *Casino Royale.* [29]

Viewers with keen eyes and encyclopaedic knowledge of stolen art will have seen Modigliani's *Woman With a Fan* behind Sévérine during this scene. This painting was stolen from the Museum of Modern Art in Paris in 2010. The inclusion of this missing artwork directly references Francisco Goya's *Portrait of The Duke of Wellington* in Dr. No's lair – another painting that was stolen at the time of the film's release.

Bond finds a casino token that Patrice intended to cash in for the assassination, which leads him to a floating casino in Macau. Bond meets Sévérine and deduces from her tattoo that she was in the Macau sex trade. This unhappy 'kept woman' character has appeared in the Bond films before. Remember Domino Derval and Lupe Lamora? There is also a hint of an 'anti-heroine' characterisation, along the lines of Pussy Galore and May Day. Either way, there's a genuine vulnerability in Bérénice Marlohe's performance as she whispers, 'how much do you know about fear?' Bond responds, 'All there is', and she trumps this with 'Not like this. Not like him.' And later, when he asks, 'I want to meet your employer', there is wonderful pregnant pause before she responds, 'Be careful what you wish for'. Her name and role as a sex slave are probably a reference to a (male) character in the novel *Venus in Furs* by Leopold von Sacher-Masoch.

Bond dispatches one of Sévérine's bodyguards with the help of a CGI Komodo dragon (Bond quips, 'It's the circle of life') and joins her on her yacht where they have sex in a shower. This made some viewers uneasy – is Bond taking advantage of a prostitute to whom he offered a chance of freedom? 'That's interesting,' Craig said when challenged. 'It's not how we wanted it to perform. Maybe it was because she was a victim. That's very valid.' [30]

They travel to an abandoned island off the coast of Macau – actually Hashima Island off the coast of Nagasaki, Japan.[31] After 67 minutes we finally we get to meet Raoul Silva, former MI6 agent who has turned to cyberterrorism. We have a series-highlight monologue, brilliantly delivered by Javier Bardem.

Silva: Hello, James. Welcome. Do you like the island? My grandmother had an island. Nothing to boast of. You could walk around it in an hour. But still it was a paradise for us. One summer, we went for a visit and discovered the place had been infested with rats. They'd come on a fishing boat and gorged themselves on coconut. So how do you get rats off an island? Hmm? My grandmother showed me. We buried an oil drum and hinged the lid, then wired coconut to the lid as bait. And the rats would come for the coconut and they would fall into the drum. And after a month, you have trapped all the rats. But what do you do then? Throw the drum into the ocean? Burn it? No. You just leave it. And they begin to get hungry. And one by one... they start eating each other until there are only two left. The two survivors. And then what? Do you kill them? No. You take them and release them into the trees. But now they don't eat coconut anymore. Now they only eat rat. You have changed their nature. The two survivors. This is what she made us.

Silva unbuttons a couple of the buttons on Bond's shirt and caresses his legs. Bond stays supernaturally cool.

Silva: Well, first time for everything. Yes?
Bond: What makes you think this is my first time?
Silva: Oh, Mr. Bond! All that physical stuff. So dull, so dull. Chasing spies. So old-fashioned!

Silva challenges Bond to a shooting competition which results in Sévérine's death. Bond has called for help ('It's the latest thing from Q-Branch. It's called a radio.').

At MI6's new underground headquarters – filmed in the tunnels under Waterloo station –Bond and M speak to Silva who notes that M is smaller than he remembers. 'Whereas I barely remember you at all,' she replies.

Q attempts to decrypt Silva's laptop, but inadvertently gives it access to the MI6 servers. This allows Silva to escape. In scenes very reminiscent of the Jason Bourne films, Bond chases Silva chase through the London Underground. The 'death-by-tube' is totally implausible and frankly not needed. Q is also involved. 'Welcome to rush hour on the Tube. Not something you'd know much about,' he says. These scenes were filmed at Charing Cross ('Temple' and 'Bank' stations), Embankment, Westminster stations and along Parliament Street. The rolling stock is from the Jubilee Line.

Bond and Mallory subsequently thwart Silva's attack on M at a Parliamentary inquiry. This entire sequence, despite its professional execution, exposes a series of massive plot holes.

Why must Silva be captured if he's a master of espionage and could infiltrate England whenever he wanted? Why doesn't Q check the laptop before merrily plugging it into the MI6 mainframe? Why is shooting M at a public inquiry a

safer bet than waiting outside her house? How does Silva even know the public inquiry exists? Why, since Silva is clearly a wizard – how else could he predict the exact moment Bond would require a tube [train] to be thrown at him – doesn't he use his magical powers to kill M from afar. Posers all.
Max Williams, *denofgeek.com*, 2016

Bond absconds with M, leaving Tanner looking bewildered.

Bond [calling Q]: Q? I need help. I need you to lay a trail of breadcrumbs impossible to follow for anyone except Silva. Think you can do it?
Q: I'm guessing this isn't strictly official.
Bond: Not even remotely.
Q: So much for my promising career in espionage.

Bond and M visit a lock-up on Arklow Road, Lewisham so they can pick up a vintage sports car. It's the car from *Goldfinger*; the same number plate and the same gadgets – ejector seat, machine guns behinds the headlights. It's not the one he won in the poker game from Dimitrios in *Casino Royale*, though, because that had a left-hand drive. 'Oh, and I suppose that's completely inconspicuous,' M observes.

They travel to Skyfall, the Bond family's ancestral home in Scotland. The house is a set, built on Hankley Common near Thursley in Surrey. Both *The World Is Not Enough* and *Die Another Day* had used the same location. Here they meet gamekeeper Kincade, played by Albert Finney. There's a rumour that Sir Sean Connery was originally considered for this role. When Bond asks Kincade if he's ready and he replies. 'I was ready before you were born, son.' He also calls Bond 'a jumped-up little shit'. We can imagine Connery delivering these lines and shiver with delight.

Bond, Kincade and 'Emma' set up a series of booby traps. They manage to deal with most of Silva's men but M is wounded. Bond sends M and Kincade through a priest hole to a nearby chapel. Names on the Bond family gravestones include Robert Bond, Celia Bond, Valentine Bond, Kathleen Bond, and James Bond's parents Andrew Bond and Monique Delacroix Bond. The latter stone is marked 'tragically departed' with the Latin phrase 'Mors Ultima Linea Rerum Est' (Death is Everything's Final Limit). This one shot disproves the ridiculous theory that 'James Bond' is a shared code name for multiple spies.

Silva follows and confronts M: 'You're hurt. You're hurt. What have they done to you?' He forces his gun into M's hand and presses his temple to hers. 'Do it. Only you can do it. Do it.'

Bond arrives and kills Silva by hurling a knife into his back. 'Last rat standing', he deadpans. M asks what took him so long. 'Well, I got into some deep water.' M dies in Bond's arms in a scene strong with symbolism: the religious implications of martyrdom – Bond and M in pieta pose – push against

the oedipal overtones of M and Bond's relationship. It's a key scene in the entire film series. It's not just Bond who sheds a tear.

We can argue, strongly, that the resolution of the Vesper story in *Quantum of Solace* and M's death in *Skyfall* affect Bond's character significantly. He is no longer the womaniser, the devil-may-care alpha male, now he is a flawed human being, a man who can be hurt and will ultimately give himself to one woman - Madeleine Swann, whose name, perhaps co-incidentally, starts with the letter M.

On the rooftop back at MI6, Eve gives Bond a box with his inheritance from M. The final scene is set in the new M's office – once again M is behind a leather-studded door, in an old-fashioned panelled office, Miss Moneypenny lodged nearby. Following M's funeral, Moneypenny formally introduces herself to Bond and tells him she is retiring from field work to become secretary for the newly appointed M, whom Bond finds to be Mallory. In the commentary for the film, director Sam Mendes reveals that the office was an exact replica of the set from *Dr. No* and *From Russia With Love*, right down to the wood panelling and coat rack. After some friendly banter and a hard-won smile from Craig's Bond, M turns to business.

M: So, OO7. Lots to be done. Are you ready to go back to work?
Bond: With pleasure, M. With pleasure.

And the gun barrel sequence ends the film. Pow! This sets up the series for its next fifty years.

'James Bond will return' promise the closing credits of almost every film in the OO7 franchise. Yes, but in what form? Set aside the series' pulpy orthodoxies – the cars, the guns, the dames – and Ian Fleming's secret agent is something of a chameleon, either blending in with or cashing in on the movie craze du jour. Think of *Moonraker*, rushed into production after *Star Wars* took popular cinema into orbit, or *Live and Let Die*, exploiting blaxploitation, or the twitchy, unsmiling *Quantum of Solace*, Bond's latter-day Bournefication.

Skyfall, the often dazzling, always audacious new entry directed by Sam Mendes, is no different. For better or worse we live in the age of the superhero, and so Mendes's film is less hardboiled spy saga than blistering comic-book escapade. The template here is Christopher Nolan's The Dark Knight, a film that has almost single-handedly reconfigured the modern blockbuster since its 2008 release, when it left *Quantum of Solace* bobbing in its wake.

Daniel Craig remains Bond incarnate, although six years on from *Casino Royale* he has become something more than a brawny cipher. There's a warmth to his banter with pretty field agent Eve, the one-liners make a tentative return, and we even learn about the loss of Bond's parents: the must-have back story for this season's conflicted superhero.

Neal Purvis, Robert Wade and John Logan's script constantly reminds us Bond's physical prowess is on the wane, but his verbal sparring, both with M and new foe Raoul Silva, a former agent turned vengeful computer hacker, is nimbler than ever.

Mendes lets the quieter moments breathe, and a conversation between Bond and Silva that's simply buttered with innuendo drew cheers at an early preview screening. But Mendes is rather good at being loud, too, and his nine times Oscar-nominated cinematographer Roger Deakins makes the wildly ambitious action sequences the most beautiful in Bond's 50-year career. The sensational Istanbul prologue is soon bettered by the Shanghai segment, where Bond pursues an assassin through a soaring glass skyscraper lit up like a neon Aurora Borealis.

It's pearls like these that give Mendes's film enough momentum to power through its scrappy third act, when Silva's diabolical plans start to feel a tad scattershot, even for a Bond villain.

'We don't go in for exploding pens anymore,' quips a fashionably tousled Q. Nor do audiences, and it's no wonder *Skyfall* was a stratospheric hit.

Robbie Collin, *The Daily Telegraph*, 24 December 2014

Spectre

Albert R Broccoli's Eon Productions Ltd presents Daniel Craig as Ian Fleming's James Bond OO7 in Spectre

Release date: 26 October 2015. Running time: 148 minutes. Distributed by MGM / Columbia. Producers: Michael G. Wilson (11 of 12), Barbara Broccoli (8 of 9).

James Bond: Daniel Craig (4 of 5), M: Ralph Fiennes (2 of 3), Judi Dench (8 of 8), Q: Ben Whishaw (2 of 3), Moneypenny: Naomie Harris (2 of 3) with Christoph Waltz (Franz Oberhauser / Ernst Stavro Blofeld) (1 of 2) Léa Seydoux (Dr. Madeleine Swann) (1 of 2), Rory Kinnear (Bill Tanner) (3 of 4), Jesper Christensen (Mr. White) (3 of 3).

With Dave Bautista (Mr. Hinx), Andrew Scott (Max Denbigh), Monica Bellucci (Lucia Sciarra).

Director: Sam Mendes (2 of 2). Screenplay: Neal Purvis (6 of 7), Robert Wade (6 of 7), John Logan (2 of 2), Jez Butterworth. Production design: Dennis Gassner (3 of 3). Main titles: Daniel Kleinman (7 of 8). Music: Thomas Newman (2 of 2). Theme song performed by Sam Smith. Cinematography: Hoyte van Hoytema. Edited by Lee Smith.

Plot

A cryptic message leads James Bond to Mexico City, Rome, Austria and Morocco, where he uncovers the existence of the sinister organization SPECTRE.

Cast

Ralph Fiennes, Judi Dench, Ben Whishaw, Naomie Harris, Rory Kinnear and Jesper Christensen reprise their roles from previous films.

The casting of Christoph Waltz as Blofeld was, in theory, a stroke of genius: watch *Inglorious Basterds* (2009) and *Django Unchained* (2012) to see just how spell-binding Waltz can be with the right script and director. French actor Léa Seydoux plays Dr. Madeleine Swann. Seydoux first came to attention when she won the Trophée Chopard at the Cannes Film Festival in 2008 for her performance in *The Beautiful Person*. She has since appeared in *Inglorious Basterds* (2009), *Robin Hood* (2010), *Midnight in Paris* (2011), *Mission: Impossible–Ghost Protocol* (2011), *Blue is the Warmest Colour* (2013) and *Grand Central* (2014). 'Madeleine needed to be soulful, feisty and complicated,' said Sam Mendes. 'It's a pivotal relationship with Bond so it couldn't have been a total newcomer. The character needed someone with a certain amount of life experience.' [32]

Dave Bautista as Mr. Hinx is a former professional wrestler, six-times world champion, who has transformed with ease to many film roles, including Drax the Destroyer in the Marvel Cinematic Universe (2014-2019) and a small but memorable part in *Bladerunner 2049* (2017). Irish-born Andrew Scott as Max Denbigh ('C') is an acclaimed stage actor, most familiar to a wider audience as the spell-binding Jim Moriarty in the BBC series *Sherlock* (2010-2017). Scott had worked with Sam Mendes in New York in the 2006 production of *The Vertical Hour*. Monica Bellucci plays the recently bereaved Lucia Sciarra. Bellucci, perhaps best known as a model for Dolce & Gabbana and Dior, became known as an actor in *Malèna* (2000), *Brotherhood of the Wolf* (2001), *Irréversible* (2002), *The Matrix Reloaded* (2003) and *The Passion of the Christ* (2004). 'When Lucia first meets Bond,' she said in 2015, 'she doesn't trust him because she comes from a world where men have all the power.' [33] 'The Bond women are always the most difficult to cast,' notes casting director Debbie McWilliams who has worked on every Bond film since 1980. 'But in my opinion, there was only one person who could play Lucia. I've been angling for Monica Bellucci to be in these films for the last twenty-five years.' [34] Despite lots of media attention in 2015 ('middle aged women are sexy too!') Bellucci's part lasts no more than a few minutes. She is fewer than four years older than Daniel Craig.

Theme Song

'The Writing's on the Wall' by Sam Smith was another Oscar-winning theme song, but it's hardly in the class of 'Skyfall'. It soars and stirs, but can you hum it? The English rock band Radiohead submitted a wonderfully brooding and dark song of their own. It's probably not right for Bond, but it's quite brilliant.

Production

Spectre was filmed between December 2014 and July 2015 at Pinewood Studios, Buckinghamshire and on location in Austria, the United Kingdom, Italy, Mexico and Morocco.

Observations

2013 saw the final resolution of legal and business disputes that had rumbled on for over fifty years. Kevin McClory had died in 2006, and MGM and Danjaq acquired all rights and interests of McClory's estate. This prevented any future remakes of *Thunderball* not under Eon's control, and also allowed Bond's nemesis, Ernst Stavro Blofeld and his international criminal organisation, Spectre, to return to the official film series. [35]

Most of *Spectre* is very good – better on repeated viewings – but the final hour lets down the film. It starts so promisingly. The opening sequence – an assassination attempt and helicopter fight in and around a Day of the Dead parade in Mexico – is a highlight of the entire film series. What seems like a single, four-minute shot, possibly influenced by the legendary three-and-a-half-minute tracking shot which opened Orson Welles's *Touch of Evil* (1958), was carefully choreographed from many different takes edited together.

0:00 The James Bond Theme and the iconic white dots.
0:21 Wide shot of the Day of the Dead parade in Mexico City.
0:56 The shot zooms in to introduce Marco Sciarra in white suit and hat.
1:05 Pan to Bond walking down the street with a lady friend played by Mexican-American actor Stephanie Sigman.
1:36 They enter the Gran Hotel Ciudad de México, on Avenue 16 de Septiembre 82. The same hotel was featured in *Licence To Kill* ('Ah, Senor Bond. You will be pleased to know your uncle has arrived. I put him in your suite'). All of this is a single take to this point. A transition occurs here, the hotel interior is on a different street. 'The first shot runs up to the door of a hotel and pauses on the Day of the Dead poster to transition as Bond enters the doorway' says cinematographer Hoyte van Hoytema. 'The lobby of the hotel is in a different part of Mexico City.' [36]
1:43 The camera follows Bond through the hotel door, across the lobby, into and up an elevator and into a hotel room. The elevator scene is one take with a Steadicam. As Bond walks towards room 327 there's another join hidden by people walking in front of the camera.
3:01 The hotel room is a set built at Pinewood studios. The view outside the window is a photograph of Mexico City.
3:42 The camera then follows Bond as he climbs out a window and onto the roof and the location reverts to Mexico City. 'There was a gigantic support scaffolding the length of the block and three stories high to accommodate the track for the Technocrane,' says Hoyte van Hoytema. Craig walks along the rooftop help up by a large safety wire. His confident strut, necessitated by a knee injury, is very effective.
4:42 Bond sets his rifle sight on his prey in a window across the street and the shot ends.

'The conventional master shots start big and go in and get more intimate,' says van Hoytema. 'But we felt it would be so nice to turn it around and suddenly sweep outside, giving it even a bigger scope. That was, of course, very difficult.'

The shootout was filmed at Pinewood. 'Where Bond is running toward camera and makes his big leap, there was a lot of material shot practically, including a large, collapsing rig and a stuntman running along the rooftop. But as it turned out in the end, the only live-action element was the body of the stuntman. Everything else is digital,' notes VFX supervisor Mark Bakowski.

Marco Sciarra, the terrorist leader, stumbles from the wreckage and phones a helicopter, as you do. Bond jumps on board for a thrilling aerial fight. This sequence uses several different approaches. The helicopter takes off for real from the Plaza de la Constitución, with a crowd of 1,500 extras. The aerobatics were shot 100 miles south of Mexico City at an aerodrome in Palenque. The wide shots combine a genuine helicopter with a computer-generated Zocalo Square and crowds. If the helicopter scene looks familiar, then re-watch the opening minutes of *For Your Eyes Only*. Furthermore, the whole Day of the Dead sequence is a call back not only to the voodoo priest Baron Samedi in *Live and Let Die* but also to the junkanoo in *Thunderball* and the carnival in *Moonraker*. These are the first of many nods to previous Bond films in *Spectre*.

'The Mexico sequence is massively impressive,' said Daniel Craig. 'Not just for a Bond movie, but for any movie.' [37]

Bond takes Sciarra's ring, which is emblazoned with a stylised octopus: the symbol of Spectre. This is an updated design of a ring worn by Blofeld in *From Russia With Love*, *You Only Live Twice* and *Diamonds Are Forever*, and by Largo and Volpe in *Thunderball*. So far, Daniel Craig has uttered just four lines of dialogue ('I won't be long'). Back in London, Bond is 'grounded' by M and suspended from field duty.

Max Denbigh, who Bond dubs 'C', presumably short for 'chief', is the Director-General of the new, privately backed Joint Intelligence Service formed by a merger of MI5 and MI6. C and M's relationship is immediately testy. C wants Britain to join a global surveillance and intelligence initiative 'Nine Eyes'. 'That all sounds lovely,' deadpans Bond. All of this plotting will be unravelled later.

Bond meets Moneypenny in the circular courtyard of the Treasury Building on Great George Street, off Whitehall, and later at his apartment in Notting Hill – 1 Stanley Gardens, not far from Portobello Market. He shows her a video message from Judi Dench's M.

> M: If anything happens to me, 007, I need you to do something. Find a man called Marco Sciarra. Kill him. And don't miss the funeral.
> Moneypenny: When's the funeral?
> Bond: Three days. In Rome.
> Moneypenny: If you think M's signing off on that, you're insane. He won't let you out of his sight.
> Bond: Yes, it's a bit of a problem.

The next day Bond and Tanner go to Q's new lab. The secret entrance was filmed on the Regent's Canal at Camden Lock yards from the crowds of tourists shopping at the famous market. Q injects Bond with a tracking device, 'smart blood', and unveils a new Aston Martin DB10. Unfortunately, it's for 009. The body of the DB5 that Silva blew up in *Skyfall* is also in the workshop. Q says, 'When I said bring it back in one piece, I didn't mean 'bring back one piece.'' Desmond Llewelyn never joked about his work.

Bond is given a watch. 'Does it do anything?' he asks. 'The watch gadget is probably the spy's most enduring piece of kit', wrote Jonathan McAloon in 2015, 'so many fans would have been pleased that Daniel Craig's exploding Omega Seamaster got him out of a tight spot in *Spectre*. A magnetised Rolex saved Bond in *Live and Let Die*, he used his Seiko to print faxes in *The Spy Who Loved Me*, and the laser built into his Omega Seamaster in *GoldenEye* could cut through metal. But it, in fact, wasn't Bond who first used a watch gadget in the films. In *From Russia With Love*, Red Grant wore one with a pull-out garrotte wire.' [38]

Bond persuades Q to give him 48 hours and pinches the DB10. In Rome, Bond is seen driving through a monumental arch at the Garibaldi Museum, in Rome, before arriving at an austere cemetery, filmed at the Museo della Civiltà Romana. Blofeld is seen from behind. Bond wastes no time in hitting on Sciarra's glamorous widow, Lucia, at her palatial house on Via Appia Antica in the outskirts of Rome.

> Bond: I hear the life expectancy of some widows can be very short.
> Lucia: How can you talk like this? Can't you see I'm grieving?
> Bond: No.

Does Bond's line deliberately echo what he said to M in *Casino Royale*? 'Well, I understand double-Os have a very short life expectancy.' After Bond kills her would-be assassins, we get the classic 'Bond, James Bond' line and Lucia tells him that Sciarra belonged to Spectre. 007 infiltrates their secret meeting ('I'm Mickey Mouse. Who are you?'). The exterior shot of the Spectre HQ is Blenheim Palace in Oxfordshire; the interior is an impressive set built at Pinewood. Of course, the classic Bond films of the 1960s include SPECTRE board meetings, most memorably in *Thunderball*.

Bond identifies the silhouetted 'Franz Oberhauser', who gives the order for the 'Pale King' to be assassinated. Franz Oberhauser is not quite a character from Fleming's books. Although not directly appearing in the story, a character called Hannes Oberhauser is a key element in Ian Fleming's *Octopussy*. You can surely hear Daniel Craig's voice in this extract:

> The man said, 'My name's Bond, James Bond. I'm from the Ministry of Defence.'
>
> Major Smythe remembered the hoary euphemism for the Secret Service. He said, with forced cheerfulness, 'Oh. The old firm?'
>
> James Bond said casually, 'Does the name of Hannes Oberhauser ring a bell?'

Major Smythe frowned, trying to remember. 'Can't say it does.' It was eighty degrees in the shade, but he shivered.

James Bond looked Major Smythe squarely in the eyes. 'It just happened that Oberhauser was a friend of mine. He taught me to ski before the war, when I was in my teens. He was a wonderful man. He was something of a father to me at a time when I happened to need one.'

From Ian Fleming's *Octopussy*. [39]

You'll recall that Dexter-Smythe was Octopussy's father in the 1983 film of the same name. In *Spectre*'s back story, Hannes Oberhauser became James Bond's temporary guardian after Bond's parents were killed. In a scene from an early draft of *Spectre*, Oberhauser's son Franz changed his name to Ernst Stavro Blofeld and joined the French Foreign Legion in Morocco. A fellow member of this battalion, called 'Les Spectre de St. Pierre', was the man who would later become known as Mr. White. Blofeld, with White's assistance, developed the shadowy terrorist organization. In the film, it is strongly hinted that Blofeld killed his father because he felt that he loved Bond more than him, his own son. [40]

Back to the film. Oberhauser rumbles Bond. 'It's funny,' he says. 'All that excitement in Mexico City rang a distant bell. And now, suddenly, this evening, it makes perfect sense. Welcome, James. It's been a long time. But, finally, here we are. What took you so long? Cuckoo.'

Bond races back to his car and is pursued across the city by Mr. Hinx, who gives chase in his Jaguar through St Peter's Square, and down the steps of the Scalo De Pinedo to Lungotevere, the road which runs along the bank of the Tiber. These scenes were filmed in the middle of the night during March 2015. There are some comedy moments as Bond impatiently uses his car to push a little Fiat along a narrow street and clicks the switch for 'atmosphere' only to be blasted with Frank Sinatra.

Sam Mendes: 'I loved the car chase being a one-on-one speed battle, a game of cat and mouse between two of the fastest cars in the world, neither of which had ever been seen before.' [41]

Bond bails out using the ejector and his Aston Martin crashes into the Tiber by the Ponte Sisto, a 15th Century bridge in Rome's historic centre.

Moneypenny tells Bond that the Pale King is Mr. White. Bond finds his former enemy in a house on Lake Altaussee in the Austrian Tyrol. The chess board here is a reference to an early scene in *From Russia With Love*, when the planner Kronsteen chooses to finish a chess game rather than leave immediately for a meeting with his superiors. In *Spectre*, this scene unveils the identity of Bond's nemesis, Blofeld. 'I always knew death would wear a familiar face,' says White. 'But not yours. To what do I owe this pleasure, Mr. Bond?'

In a tautly acted scene, White asks Bond to find and protect his daughter, psychiatrist Dr. Madeleine Swann, who will take him to 'L'Américain' in order to locate Oberhauser. He then shoots himself.

Bond meets Swann at the Hoffler Klinik. This scene references Piz Gloria, Blofeld's alpine research facility in *On Her Majesty's Secret Service* and was filmed at the Ice Q restaurant on the Gaislachkogl mountain peak in January and February 2015. Bond enjoys some flirtatious banter with her.

Swann: I hope you don't mind. The view can be distracting.
Bond: [without taking his eyes off her]: I hadn't noticed.

Q arrives.

Bond: If you've come for the car, I parked it at the bottom of the Tiber.
Q: Well, not to worry, OO7. It was only a £3,000,000 prototype.
Bond: Why are you here, Q?
Q: Oh, I just fancied a break, to be honest. I've been a tad stressed at work recently. What with C's people crawling all over us and the fact that M wants my balls for Christmas decorations.

Swann is captured: Bond sees her being led away by Mr Hinx. The obligatory chase scene was filmed in and around Obertilliach in Austria. The plane that Bond flies was a full-size replica, travelling on a high wire that was removed in post-production. As in *Live and Let Die*, the plane loses its wings; from there, another large prop was driven with skidoos inside. The barn it bursts through was found elsewhere in Austria, dismantled, reconstructed and rigged to allow Bond to fly through it. Q links Oberhauser to Bond's previous missions, identifying Le Chiffre, Dominic Greene and Raoul Silva as agents of the same organisation, which Swann identifies as Spectre.

Bond and Swann travel to Tangier, to the hotel L'Americain to find whatever clues Mr White has led them to. You'll recall that Timothy Dalton's Bond had visited the city in *The Living Daylights*. 'Come anywhere near me and I'll kill you,' Swann says. Bond keeps watch while Miss Swann sleeps. He sips beer and watches a mouse. 'Who sent you?' asks Bond. A hidden room yields the coordinates to Oberhauser's base.

Back in London, M meets C. The scenes at Joint Intelligence Service's offices were filmed at London's City Hall.

C: I should tell you I've spoken with the Home Secretary. And in light of the new information I've given him, he's decided to close down the double-O program with immediate effect.
M: You don't know what you're doing.
C: It's not personal. It's the future. And... you're not.
M: You're a cocky little bastard, aren't you?
C: I'll take that as a compliment.
M: I wouldn't. This isn't over yet.

Unfortunately, it is. After 84 minutes of a really good film, the rest just fizzles out.

Bond and Swann take a train to Oberhauser's base in a crater in the Sahara. This is the Oriental Desert Express, which runs 200 miles between Oujda and Bouarfa in north-eastern Morocco.

Note the throwaway snatch of dialogue here that triggers the plot of the forthcoming *No Time To Die*: 'A man once came to our house to kill my father,' she says. 'He didn't know I was upstairs playing in my bedroom.'

The scene in the restaurant car is very reminiscent of Bond's first meeting with Vesper Lynd. Bond wears a white dinner jacket, complete with red carnation, similar to the opening scene in *Goldfinger*. Mr Hinx attacks them in a direct reference to previous rail-bound fights in *From Russia With Love*, *Live and Let Die*, *The Spy Who Loved Me* and *Octopussy*. Ian Fleming often associated trains with death. Breathless after Hinx's death, Swann looks at Bond. 'What do we do now?', she asks. Can you guess?

They alight in the middle of nowhere, for no obvious reason, and are eventually picked up by a Rolls Royce. The Rolls is a similar model to Kerim-Bey's and Goldfinger's cars from the second and third Bond films; the chauffeur is wearing the same design of uniform as Mr Jones, the chauffeur hired by *Dr. No* to pick up Bond from the airport in Jamaica. Bond is wearing a brown jacket and tie that are very similar to the tweed worn by Sean Connery in *Goldfinger*.

The couple arrive at the secret Spectre base. The exterior scenes were filmed at Gara Medouar, a horseshoe-shaped geological formation and former military garrison near Sijilmasa in Morocco. *The Mummy* and *Prince of Persia* were both shot nearby. They are offered a glass of champagne before going to meet Oberhauser – remember *Dr. No*? – but they decline. There follows a very subtle scenic design nod to the very first Bond film. You may recall that when Bond meets *Dr. No* he recognises a portrait of the Duke of Wellington by Goya which had been stolen from the National Gallery in London in 1961. Blink-and-you'll-miss-it, but Modigliani's *Woman with Fan* hangs in Bond's guest room, and Madeleine's has Picasso's *Dove with Green Peas*. These two paintings were stolen from the Paris Museum of Modern Art in 2010 and are still missing. *Woman with Fan* is also seen in *Skyfall* when Sévérine shows it to a potential buyer in Shanghai.

We learn that Oberhauser has been behind all the threats 007 has faced in the previous three films, and has caused the deaths of both Vesper and M. Note that Oberhauser is wearing a Nehru-collared suit, as did Donald Pleasance (*You Only Live Twice*), Telly Savalas (*On Her Majesty's Secret Service*), Charles Gray (*Diamonds Are Forever*) and Hugo Drax (*Moonraker*). There is even a Persian cat.

For no obvious reason, Bond is tortured with a tiny robotic drill as Oberhauser discusses their shared history.

> Blofeld: You came across me so many times and yet you never saw me. Le Chiffre, Greene, Silva. You interfered in my world, I destroyed yours. Or did

> you think it was coincidence that all the women in your life ended up dead? Vesper Lynd, for example. She was the big one. Has he told you about her? And then, of course, your beloved M. Gone forever. Me. It was all me, James. It's always been me. The author of all your pain. You probably know that James here lost his parents when he was young. But did you know that it was my father who helped him through this difficult time? Over the course of two winters, he taught him to ski, and climb, and hunt. He soothed the wounds of the poor little blue-eyed orphan. Asked me to treat him as a brother. My little brother. You know what happens when a cuckoo hatches inside another bird's nest? It forces the other eggs out. Well, this cuckoo made me realize my father's life had to end. In a way, he's responsible for the path I took.

Oberhauser reveals that Spectre has funded the Joint Intelligence Service while staging terrorist attacks around the world, creating a need for the Nine Eyes programme. In return, Spectre will get unlimited access to intelligence gathered by Nine Eyes, allowing them to anticipate and counter-act investigations into their operations.

Bond manages to slip Madeleine his Q watch, which explodes ('Tempus fugit,' quips Bond), allowing them to escape back to the UK, meeting up with M, Tanner, Q and Moneypenny.

The finale in London feels tacked on. M confronts C.

> C: Take a look at the world. Chaos. Because people like you, paper-pushers and politicians, are too spineless to do what needs to be done. So I made an alliance to put the power where it should be. And now you want to throw it away for the sake of 'democracy'. Whatever the hell that is. How predictably moronic. But then, isn't that what M stands for? 'Moron.'
> M: [revealing the bullets he has removed from C's gun] And now we know what C stands for.

The last line got a laugh-out-loud response in cinemas, with many viewers missing M's response: 'careless'. This clash ends with C falling to his death. Bond and Swann say goodbye, but she is seized by Blofeld.

The finale sees Bond face up to Blofeld in the ruins of the MI6 building. The shooting gallery of ghosts from the past recalls Scaramanga's funhouse in *The Man With the Golden Gun*, but with less panache. Blofeld sets a timer to detonate three minutes hence. 'In three minutes, this building will be demolished,' he declares. 'I can get out easily. Now, you have a choice. Die trying to save her or save yourself and live with the pain.'

After saving Madeleine, Bond shoots down Blofeld's helicopter, which crashes onto Westminster Bridge. This was filmed on a full-scale replica on the 007 Stage at Pinewood. Bond has Blofeld at gunpoint and the villain urges Bond to shoot, but he replies, 'Out of bullets. And besides, I've got something better to do.' He looks at Madeleine Swann.

The image of Bond walking across Westminster Bridge evokes the last few paragraphs of Ian Fleming's third book, 1955's *Moonraker*.

> And now what? wondered Bond. He shrugged his shoulders to shift the pain of failure – the pain that is so much greater than the pleasure of success. The exit line. There must be no regrets. No false sentiment. The tough man of the world. The Secret Agent. The man who was only a silhouette. [42]

The ending of the film is open to interpretation, as Bond and Swann drive away from Whitehall in his Aston Martin. It was not clear at that time whether Daniel Craig would return to the role; it certainly feels like a valediction.

In the end, *Spectre* has much to admire and lots to enjoy. Its biggest problem, perhaps, is simply that it's not *Skyfall*. *Spectre* remains however, at the time of writing, the third highest-grossing film of all time the United Kingdom.

> There has been much whining in the run-up to the release of this latest Bond outing – from the strangulated cry of Sam Smith's wailing theme tune (and the reaction it provoked) to the sound of leading man Daniel Craig complaining that he would rather slash his wrists than play 007 again. After the high-water mark of *Skyfall*, there was a very real fear that director Sam Mendes's second 007 adventure may go the misbegotten way of *Quantum of Solace*. Terrific to report, then, that while *Spectre* may not be the equal of its immediate predecessor, it's still bang on target in delivering what an audience wants from this seemingly indestructible franchise: globetrotting locations, spectacular stunts, impossible intrigue, inconceivable costume changes, laugh-out-loud zingers and a plot that is at once utterly preposterous yet oddly apposite.
>
> We open with a ... tracking shot that leads us through Mexico City's Day of the Dead parade. It's a sinewy curtain-raiser to a bravura prologue involving scenic vistas, collapsing buildings and loop-de-looping helicopters.
>
> But it's not until the introduction of Léa Seydoux's Madeleine Swann that the plot really starts to tick, Bond meeting his match in a woman who can strip a handgun and order 'a vodka martini, dirty' while he's brushed off with a protein shake. Seydoux is the film's secret weapon, bringing emotional heft to the pantomime elements, a winning mixture of strength and sultriness.
>
> Together, James and Madeleine square up to Christoph Waltz's Franz Oberhauser, a nominal relative of a character from Fleming's short story *Octopussy*, who's introduced in shadowy silhouette, whispering menacing nothings in his disposable henchmen's ears. With his European vowels and playfully threatening manner, Waltz is an old-school Bond villain, one of many throwback elements that make *Spectre* such fun.
>
> Add to this a button-pushing score that goes jaga-jaga-jaga when Bond turns a plane into a snowplough or plays dodgems with a helicopter, a fleeting visual gag about Butch and Sundance in Bolivia, and an impressively forceful showing from Naomie Harris as Moneypenny 2.0, and *Spectre* pretty much shoots to

kill. I'll be sad if this turns out to be Craig's last hurrah (he's been the best screen Bond to date), but if he walks away now, he does so on a high note.
Mark Kermode, *The Observer*, 25 October 2015

No Time to Die

Albert R Broccoli's Eon Productions Ltd presents Daniel Craig as Ian Fleming's James Bond 007 in *No Time To Die*.
Release date: 30 September 2021. Running time: 163 minutes. Distributed by United Artists / Universal. Producers: Michael G. Wilson (12 of 12), Barbara Broccoli (9 of 9).
James Bond: Daniel Craig (5 of 5), M: Ralph Fiennes (3 of 3), Q: Ben Whishaw (3 of 3), Moneypenny: Naomie Harris (3 of 3), Christoph Waltz (Ernst Stavro Blofeld) (2 of 2), Léa Seydoux (Dr. Madeleine Swann) (2 of 2), Rory Kinnear (Bill Tanner) (4 of 4), Jeffrey Wright (Felix Leiter) (3 of 3).
With Rami Malik (Lyutsifer Safin) and Lashana Lynch (Nomi), Ana de Armas (Paloma), Dali Benssalah (Primo), David Dencik (Valdo Obruchev), Billy Magnussen (Logan Ash).
Director: Cary Joji Fukunaga. Screenplay: Neal Purvis (7 of 7), Robert Wade (7 of 7), Cary Joji Fukunaga, Phoebe Waller-Bridge, Paul Haggis (uncredited), Scott Z. Burns (uncredited). Production design: Mark Tildesley. Main titles: Daniel Kleinman (8 of 8). Music: Hans Zimmer. Theme song performed by Billie Eilish. Cinematography: Linus Sandgren. Edited by Elliot Graham, Tom Cross.

Plot

James Bond is retired. CIA pal Felix Leiter wants Bond to help him find a missing scientist. The mission sets Bond on a collision course with terrorist Lyutsifer Safin who threatens to release a DNA-based bioweapon.

Cast

***Time Out* (7 October 2015)**:
Time Out: Can you imagine doing another Bond movie?
Daniel Craig: Now? I'd rather break this glass and slash my wrists. No, not at the moment. Not at all. That's fine. I'm over it at the moment. We're done. All I want to do is move on.
Time Out: You want to move on from Bond for good?
Craig: I haven't given it any thought. For at least a year or two, I just don't want to think about it. I don't know what the next step is. I've no idea. Not because I'm trying to be cagey. Who the f*** knows? At the moment, we've done it. I'm not in discussion with anybody about anything. If I did another Bond movie, it would only be for the money.
Time Out: Do you care who plays Bond after you?'

Craig: Look, I don't give a f***. Good luck to them! All I care about is that if I stop doing these things we've left it in a good place and people pick it up and make it better. Make it better, that's all.

The Late Show with Stephen Colbert (16 August 2017):
Colbert: You've been reported to have accepted the role of James Bond again…'
Daniel Craig: I have been quite cagey about it. I have been doing interviews all day and people have been asking me and I think I've been rather coy. But kind of felt like if I was going to speak the truth, I should speak truth to you.
Colbert: We could use some good news here. Will you return as James Bond?
Craig: Yes. I couldn't be happier.
Colbert: How long have you known that you were going to be the next James Bond?
Craig: It's been a couple of months. We've been discussing it; we've just been trying to figure things out. I always wanted to, I needed a break. I think this is it. I just want to go out on a high note and I can't wait.

Rami Malek (Oscar winner as Freddie Mercury in *Bohemian Rhapsody*) was added to the cast in April 2019. Malek is given little to do other than say his lines and carry his disfigurement. Ralph Fiennes, Ben Whishaw, Naomie Harris, Léa Seydoux, Rory Kinnear and Jeffrey Wright reprise their roles from previous films. Cuban actor Ana De Arnas, spell-binding in *Knives Out* (2019), plays CIA agent Paloma.

The first trailer dropped on 4 December 2019, officially confirming that Christoph Waltz would return as Blofeld. He had been spotted at Pinewood in July 2019, and his name had appeared, without fanfare, buried in the credits for the MGM press release for a poster release in September 2019. And, long-rumoured, Lashana Lynch, Maria Rambeau in *Captain Marvel* (2019), would play a new OO agent

'I didn't want [to play] someone who was slick,' Lashana Lynch said to *Esquire* in 2019. 'I wanted someone who was rough around the edges and who has a past and a history and has issues with her weight and maybe questions what's going on with her boyfriend.'

The second trailer was published in September 2020 after the release date of the film was pushed back seven months due to the restrictions placed by the coronavirus lockdown. After further delays, it would be September 2021 before the film's premiere.

Theme Song

The title song is by Billie Eilish, written with her brother Finneas O'Connell. It was released ahead of the original premiere date in early 2020 and won the Grammy for Best Song Written for Visual Media at the 63rd Annual Grammy Awards on 14 March 2021, six months before the film's release date.

Production

No Time To Die was filmed between April and October 2019 at Pinewood Studios, Buckinghamshire and on location in Italy, Jamaica, Norway, the Faroe Islands, Scotland and London.

Observations

Development of *Bond 25*, as it was known until August 2019, began in 2016. Scriptwriters Neal Purvis and Robert Wade were once again approached, and *Trainspotting* and *Slumdog Millionaire* director Danny Boyle was confirmed as director in 2018. Boyle's long-time writing partner John Hodge was brought in to write a new screenplay: Purvis and Wade's first version was scrapped. Production was due to start in December 2018, but Boyle left the project in August 2018 due to 'creative differences'. A spokeswoman for Hodge confirmed that he also was no longer involved.

'Danny had ideas,' Daniel Craig told *GQ*, 'and the ideas didn't work out, and that was just the way it was.'

Subsequently, Cary Joji Fukunaga was announced as the new director in September 2018. He was the first American to direct an Eon James Bond film and first gained recognition for writing and directing the 2009 film *Sin Nombre*, and the 2011 adaptation of *Jane Eyre*. He was the director and executive producer of the first season of *True Detective*, for which he won the Primetime Emmy Award for Outstanding Directing for a Drama Series.

'There was no script when I joined,' Fukunaga told *Entertainment Weekly*. 'It was a complete wipe-the-chalkboard-clean, start over again. Barbara and Michael had some things that they wanted to take place in the story, some characters they were excited about but didn't know what their part was in the story. I sat down with Purvis and Wade initially, and we hashed out a treatment and a screenplay, and I took that screenplay and worked on it a bit myself.'

Purvis and Wade returned to receive their seventh consecutive credit. At Daniel Craig's insistence, the dialogue was polished by Phoebe Waller-Bridge, the first woman to be credited on a Bond script since Johanna Harwood on *Dr. No* and *From Russia With Love*. Waller-Bridge had written the first series of the hugely acclaimed *Killing Eve*, as well as creating, writing and acting in the much-admired comedy series *Fleabag* (2016-2019). 'There's been a lot of talk about whether or not [the Bond series] is relevant now because of who he is and the way he treats women,' she told *Deadline* in June 2019. 'I think that's bollocks. I think he's absolutely relevant now. It has just got to grow. It has just got to evolve, and the important thing is that the film treats the women properly. He doesn't have to. He needs to be true to this character.'

'She's just brilliant,' Daniel Craig told *The Times* in November 2019. 'I had my eye on her ever since the first *Fleabag*, and then I saw *Killing Eve* and what she did with that and just wanted her voice. It is so unique. We are very privileged to have her on board.'

'I really like her mind,' notes Cary Joji Fukunaga. 'I really like the way she thinks about character, and especially scenes. It's almost like a science for her. We talked about what we had; I talked about what characters I wasn't happy with yet, and about situation and dialogue. Dialogue is often times the last thing you do, it's the most cosmetic thing, but great dialogue just elevates a scene to a whole other level. So we talked a lot about the different characters and how to sprinkle in some better dialogue throughout, and it was a lot of fun actually.'

The twenty-four minutes long pre-credits sequence starts as a flashback. We seem to be watching a French art film, in which a young Madeleine Swann witnesses the murder of her mother by a masked terrorist, Safin. Clues such as the Tamagotchi, the CD Walkman and *The Wrong Trousers* on TV place this scene in the early 1990s.

In a tense moment teased in *Spectre* ('Papa kept a Beretta Nine-millimetre under the sink with the bleach', she says in that film), Madeleine shoots Safin. She flees onto a nearby frozen lake but falls through the ice; Safin rescues her.

Flash forward to five years before the present. Swann is in Italy with James Bond.

Bond: Where did you go to? Today, at the water. Tell me.
Swann: I'll tell you if you tell me about Vesper.
Bond: Is that why we're here?
Swann: She's buried at the acropolis…
Bond: I know where she's buried. I left her behind a long time ago.
Swann: As long as we are looking over our shoulders, Vesper's not dead. Can you forgive her? For us?

He visits Vesper Lynd's grave. The dates shown are 1983-2006, making her twenty-three when she died: this seem unlikely for a senior employee of Her Majesty's Treasury with $10 million in her purse. Bond burns a note which reads 'forgive me'. He picks up a Spectre calling card which triggers an explosion and an ambush by assassins from Spectre. Violent action abounds until Bond returns to his hotel and accuses Swann of betraying him.

Bond: You're right. Letting go is hard.
Swann: James! What happened?
Bond: How did they know I was here?
Swann: What are you talking about?
Bond: Madeleine, how did they know I was here? Spectre! How did they know?
Swann: I didn't do anything…
Bond: We're leaving.
Swann: There's something I have to tell you… [The phone rings.]
Bond: Pick it up!
Voice on phone: Your father will be so proud of you. You're sacrifice will be our glory.

Swann: James… why are they after you?
Bond: We all have our secrets. We just didn't get to yours yet.

He despatches Spectre's goons with his modified Aston Martin and puts her on a train. Madeleine's secret will, of course, be revealed in due course. Cue titles.

Five years later, MI6 scientist Valdo Obruchev is kidnapped by Spectre. Obruchev has developed an 'off-the-books' DNA-targeted virus codenamed Heracles. The virus has been coded to specific DNA strands, rendering it lethal against a target but harmless to anyone else. James Bond, meanwhile, has retired to Jamaica. He is contacted by CIA agents Felix Leiter and Logan Ash at a club called XXV – a nod to this, the 25th Eon Bond film. Ash is portrayed as a 'dumb blond', or, as Leiter notes, 'seems like intelligence isn't central any more'. Bond is recruited to track down Obruchev. A major character is introduced here: Nomi, the current 007. She is not instantly taken with Bond – and some frosty dialogue follows. At his hotel, Nomi removes her wig in a scene which is strongly reminiscent of a similar scene with agent Rosie Carver in *Live and Let Die*. Bond's response is the sub-Moore 'that's not the first thing I thought you'd take off'.

In Santiago, Bond meets Paloma, a CIA agent, and they infiltrate a Spectre meeting to celebrate Blofeld's birthday. Blofeld attends virtually, courtesy of, I'm afraid to say, a bionic eye. Drop-dead-gorgeous Ana de Armas as Paloma fills the traditional female juvenile lead in a deep v-neck dress. 'She's a CIA agent from Cuba,' de Armas told *Vogue* in September 2020 'and she's wearing this dress and these diamonds because she's on a mission and she needs to blend in, so everything is there for a reason.'

'She's very irresponsible,' she had told *Esquire* in November 2019. 'She's got this bubbliness of someone who is excited to be on a mission, but she plays with this ambiguity — you don't really know if she's like a really trained, prepared partner for Bond. She's very smart. She helps Bond navigate through certain things that he wouldn't be able to do alone.'

But her time on screen is, unfortunately, brief. And, because it's not that sort of film, Bond and Paloma do not end up in bed together: an unavoidable trope in every other Bond film.

Bond: Is this your room?
Paloma: It's the wine cellar.

She starts to undress him.

Bond: Don't you think that we ought to get know each other just a little bit before we, erm…

She has supplied his dinner suit. As a musical theme from *Casino Royale* plays, they join the meeting and drink vodka martinis.

Bond: What shall we drink to?
Paloma: Felix?
Bond: To Felix. Remind me to get him a cigar.

Blofeld orders Bond to be killed by the virus, but both Ash and Obruchev are double agents working for Safin and it's the Spectre members who fall dead. Paloma holds her own in a terrific fight sequence and also provides some much-needed humour. Nomi initially captures Obruchev but in a tightly-directed sequence filmed in a remarkable set at Pinewood, Bond retrieves a USB data stick and then Obruchev himself before parting ways with Paloma. At a safe-ship, Ash is revealed as double agent, shoots Leiter ('I was such a big fan of his') and escapes with Obruchev. Leiter dies from drowning in a shot that is beat-for-beat repeated from Vesper's demise in *Casino Royale*.

In London, Moneypenny takes Bond to see Q in a light-hearted scene in which Q is attempting to cook dinner for his date.

Bond: Hello, Q. I've missed you. Were you expecting somebody? I need you to tell me what's on this…
Q: No, I need to lay the table… It's never nine to five is it?

Note that Q shoos his cats away when he spots Bond through the peep hole of his front door – a neat tie in to *Spectre* when Q reminds Bond that he has 'a mortgage and two cats to feed', and Bond replies, 'Well, then I suggest you trust me, for the sake of the cats.'

They analyse the USB stick retrieved from Obruchev and realise the scope of the plan, if not the perpetrator. Nomi is sent to find him. Safin, meanwhile, visits Madeleine and reminds her of the life debt she owes him. 'Instead of taking a life,' he says, 'they belong to you.'

He blackmails her into dosing herself with the virus with the intention of infecting Blofeld. Bond visits Blofeld but encounters Madeleine, who flees, but not before passing the Blofeld-specific virus to Bond.

Blofeld: Oh my sweet James. What do you want?
Bond: Your enemies are closing in, Blofeld. But the biggest twist here is that if you tell me who they are, I could save your life.
Blofeld: My avenging angel… my chaser of lost causes. Now you even chase mine. But you're asking the wrong question. Look at us. Two old men in a hole trying to work out who's playing tricks on us. She still loves you, do you know that? And you broke her heart. And she betrayed you.
Bond: She's irrelevant.
Blofeld: I wouldn't be so quick to dismiss… you said it yourself, she's very good at hiding things. And when her secret finds its way out, and it will, it will be the death of you.

Bond: Just give me a name.
Blofeld: Madeleine. Cuckoo.

Bond goes to strangle Blofeld, but pulls back. In doing so, he infects Blofeld, killing him by proxy. Bond tracks Madeleine down to her childhood home in Norway.

Swann: Is he dead?
Bond: Yes, he's dead. He told me you didn't betray me.
Swann: I understand you're not built to trust people.
Bond: Neither are you. I came here to find out who gave you the poison. And I'm not going to leave here without you knowing that I have loved you and I will love you, and I do not regret a single moment of my life that led me to you. Except when I put you on that train.

Star-crossed lovers? Both poisoned? James Bond in *Romeo and Juliet* anyone?

Swann: Do you know the worst thing about you?
Bond: My timing?

Just as they prepare to embrace, Bond learns that Madeleine has a five-year-old daughter, Mathilde (another name beginning with the letter M, we observe).

Swann: She's not yours.
Bond: But… the blues eyes?
Swann: She's not yours.
Bond: OK.
Swann: I have something to show you.
Bond: Another child?

Swann takes Bond to her father's secret room and tells him about Safin, his motives, how he saved her life years before and how he now wants revenge. Safin, Ash and their men locate them and give chase through Norwegian pine forests in a long set-piece which includes a thrilling shot of three 4x4s powering across the snow. Bond kills Ash – 'I'm doing this for my brother', Leiter, the 'brother from Langley' – but Safin captures Madeleine and Mathilde.

Bond returns to active service now with fellow Double-O agent Nomi. Relationships are still cool as Nomi tells Moneypenny: 'I get why you shot him.'

They locate Safin in a former missile base on an island between Japan and Russia. Here, he is mass-producing the deadly virus. Bond orders an air strike from nearby HMS Dragon as Nomi, Madeleine, and Mathilde escape. In a final clash, Safin infects Bond with a virus programmed to kill Madeleine and Mathilde. 'Now we are both poisoned with heartbreak', he says, as Bond realises that he will be unable to touch Madeleine or Mathilde without killing

them. In an unexpected and very powerful conclusion Bond chooses a heroic sacrifice. Bond and Madeleine's final dialogue is taut and memorable. 'You have all the time in the world,' he says. 'She does have your eyes,' she responds, confirming that Mathilde is his daughter. 'I know,' he says, as missiles come down on the base. 'I know.'

That line 'we have all the time in the world' is the unforgettable conclusion to *On Her Majesty's Secret Service*, a film that saw Bond growing beyond his spying role and being ready to settle down with a wife and, perhaps, a family. In both instances, fate intervenes. If you're reading this book and haven't yet seen the film, then I won't spoil the ending, other to say that *No Time To Die* has a powerful conclusion that is unprecedented in the Bond series and categorically draws to a close the narrative of the five films of the Daniel Craig era. Pardon me, I have something in my eye.

With beautiful and luminous cinematography, *No Time To Die* references each of the previous Bond eras: the dancing circles in the opening titles hark back to the same visual effect in *Dr. No*, as does Safin's island lair (which itself has missile silos from Fleming's *Moonraker* novel) and later scenes within the complex reference the work of Ken Adam in the very first Bond film; several parts of the score reprise themes from *On Her Majesty's Secret Service*; Lashana Lynch as Nomi wears a safari suit, neatly updating the easily-scorned outfit worn by Roger Moore; Bond visits his lover's grave, revisiting the opening moments of *For Your Eyes Only*; the look of the interior of the missile silos is very suggestive of the submarine-swallowing ship The Liparus in *The Spy Who Loved Me*; the Brosnan films are referenced by Leiter smoking a Delectado cigar – this same brand name is used by Bond in *Die Another Day* as codeword to wake a sleeper agent; best of all, Bond drives the Aston Martin V8 Vantage, previously used by Timothy Dalton in 1987's *The Living Daylights* – even the registration plate, B549 WUU, is carried over in a neat touch. Look out also for paintings of former M's in the secret service offices: portraits of Judi Dench, Bernard Lee and Robert Brown pay tribute to previous heads of MI6.

There are also two references to Ian Fleming's last fully-realised novel, *You Only Live Twice*. Firstly, Lyutsifer Safin's poisoned garden in *No Time Do Die* is a plot point that mirror's Blofeld's Garden of Death in Fleming's novel. It's clear that the writers' originally planned for Safin's garden to be the source of the poison used in his plan – perhaps the introduction of 'nanobots' was a late change to move away from a natural-born virus? Intriguingly in *You Only Live Twice*, Tiger Tanaka refers to Blofeld as 'a devil who has taken human form' – Lyutsifer = Lucifer. And secondly, M's eulogy to Bond uses a quote widely attributed to author Jack London: 'The proper function of man is to live, not to exist. I shall not waste my days in trying to prolong them. I shall use my time.' Fleming used these words in an obituary for Bond when he was presumed dead in *You Only Live Twice.* The working title of *No Time To Die*, *Shatterhand*, references the name adopted by Blofeld as the book's villain. The original novel ends with Bond suffering from amnesia and settling down to a quiet life with his new family before regaining his memory for next book in the series: some fans have speculated that the same will happen in the follow-up to *No Time To Die*, conveniently forgetting that there has been no consistent continuity in the James Bond series since 1969.

> *No Time to Die* includes Bond movie staples like gravity-defying car chases, ridiculous doomsday weapons and vast brutalist hideouts full of henchmen with silly facial tics to mow down. And it continues the many through-lines from *Skyfall* and *Spectre*. But at the same time, *No Time to Die* revels in blasting canon out of a cannon. You can feel an iconoclastic freedom running through the film, a school's-out delirium, a righteous urge to throw everything at the wall. We all know there's a reset coming when the role is recast at some unspecified point in the future, so for now the gloves are well and truly off.
> Richard Trenholm, *CNET.com*, 30 September 2021

And so, *No Time to Die* boldly and definitively ends the fifteen-year tenure of Daniel Craig as James Bond – the longest continuous association of any actor with the iconic role. As Craig told *The Times* on 3 November 2019: 'This may be hard to believe, but I love the fact I'm Bond. We're in rare air, making Bond movies. It is one of the most intense, fulfilling things I've ever done, but it takes a lot of energy and I'm getting old. I'm getting creaky.'

When asked by *GQ* in 2020 how she was going to cope without Craig, Broccoli replied, 'honestly, I don't know. I can't…I don't want to think about it.'

Even whilst the film was in production, the rumours of 'who will replace Daniel Craig' would fill the pages of magazines and websites. Idris Elba, outstanding in *Luther* (2010-2019), has long been linked to the role, as has Tom Hiddleston, suave and very watchable in *The Night Manager* (2016) and as Loki in the Marvel films (2011-2021). Hiddleston is rumoured to have met Barbara Broccoli in 2016 but his and Elba's chances have surely passed. Other names include: Irish actor Cillian Murphy from *Peaky Blinders* (since 2013); *Harry Potter* actor Matthew Lewis; Tom Hardy, who is surely too well-known; Tom Ellis from *Miranda* and the title role of Netflix' *Lucifer* since 2016; James Norton from *Happy Valley*, *Little Women*, *Grantchester* and *McMafia*; Henry Cavill who was Superman in *Man of Steel* and will be lead in the reboot of *Highlander*; *Nine Perfect Strangers'* and *The Hobbit*'s Luke Evans; Nicholas Hoult from *X-Men*, *Mad Max* and *Tolkien*, and former *Sherlock* Benedict Cumberbatch. Speaking at the premiere of *Black Mass* in October 2015, Cumberbatch quipped, 'I can wear a suit, and I can fight! I can raise my eyebrow, but that's not what it takes to play Bond.'

Umbrella Academy star Tom Hopper had bookies' odds of 3/1 in the weeks following the release of *No Time To Die*.

But it's Scottish actors Sam Heughan (born April 1980, a key player in the dismal *Outlander* since 2014) and Richard Madden (born June 1986 and compelling in *Bodyguard*, 2018) who have the strongest pedigrees.

'I actually have auditioned for James Bond back when they were rebooting Bond 21,' Heughan told *Harper's Bazaar* in March 2020. 'When Daniel Craig came on board, they were talking about making him younger. I don't know what happened, but very recently, I became the bookies' favourite to play Bond, which is kind of random and very strange. I mean, we want a Scottish James Bond, don't we?'

'I'm more than flattered to be mentioned,' Madden told *GQ* in 2018. 'I don't want to curse anything by saying anything.'

Stick around. James Bond will return…

[1]*New York Times* (14 November 2004).
[2] Quoted in *Some Kind of Hero: The Remarkable Story of the James Bond Films* (2015).
[3] *No Remission* at the Lyric Studio, London, reviewed by Georgina Brown in *The Independent* (July 1992).
[4] Interviewed at mi6-hq.com (2006).
[5] *The Boston Globe* (2006).
[6] *The Player* (2012) and *The Boston Globe* (2006).
[7] *The Daily Telegraph* (12 April 2008).
[8] *The New Yorker* (8 November 2012).
[9] *Entertainment Weekly* (November 2010) and *GQ* (November 2012).
[10] Press conference (14 September 2006).
[11] *'Daniel Craig: A very secret agent'*, in *GQ* (2012).
[12] *And Furthermore* (2010).
[13] Copyright the Ian Fleming Estate.
[14] *The Daily Telegraph* (10 October 2015).
[15] *The Daily Telegraph* (12 January 2011).
[16] *The South Bank Show* (2008).
[17] Copyright the Ian Fleming Estate.
[18] Mark O'Connell in *Catching Bullets* (2012).
[19] *The Boston Globe* (2006).
[20] Copyright the Ian Fleming Estate.
[21] *Collider* (10 November 2008).
[22] *Collider* (10 November 2008).
[23] *Collider* (10 November 2008). The UN was used in the pre-titles sequence of *Live and Let Die*.
[24] *James Bond: A History in 25 Objects* published at denofgeek.com (23 October 2015).
[25] *The Guardian* (5 December 2014).
[26] *www.theartofthetitle.com* (2013).
[27] Copyright the Ian Fleming Estate.
[28] *The Daily Telegraph* (10 October 2015).
[29] Copyright the Ian Fleming Estate.
[30] *'Daniel Craig: Bond's got 'serious f***ing problems''* in the *New Zealand Herald* (October 2015).
[31] You can take a virtual tour of the island at Google Maps.
[32] Quoted in *Blood, Sweat and Bond: Behind the Scenes of Spectre* (2015).
[33] Quoted in *Blood, Sweat and Bond: Behind the Scenes of Spectre* (2015).
[34] Quoted in *Blood, Sweat and Bond: Behind the Scenes of Spectre* (2015).
[35] In the 2015 film, Blofeld's organisation is simply referred to as 'Spectre', not

'SPECTRE'. The acronym is not mentioned.

[36] This and subsequent quotes by van Hoytema and Mark Bakowski are taken from 'How They Pulled Off the 'Spectre' of Death Opening in Mexico City' published at *IndieWire*, 23 November 2015.

[37] Quoted in *Blood, Sweat and Bond: Behind the Scenes of Spectre* (2015).

[38] *The Daily Telegraph* (10 November 2015).

[39] Copyright the Ian Fleming Estate.

[40] Interestingly, a character called Franz discovered the frozen corpse of Hannes Oberhauser at the beginning of the 1967-68 comic adaptation of *Octopussy* published in *The Daily Express*, written by Jim Lawrence and drawn by Yaroslav Horak.

[41] Quoted in *Blood, Sweat and Bond: Behind the Scenes of Spectre* (2015).

[42] Copyright the Ian Fleming Estate.

'Farewell Mr. Bond, But Not Goodbye'

To conclude, let's go back to 1967, when the entire milieu of critical Bond literature numbered precisely five: *The James Bond Dossier*, *The Bond Affair*, *007–James Bond–A Report*, *The Life of Ian Fleming* and *The Devil with James Bond!*

The last-named compares James Bond to a modern-day St. George. The various Bond villains are representations of the seven deadly sins of contemporary urban mankind (Goldfinger = avarice, for example).

> Regardless of what anyone says now and whatever significance people might consider the Bond phenomenon to have a century from now, there can be little doubt concerning the impact it made when it struck the cultural mainland with full-fledged hurricane force in the 1960s. The ubiquitous symbol of secret agent 007 was found everywhere, from bread and bubble gum to men's fashions and toiletries, from parlor games to children's dolls and paper dolls, from his own image to that of imitations in books, films, and television series. More than two hundred commercial products were authorized to carry the official trademark, while hundreds of others hitched onto the Bond-wagon surreptitiously. The James Bond syndrome was soon a universal focal point for countless Walter Mittys. As Kingsley Amis said, 'We don't want to have Bond to dinner, or go golfing with Bond, or talk to Bond. We want to be Bond!'
> **Ann Boyd, *The Devil with James Bond!*, 1967**

Kingsley Amis in *The James Bond Dossier* (1966), suggests:

> Ian Fleming has set his stamp on the story of action and intrigue, bringing to it a sense of our time, a power and a flair that will win him readers when all the protests about his supposed deficiencies have been forgotten.

Fifty-plus years later, these statements still ring true – that phenomenon is still with us, earning millions for the books' publishers and the films' producers. It is perhaps ironic to think that without the success of the film series, Ian Fleming's books, as good as they are, might now be forgotten.

Where the Bond film series will go next is anyone's guess. My money's on Richard Madden and a reset in the 1950s. Wouldn't that be cool?

> Major Anya Amasova: Goodbye, Mr Bond.
> James Bond: Well, let's say 'au revoir'. I have the oddest feeling we'll meet again some time.

Bibliography

Amis, K., *The James Bond Dossier* (Pan Books, London, 1966)

Armes, R., *A Critical History of British Cinema* (Oxford University Press, Oxford, 1978)

Armstrong, V. & Sellers, R., *The True Adventures of the World's Greatest Stuntman: My Life as Indiana Jones, James Bond, Superman and Other Movie Heroes* (Titan Books, London, 2012)

Barnes, A. & Hearn, M., *Kiss Kiss Bang! Bang!* (Batsford, London, 1997)

Bennett, T. & Wollacott, J., *Bond and Beyond: The Political Career of a Popular Hero* (Macmillan, Basingstoke, 1987)

Benson, R., *The James Bond Bedside Companion* (Boxtree, London, 1984)

Bergan, R., *The Film Book* (Dorling Kindersley, London, 2011)

Betts, E., *Film Business–History of the British Cinema 1896-1972* (George Allen & Unwin, 1973)

Black, J., *The Politics of James Bond: From the Fleming Novels to the Big Screen* (Bison Books, Lincoln, 2000)

— *The World of James Bond: The Lives and Times of 007* (Rowman & Littlefield, Lanham, 2017)

Boxall, P. (ed), *1001 Books You Must Read Before You Die* (Cassell, London, 2008)

Boyd, AS., *The Devil with James Bond!* (John Knox Press, Richmond, 1967)

Bray, C., *Sean Connery – The Measure of a Man* (Faber & Faber, London, 2011)

Broccoli, A. & Zec, D., *When the Snow Melts–The Autobiography of Cubby Broccoli* (Boxtree, London, 1999)

Brosnan, J., *James Bond in the Cinema* (first edition, Tantivy Press, London, 1972)

—*James Bond in the Cinema* (second edition, Tantivy Press, London, 1981)

Bouzereau, L., *The Art of Bond* (Boxtree, London, 2006)

Burlingame, J., *The Music of James Bond* (Oxford University Press, New York, 2012)

Caplen, R.A., *Shaken and Stirred–the Feminism of James Bond* (Xlibris Corporation, Bloomington, 2010)

Chapman, J., *Licence to Thrill–A Cultural History of the James Bond Films* (I.B. Tauris, Chichester, 2000)

Chancellor, H., *James Bond, the Man and his World: The Official Companion to Ian Fleming's Creation* (John Murray, London, 2005)

Cork, J., & Scivally, B., *James Bond, the Legacy* (Boxtree, London, 2002)

Del Bueno, O. & Eco, U, *The Bond Affair* (MacDonald, London, 1966)

Dench, J. with Miller, J., *And Furthermore* (Phoenix, London, 2010)

Dougall, A., *James Bond: The Secret World of 007* (Dorling Kindersley, London, 2000)

— *Bond Girls* (Dorling Kindersley, London, 2010)

Duncan, P. (ed), *The James Bond Archives* (Taschen, Köln, 2015)
Duns, J., *Rogue Royale–The Lost Bond Film by the Shakespeare of Hollywood* (Skerry, Norwich, 2016)
Edlitz, M., *The Lost Adventures of James Bond: Timothy Dalton's Third and Fourth Bond Films, James Bond Jr., and Other Unmade or Forgotten 007 Projects* (Bowker, 2020)
Edwards, C., *He Disagreed with Something That Ate Him* (CreateSpace Independent Publishing, 2018)
Egan, S., *James Bond–The Secret History* (John Blake Publishing, London, 2016)
Field, M. & Chowdhury, A., *Some Kind of Hero: The Remarkable Story of the James Bond Films* (The History Press, Stroud, 2015)
Fleming, F. (ed), *The Man with the Golden Typewriter* (Bloomsbury, London, 2016)
Fleming, I. *Casino Royale* (Jonathan Cape, London, 1953)
–*Live and Let Die* (Jonathan Cape, London, 1954)
–*Moonraker* (Jonathan Cape, London, 1955)
–*Diamonds Are Forever* (Jonathan Cape, London, 1956)
–*From Russia With Love* (Jonathan Cape, London, 1957)
–*Dr. No* (Jonathan Cape, London, 1958)
–*Goldfinger* (Jonathan Cape, London, 1959)
–*For Your Eyes Only* (Jonathan Cape, London, 1960)
–*Thunderball* (Jonathan Cape, London, 1961)
–*The Spy Who Loved Me* (Jonathan Cape, London, 1962)
–*On Her Majesty's Secret Service* (Jonathan Cape, London, 1963)
–*You Only Live Twice* (Jonathan Cape, London, 1964)
–*The Man With the Golden Gun* (Jonathan Cape, London, 1965)
– *Octopussy and The Living Daylights* (Jonathan Cape, London, 1966)
Frayling, C., *Ken Adam –The Art of Production Design* (Faber & Faber, London, 2005)
Friedman, L. (ed.), *American Films of the 1970s–Themes and Variations* (Rutgers University Press, New Brunswick, 2007)
Funnel. L. (ed), *For His Eyes Only: The Women of James Bond* (Wallflower Press, New York, 2015)
Funnell, L., & Dodds, K., *Geographies, Genders and Geopolitics of James Bond* (Palgrave Macmillan, London, 2016)
Gassner, D., *James Bond–50 Years of Movie Posters* (Dorling Kindersley, London, 2012)
Giammarco, D., *For Your Eyes Only–Behind the Scenes of the James Bond Films* (ECW Press, Toronto, 2002)
Glen, J., *For My Eyes Only: My Life with James Bond* (Brassey's, Washington, 2001)
Griswold, J., *Ian Fleming's James Bond–Annotations and Chronologies for Ian Fleming's Bond Stories* (AuthorHouse, Bloomington, 2006)

Haining, P., *James Bond–A Celebration* (The Book Service Ltd, Colchester, 1987)
Helfenstein, C., *The Making of On Her Majesty's Secret Service* (Spies, United States, 2009)
— *The Making of The Living Daylights* (Spies, United States, 2012)
Hill, J., *British Cinema in the 1980s* (Oxford University Press, Oxford, 1999)
Hines, C., *The Playboy and James Bond: 007, Ian Fleming, and Playboy Magazine* (Manchester University Press, Manchester, 2018)
Hernu, S., *Q: The Biography of Desmond Llewelyn* (SB Publications, Seaford, 1999)
Johnstone, I., *The World Is Not Enough: A Companion* (Boxtree, London, 1999)
Lane, A. & Simpson, P., *The Bond Files* (Virgin Publishing, London, 1998)
Life Books, *50 Years of James Bond* (Life Books, New York, 2012)
Lee, C., *Tall, Dark and Gruesome* (Vista, London, 1997)
Linder, C. (ed), *The James Bond Phenomenon* (Manchester University Press, Manchester, 2003)
— *Revisioning 007* (Wallflower Press, London, 2009)
Lisa, P. & Pfeiffer, L., *The Incredible World of 007* (Boxtree, London, 1992)
Lycett, I., *Ian Fleming* (W&N, London, 1996)
Macintyre, B., *For Your Eyes Only: Ian Fleming and James Bond* (Bloomsbury, London, 2009)
McKay, S., *The Man With the Golden Touch* (Aurum Press, London, 2008)
McNess, A., *A Close Look at 'A View to a Kill'* (CreateSpace Independent Publishing Platform, 2015)
Membery, Y., *Pierce Brosnan The Biography* (Virgin Books, London, 2002)
Mills, A., *Shooting 007 and Other Celluloid Adventures* (The History Press, Stroud, 2014)
Millard, A., *Equipping James Bond: Guns, Gadgets, and Technological Enthusiasm* (Johns Hopkins University Press, Baltimore, 2018)
Moore, R., *Roger Moore as James Bond* (Macmillan, London, 1973)
–*Last Man Standing: Tales from Tinseltown* (Michael O'Mara, London, 2014)
Moore, R. with Owen. G., *My Word Is My Bond* (harpercollins, London, 2008)
–*Bond on Bond: Reflections on 50 Years of James Bond Movies* (Michael O'Mara Books, London, 2012)
–*Bond on Bond: The Ultimate Book on Over 50 Years of 007* (Michael O'Mara Books, London, 2015)
Mulder, M. & Kloosterboer, K., *On the Tracks of 007* (DMD Digital, 2008)
Murphy, R., *Sixties British Cinema* (British Film Institute, London, 1992)
O'Brien, D., *Daniel Craig–Ultimate Professional* (Reynolds & Heath, Richmond, 2007)
O'Brien, H., *Action Moves: The Cinema of Striking Back* (Wallflower Press, New York, 2012)
O'Connell, M., *Catching Bullets: Memoirs of a Bond Fan* (Splendid Books, Bishops Waltham, 2012)

Parker, M., *GoldenEye–Where Born Was Born: Ian Fleming's Jamaica* (Windmill, London, 2014)
Pearce, G., *The Making of Tomorrow Never Dies* (Boxtree, London, 1997)
Pearson, J., *The Life of Ian Fleming* (Bloomsbury, London, 1966)
–James Bond–The Authorised Biography (Sidgewick & Jackson, London, 1976)
Peary, D., *Guide for the Film Fanatic* (Simon & Schuster, London, 1987)
Perry, G., *Movies from the Mansion: History of Pinewood Studios* (Pavilion Books, London. 1986)
Picker, D., *Musts, Maybes, and Nevers: A Book About the Movies* (CreateSpace, North Charleston, 2013)
Radatz, B., *James Bond: 50 Years of Main Title Design* (Art of the Title, published online, 2012)
Rankin, *Blood, Sweat and Bond: Behind the Scenes of Spectre* (Dorling Kindersley, London, 2015)
Reynolds, B. & Winokur, J., *But Enough About Me* (Blink Publishing, London, 2015)
Rubin, S.J., *The Complete James Bond Movie Encyclopaedia* (McGraw Hill, New York, 2003)
Sandbrook, D., *Never Had It So Good: A History of Britain from Suez to the Beatles* (Little Brown, London, 2005)
–White Heat: A History of Britain in the Swinging Sixties (Little Brown, London, 2006)
–State of Emergency: The Way We Were: Britain, 1970-1974 (Little Brown, London, 2010)
–Seasons in the Sun: The Battle for Britain, 1974-1979 (Little Brown, London, 2012)
Schneider, S.J., *1001 Movies You Must See Before You Die* (Cassell, London, 2007)
Sellers, R., *The Films of Sean Connery* (Vision Press, Chailey, 1990)
–Sean Connery A Celebration (Robert Hale, London, 1999)
–The Battle for Bond (Tomahawk Press, Sheffield, 2007)
–Don't Let the Bastards Grind You Down: How One Generation of British Actors Changed the World (Preface Publishing, London, 2011)
Sepati, J.P., *James Bond on Location: Volume 1–London* (Irregular Special Press, Sawston, 2013)
–James Bond on Location: Volume 2–UK (Irregular Special Press, Sawston, 2013)
Shone, T., *Blockbuster* (Simon & Schuster, London, 2004)
Simpson, P., *The Rough Guide to James Bond* (Rough Guides, London, 2002)
–Bond vs. Bond (Race Point Publishing, New York, 2015)
Snelling, O.F., *007–James Bond–A Report* (Panther, London, 1965)
South, J., & Held, J.M., *James Bond and Philosophy: Questions are Forever* (Open Court, Chicago, 2006)
Speed, J., *The Films of Roger Moore* (self-published, 2016)

Spicer, A., *Typical Men–The Representation of Masculinity in Popular British Cinema* (IB Tauris, London, 2003)
Sterling, M. & Morecambe, G., *Martinis, Girls and Guns–50 Years of 007* (Robson, London, 2003)
Street, S., *British National Cinema* (Routledge, London, 1997)
Strong, J., *James Bond Uncovered* (Palgrave Macmillan, London, 2018)
Tasker, Y. (ed), *Action and Adventure Cinema* (Routledge, London, 2004)
Thomas, G., *The Definitive Story of You Only Live Twice: Fleming, Bond and Connery in Japan* (self-published, 2019)
Turner, A., *Goldfinger* (Bloomsbury, London, 2000)
Walker, A., *Hollywood England: The British Film Industry in the 60s* (Harrop, London, 1986)
–National Heroes: British Cinema in the 70s and 80s (Orion, London, 2005)
Walker, J., *Once and Future Film: British Cinema in the Seventies and Eighties* (Methuen, London, 1985)
Weiner, R.G., Whitfield, B.L., & Becker, J., *James Bond in World and Popular Culture: The Films are Not Enough* (Cambridge Scholars Publishing, Newcastle upon Tyne, 2011)
Winder, S., *The Man Who Saved Britain: A Personal Journey into the Disturbing World of James Bond* (Picador, London, 2006)
Winter, H., *Fifty Years of Hurt: The Story of England Football and Why We Never Stop Believing* (Bantam, London, 2016)
Yeffeth G. (ed.), *James Bond in the 21st Century: Why we still need 007* (SmartPop, Dallas, 2006)

Would you like to write for Sonicbond Publishing?

We are mainly a music publisher, but we also occasionally publish in other genres including film and television. At Sonicbond Publishing we are always on the look-out for authors, particularly for our two main series, On Track and Decades.

Mixing fact with in depth analysis, the On Track series examines the entire recorded work of a particular musical artist or group. All genres are considered from easy listening and jazz to 60s soul to 90s pop, via rock and metal.

The Decades series singles out a particular decade in an artist or group's history and focuses on that decade in more detail than may be allowed in the On Track series.

While professional writing experience would, of course, be an advantage, the most important qualification is to have real enthusiasm and knowledge of your subject. First-time authors are welcomed, but the ability to write well in English is essential.

Sonicbond Publishing has distribution throughout Europe and North America, and all our books are also published in E-book form. Authors will be paid a royalty based on sales of their book. Further details about our books are available from www.sonicbondpublishing.com. To contact us, complete the contact form there or email info@sonicbondpublishing.co.uk